Simulation: The Practice of Model Development and Use

Simulation: The Practice of Model Development and Use

Stewart Robinson
Warwick Business School

John Wiley & Sons, Ltd

Telephone (+44) 1243 779777

Email (for orders and customer service enquiries): cs-books@wiley.co.uk
Visit our Home Page on www.wileyeurope.com or www.wiley.com

Reprinted October 2004, March 2007

Other Wiley Editorial Offices

John Wiley & Sons Inc., 111 River Street, Hoboken, NJ 07030, USA

Jossey-Bass, 989 Market Street, San Francisco, CA 94103-1741, USA

Wiley-VCH Verlag GmbH, Boschstr. 12, D-69469 Weinheim, Germany

John Wiley & Sons Australia Ltd, 33 Park Road, Milton, Queensland 4064, Australia

John Wiley & Sons (Asia) Pte Ltd, 2 Clementi Loop #02-01, Jin Xing Distripark, Singapore 129809

John Wiley & Sons Canada Ltd, 22 Worcester Road, Etobicoke, Ontario, Canada M9W 1L1

Wiley also publishes its books in a variety of electronic formats. Some content that appears in print may not be available in electronic books.

Library of Congress Cataloging-in-Publication Data

Robinson, Stewart, 1964-
Simulation : the practice of model development and use / Stewart Robinson.
p. cm.
Includes bibliographical references and index.
ISBN 0-470-84772-7 (pbk.)
1. Computer simulation. 2. Simulation methods. I. Title.

QA76.9.C65R63 2003
003′.3 – dc22

2003063093

British Library Cataloguing in Publication Data

A catalogue record for this book is available from the British Library

ISBN 978-0-470-84772-5 (pbk)

Typeset in 10/12pt Goudy by Laserwords Private Limited, Chennai, India
Printed and bound in Great Britain by Biddles Ltd, King's Lynn, Norfolk
This book is printed on acid-free paper responsibly manufactured from sustainable forestry in which at least two trees are planted for each one used for paper production.

For Jane, Naomi, Martha and Aaron

Contents

ACKNOWLEDGEMENTS

Various people have offered advice and reviewed sections and chapters of the book during its writing. In particular I would like to thank (in alphabetical order) Russell Cheng, Ruth Davies, Geoff Hook, Maureen Meadows and Durk-Jouke van der Zee.

PREFACE

It was in the mid-1980s that I stumbled upon a career in simulation modelling, a career that can be split roughly into two parts. In the first part I spent my time as an external consultant, developing and using simulations for manufacturing and service organizations, and training and supporting simulation users. At first the simulations were developed in a programming language. Later I was able to take advantage of more user-friendly simulation software. The second part of my career has largely been spent reflecting upon my time as a consultant and researching the way in which others practise simulation. I also teach simulation to undergraduates, postgraduates and industrialists, and occasionally find time to do a little consulting, keeping fresh those memories of the first part of my career. Over this period a wide range of lessons has been learnt, revealing "the good, the bad and the ugly" of simulation practice. It is these lessons that are described in the pages that follow.

The aim of this book is to provide the reader with a clear understanding of the requirements for the successful development and use of simulation models. The specific objectives of the book are for the reader:

- To understand how simulation software works and the types of software that are available for simulation modelling.
- To know the processes involved in a simulation project.
- To be able to develop an appropriate model for a problem situation.
- To be able to collect and analyse the data required for a simulation model.
- To be able to perform simulation experiments, analyse the results and draw conclusions.
- To ensure that a simulation model has been verified and validated so there is sufficient confidence to use the model in decision-making.
- To know how to manage a simulation project successfully.

The assumption is that the reader has access to, and some level of competence with, a simulation software package. In this respect the book takes a non-software specific view and so should be useful whatever software is being used. Indeed, almost all the principles and techniques described apply to the use of non-specialist simulation software (e.g. programming languages and spreadsheets) as well.

At whom is this book aimed? In short, to *anyone* who has a *problem* that needs to be tackled with simulation. Who is *anyone*? Undergraduates and postgraduates who are learning about the principles of simulation, particularly from the perspective of how to investigate a problem with a simulation model. My observation is that most simulation courses now ask students to tackle a (pseudo-) real problem as part of the assessment. Meanwhile, some students are asked to take on larger-scale problems as part of a practical or research project. Both should find this book useful. Beyond those in education, practitioners, both novice and longer-in-the-tooth, who are trying to develop and hone their simulation skills should also benefit from the content of this book.

What types of *problems* are we considering? In summary, those that relate to *operations systems*. These systems are described in Section 1.2. For now it is enough to say that the hub of almost any organization is its operations systems. Included in this description are manufacturing systems, service systems, health care systems, transportation systems, business processes, military operations and many more. As such, the focus is on simulation as it is used in operational (or operations) research. The underlying simulation method most commonly used in this field is discrete-event simulation (Section 2.2.2), although many of the ideas presented in this book could be applied to other methods of simulation.

The practice of simulation requires both technical and socio-political skills. Indeed, a mix of skills is needed including problem solving, computing, statistics, project management, people management and communication. It has been my aim to describe the core skills required for the successful application of simulation, while at the same time not giving undue emphasis to any one area. Although some give great emphasis to, say, the computing or statistical aspects of simulation, and rightly so within a specific context, my contention is that successful simulation studies require well-rounded modellers whose skills lie across the range of areas listed above. Of course, some may wish to delve into specific areas in more depth. It is hoped that the references provided at the end of each chapter will provide a starting point for such investigations.

The first three chapters provide a background to simulation and simulation software. Chapter 1 explains what simulation is, why it would be used and the sorts of applications to which it might be applied. Chapter 2 then goes on to describe how simulation software works. Two specific areas are discussed: modelling the progress of time and modelling variability. Meanwhile, Chapter 3 describes the different types of simulation software and the selection of an appropriate package.

Following this introduction to simulation the attention turns to the process of performing a simulation study: the main content of the book. Chapter 4 provides an outline of this process and discusses the issues surrounding project time-scales, the simulation project team, hardware and software requirements, project costs and the selection of projects. In the outline of a simulation study, four key processes are identified: conceptual modelling, model coding, experimentation and implementation. These processes are described in detail in Chapters 5 to 11.

Chapters 5 and 6 explain the requirements for and process of conceptual modelling. The role of a "project specification" is explained and some methods for simplifying simulation models are also described. Chapter 7 discusses data requirements, and data collection and analysis. Various methods for representing variability are described and the identification of an appropriate method is discussed. Chapter 8 focuses on the coding of the simulation model.

Chapters 9 and 10 explain the process of experimentation. The focus of Chapter 9 is on obtaining accurate results by ensuring that the simulation has been run for long enough. Meanwhile, methods for searching for improvements to the system being simulated are described in Chapter 10. The fourth process, implementation, is discussed in Chapter 11.

Up to this point there is little mention of the verification and validation of the simulation model. This subject is left to Chapter 12 where the need continuously to perform verification and validation throughout a simulation study is highlighted. The difficulties encountered in validating models are discussed and methods of verification and validation are described. The final chapter (Chapter 13) discusses the practice of simulation in terms of simulation model types and the way in which simulation models are developed and used.

In Appendix 1 and 2, two case study examples are presented: Wardeon Cinema and Panorama Televisions. The purpose of these examples is to provide an illustration of how the principles and techniques described in the book can be applied to semi-real problems. The reader is encouraged to follow these examples and possibly to develop and use models of each case in order to gain practice with simulation.

Exercises are given at the end of many of the chapters. These are intended to give the reader practice with the concepts presented in a chapter and to encourage some further investigation into important areas. A web site (www.wileyeurope.com/go/robinson) provides data for the exercises and Excel spreadsheets for some of the analytical methods presented in the book. It also provides simulation models for the Wardeon Cinema and Panorama Televisions cases (Appendix 1 and 2). These have been developed in various simulation software packages.

Stewart Robinson
July 2003

1 WWW.SIMULATION: WHAT, WHY AND WHEN?

1.1 Introduction

The management of an airport are planning the facilities that are required in a new terminal building. Important decisions need to be made about, among other things, the number of check-in desks devoted to each airline, the size of the baggage handling system, the amount of security check positions and the number of departure gates. On top of this, the number of staff to employ and the shifts they should work need to be determined. The total investment is in the tens of millions and it is critical that these decisions are made correctly. How can the management determine the number of resources that are required in each area of the airport?

One approach would be to build the terminal and hope that it works! This seems very risky with so much at stake. Only slightly better would be to rely upon gut feel, no doubt based on some past experience with designing and managing airport terminals. A few paper calculations, or even a spreadsheet, may help, but these are unlikely to be able to handle the full complexity of the situation.

A much more effective approach is likely to be a simulation of the proposed airport terminal. This could imitate the flow of passengers and their bags through each of the key stages from arrival to departure and would act as a basis for planning airport facilities. Indeed, simulation models are used by many organizations to plan future facilities and to improve current ones. Manufacturing companies simulate their production lines, financial services organizations simulate their call centres and transport companies simulate their delivery networks. There are many examples of simulation being used in practice.

This chapter aims to answer three questions concerning simulation:

- What exactly is a simulation?
- Why would an organization choose to develop and use a simulation model?
- When is simulation appropriate?

1.2 What is Simulation?

Simulation models are in everyday use and so simulation is a concept that is not alien to us. For instance, weather forecasters daily show us simulations of the weather system, where we see the movement of weather fronts over the days ahead. Many of us have game consoles that simulate a whole variety of activities, enabling us to test our skills as racing drivers, adventurers and city planners. Simulations need not be computer based. Model railways and remote control boats are familiar examples of physical simulations.

So what does the term simulation mean? In its most general sense a simulation can be defined as:

An imitation of a system.

Imitation implies mimicking or copying something else. For instance, a forger imitates the work of a great artist. The Strip in Las Vegas is full of imitations: the Eiffel Tower, the New York skyline, Venice and so on. In the 2002 soccer world cup, if a player imitated being the recipient of foul play, it was referred to as a "simulation". Computer aided design (CAD) systems provide imitations of production facility designs and a business process map is an imitation of a business organization. All of these can be described as a simulation in its most general sense.

There is, however, a key difference between these imitations and those examples described in the first paragraph of this section. The earlier examples involve the passage of time, whether it is the movement of trains on a track or clouds in a weather system. The second set of examples does not involve the passage of time. Hence there is a difference between the concepts of a *static simulation*, which imitates a system at a point in time, and a *dynamic simulation*, which imitates a system as it progresses through time (Law and Kelton 2000). The term simulation is mostly used in the context of dynamic simulation.

This book is concerned only with dynamic simulations. Further to this, the focus is on computer based simulations rather than physical simulations, although many of the principles that are described would still apply to the latter. Building on the previous definition, computer based dynamic simulation can be defined as follows:

An imitation (on a computer) of a system as it progresses through time.

Some aspects of this definition need exploring a little further. First, the concept of a *system* needs to be explained. In general terms a system is a collection of parts organized for some purpose (Coyle 1996). The weather system, for instance, is a collection of parts, including the sun, water and land, that is designed (assuming we believe in a Creator) for the purpose of maintaining life.

Checkland (1981) identifies four main classes of system:

- *Natural systems*: systems whose origins lie in the origins of the universe, e.g. the atom, the Earth's weather system and galactic systems.
- *Designed physical systems*: physical systems that are a result of human design, e.g. a house, a car and a production facility.

- *Designed abstract systems*: abstract systems that are a result of human design, e.g. mathematics and literature.
- *Human activity systems*: systems of human activity that are consciously, or unconsciously, ordered, e.g. a family, a city and political systems.

All such systems can be, and indeed are, simulated. This book, however, is concerned with simulation as it is used for modelling in private and public sector organizations. When describing and understanding these organizations two classes of system are of prime concern, that is, designed physical and human activity systems. For instance, a simulation might be developed of an automated production facility or warehouse (a designed physical system), or at the other extreme a model of regional health care delivery (a human activity system). Many situations cannot be defined simply as either a designed physical system or a human activity system, but they lie at the interface between the two. A bank, for instance, consists of a designed physical system (the service counters, automatic tellers, etc.), but it is also a human activity system where the staff and customers interact between and with one another. Indeed, many of the situations in which simulation is used lie at the interface between designed physical systems and human activity systems. For instance, service operations (banks, call centres and supermarkets), manufacturing plants, supply chains, transport systems, hospital emergency departments and military operations all involve elements of both classes of system. In general terms, these systems can be referred to as *operations systems* or *operating systems*. "An operating system is a configuration of resources [parts] combined for the provision of goods or services [purpose]" (Wild 2002; words in brackets added by author). Wild identifies four specific functions of operating systems: manufacture, transport, supply and service.

There are, of course, cases where other types of system need to be modelled as well. For instance, in a simulation of a port it may be necessary to model the tidal and weather conditions, since adverse conditions may prevent a ship from entering the port. As such, it is necessary to model, at least simply, some natural systems. In general this would involve modelling the outcome of the natural system (e.g. high winds) rather than the system itself.

A second aspect of the definition that needs exploring further is to consider the purpose of simulation models. Pidd (2003), in a more general discussion about models in management science, identifies the purpose of models as understanding, changing, managing and controlling reality. Following this theme, the purpose of a simulation can be described as obtaining a better understanding of and/or identifying improvements to a system. Improved understanding of a system, as well as the identification of improvements, is important since it informs future decision-making in the real system.

Another feature of Pidd's description of models is his emphasis on simplification. It is unlikely that a simulation of an operations system, particularly the elements of human activity, could represent its full detail. Indeed, even if it were possible, it is probably not desirable, since the time required to collect data on and model every aspect of a system would be excessive. Note that even the Las Vegans only built a half-size replica of the Eiffel Tower, and this for a "simple" physical structure!

A final aspect to consider is the nature of simulation model use. Some modelling approaches attempt to provide optimum answers (e.g. linear programming) or near optimum answers (e.g. heuristic methods). This is not the case for a simulation model. A simulation simply predicts the performance of an operations system under a specific set of inputs. For instance, it might predict the average waiting time for telephone customers at a call centre when a specific number of operators are employed. It is the job of the person using the simulation model to vary the inputs (the number of operators) and to run the model in order to determine the effect. As such, simulation is an experimental approach to modelling, that is, a "what-if" analysis tool. The model user enters a scenario and the model predicts the outcome. The model user continues to explore alternative scenarios until he/she has obtained sufficient understanding or identified how to improve the real system. As a consequence, simulation should be seen as a form of decision support system, that is, it supports decision-making rather than making decisions on behalf of the user. It should be noted, however, that most modern simulation software provide facilities for automating the experimentation process with the aim of finding an optimum scenario. These facilities and their application are discussed in Section 10.5.4.

These four aspects (operations systems, purpose, simplification and experimentation) are now added to the previous definition so that simulation is defined as:

Experimentation with a simplified imitation (on a computer) of an operations system as it progresses through time, for the purpose of better understanding and/or improving that system.

This is the nature of the simulations that are described in this book. Note that some specifics of this definition are discussed in detail in later chapters, in particular, the methods of imitating a system as it progresses through time (Section 2.2), approaches to simplification (Section 6.3) and experimentation (Chapters 9 and 10). From here on the term simulation will be taken to mean simulation as defined above, unless otherwise stated.

1.3 Why Simulate?

In order to answer this question, three perspectives are adopted. First, the need to use simulation because of the nature of operations systems is discussed. Secondly, the advantages of simulation over other approaches to understanding and improving a system are described. Finally, the disadvantages of simulation are discussed, on the grounds that it is important to be cognizant of these when determining whether or not to use the approach.

1.3.1 The nature of operations systems: variability, interconnectedness and complexity

Many operations systems are subject to *variability*. This might be predictable variations, for instance, changing the number of operators in a call centre during the day to meet changing call volumes or planned stoppages in a production facility. It might also be variations that are unpredictable, such as the arrival rate of patients at a hospital emergency department or the breakdown of equipment in a flexible manufacturing cell. Both forms of variability are present in most operations systems.

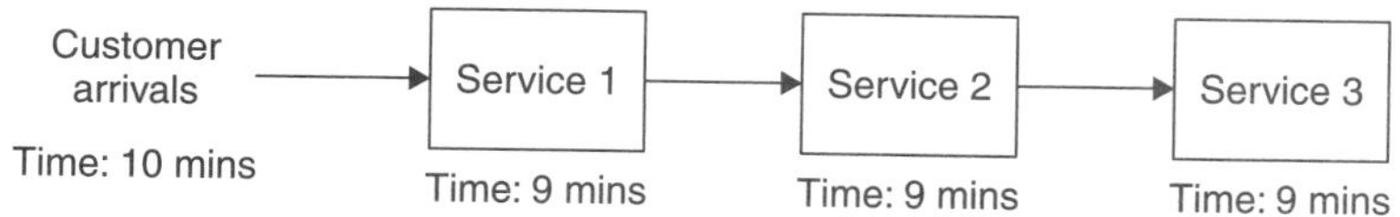

Figure 1.1 Example of an Interconnected System Subject to Variability.

Operations systems are also *interconnected*. Components of the system do not work in isolation, but affect one another. A change in one part of a system leads to a change in another part of the system. For instance, if a machine is set to work faster this is likely to cause a reduction in work-in-progress up-stream and a build-up of parts down-stream.

It is often difficult to predict the effects of the interconnections in a system, especially when variability is present. Take the following example. Customers in a service process pass through three (interconnected) stages (Figure 1.1). Each stage takes exactly 9 minutes. Customers arrive exactly every 10 minutes. What is the average time a customer spends in the system? This is a relatively simple question to answer, since there is no variability in the system. The average time customers spend in the system is 27 minutes; in fact each customer spends exactly 27 minutes in the system.

Now assume that the times given above are averages, so customers arrive on average every 10 minutes and it takes on average 9 minutes to serve a customer at each stage. What is the average time a customer spends in the system? This is not an easy question to answer since there is variability in both customer arrivals and service times. It is also expected that queues will develop between the service stages. Added to this, the range of variability around the average is not known. Most people would estimate that the average is still 27 minutes or maybe slightly longer. In fact, assuming a typical range of variability (a negative exponential distribution – Section 7.4.3), the average is near to 150 minutes. The compound effect of variability and the interconnections in the system make it very difficult to predict the overall performance of the system.

Many operations systems are also *complex*. It is difficult to provide an exact definition of the word complexity; an interesting discussion can be found in Gell-Mann (1994) and in relation to simulation and modelling in Brooks and Tobias (1996). For our purposes it is useful to distinguish between *combinatorial complexity* and *dynamic complexity*. Combinatorial complexity is related to the number of components in a system or the number of combinations of system components that are possible. The travelling salesman problem is a useful illustration of this. A salesperson has to make a series of visits to potential customers during a day. The aim is to find the shortest route around those customers. If there are eight "cities" (customers) to visit, then the sales person is faced with 2520 possible combinations of routes (this is calculated by $(n - 1!)/2$, where n is the number of cities). As the number of cities increases, so the number of combinations grows at an increasing rate. A 16 city tour gives 6.5×10^{11} combinations of routes! The problem is subject to combinatorial complexity.

Combinatorial complexity is present in some operations systems. Take, for instance, a job shop. Parts are processed through a series of machines. Once the processing is complete on one machine, a part is passed to any one of the other machines, depending on the type of part and the next process required. The more machines there are in the job shop, the more the

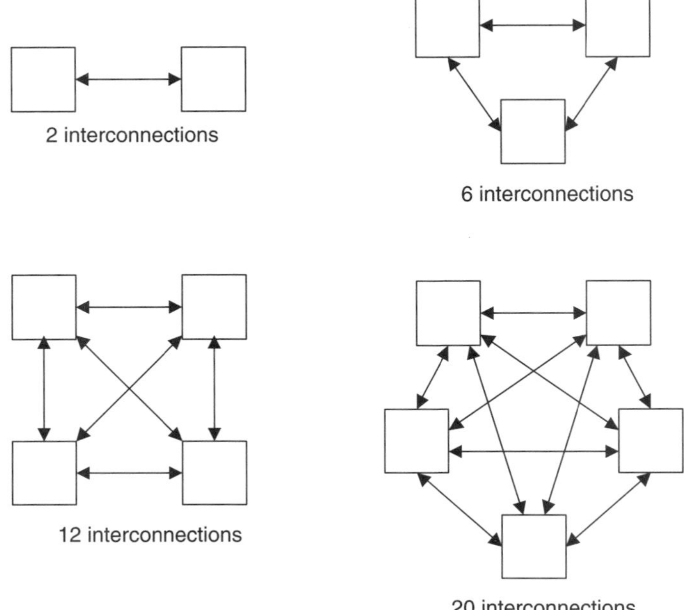

Figure 1.2 Job Shop Systems: Interconnections and Combinatorial Complexity.

potential interconnections. As the number of machines increases so the interconnections increase at an even faster rate. Figure 1.2 shows the possible interconnections for job shops with two, three, four and five machines. There are two interconnections between any two machines since parts can move in either direction. The total number of interconnections can be calculated as $n(n - 1)$, where n is the number of machines in the job shop.

On the other hand, dynamic complexity is not necessarily related to size. Dynamic complexity arises from the interaction of components in a system over time (Sterman 2000). This can occur in systems that are small, as well as large. Systems that are highly interconnected are likely to display dynamic complexity.

Senge (1990) illustrates dynamic complexity with the "beer distribution game". This represents a simple supply chain consisting of a retailer, wholesaler and factory. The retailer orders cases of beer from the wholesaler, who in turn orders beer from the factory. There is a delay between placing an order and receiving the cases of beer. The game demonstrates that a small perturbation in the number of beer cases sold by the retailer can cause large shifts in the quantity of cases stored and produced by the wholesaler and factory respectively. Such a system is subject to dynamic complexity.

Senge (1990) describes three effects of dynamic complexity:

- An action has dramatically different effects in the short and long run.
- An action has a very different set of consequences in one part of the system to another.
- An action leads to non-obvious consequences (counter intuitive behaviour).

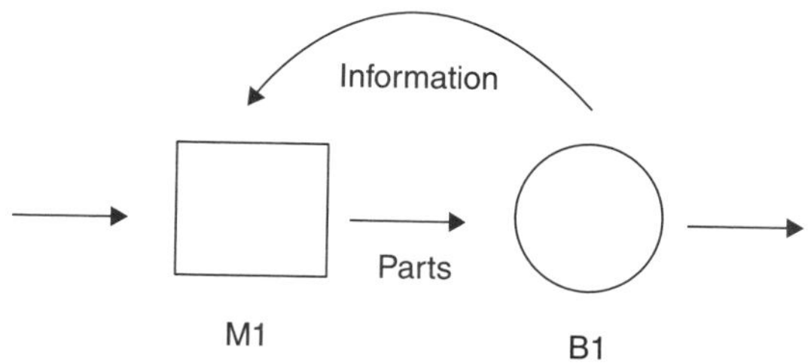

Figure 1.3 Simple Kanban System Demonstrating Feedback.

These effects make it very difficult to predict the performance of a system when actions are taken, or changes are made.

The effects described above often arise because of feedback within a system. Feedback occurs when the components of a system are interconnected in a loop structure. As a result an action taken at one point in a system eventually leads to a feedback effect on that same point in the system. A simple example is a kanban system (Figure 1.3). Machine M1 feeds buffer B1. The rate at which M1 works depends upon the number of parts in B1. The smaller the inventory in B1 the faster M1 works, and vice versa. M1 is connected to B1 through the flow of parts and B1 is connected to M1 through the flow of information about the quantity of parts in the buffer. There is, therefore, a loop structure and so feedback occurs. For instance, if M1 is made to work faster, this increases the number of parts in B1, which in turn reduces the speed at which M1 works. This is, of course, a very simple example.

The interconnections in operations systems are often not unidirectional, and so loop structures and feedback are quite common. In particular, physical items and information often flow in opposite directions. In a supply chain, for instance, physical items often move towards the customers while information about orders for more stock move towards the producers. In some cases the loop structures are very complex, involving many system components.

The need for simulation

Many operations systems are interconnected and subject to both variability and complexity (combinatorial and dynamic). Because it is difficult to predict the performance of systems that are subject to any one of variability, interconnectedness and complexity, it is very difficult, if not impossible, to predict the performance of operations systems that are potentially subject to all three. Simulation models, however, are able explicitly to represent the variability, interconnectedness and complexity of a system. As a result, it is possible with a simulation to predict system performance, to compare alternative system designs and to determine the effect of alternative policies on system performance.

The methods for modelling variability in simulation are discussed in Section 2.3 and Section 7.4. Section 6.2.4 discusses the need to account for the interconnections in a system. The combination of modelling variability and interconnectedness means that the complexity in a system can be represented by a simulation model.

1.3.2 The advantages of simulation

Simulation is not the only method of analysing and improving operations systems. In particular, it might be possible to experiment with the real system or to use another modelling approach (Pidd 1998). What are the specific advantages of simulation over these approaches?

Simulation versus experimentation with the real system

Rather than develop and use a simulation model, experiments could be carried out in the real system. For instance, additional check-in desks could be placed in an airport departure area, or a change in the flow around a factory floor could be implemented. There are some obvious, and less obvious, reasons why simulation is preferable to such direct experimentation.

- *Cost.* Experimentation with the real system is likely to be costly. It is expensive to interrupt day-to-day operations in order to try out new ideas. Apart from the cost of making changes, it may be necessary to shut the system down for a period while alterations are made. Added to this, if the alterations cause the operation's performance to worsen, this may be costly in terms of loss of custom and customer dissatisfaction. With a simulation, however, changes can be made at the cost of the time it takes to alter the model and without any interruption to the operation of the real world system.
- *Time.* It is time consuming to experiment with a real system. It may take many weeks or months (possibly more) before a true reflection of the performance of the system can be obtained. Depending on the size of the model and speed of the computer, a simulation can run many times faster than real time. Consequently, results on system performance can be obtained in a matter of minutes, maybe hours. This also has the advantage that results can be obtained over a very long time frame, maybe years of operation, if required. Faster experimentation also enables many ideas to be explored in a short time frame.
- *Control of the experimental conditions.* When comparing alternatives it is useful to control the conditions under which the experiments are performed so direct comparisons can be made. This is difficult when experimenting with the real system. For instance, it is not possible to control the arrival of patients at a hospital. It is also likely that experimentation with the real system will lead to the Hawthorne effect, where staff performance improves simply because some attention is being paid to them. In some cases the real system only occurs once, for example, a military campaign, and so there is no option to repeat an experiment. With a simulation model the conditions under which an experiment is performed can be repeated many times. The same pattern of patient arrivals can be generated time and time again, or the events that occur during a military campaign can be reproduced exactly as often as is required.
- *The real system does not exist.* A most obvious difficulty with real world experimentation is that the real system may not yet exist. Apart from building a series of alternative real world systems, which is unlikely to be practical in any but the most trivial of situations, direct experimentation is impossible in such circumstances. The only alternative is to develop a model.

Simulation versus other modelling approaches

Simulations are not the only models that can be used for understanding and improving the real world. Other modelling approaches range from simple paper calculations, through spreadsheet models, to more complex mathematical programming and heuristic methods (e.g. linear programming, dynamic programming, simulated annealing and genetic algorithms). Queuing theory provides a specific class of model that looks at similar situations to those often represented by simulations, arrivals, queues and service processes (Winston 1994). There are some reasons why simulation would be used in preference to these other methods.

- *Modelling variability*. It has already been stated that simulations are able to model variability and its effects. Meanwhile, many of the methods mentioned above are not able to do so. (It should be noted that some modelling approaches can be adapted to account for variability, but this often increases their complexity.) If the systems being modelled are subject to significant levels of variability, then simulation is often the only means for accurately predicting performance. Some systems cannot be modelled analytically. This is illustrated by Robinson and Higton (1995) who contrast the results from a "static" analysis of alternative factory designs with a simulation. In the static analysis the variability, largely resulting from equipment failures, was accounted for by averaging their effects into the process cycle times. In the simulation, the variability was modelled in detail. Whilst the static analysis predicted each design would reach the throughput required, the simulation showed that none of the designs were satisfactory. It is vital that variability is properly accounted for when attempting to predict performance.
- *Restrictive assumptions*. Simulation requires few, if any, assumptions, although the desire to simplify models and a shortage of data mean that some appropriate assumptions are normally made. Many other modelling approaches require certain assumptions. Queuing theory, for instance, often assumes particular distributions for arrival and service times. For many processes these distributions are not appropriate. In simulation, any distribution can be selected.
- *Transparency*. A manager faced with a set of mathematical equations or a large spreadsheet may struggle to understand, or believe, the results from the model. Simulation is appealing because it is more intuitive and an animated display of the system can be created, giving a non-expert greater understanding of, and confidence in, the model.

Of course, there are occasions when another modelling approach is appropriate and simulation is not required. Because simulation is a time consuming approach, it is recommended that it is used as a means of last resort, rather than the preferred option (Pidd 1998). That said, simulation is often the only resort. Indeed, surveys of modelling practice demonstrate that simulation is one of the most commonly used modelling techniques (Jeffrey and Seaton 1995; Fildes and Ranyard 1997; Clark 1999).

Simulation: the management perspective

Among the most compelling reasons for using simulation are the benefits that are gained by managers.

- *Fostering creativity.* "Ideas which can produce considerable improvements are often never tried because of an employee's fear of failure" (Gogg and Mott 1992). With a simulation, however, ideas can be tried in an environment that is free of risk. This can only help to encourage creativity in tackling problem situations.
- *Creating knowledge and understanding.* At the end of many months of simulation modelling, the manager of the organization informed me that all of the benefits could have been obtained without the use of simulation by simply thinking about the problem in more detail. My defence lay in the fact that they would not have thought through the issues had the simulation not been there to act as a catalyst. The development and use of a simulation model forces people to think through issues that otherwise may not have been considered. The modeller seeks information, asks for data and questions assumptions, all of which lead to an improved knowledge and understanding of the system that is being simulated. Shannon (1975) recognizes that the development of the model alone, without the need for experimentation, may create sufficient understanding to bring about the necessary improvement to the real system. As the old adage states "a problem stated is a problem half solved".
- *Visualization and communication.* Many good ideas have been trampled under foot because the benefits could not be demonstrated to a senior manager. Visual simulations prove a powerful tool for communication. It may be that an idea has already been proven but it is deemed necessary to build a simulation model in order to convince senior managers and colleagues of its validity.
- *Consensus building.* Many simulation studies are performed in the light of differing opinions as to the way forward. In the health sector, clinicians may be at odds with managers over the resources required. In a factory, managers and workers may not be in agreement over working hours and shifts. Sitting opposing parties around a simulation model of the problem situation can be a powerful means of sharing concerns and testing ideas with a view to obtaining a consensus of opinion.

1.3.3 The disadvantages of simulation

There are a number of problems with using simulation and these must not be ignored when deciding whether or not it is appropriate.

- *Expensive.* Simulation software is not necessarily cheap and the cost of model development and use may be considerable, particularly if consultants have to be employed.
- *Time consuming.* It has already been stated that simulation is a time consuming approach. This only adds to the cost of its use and means that the benefits are not immediate.
- *Data hungry.* Most simulation models require a significant amount of data. This is not always immediately available and, where it is, much analysis may be required to put it in a form suitable for the simulation.
- *Requires expertise.* Simulation modelling is more than the development of a computer program or the use of a software package. It requires skills in, among other things, conceptual modelling, validation and statistics, as well as skills in working with people and project management. These are the skills that are discussed in this book. This expertise is not always readily available.

- *Overconfidence*. There is a danger that anything produced on a computer is seen to be right. With simulation this is further exacerbated with the use of an animated display, giving an appearance of reality. When interpreting the results from a simulation, consideration must be given to the validity of the underlying model and the assumptions and simplifications that have been made.

1.4 When to Simulate

In general terms simulation, at least as it is described in this book, is used for modelling queuing systems. These consist of entities being processed through a series of stages, with queues forming between each stage if there is insufficient processing capacity. On the surface this may seem to be a limited set of circumstances, but the applications are many and various. Many systems can be conceived as queuing systems, whether it is people, physical items or information that are represented by the entities moving through the system.

It is impossible to give a full list of applications for which simulation might be used. It is, however, useful to give some indication of the range of systems that can be modelled. Banks *et al.* (1996) suggest the following list:

- Manufacturing systems
- Public systems: health care, military, natural resources
- Transportation systems
- Construction systems
- Restaurant and entertainment systems
- Business process reengineering/management
- Food processing
- Computer system performance

There are no doubt other applications that can be added to this list, for instance, service and retail systems.

1.5 Conclusion

This chapter discusses the nature of simulation that is described in this book. While a specific definition of simulation for modelling operations systems is provided, it is also shown that the term "simulation" has many meanings. The reasons for using simulation are discussed based on the nature of operations systems and the advantages of simulation. The latter describes why simulation is often preferable to other improvement approaches that could be adopted. The disadvantages of simulation are also identified. Finally, some common application areas for simulation modelling are listed. Having set the scene, the next chapter describes how a simulation model works by showing how the progression of time and variability are modelled.

Exercises

E1.1 Think of situations where simulation could be used, for instance, from day-to-day life, a place of study or work. What aspects of each situation make simulation appropriate?

E1.2 Take a typical operations system, preferably one that can be observed (e.g. a bank or supermarket), and identify the elements of variability, interconnectedness and complexity.

E1.3 There are many case studies describing the application of simulation to real problems. Obtain and read some simulation case studies. Why was simulation used? What benefits were obtained? Some journals that often publish simulation case studies are: IIE Solutions, Interfaces, OR Insight and the Journal of the Operational Research Society. The Winter Simulation Conference proceedings (www.wintersim.org) include many case studies. Simulation software suppliers also publish case studies on their web sites (Section 3.3.3).

References

Banks, J., Carson, J.S. and Nelson, B.L. (1996) *Discrete-Event System Simulation*, 2nd edn. Upper Saddle River, NJ: Prentice-Hall.

Brooks, R.J. and Tobias, A.M. (1996) "Choosing the best model: level of detail, complexity and model performance". *Mathematical and Computer Modelling*, 24(4), 1–14.

Checkland, P. (1981) *Systems Thinking, Systems Practice*. Chichester, UK: Wiley.

Clark, D.N. (1999) "Strategic level MS/OR tool usage in the United Kingdom and New Zealand: a comparative survey". *Asia-Pacific Journal of Operational Research*, 16(1), 35–51.

Coyle, R.G. (1996) *System Dynamics Modelling: A Practical Approach*. London: Chapman & Hall.

Fildes, R. and Ranyard, J.C (1997). "Success and survival of operational research groups – a review". *Journal of the Operational Research Society*, 48(4), 336–360.

Gell-Mann, M. (1994) *The Quark and the Jaguar: Adventures in the Simple and the Complex*. London: Abacus.

Gogg, T. and Mott, J. (1992) *Improve Quality and Productivity with Simulation*. Palos Verdes Pnsl., CA: JMI Consulting Group.

Jeffrey, P. and Seaton, R. (1995) "The use of operational research tools: a survey of operational research practitioners in the UK". *Journal of the Operational Research Society*, 46(7), 797–808.

Law, A.M. and Kelton, W.D. (2000) *Simulation Modeling and Analysis*, 3rd edn. New York: McGraw-Hill.

Pidd, M. (1998) *Computer Simulation in Management Science*, 4th edn. Chichester, UK: Wiley.

Pidd, M. (2003) *Tools for Thinking: Modelling in Management Science*, 2nd edn. Chichester, UK: Wiley.

Robinson, S. and Higton, N. (1995) "Computer simulation for quality and reliability engineering". *Quality and Reliability Engineering International*, 11, 371–377.

Senge, P.M. (1990) *The Fifth Discipline: The Art and Practice of the Learning Organization*. London: Random House.

Shannon, R.E. (1975) *Systems Simulation: The Art and Science*. Englewood Cliffs, NJ: Prentice-Hall.

Sterman, J.D. (2000) *Business Dynamics: Systems Thinking and Modeling for a Complex World*. New York: McGraw-Hill.

Wild, R. (2002) *Operations Management*, 6th edn. London: Continuum.

Winston, W.L. (1994) *Operations Research: Applications and Algorithms*, 3rd edn. Belmont, CA: Duxbury Press.

Inside Simulation Software

2

2.1 Introduction

In most cases simulation models of operations systems are developed using specialist software and they are not programmed from scratch. Such is the power of modern simulation software that it is rarely necessary to resort to a programming language. One danger of using packaged software, however, is that the user has little understanding of the principles of the underlying technique. Whereas much of the software we use (for instance, spreadsheets) simply automate everyday tasks and help to perform them on a larger scale, simulation is not a day-to-day activity. Therefore, this danger is even greater.

In this chapter the principles of the simulation technique are explained to give an understanding of what is inside simulation software. In short, the software involves two key elements: modelling the progress of time and modelling variability. The first is present in all dynamic simulations, the second is present in the majority. Indeed, these two elements enable a simulation to model the variability, interconnectedness and complexity in an operations system: the first directly by modelling the variability, the latter two by modelling the progress of time. Modelling the progress of time is described first, followed by a discussion on modelling variability.

Only a brief introduction to modelling the progress of time and variability is given, along with some simple illustrative examples. This is certainly not meant to provide sufficient detail for those wishing to program a simulation from scratch. It is aimed at giving a basic grounding in the simulation technique. For those wishing to develop a more detailed knowledge of the simulation technique, references are provided at suitable points.

2.2 Modelling the Progress of Time

There are a number of means for modelling the progress of time. Two specific approaches are described here. The time-slicing method is described first since it is useful for understanding the basics of the simulation approach. Discrete-event simulation is then described, this being the simulation approach upon which this book concentrates and the method that underlies the commercial simulation software referred to in Chapter 3. In both cases "hand" simulations are used to demonstrate the methods. There is also a brief discussion on continuous simulation, which is sometimes used for modelling operations systems. Pidd (1998) and Law and Kelton (2000) provide more in-depth discussions on these topics for those wishing to develop a more detailed understanding.

2.2.1 The time-slicing approach

The simplest method for modelling the progress of time is the time-slicing approach in which a constant time-step (Δt) is adopted. This is best explained with an example. In a telephone call centre, calls arrive every 3 minutes and are passed to one of two operators who take 5 minutes to deal with the customer (Figure 2.1). It is assumed for now that there is no variation in the inter-arrival time and the service time.

Table 2.1 shows 24 minutes of simulation of the call centre with Δt set to 1 minute. Column two shows the time remaining until a call arrives. Columns three and four show the time remaining until a customer service is complete. The number of calls completed by each operator is calculated.

It is relatively simple to set up a time-slicing simulation for this situation. The same approach could be used for more complex situations, although the table would soon become very large and possibly unmanageable by hand. By devising a flow chart outlining the sequence of activities it would be possible to develop a computer program to perform the simulation, making larger-scale simulations possible. The time-slicing approach can also be modelled easily in a spreadsheet.

There are two main problems with the time-slicing approach. First, it is very inefficient. During many of the time-steps there is no change in the system-state and as a result many computations are unnecessary. In Table 2.1 the only points of interest are when a call arrives, when an operator takes a call and when an operator completes a call. In total there are 22 such points as opposed to the 72 (24×3) calculations performed in Table 2.1. This problem is only likely to be exacerbated the larger the simulation becomes.

A second problem is determining the value of Δt. Albeit that a one-minute time-step seems obvious for the example above, in most simulations the duration of activities cannot

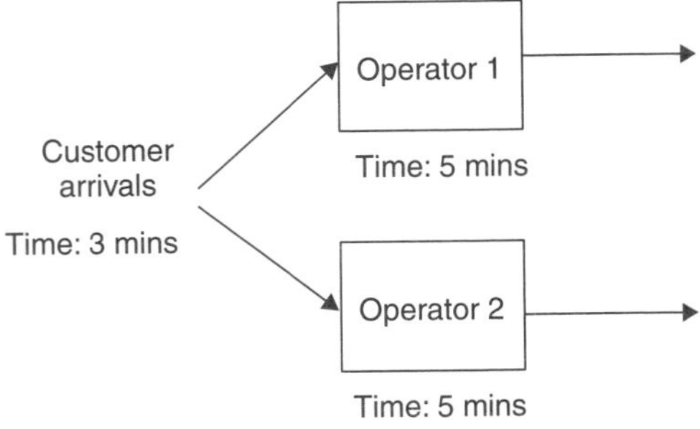

Figure 2.1 **Time-Slicing Approach: Simple Telephone Call Centre Simulation.**

Table 2.1 Time-Slicing Approach: Simple Telephone Call Centre Simulation.

Time	Call arrival	Operator 1	Operator 2
0	3		
1	2		
2	1		
3	3	5	
4	2	4	
5	1	3	
6	3	2	5
7	2	1	4
8	1		3
9	3	5	2
10	2	4	1
11	1	3	
12	3	2	5
13	2	1	4
14	1		3
15	3	5	2
16	2	4	1
17	1	3	
18	3	2	5
19	2	1	4
20	1		3
21	3	5	2
22	2	4	1
23	1	3	
24	3	2	5
Completed calls		3	3

be counted in whole numbers. Also, there is often a wide variation in activity times within a model from possibly seconds (or less) through to hours, days, weeks or more. The discrete-event simulation approach addresses both of these issues.

2.2.2 The discrete-event simulation approach (three-phase method)

In discrete-event simulation only the points in time at which the state of the system changes are represented. In other words the system is modelled as a series of events, that is, instants in time when a state-change occurs. Examples of events are a customer arrives, a customer starts receiving service and a machine is repaired. Each of these occurs at an instant in

Table 2.2 Discrete-Event Simulation Approach: Simple Telephone Call Centre Simulation.

Time	Event
3	Customer arrives
	Operator 1 starts service
6	Customer arrives
	Operator 2 starts service
8	Operator 1 completes service
9	Customer arrives
	Operator 1 starts service
11	Operator 2 completes service
12	Customer arrives
	Operator 2 starts service
14	Operator 1 completes service
15	Customer arrives
	Operator 1 starts service
17	Operator 2 completes service
18	Customer arrives
	Operator 2 starts service
20	Operator 1 completes service
21	Customer arrives
	Operator 1 starts service
23	Operator 2 completes service
24	Customer arrives
	Operator 2 starts service

time. To illustrate this point, the call centre simulation is summarized as a discrete-event simulation in Table 2.2.

Table 2.2 has been created by simply identifying the events in Table 2.1. This obviously requires a time-slicing simulation to be carried out first. It is normal, however, to perform the discrete-event simulation directly. A number of mechanisms have been proposed for carrying out discrete-event simulation, among them are the event-based, activity-based, process-based and three-phase approaches. For a detailed discussion on these see Pidd (1998). In order to develop an understanding of discrete-event simulation, the three-phase approach is described here (Tocher 1963). This approach is used by a number of commercial simulation software packages, but this is not to say that the other mechanisms are not in common use within commercial software as well. From the software user's perspective, however, the specifics of the underlying simulation method are generally hidden.

The three-phase simulation approach

In the three-phase simulation approach events are classified into two types.

- *B (bound or booked) events*: these are state changes that are scheduled to occur at a point in time. For instance, the call arrivals in the call centre model occur every 3 minutes. Once a call has been taken by an operator, it can be scheduled to finish 5 minutes later. This principle applies even when there is variability in the model, by predicting in advance how long a particular activity will take. In general B-events relate to arrivals or the completion of an activity.
- *C (conditional) events*: these are state changes that are dependent on the conditions in the model. For instance, an operator can only start serving a customer *if* there is a customer waiting to be served and the operator is not busy. In general C-events relate to the start of some activity.

In order to demonstrate the three-phase approach a slightly more complex call centre example is now introduced (Figure 2.2). Two types of customer (X, Y) make calls to the centre. Calls arrive from a customer type X every 5 minutes and from a customer type Y every 10 minutes. Arriving calls are placed in a queue (denoted by a circle) before the call router (a touch tone menu system) directs the call to the right operator; an activity that takes 1 minute. There are two operators, the first takes all customer X calls, the second all customer Y calls. Operator 1 takes exactly 4 minutes to deal with a call and operator 2 exactly 7 minutes.

As a first step all of the B and C events for the system need to be defined. These are shown in Tables 2.3 and 2.4 respectively. Note the column that specifies which events are to be scheduled following an event, for instance, the arrival of a customer type X leads to the next arrival being scheduled (event B1). Since each C-event represents the start of an activity, they schedule the B-event that represents the completion of that activity. For events B4 and B5 the calls are output to the "world". This term means that the calls are passed out of the model. Also note that for event B4 and B5 statistics are collected on the number of customers served. For each C-event the conditions for it to be executed are specified.

Having identified all the events, the system can be simulated. Figure 2.3 outlines the three-phase approach. At the start of the simulation the initial state of the model is

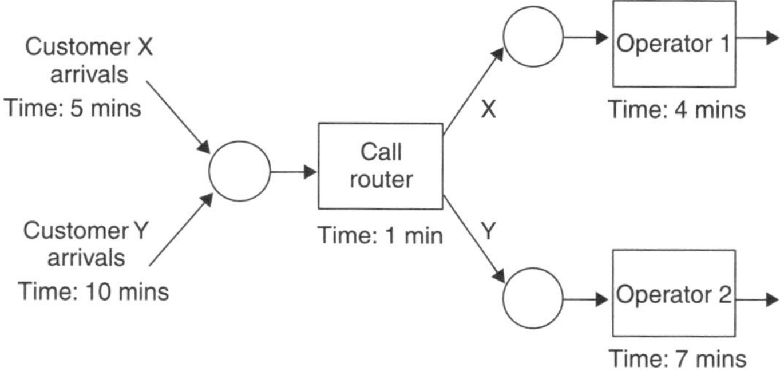

Figure 2.2 Discrete-Event Simulation Approach: Telephone Call Centre Simulation.

Table 2.3 Telephone Call Centre Simulation: B-Events.

Event	Type	Change in state	Future events to schedule
B1	Arrival	Customer X arrives and enters router queue	B1
B2	Arrival	Customer Y arrives and enters router queue	B2
B3	Finish activity	Router completes work and outputs X to operator 1 queue, Y to operator 2 queue	
B4	Finish activity	Operator 1 completes work and outputs to world (increment result work complete X by 1)	
B5	Finish activity	Operator 2 completes work and outputs to world (increment result work complete Y by 1)	

Table 2.4 Telephone Call Centre Simulation: C-Events.

Event	Type	Condition	Change in state	Future events to schedule
C1	Start activity	Call in router queue and router is idle	Router takes call from router queue and starts work	B3
C2	Start activity	Call is in operator 1 queue and operator 1 is idle	Operator 1 takes call from operator 1 queue and starts work	B4
C3	Start activity	Call is in operator 2 queue and operator 1 is idle	Operator 2 takes call from operator 2 queue and starts work	B5

determined. This may involve placing work-in-progress in the model in order to create a realistic initial condition (Section 9.5.2). The initial B-events are also scheduled, for instance, the arrival of the first customers. Scheduled events are placed into an event list that keeps a record of all future events that have been scheduled. The simulation then moves into three phases that are continuously repeated.

In the A-phase, which is also known as the simulation executive, the time of the next event is determined by inspecting the event list. The simulation clock is then advanced to the time of the next event. In the B-phase all B-events due at the clock time are executed. In the C-phase all C-events are attempted and those for which the conditions are met are executed. Since the successful execution of a C-event may mean that another C-event can now be executed, the simulation continues to attempt C-events until no further events can be executed. The simulation then returns to the A-phase unless it is deemed that the simulation is complete. Typically a simulation is run for a predetermined run-length or possibly a set number of arrivals (Section 9.6).

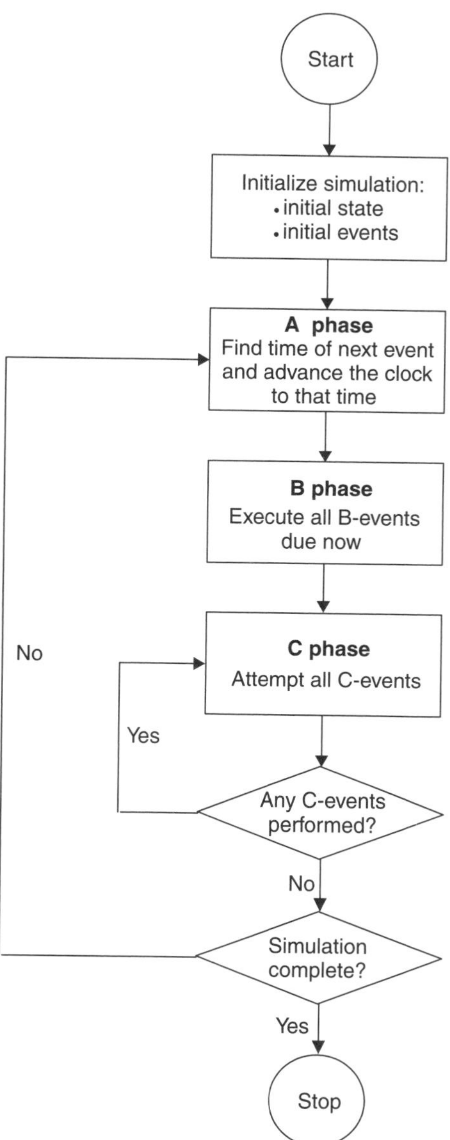

Figure 2.3 The Three-Phase Simulation Approach.

Telephone call centre example: hand simulation

A computer can easily be programmed to follow the stages in the three-phase approach. For the purpose of understanding, however, it is useful to perform a simulation by hand. Tables 2.5 to 2.13 show the three-phase method in operation for the call centre example.

Table 2.5 Call Centre Simulation: Clock = 0 (Initialize Simulation).

Model Status

Phase	Router queue	Router	Oper. 1 queue	Oper. 1	Oper. 2 queue	Oper. 2
	Empty	Idle	Empty	Idle	Empty	Idle

Event List

Event	Time
B1	5
B2	10

Results

Work complete	
X	0
Y	0

Table 2.6 Call Centre Simulation: Clock = 5 (Event B1).

Model Status

Phase	Router queue	Router	Oper. 1 queue	Oper. 1	Oper. 2 queue	Oper. 2
B	X1	Idle	Empty	Idle	Empty	Idle
C	Empty	X1	Empty	Idle	Empty	Idle

Event List

Event	Time
B3	6
B2	10
B1	10

Results

Work complete	
X	0
Y	0

Each table shows a successive iteration of the method for a total of 18 minutes of simulation. The status of the model following the B-phase and the C-phase in each iteration is shown. It is recommended that the reader follows this example in conjunction with the flow chart in Figure 2.3. It may be useful to create a visual simulation by drawing the diagram in Figure 2.2 and using pieces of paper with X and Y written on them to show the movement of customers as described in the tables below.

Table 2.5 shows the initial state of the simulation. It is assumed that there are no calls in the call centre, although some calls could be placed in the queues if it were seen as necessary.

Table 2.7 **Call Centre Simulation: Clock = 6 (Event B3).**

Model Status

Phase	Router queue	Router	Oper. 1 queue	Oper. 1	Oper. 2 queue	Oper. 2
B	Empty	Idle	X1	Idle	Empty	Idle
C	Empty	Idle	Empty	X1	Empty	Idle

Event List

Event	Time
B2	10
B1	10
B4	10

Results

Work complete	
X	0
Y	0

Table 2.8 **Call Centre Simulation: Clock = 10 (Events B2, B1, B4).**

Model Status

Phase	Router queue	Router	Oper. 1 queue	Oper. 1	Oper. 2 queue	Oper. 2
B	X2, Y1	Idle	Empty	Idle	Empty	Idle
C	X2	Y1	Empty	Idle	Empty	Idle

Event List

Event	Time
B3	11
B1	15
B2	20

Results

Work complete	
X	1
Y	0

Two initial events are scheduled for the arrival of the first customers X and Y, which will occur at time 5 minutes and 10 minutes respectively. Note that the event list is placed in chronological sequence so the A-phase can simply pick the event at the top of the list.

The simulation then enters the A-phase which advances the clock to time 5 minutes when the first B-event, B1, is due (Table 2.6). In the B-phase, the call from the first

Table 2.9 Call Centre Simulation: Clock = 11 (Event B3).

Model Status

Phase	Router queue	Router	Oper. 1 queue	Oper. 1	Oper. 2 queue	Oper. 2
B	X2	Idle	Empty	Idle	Y1	Idle
C	Empty	X2	Empty	Idle	Empty	Y1

Event List

Event	Time
B3	12
B1	15
B5	18
B2	20

Results

	Work complete
X	1
Y	0

Table 2.10 Call Centre Simulation: Clock = 12 (Event B3).

Model Status

Phase	Router queue	Router	Oper. 1 queue	Oper. 1	Oper. 2 queue	Oper. 2
B	Empty	Idle	X2	Idle	Empty	Y1
C	Empty	Idle	Empty	X2	Empty	Y1

Event List

Event	Time
B1	15
B4	16
B5	18
B2	20

Results

	Work complete
X	1
Y	0

customer type X arrives (X1) at the router queue. The next arrival of a customer type X call is scheduled to occur at time 10 (event B1). Note that the event is due to take place at the same time as event B2, but is placed after B2 in the event list since its scheduling took place after. This becomes important when these events are executed in Table 2.8. On

Table 2.11 Call Centre Simulation: Clock = 15 (Event B1).

Model Status

Phase	Router queue	Router	Oper. 1 queue	Oper. 1	Oper. 2 queue	Oper. 2
B	X3	Idle	Empty	X2	Empty	Y1
C	Empty	X3	Empty	X2	Empty	Y1

Event List

Event	Time
B4	16
B3	16
B5	18
B2	20
B1	20

Results

	Work complete
X	1
Y	0

Table 2.12 Call Centre Simulation: Clock = 16 (Events B4, B3).

Model Status

Phase	Router queue	Router	Oper. 1 queue	Oper. 1	Oper. 2 queue	Oper. 2
B	Empty	Idle	X3	Idle	Empty	Y1
C	Empty	Idle	Empty	X3	Empty	Y1

Event List

Event	Time
B5	18
B2	20
B1	20
B4	20

Results

	Work complete
X	2
Y	0

entering the C-phase, event C1 is executed. Call X1 is moved to the router and the router is scheduled to complete at time 6 minutes (event B3). No further C-events can be executed.

Returning to the A-phase, the clock is advanced to time 6 minutes and event B3 is executed in the B-phase. As a result, call X1 is transferred to the operator 1 queue

Table 2.13 Call Centre Simulation: Clock = 18 (Event B5).

Model Status

Phase	Router queue	Router	Oper. 1 queue	Oper. 1	Oper. 2 queue	Oper. 2
B	Empty	Idle	Empty	X3	Empty	Idle
C	Empty	Idle	Empty	X3	Empty	Idle

Event List

Event	Time
B2	20
B1	20
B4	20

Results

Work complete	
X	2
Y	1

(Table 2.7). In the C-phase the call is transferred to operator 1, who is scheduled to complete the call at time 10 via event B4.

At time 10, three B-events are executed, B2, B1 and B4 respectively (Table 2.8). These events are all executed before entering the C-phase. As a result of their ordering, call Y1 is selected to enter the router queue before call X2. Here a first-in-first-out priority is used, but an alternative priority could be adopted if required, for instance, answer customer type X calls before customer type Y.

The two arrival events lead to further arrival events being scheduled, B1 at 15 minutes and B2 at 20 minutes. When event B4 is executed, call X1 leaves the model and the work complete count is incremented by 1. Event C1 is executed in the C-phase making call Y1 move to the router and scheduling event B3. No further C-events can be executed.

The simulation then continues in a similar manner through the three phases (Tables 2.9–2.13). For the purposes of this example the simulation is stopped at time 18 minutes (Table 2.13). At this point two calls from customer type X have been completed and one from a customer type Y. Call X3 is being served by operator 1.

2.2.3 The continuous simulation approach

In a whole range of situations, operations are not subject to discrete changes in state, but the state of the system changes continuously through time. The most obvious of these is in operations involving the movement of fluids, for instance, chemical plants and oil refineries. In these systems tanks of fluid are subject to continuously changing volumes. Systems that involve a high volume of fast moving items may also be thought of as continuous, for instance, food manufacturing plants and communications systems. In these situations the level of granularity with which the system is to be analysed determines whether it is seen as discrete or continuous.

Digital computers cannot model continuous changes in state. Therefore, the continuous simulation approach approximates continuous change by taking small discrete time-steps (Δt). Figure 2.4 illustrates how the changes in a level of, say, fluid in a tank might be simulated through time. In this example changes in state over the time-step are approximated linearly. The smaller the time-step the more accurate the approximation, but the slower the simulation runs, because the level is being recalculated more frequently per simulated time unit. This approach is, of course, the same as the time-slicing method described above.

Continuous simulation is widely used in, for instance, engineering, economics and biology. It is less often used for modelling operations systems, although it is not in infrequent use. Some discrete-event simulation packages also have facilities for continuous simulation, while it is always possible to imitate a continuous simulation in a discrete-event package by including a regular event that mimics a time-step (Δt). This is useful because there are circumstances in which discrete and continuous changes need to be combined, for instance, process failures (discrete change) in a chemical plant (continuous change). Huda and Chung (2002) describe an example of a combined discrete and continuous simulation that models a coffee production plant using commercial simulation software.

System dynamics is a specific form of continuous simulation that represents a system as a set of stocks and flows (Forrester 1961; Coyle 1996; Sterman 2000). Among its many applications, the method is particularly useful for looking at strategic issues within organizations. There are a number of situations where system dynamics could be used in place of a discrete-event simulation, or vice versa. For instance, both are used to model supply chains (Anderson *et al.* 2000; Jain *et al.* 2001) and health care issues (Lane *et al.* 1998; Taylor *et al.* 1998). Not many have ventured to discuss the interface between the two approaches, Lane (2000) being one of the few examples. In general, discrete-event simulation is more appropriate when a system needs to be modelled in detail, particularly when individual items need to be tracked through the system.

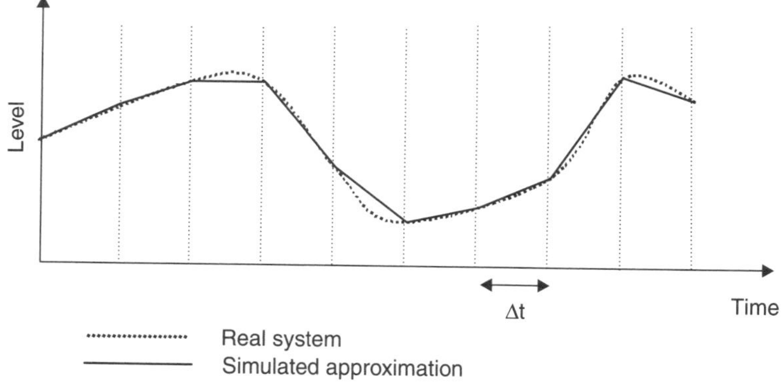

Figure 2.4 Continuous Simulation: Discrete Approximation of a Continuous System.

2.2.4 Summary: modelling the progress of time

Three approaches for modelling the progress of time are described above: time-slicing, discrete-event simulation and continuous simulation. The main focus of this book is on discrete-event simulation. This approach is embodied in a variety of commercial simulation software packages (Chapter 3).

2.3 Modelling Variability

Having described the modelling of the progress of time, the attention now turns to the second aspect that is central to simulation, modelling variability. In this respect the modelling of unpredictable variability presents the key challenge and so much of the discussion that follows focuses on this. There is, however, a brief discussion on the modelling of predictable variability at the end of the section.

2.3.1 Modelling unpredictable variability

So far the call centre simulation has not included any elements of variability and, in particular, unpredictable variability. It is unrealistic to expect the time callers spend at the router and the operators to be fixed. Nor will calls arrive at fixed intervals with exactly two X customers for every Y. How can such unpredictable variability be represented within a simulation?

To answer this question, first take the example of the ratio of X and Y customers. Rather than model the arrival of these customers as separate events, it is common practice to model a single arrival event and to determine the call type as a customer arrives. If there were many customer types this negates the need for a large number of B-events; one for each customer type. For now we will assume that a customer arrives every 3 minutes exactly.

A simple way of determining the call type would be to toss a coin every time a customer arrives in the model. A head could represent an X customer and a tail a Y customer. The shortcoming of this approach is that it assumes an equal proportion of X and Y customers (unless the coin is biased). What if 60% of customers are of type X and only 40% of type Y? This could be represented by taking 10 pieces of paper and writing X on six of them and Y on four. The pieces of paper could then be placed into a hat and every time a customer arrives in the model a piece of paper could be drawn out to determine the customer type. It is important that the paper is replaced each time to maintain the ratio of customers at 60:40.

Although the second approach would enable different customer ratios to be modelled, it is only suitable for hand simulations; a computer cannot draw pieces of paper from a hat! In computer simulation a similar principle is adopted based upon the use of random numbers.

2.3.2 Random numbers

Random numbers are a sequence of numbers that appear in a random order. They are presented either as integer (whole) numbers on a scale of say 0 to 9 or 0 to 99, or as real (with decimal places) numbers on a scale of 0 to 1. A sequence of integer random numbers, on a scale of 0–99, could be generated by placing 100 pieces of paper into a hat, each with a number written on it, and withdrawing numbers from the hat. The pieces of paper are replaced each time. This is known as the top hat method.

Random numbers generated in this fashion have two important properties:

- *Uniform*: there is the same probability of any number occurring at any point in the sequence;
- *Independent*: once a number has been chosen this does not affect the probability of it being chosen again or of another number being chosen.

These properties are maintained because the pieces of paper are replaced each time.

Table 2.14 shows a list of random numbers. Books containing such tables can be obtained (RAND Corporation 1955) and spreadsheets provide functions from which tables of random numbers can be created (e.g. 'RAND' function in Excel). Such tables could be stored for use by a simulation, although this is quite inefficient in terms of computer memory usage. It is, therefore, more usual to generate the random numbers as they are required (Section 2.3.6).

2.3.3 Relating random numbers to variability in a simulation

The random numbers in Table 2.14 can be used to sample the type of an arriving call. They can be associated with the customer type such that 60% of the random numbers relate to type X calls and 40% to type Y calls as follows:

Random numbers	Customer type
00–59	X
60–99	Y

Reading across the top row of random numbers, the first customer to arrive would be a type Y (93), the second a type X (43) and so on. The sequence for the first 10 customers is Y (93), X (43), X (08), X (21), Y (61), X (40), Y (88), X (36), X (10), X (09). Note that the ratio of X to Y customers is 7:3 for this sequence. When a coin is tossed 10 times there will not necessarily be five heads and five tails. At an extreme it is in fact possible that there will be 10 of one or the other. This is not because the coin is biased, but because the process is random. Over very many tosses it is expected that the ratio of heads to tails will be exactly 1:1. In the same way, using random numbers to determine whether customers are of type X or Y over a few arrivals is not expected to give an exact ratio of 6 (X): 4 (Y). Over a great many arrivals, however, the ratio will be more-or-less achieved.

2.3.4 Modelling variability in times

The method described above is useful for modelling proportions. In order to model activity times (or other continuous real variables) a small extension to the approach needs to be adopted. This is best illustrated with an example.

Table 2.14 Integer Random Numbers on a Scale 0–99.

93	43	08	21	61	40	88	36	10	09
34	47	17	99	81	54	44	37	12	97
02	22	48	12	45	00	24	38	43	41
78	71	51	66	19	07	83	29	51	30
82	19	46	05	24	50	09	78	17	64
41	44	39	90	81	22	56	79	25	24
54	32	60	60	32	30	42	50	93	86
23	23	64	16	56	61	21	09	72	36
09	06	82	14	81	05	40	37	55	33
66	86	57	85	63	69	47	56	86	08
27	24	31	05	15	43	45	23	62	03
19	36	86	85	43	17	99	74	72	63
22	00	88	14	84	56	89	95	05	94
87	43	20	07	35	41	51	10	11	31
66	00	05	46	23	22	22	25	21	70
43	28	43	18	66	86	42	91	55	48
28	20	62	82	06	82	79	60	73	67
77	78	43	27	54	89	22	02	78	35
72	67	13	42	46	33	27	66	34	24
06	70	58	78	07	89	71	75	03	60

Up to this point it has been assumed that calls arrive at a fixed interval. This is obviously unrealistic and there is likely to be some level of variation in the time between call arrivals. Figure 2.5 shows a frequency distribution for the inter-arrival time of calls at the call centre. The mean of this distribution is 3 minutes, but actual inter-arrival times can vary from zero (calls arriving together) to 7 minutes.

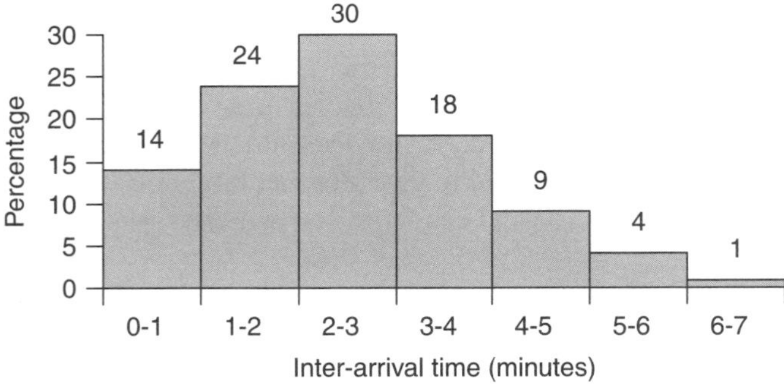

Figure 2.5 Frequency Distribution for Inter-Arrival Time of Calls.

Table 2.15 Relation of Random Numbers to Sampled Inter-Arrival Times.

Random numbers	Inter-arrival time (minutes)
00–13	0–1
14–37	1–2
38–67	2–3
68–85	3–4
86–94	4–5
95–98	5–6
99	6–7

Random numbers can be related to the frequencies in Figure 2.5 in a similar fashion to that used for the proportion of customer types above (Table 2.15). In this way, the correct proportion of inter-arrival times in each range can be obtained. This, however, only gives the range within which the inter-arrival time falls. In order to obtain the actual inter-arrival time, a second random number could be selected, divided by 100 and added to the lower end of the range.

To illustrate, Table 2.16 shows the inter-arrival time for the first 10 calls. Random numbers are taken from row six and row 11 of Table 2.14. Different rows are used for these samples, as well as for the sampling of customer type, to ensure complete independence. Note that the mean of the 10 samples is only 2.38 minutes and the frequency of samples in each range is very different from the distribution in Figure 2.5. It would only be after many samples are taken that the mean and shape of the sampled distribution would become similar to the original data.

Table 2.16 Inter-Arrival Time of the First 10 Calls: Sampled using Random Numbers.

Customer	First random number (row 6)	Inter-arrival time range	Second random number (row 11)	Inter-arrival time (minutes)
1	41	2–3	27	2.27
2	44	2–3	24	2.24
3	39	2–3	31	2.31
4	90	4–5	05	4.05
5	81	3–4	15	3.15
6	22	1–2	43	1.43
7	56	2–3	45	2.45
8	79	3–4	23	3.23
9	25	1–2	62	1.62
10	24	1–2	03	1.03
Mean				2.38

A known sequence of random numbers is used to generate the variability. As a result the sequence of events, in this case the inter-arrival times, can be generated over and over again by using the same set of random numbers. Here this would mean always starting in row 6 and 11 to sample the arrival times. This approach enables experiments with a simulation model to be repeated under the same conditions as many times as is required and so provides the benefit of being able to control the experimental conditions as discussed in Section 1.3.2. In order to change the conditions in terms of variability, a different set of random numbers needs to be selected, for instance, starting in rows 15 and 20. The control of random numbers during simulation experiments is discussed in more detail in Section 8.3.2 and Section 9.6.2.

A hand simulation could now be performed using the three-phase approach described in Section 2.2.2, but instead of using the fixed data, the inter-arrival times and customer types could be sampled using the process described above. Each time a call arrives its type would be sampled along with the arrival time of the next call. There would be only one B-phase arrival event, say B1, instead of two. The activity times at the router and operators should also be made to vary. A distribution for each process could be specified and the same approach could be adopted for sampling the activity times.

2.3.5 Sampling from standard statistical distributions

In the previous sub-section, samples are taken by relating random numbers to an empirical distribution. Often, samples are required from standard statistical distributions, for instance, the normal distribution. The sampling concept is very similar to that above. Take, for instance, a normal distribution with a mean of 5 and standard deviation of 1, as shown in Figure 2.6. To sample a value from this distribution, the random number selected is taken to be a percentage of the area under the curve. Working from the left-hand end of the distribution, the sample value is the point on the *x*-axis at which the area under the curve is equal to that percentage. If, for instance, the random number is 30, then the sample would be selected from the point at which 30% of the area under the curve is found. In the example this gives a sample value of 4.48, as shown in Figure 2.6.

It is quite difficult to think in terms of identifying the area under a curve. Therefore, rather than sampling directly from a distribution's probability density function (PDF), as in Figure 2.6, samples are taken using the cumulative distribution function (CDF). This specifies the percentage of the area under the curve for any given value of *x*. Figure 2.7 shows the cumulative distribution function for the normal distribution displayed in Figure 2.6. By identifying the point at which the cumulative distribution function is equal to a random number (say, 30), then the sample value of *x* can be determined.

Although the principle is fairly straightforward, in practice sampling from such distributions requires either direct or numerical integration of the distribution's probability density function (to obtain its cumulative distribution function). Thankfully simulation software packages provide functions that give samples from a range of useful statistical distributions (Section 7.4.3 and Appendix 4) without the need to refer to the underlying theory. As a result, this process is not described in any more detail here. Pidd (1998) and Law and Kelton (2000) both describe procedures for sampling from distributions in some detail.

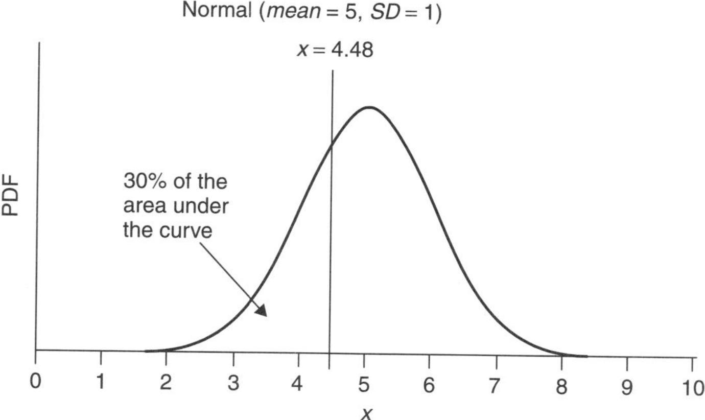

Figure 2.6 Sampling from a Normal Distribution.

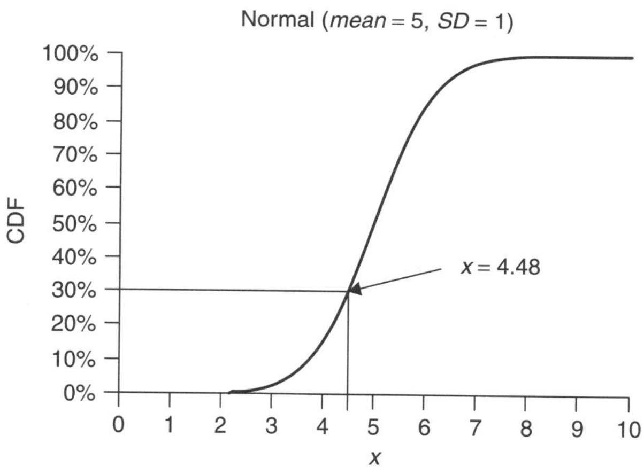

Figure 2.7 Sampling from the Cumulative Distribution Function for a Normal Distribution.

2.3.6 Computer generated random numbers

Large-scale simulation models can require thousands or even millions of random numbers during a run. Generating so many numbers manually, using say the top hat method, is obviously impractical. A lot of computer memory is also required to store so many numbers. In order to address this issue, it is more normal for the computer to generate the random numbers as they are required.

By nature, computers do not behave in a random fashion, and so they are not apt at creating random numbers. There are, however, algorithms that give the appearance of producing random numbers, albeit that the results are completely predictable! Although it is always possible to predict the next number in the sequence (using the algorithm), when a stream of the numbers is inspected, they have the properties of uniformity and independence required for randomness. As a result, random numbers generated in this fashion are known as *pseudo random numbers*.

A simple, but commonly used, algorithm for generating random numbers is as follows:

$$X_{i+1} = aX_i + c \ (mod\ m)$$

where:

X_i : stream of random numbers (integer) on the interval $(0, m - 1)$
a : multiplier constant
c : additive constant
m : modulus; *mod* m means take the remainder having divided by m

Values for each of the constants are selected along with a starting value for X (X_0), otherwise known as the "seed". If the random numbers are required on a scale of 0–1, as is more common with computer generated numbers, then the X_i can be divided by m.

Table 2.17 illustrates the algorithm with $X_0 = 8$, $a = 4$, $c = 0$ and $m = 25$. This gives random numbers on a range of 0 to 24, the maximum always being one less than the value of m. Note that the stream repeats itself after $i = 9$. This is a common problem with this algorithm and the values of the constants need to be carefully selected to ensure that the cycle is sufficiently long so it does not repeat itself during a simulation run. This example

Table 2.17 Generation of Random Numbers from an Algorithm.

i	X_i	$4X_i$
0	8	32
1	7	28
2	3	12
3	12	48
4	23	92
5	17	68
6	18	72
7	22	88
8	13	52
9	2	8
10	8	32
11	7	28
12	3	12
13	12	48
14	23	92
15	17	68

is purely illustrative and normally much larger values, at least of m, are used to ensure the cycle is very long.

This type of approach gives complete control over the random numbers that are generated. By using the same seed and constants, the same stream of random numbers can be generated over and over again. This gives the same control over the experimental conditions as with the use of the random number table (Table 2.14). In order to change the model conditions in terms of variability, a different random number seed (X_0) needs to be selected. By changing the seed different streams of pseudo random numbers are generated. These streams are referred to as *pseudo random number streams*.

More detailed discussion on generating random numbers can be found in Kleijnen and van Groenendaal (1992), L'Ecuyer (1994), Pidd (1998) and Law and Kelton (2000). These also describe methods for testing whether the generated random numbers meet the conditions of uniformity and independence.

2.3.7 Modelling predictable variability

The discussion above focuses on the modelling of unpredictable variability. Predictable variability does not require the use of random numbers, but simply some means for specifying when a variation (event) will occur. For instance, the time at which an operator comes on, or goes off, shift is stated as an item of data. The event can then be executed in the normal manner through the B and C-phases of the simulation.

2.3.8 Summary on modelling variability

This section covers the fundamental issues in modelling variability. Central to the modelling of unpredictable variability is the use of random numbers and the means of relating these numbers to empirical and statistical distributions to obtain samples. There is also some discussion on the computer generation of random numbers and the modelling of predictable variability.

Figure 2.8 summarizes the issues in modelling variability. For predictable variability it is necessary to specify the time at which the variation will occur and then to execute the event. For unpredictable variability the distribution must be specified, random numbers generated and a sample taken from the distribution before the event can be executed. The range and selection of distributions for modelling unpredictable variability is discussed in detail in Sections 7.4 and 7.5.

2.4 Conclusion

An overview of how a simulation works has been given, showing how the progression of time and variability can be represented. Three methods for modelling the progress of time are discussed: time-slicing, discrete-event and continuous. Discrete-event is the most commonly used for modelling operations systems, although continuous simulation (which is based on a time-slicing approach) is sometimes required. One specific approach to discrete-event

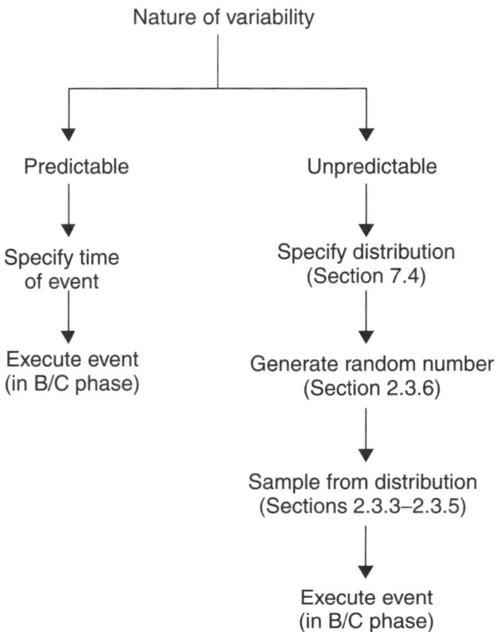

Figure 2.8 Summary of Issues in Modelling Variability.

simulation, the three-phase method, is described. The use of random numbers as the basis for modelling variability is also described, along with the generation of random numbers on a computer. All of this is described at an introductory level with the aim of understanding the fundamentals. References are given which provide a more in-depth treatment of these topics. Having understood the basics of what is inside simulation software, the next task is to discuss the nature and range of the software that are available.

Exercises

E2.1 An airport is planning its requirements for runway facilities and wishes to know whether the current plan to have a single full-length runway is sufficient. It is expected that during peak periods aeroplanes will land every 4 minutes (exactly) and that aeroplanes will take-off with the same frequency. For reasons of safety both landing and taking-off aeroplanes are given a 2-minute slot on the runway. If the runway is in use, then both landing and taking-off aeroplanes queue until the runway is available. Priority is then given to landing aeroplanes.

Develop a time-slice simulation showing 20 minutes of operation at the airport.

E2.2 For the airport problem described in Exercise E2.1 develop a three-phase discrete-event simulation of the problem.

a) Define the B-events and C-events for the problem.
b) Simulate 20 minutes of operation at the airport.

E2.3 Following a discussion with the airport's operations manager, more accurate data on the take-off and landing of aeroplanes have come to light. Aeroplanes are classified into two sizes: small and large. Small aeroplanes only require a 1.5-minute slot on the runway, while large aeroplanes require 2.5 minutes. It is expected that 70% of aeroplanes will be small. The time between aeroplanes arriving for landing is expected to be as follows:

Time between arrival for landing (minutes)	Percentage
2–3	30%
3–4	35%
4–5	25%
5–6	10%

The time between arrivals for take-off is expected to be the same.
Develop a three-phase discrete-event simulation of the problem.

a) Define the B-events and C-events for the problem.
b) Create samples from the distributions for inter-arrival time and aeroplane size.
c) Simulate a period of operation at the airport.

E2.4 Section 2.3.6 describes an algorithm for generating random numbers. Research and identify alternative mechanisms for generating random numbers. What are the benefits and problems with alternative generators? How can the efficacy of a random number generator be tested? (Hint: use the references in Section 2.3.6 as a starting point.)

E2.5 Section 2.3.5 describes how samples can be taken from a normal distribution. Various algorithms are available for sampling from a range of statistical distributions. For each of the distributions described in Appendix 4 identify a sampling algorithm. (Hint: use the references in Section 2.3.5 as a starting point.)

References

Anderson, E.G., Fine, C.H. and Parker, G.G. (2000) "Upstream volatility in the supply chain: the machine tool industry as a case study". *Production and Operations Management*, 9(3), 239–261.

Coyle, R.G. (1996) *System Dynamics Modelling: A Practical Approach*. London: Chapman & Hall.

Forrester, J.W. (1961) *Industrial Dynamics*. Cambridge, MA: MIT Press.

Huda, A.M. and Chung, C.A. (2002) "Simulation modeling and analysis issues for high-speed combined continuous and discrete food industry manufacturing processes". *Computers and Industrial Engineering*, 43, 473–483.

Jain, S., Workman, R.W., Collins, L.M., Ervin, E.C. and Lathrop, A.P. (2001) "Development of a high-level supply chain simulation model". *Proceedings of the 2001 Winter Simulation Conference* (Peters, B.A., Smith, J.S., Medeiros, D.J. and Rohrer, M.W., eds). Piscataway, NJ: IEEE, pp. 1129–1137.

Kleijnen, J.P.C. and van Groenendaal, W. (1992) *Simulation: A Statistical Perspective*. Chichester, UK: Wiley.

Lane, D.C. (2000) "You just don't understand me: modes of failure and success in the discourse between system dynamics and discrete event simulation". Working Paper OR.00.34, London School of Economics and Political Science, Operational Research.

Lane, D., Monefeldt, C. and Rosenhead, J. (1998) "Emergency – but no accident". *OR Insight*, 11(4), 2–10.

Law, A.M. and Kelton, W.D. (2000) *Simulation Modeling and Analysis*, 3rd edn. New York: McGraw-Hill.

L'Ecuyer, P. (1994) "Uniform random number generation". In *Annals of Operations Research Vol 23: Simulation and Modeling* (O. Balci, ed.). Basel: J.C. Balzer.

Pidd, M. (1998) *Computer Simulation in Management Science*, 4th edn. Chichester, UK: Wiley.

RAND Corporation (1955) *A Million Random Digits with 100,000 Normal Deviates*. Glencoe, IL: The Free Press.

Sterman, J.D. (2000) *Business Dynamics: Systems Thinking and Modeling for a Complex World*. New York: Irwin/McGraw-Hill.

Taylor, S., Eldabi, T. and Paul, R.J. (1998) "Clinical trials, economic evaluation and simulation". *OR Insight*, 11(4), 22–28.

Tocher, K.D. (1963) *The Art of Simulation*. London: The English Universities Press.

Software for Simulation 3

3.1 Introduction

The development of (discrete-event) simulation software has been very closely allied to the development of computing. As hardware and software have improved, so has the software for computer simulation. The 1950s saw the first computer simulations. In the decade that followed, the advent of programming languages such as Fortran greatly benefited the simulation community. The 1960s also saw the first specialist simulation languages such as GPSS (Schriber 1974) and SIMULA (Dahl and Nygaard 1966). The early simulations were lines of computer code; to the non-expert a black box into which data were input and results were output following a simulation run. Amiry (1965) was among the first to provide an animation of the running model giving greater understanding to the model user.

In the 1970s computer technology continued to advance with the introduction of the microprocessor and the microcomputer. Hurrion (1976) published his PhD thesis outlining the potential for simulations that are both visual and interactive. This resulted in the development of the first visual interactive simulation (VIS) language in 1979, SEE-WHY (Fiddy *et al.*, 1981). The 1980s and 1990s saw the continued development of computing, with the introduction of the PC (personal computer) and windows technology. During this period a wide range of simulation languages and simulators became available (Law and Kelton 2000). Recent developments have seen improvements in the functionality and animation capabilities of the software (3D displays), greater compatibility with other software packages (e.g. spreadsheets and databases), use of simulation across the world wide web and the introduction of simulation optimizers.

A wide range of software is now available for developing simulation models. As a result, simulation modellers need to be aware of the possibilities in order to select the appropriate tool for model development. This chapter attempts to create this awareness by answering the following three questions:

- What types of software can be used for developing simulation models?
- What specific packages are available?
- How can an appropriate package be selected?

First there is a description of the nature and range of modern simulation software. The advantages and disadvantages of the different types are discussed. Following this, the process of selecting an appropriate simulation package is described. The focus throughout is on software for discrete-event simulation, although some of the software also have capabilities for performing continuous simulation.

3.2 Visual Interactive Simulation

Today, the majority of simulation models could be described as being visual interactive simulations (VIS). As stated above, this was a concept first introduced by Hurrion (1976). The idea is that the model provides a *visual* display showing an animation of the model as it runs. Figure 3.1 shows an example of such a display for a model of a bank. The display shows people queuing and being served at different locations (information desk, tellers, automated tellers, etc.). It is quite common to use different colours to represent the status of an element, for instance, whether a machine is working, idle or broken. The display can range from a simple schematic to a highly complex 3D animation.

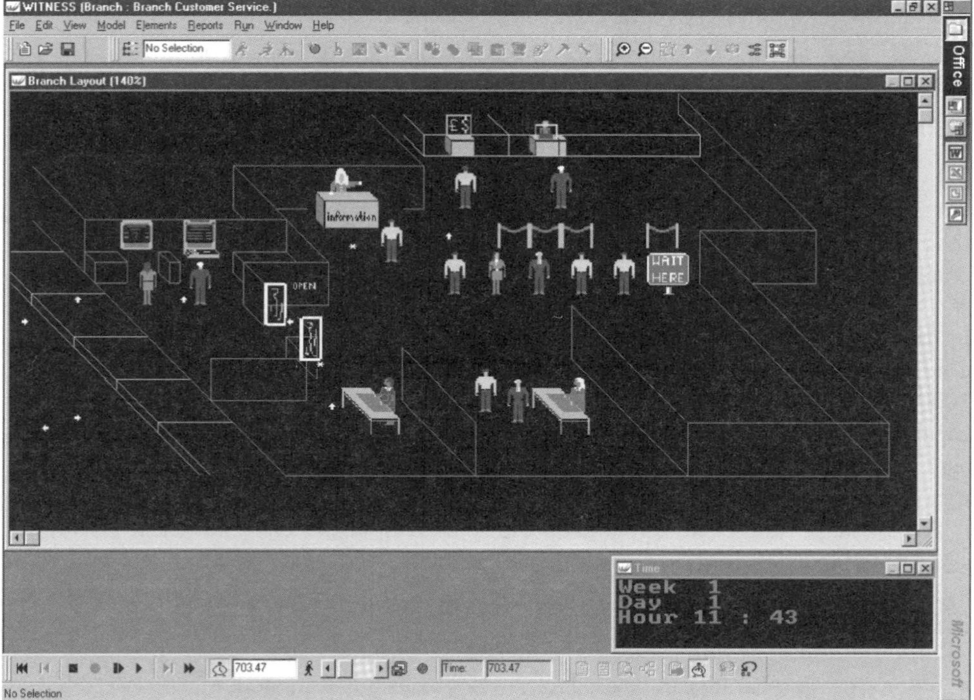

Figure 3.1 Example of a Visual Interactive Simulation of a Bank.

The user is also able to *interact* with the running model. The user can stop the simulation run at any point and obtain information (additional to that on the animated display) about the status of the model and the performance of the system being modelled. The user can then make alterations to the model before running it further. For example, an additional teller might be added to the model in Figure 3.1 when it is identified that large queues are building up. The simulation can also stop automatically at a point when it requires the user to interact with it. For instance, in the bank model, if the queues reach a certain length the simulation could stop and ask the user what action he/she wishes to take.

The main benefits of VIS are as follows:

- *Greater understanding of the model.* The visual display enables the model user to track events as they occur in the simulation and to identify potential shortcomings in the operations system.
- *Easier model verification and validation (Chapter 12).* Coding errors can be identified by spurious events that occur while the model runs. The interactive capability can be used to force the model into specific conditions, and so to test its correctness. Non-simulation experts can view the model as it runs and comment on its validity.
- *Enables interactive experimentation (Section 10.2.1).* New ideas can be implemented in the model, improving the understanding of the model and the operations system, and enabling potential improvements to be identified.
- *Improved understanding of the results.* The results can be related to specific events that have been observed during model runs. The simulation can also be re-run and observed to understand why specific results have been obtained.
- *Improved communication of the model and its findings to all parties.* Non-simulation experts are able to relate to the model, enabling a wider group to participate in a simulation study.
- *Provides the potential for using simulation in group problem solving.* Validation and experimentation can be carried out in a group setting with input from a range of interested parties (Robinson 2001). This can facilitate greater creativity and consensus in problem solving.

3.3 Simulation Software

In general terms, today's simulation modellers are faced with three options for developing computer models: spreadsheets, programming languages and specialist software.

3.3.1 Spreadsheets

Spreadsheet packages, such as Excel, provide some rudimentary capabilities for simulation modelling. It is relatively straightforward to develop a simple time-slice model using the basic capabilities of a spreadsheet. In Excel, random numbers can be generated using the "RAND" function. Samples can be taken from empirical distributions using the "IF" function or more succinctly with a lookup function ("VLOOKUP" or "HLOOKUP"). Some functions for sampling from statistical distributions are provided by Excel, for instance, normal and gamma distributions (Section 7.4.3 and Appendix 4). Various spreadsheet add-ins can be obtained that provide specific simulation capabilities. @RISK is one such add-in that provides capabilities for distribution sampling and modelling the progression of time (Winston 1998).

Beyond a very rudimentary level, however, it becomes necessary to use some programming capabilities within the spreadsheet, for instance, macros or Visual Basic for Applications in Excel. It is also difficult to develop a model animation using a spreadsheet, although a basic display can be provided.

For a useful discussion on spreadsheet simulation see Seila (2002). Meanwhile, Greasley (1998) describes an example of a simulation model developed in a spreadsheet.

3.3.2 Programming languages

Simulation models can be developed using general purpose programming languages such as Visual Basic, C++ and Java. The use of languages gives the modeller a great deal of flexibility in model design. It can be time consuming, however, since the modeller needs to develop the simulation capabilities from scratch, for instance, the three-phase executive set out in Section 2.2.2. Modern programming languages such as C++ support object orientated approaches which can be beneficial for simulation modelling (Pidd 1992). Java is particularly useful for developing simulations that are to run across the world wide web.

3.3.3 Specialist simulation software

Many specialist simulation software packages are available. Law and Kelton (2000) identify two broad types of specialist simulation package. *General purpose simulation packages* are intended for use on a wide range of applications, albeit they might have special features for some applications. *Application orientated simulation packages* are focused on specific applications, for instance, medical, production scheduling or call centres. A more focused package tends to be easier to use, possibly only requiring the entry of relevant data, but it obviously has a much narrower range of application.

The majority of these specialist packages could be described as visual interactive modelling systems (VIMS) (Pidd 1998). VIMS enable a simulation to be built as well as run in a visual and interactive manner. The software provides a predefined set of simulation objects. The modeller selects the required objects and defines the logic of the model through a series of menus. The visual display is also developed through a set of menus. As a result, the modeller requires little in the way of programming skills, although most VIMS either link to a programming language or have their own internal language to enable the modelling of more complex logic. For the majority of models it is necessary to use the programming interface to a greater or lesser degree.

The terms VIS and VIMS should not be confused. VIS refers to the nature of the model while VIMS refers to how it is developed. Indeed, a VIS does not necessarily have to be developed using a VIMS, but could be developed in a programming language or a spreadsheet. Meanwhile, a simulation model built using a VIMS is not necessarily a VIS, since, for instance, the modeller may decide not to have a visual display.

Table 3.1 Examples of Specialist Simulation Software.

Software	Supplier
Arena	Rockwell Software
AutoMod	Brooks-PRI Automation
Awe Sim	Frontstep, Inc.
Enterprise Dynamics	Incontrol Enterprise Dynamics
Extend	Imagine That, Inc.
Flexsim	Flexsim Software Products, Inc.
GPSS/H	Wolverine Software Corporation
Micro Saint	Micro Analysis and Design
ProModel (MedModel, ServiceModel)	ProModel Corporation
Quest	DELMIA Corporation
ShowFlow	Webb Systems Limited
SIGMA	Custom Simulation
Simprocess	CACI Products Company
Simul8	Visual8 Corporation
SLX	Wolverine Software Corporation
Visual Simulation Environment	Orca Computer, Inc.
Witness	Lanner Group, Inc.

There is no attempt here to provide a comprehensive list of simulation software or to review the packages that are available. Any such attempt would be futile, since the available packages are constantly being updated, new packages are being made available and old packages are disappearing. As a result, any review or list of software is out-of-date almost as soon as it is written. To provide a starting point, however, a list of some of the software packages available at the time of writing is provided in Table 3.1. Useful places for finding information on the available software are:

- IIE Solutions have regular simulation software surveys (e.g. Elliott 2001).
- ORMS Today also provide surveys of simulation software (e.g. Swain 2001).
- The Winter Simulation Conference (www: Winter Simulation Conference) includes a fairly comprehensive exhibition and tutorial papers on simulation software.
- The INFORMS (Institute for Operations Research and the Management Sciences) College on Computer Simulation provides a list of simulation software and links to the associated vendors through their web site (www: INFORMS-Computer Simulation).

3.3.4 Comparing spreadsheets, programming languages and specialist simulation software

Table 3.2 provides a broad comparison of the approaches to simulation modelling described above. This is only intended to give a general sense of where the advantages and

Table 3.2 A Comparison of Spreadsheets, Programming Languages and Specialist Simulation Software for Simulation Modelling.

Feature	Spreadsheet	Programming language	Specialist simulation software
Range of application	Low	High	Medium
Modelling flexibility	Low	High	Medium
Duration of model build	Medium	Long	Short
Ease of use	Medium	Low	High
Ease of model validation	Medium	Low	High
Run-speed	Low	High	Medium
Time to obtain software skills	Short (medium for macro use)	Long	Medium
Price	Low	Low	High

disadvantages of the different approaches lie; it is not a detailed comparison. What it shows is that programming languages generally provide the greatest range of applications and modelling flexibility. Models developed in programming languages are also likely to run faster than equivalent models in the other software. Meanwhile, specialist simulation software tends to win on speed of model build and ease of use. Spreadsheets are probably better than programming languages in respect of speed of model build and ease of use (at least for smaller applications), but they are not as quick or straightforward to use as the specialist software. Indeed, the only area in Table 3.2 in which spreadsheets are likely to be preferred is in the time required to obtain the software skills. Because many people are already familiar with spreadsheets, very little time is required to adapt to simulation modelling in a spreadsheet. The time for learning is increased, however, if the macro language is required for model development. Spreadsheets and programming languages are similarly priced, while specialist simulation software tends to be priced from around $1000 (similar to a spreadsheet) up to $20,000 or more. Price reductions are normally available for multiple copies.

The choice of software depends upon the nature of the study, particularly its level of complexity. For very simple applications a spreadsheet may suffice and is probably the best option, because in most cases the software and skills are already available within an organization. Most applications, however, are more complex and it soon becomes necessary to adopt more powerful software. Specialist (general purpose) simulation packages are able to model a very wide range of applications (their capabilities have increased over the years) and should suffice unless the model is highly complex. In this case a programming language is probably required.

The assumption in this book is that the modeller is using a specialist simulation package, since these are suitable for modelling most operations systems. That said, the modelling process described in the chapters that follow also applies to the use of spreadsheets and programming languages.

3.4 Selection of Simulation Software

Having outlined the nature of simulation software, this section discusses the selection of a simulation package for an organization. It is assumed that the decision has already been made to use specialist simulation software, so the decision at this point is which software package. Below a series of steps for software selection is described.

Before describing the selection process it is worth commenting on the importance of package selection. Some authors stress the vital role of package selection in successful simulation modelling, for instance, Law and McComas (1989). Meanwhile, there is some evidence to the contrary, suggesting that the simulation software only plays a small part in the success of a study (Robinson and Pidd 1998). It is notable that many modellers use the same simulation software repeatedly on quite different problems. They seem to be quite adept at flexing the software to meet the requirements of the project and there is a natural preference to use software that is already available and familiar.

This apparent difference in view can be explained as follows. Within a certain domain of application, most of the "more powerful" simulation packages are quite capable of modelling what is required. Indeed, with their growing capabilities over the past years, this domain of application has steadily increased. There are always, of course, applications that go beyond the capabilities of a software package. It is when we are dealing with these applications that careful software selection is needed. Because much of the available software has been designed specifically for modelling operations systems, there are few occasions on which the software simply cannot model these systems. As a result, software selection becomes more a matter of the convenience with which the system can be modelled than the capability of modelling the system. It has to be said that as long as the software suffices, the expertise of the modeller (e.g. in problem solving, statistics, project management, people management and communication) is probably of far greater importance to successful simulation modelling.

3.4.1 The process of software selection

A number of authors describe a series of steps for selecting simulation software, among them are, Holder (1990), Hlupic and Paul (1996) and Nikoukaran and Paul (1999). Bard (1997) describes an interesting case study of software selection for modelling postal operations. The steps suggested by these authors are quite similar, although there are some variations. The selection process could be summarized as follows:

- *Step 1*: establish the modelling requirements
- *Step 2*: survey and shortlist the software
- *Step 3*: establish evaluation criteria
- *Step 4*: evaluate the software in relation to the criteria
- *Step 5*: software selection

This process is likely to be fairly linear, moving from step 1 through to 5. There may be some cause for iteration, particularly between steps 3 to 5, as the evaluation process will probably change opinions about the criteria and their importance. Each step is now described in a little more detail.

3.4.2 Step 1: Establish the modelling requirements

The requirements for simulation modelling within the organization need to be established. First, the nature of the systems which are to be modelled should be identified. Is the software to be used for a single application or is it intended for more general use? Does this general use involve only a narrow domain of application (e.g. flexible manufacturing systems), or does it entail modelling a wide variety of systems (e.g. if the software is to be used in consulting work)?

The modelling approach is also important. In particular whether the software is for "quick and dirty" modelling or complex/detailed modelling (Hlupic and Paul 1996). The former primarily requires ease-of-use, while the latter needs a much greater level of functionality.

Any constraints that exist within the organization must also be considered. These might include the availability of finance, the level of software and modelling skills, and the hardware and software policy of the organization.

3.4.3 Step 2: Survey and shortlist the software

Having identified at a general level the modelling requirements, the next task is to create a shortlist of simulation software. A longlist can be obtained using the sources described in Section 3.3.3. Shortlisting can then take place by obtaining outline information on the software to determine whether they meet the organization's modelling requirements. This outline information can probably be obtained from vendor web sites, with some need for direct contact to answer specific questions. Further to this, the surveys carried out in IIE Solutions and ORMS Today provide some useful information. It may also be useful to seek the advice of simulation experts who have some knowledge of a range of packages. The aim should be quickly to eliminate packages that obviously do not meet the organization's requirements, with a view to having a shortlist of five or less packages to include in a more detailed evaluation.

3.4.4 Step 3: Establish evaluation criteria

Criteria for comparing the shortlisted simulation packages need to be established. Table 3.3 provides a list of criteria, grouped under a series of headings, that might be used. Note that some of these criteria (e.g. ability to perform multiple replications) are explained in the proceeding chapters. Other useful lists of criteria can be found in Holder (1990), Van Breedman *et al.* (1990), Banks and Gibson (1997), Nikoukaran *et al.* (1999) and Law and Kelton (2000). Hlupic *et al.* (1999) provide the most comprehensive list with over 250 criteria.

It is not suggested that every criterion from these lists should be included in a software evaluation. The criteria should be selected on the basis of the organization's needs and the modelling requirements, as discussed in step 1. The list of criteria is probably best negotiated between key members of the organization, possibly with the help of some expert opinion.

Table 3.3 Some Criteria for Simulation Software Selection.

Hardware/software requirements
Hardware platform required
Operating system required
Software protection (hardware security device?)
Availability of network licences
Features for use on the world wide web

Model coding and testing
Ease of model development
Can a model be built and run in small steps?
Availability of debugging aids (e.g. syntax checking, consistency checking, trace)
Maximum model size
Maximum dimensions of objects (e.g. arrays)
Features for documenting a model
Availability of help facility
Availability of software wizard

Visual features
Is the display concurrent with the run, or is it a playback feature?
Speed with which display can be developed
Can user icons be drawn?
Availability of icon libraries
Ability to pan and zoom
Ability to locate objects on the display
Smoothness of animation
Availability of 3D animation

Input data and analysis features
Distribution fitting
Ability to sample from empirical distributions
Which statistical distributions are available?
Ability to import data from other software

Reporting and output analysis features
Availability of standard reports for model objects
Availability of graphical reporting
Ability to develop customized reports
Ability to export results to other software
Statistical analysis of results

Experimentation
Probable run-speed
Run control (step, animated, batch)
Interactive capability
Number of random number streams available
Control of random number streams
Ability to perform multiple replications
Facilities for organizing batches of runs
Provision of advice on warm-up, run-length and multiple replications
Availability of an optimizer
Ability to distribute runs across networked computers

Support
Availability of a help desk
Availability of consultancy support
Type of training given
Frequency of software upgrades
What is in the next upgrade?
Foreign language versions and support
Quality of documentation

Pedigree
Size of vendor's organization
How long has the package been available?
Have similar applications been modelled with the package?
Number of users (in industry sector)
Geographic usage of the package
Availability of literature on the package and package use

Cost
Purchase price
Maintenance fee
Cost of support
Cost of training
Time to learn the software
Availability of lower cost run-only licence

3.4.5 Step 4: Evaluate the software in relation to the criteria

Each of the shortlisted packages needs to be evaluated in relation to the criteria. A number of means can be employed for establishing the extent to which the criteria are met by a package:

- *Discussion with the software vendor.* As far as possible get information from technical staff rather than sales staff, they know the product better! Be sceptical of the claims of software vendors (Pidd 1989), this is not to say that they are dishonest, but they are trying to sell you their software.
- *Software demonstrations.* Ask the vendor to demonstrate the capabilities of the software, but be wary of demonstrations particularly if they only solve a test problem (Banks *et al.*, 2001). Such demonstrations may show the cleverness of the software, but they do not necessarily show how well the software suits the intended application.
- *Demonstration models.* Ask the software vendor to develop a demonstration model of a simplified version of the intended application. This helps to assess the suitability of the software for the application. If possible, get them to develop the model in front of you.
- *Discussion with users of the software.* Speak with other users of the software and where possible try to locate them yourself, rather than rely upon the vendor to nominate a reference site.
- *Obtaining a free evaluation copy of the software.* Many vendors provide free evaluation copies of the software. This is a useful idea if there is sufficient time to learn and use the package during the evaluation.
- *Software documentation.* Try to obtain copies of the documentation.
- *Literature.* From time-to-time written descriptions and reviews of simulation software appear, largely in books and conference and journal papers. Be wary of software reviews, however. Most reviews I have seen of packages I know well contain significant inaccuracies. This is either because the software has been enhanced since the review was written, or because the reviewer simply did not have sufficient knowledge of the package and so makes incorrect statements about its capabilities.
- *Expert opinion.* Obtain the views of independent simulation experts, but bear in mind that they may be subject to some bias.

The extent to which all of these sources can be used depends upon the time available for the evaluation. Obviously any evaluation approach that requires the development of models is going to require significantly more time.

The evaluation should lead to an assessment of the extent to which each package meets the criteria set out in Section 3.4.4. A simple "yes" or "no" by each criterion to indicate whether or not a package has that capability may suffice. However, because there are degrees of capability, it is probably better to devise a scale for scoring the criteria, say 1 to 5, indicating the level of adherence. Some criteria can be assessed objectively (e.g. purchase price), while for others subjective judgements must be made (e.g. quality of documentation). As far as possible, it is best to find objective measures to evaluate the criteria.

3.4.6 Step 5: Software selection

A specific package can be selected based upon the extent to which it meets the chosen criteria. This may simply entail a subjective judgement based on a comparison of the package evaluations (step 4). To provide a more objective view, it may be useful to devise an overall score. Because each criterion does not have the same level of importance, the simple calculation of a total score is unlikely to be meaningful. Instead, it is useful to weight the criteria according to their importance.

In the same way that the criteria to be evaluated vary depending upon the organizational context and modelling requirements, so do their importance weights. Therefore, the importance weights need to be obtained from key members of the organization. Where there are only a few criteria this can be done by assigning percentages to each criterion, such that they total to 100; the higher the percentage, the greater the importance. An overall score could then be calculated for each package as follows:

$$S_i = \sum_j W_j E_{ji}$$

where:

S_i overall score for package i
W_j importance weight for criterion j
E_{ji} evaluated score for criterion j for package i

If there are a large number of criteria, however, it is impossible to assign percentage weights with any degree of consistency. One means for addressing this issue is to adopt the Analytic Hierarchy Process (AHP) (Saaty 1980). In the AHP importance weights are derived by pair-wise comparisons between criteria. The consistency of the assigned importance weights is tested as part of the procedure. An overall score for each package is calculated by combining the importance weights and scores from the evaluation of the criteria. Another feature of the AHP is the ability to develop a hierarchy of criteria and sub-criteria. For instance, importance weights could be assigned to each of the criteria headings in Table 3.3 (e.g. hardware/software requirements) and then further importance weights to each of their sub-criteria (e.g. hardware platform required). This helps to perform quite complex evaluations. Davis and Williams (1994) describe the use of the AHP for selecting simulation software.

3.5 Conclusion

This chapter describes the nature and range of simulation software and the process of selecting a simulation package. Most simulation models are developed as visual interactive simulations (VIS) giving the user an animated display of the model as it runs and the ability to interact with the running model. Three broad types of software are available for developing simulations: spreadsheets, programming languages and specialist simulation software. The choice of software depends upon the nature of the study being performed. In general, as the complexity of the model increases it soon becomes necessary to move from spreadsheets to specialist simulation software. For very complex models a programming language is probably required.

A range of specialist simulation software is available. Most could be described as visual interactive modelling systems (VIMS) that enable the modeller to develop the simulation from a predefined set of objects through a series of menus. Many of these packages also provide some form of programming interface that enhances their modelling capability.

The process of selecting a specialist simulation package involves the establishment of modelling requirements, shortlisting of packages, and the selection and evaluation of criteria that reflect the needs of the organization. It is also useful to determine importance weights for the criteria. It should be noted, however, that most simulation modellers simply use and re-use the software that they are familiar with and that is available to them.

References

Amiry, A.P. (1965) The simulation of information flow in a steelmaking plant. In: *Digital Simulation in Operational Research* (Hollingdale, S., ed.). London: English University Press, pp. 347–356.

Banks, J., Carson, J.S., Nelson, B.L. and Nicol, D.M. (2001) *Discrete-Event System Simulation*, 3rd edn. Upper Saddle River, NJ: Prentice Hall.

Banks, J. and Gibson, R.R. (1997) "Selecting simulation software". *IIE Solutions*, 29(5), 30–32.

Bard, J.F. (1997) "Benchmarking simulation software for use in modeling postal operations". *Computers and Industrial Engineering*, 32(3), 607–625.

Dahl, O. and Nygaard, K. (1966) "SIMULA: an Algol-based simulation language". *Communications of the ACM*, 9(9), 671–678.

Davis, L. and Williams G. (1994) "Evaluating and selecting simulation software using the analytic hierarchy process". *Integrated Manufacturing Systems*, 5(1), 22–32.

Elliott, M. (2001) "Buyer's guide: simulation software". *IIE Solutions*, 33(5), 41–50.

Fiddy, E., Bright, J.G. and Hurrion, R.D. (1981) "SEE-WHY: interactive simulation on the screen". *Proceedings of the Institute of Mechanical Engineers C293/81*, pp. 167–172.

Greasley, A. (1998) "An example of a discrete-event simulation on a spreadsheet". *Simulation*, 70(3), 148–166.

Hlupic, V. and Paul, R.J. (1996) "Methodological approach to manufacturing simulation software selection". *Computer Integrated Manufacturing Systems*, 9(1), 49–55.

Hlupic, V., Irani, Z. and Paul, R.J. (1999) "Evaluation framework for simulation software". *The International Journal of Advanced Manufacturing Technology*, 15(5), 366–382.

Holder, K. (1990) "Selecting simulation software". *OR Insight*, 3(4), 19–24.

Hurrion, R.D. (1976) The design, use and required facilities of an interactive visual computer simulation language to explore production planning problems. PhD Thesis, University of London.

Law, A.M. and Kelton, W.D. (2000) *Simulation Modeling and Analysis*, 3rd edn. New York: McGraw-Hill.

Law, A. and McComas, M. (1989) "Pitfalls to avoid in the simulation of manufacturing systems". *Industrial Engineering*, 21(5), 28–69.

Nikoukaran, J. and Paul, R.J. (1999) "Software selection for simulation in manufacturing: a review". *Simulation Practice and Theory*, 7(1), 1–14.

Nikoukaran, J., Hlupic, V. and Paul, R.J. (1999) "A hierarchical framework for evaluating simulation software". *Simulation Practice and Theory*, 7(3), 219–231.

Pidd, M. (1989) "Choosing discrete simulation software". *OR Insight*, 2(3), 22–23.

Pidd, M. (1992) "Object orientation and three phase simulation". *Proceedings of the 1992 Winter Simulation Conference* (Swain, J.J., Goldsman, D., Crain, R.C. and Wilson, J.R., eds). Piscataway, NJ: IEEE, pp. 689–693.

Pidd, M. (1998) *Computer Simulation in Management Science*, 4th edn. Chichester, UK: Wiley.

Robinson, S. (2001) "Soft with a hard centre: discrete-event simulation in facilitation". *Journal of the Operational Research Society*, 52(8), 905–915.

Robinson, S. and Pidd, M. (1998) "Provider and customer expectations of successful simulation projects". *Journal of the Operational Research Society*, 49(3), 200–209.

Saaty, T.L. (1980) *The Analytic Hierarchy Process*. New York: McGraw-Hill.

Schriber, T. (1974) *Simulation Using GPSS*. New York: Wiley.

Seila, A.F. (2002) "Spreadsheet simulation". *Proceedings of the 2002 Winter Simulation Conference* (Yucesan, E., Chen, C.-H., Snowden, S.L., Charnes, J.M., eds). IEEE, Piscataway, NJ, pp. 17–22.

Swain, J.J. (2001) "Power tools for visualization and decision-making". *ORMS Today*, 28(1), 52–63.

Van Breedman, A., Raes, J. and van de Velde, K. (1990) "Segmenting the simulation software market". *OR Insight*, 3(2), 9–13.

Winston, W.L. (1998) *Financial Models Using Simulation and Optimization: A Step-by-Step Guide with Excel and Palisade's Decisiontools Software*. Newfield, NY: Palisade Corp.

Internet addresses

INFORMS-Computer Simulation: www.informs-cs.org (July 2003)
Winter Simulation Conference: www.wintersim.org (July 2003)

SIMULATION STUDIES: AN OVERVIEW

4

4.1 Introduction

Before entering into a detailed description of each process involved in a simulation study, it is important to develop an overall view in order to understand how the processes interconnect. The aim of this chapter is to provide such a perspective by giving an overview of a simulation study. There are also a number of related issues concerning the time-scales for simulation studies, the membership of the project team, the software and hardware requirements, project costs and project selection. Having given an overview of a simulation study, each of these issues is discussed in turn. This chapter sets out the basics of performing simulation studies before the rest of the book goes on to describe each process in more detail.

4.2 Simulation Studies: An Overview of Key Modelling Processes

There are as many diagrams and descriptions that outline the key processes in a simulation study as there are authors who have written about the subject. Among them are Shannon (1975), Szymankiewicz *et al.* (1988), Hoover and Perry (1990), Ulgen (1991), Dietz (1992), Gogg and Mott (1992), Musselman (1992), Nordgren (1995), Shannon (1998), Law and Kelton (2000) and Banks *et al.* (2001). Each has their preferred way of explaining how to approach simulation modelling. A detailed inspection of these explanations shows that they are in the main very similar, outlining a set of processes that must be performed. The main differences lie in the naming of the processes and the number of sub-processes into which they are split. The outline of a simulation study described below is based in part on the work of Landry *et al.* (1983).

Figure 4.1 shows an outline of a simulation study. The boxes are the key stages in a study and represent the important deliverables:

- A *conceptual model*: a description of the model that is to be developed.
- A *computer model*: the simulation model implemented on a computer.

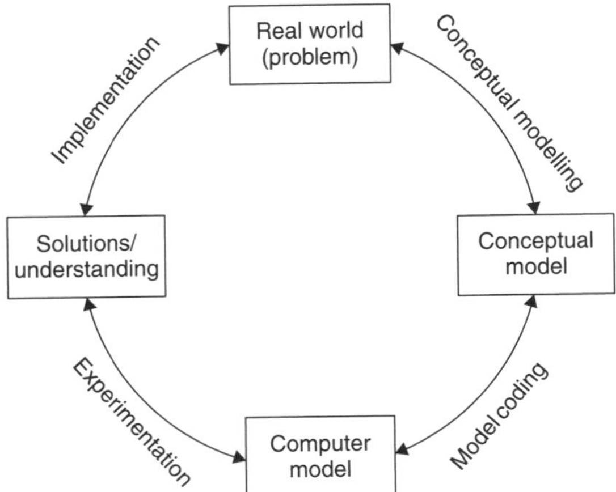

Figure 4.1 Simulation Studies: Key Stages and Processes. (Brooks, R.J. and Robinson, S., Simulation 2000, Palgrave Macmillan, Reproduced with Permission of Palgrave Macmillan.)

- *Solutions and/or understanding*: derived from the results of the experimentation.
- *An improvement in the real world*: obtained from implementing the solutions and/or understanding gained.

The arrows are the processes that enable movement between the stages. Each process is briefly described below, with detailed discussions in the chapters that follow.

Conceptual modelling

The motivation for a simulation study is a recognition that some problem exists in the real world. This might be a problem within an existing system or a concern about a proposed system. For instance, customers in an existing supermarket may be experiencing long queues, or the management of a supermarket chain may be concerned about the design of a new superstore. The job of the modeller is to understand the nature of the problem and to propose a model that is suitable for tackling it. As such, conceptual modelling consists of the following sub-processes:

- Develop an understanding of the problem situation
- Determine the modelling objectives
- Design the conceptual model: inputs, outputs and model content
- Collect and analyse the data required to develop the model

Part of the process of designing the conceptual model should also involve determining the modelling approach and whether simulation is suitable. Modellers, even if they are experts in simulation, should always ask whether an alternative modelling approach would be more suitable, especially in the light of comments on simulation as a last resort (Section 1.3.2) and its disadvantages (Section 1.3.3).

Data collection and analysis is included as part of conceptual modelling for two reasons. First, it is necessary to obtain preliminary or contextual data in order to develop an understanding of the problem situation. Secondly, the detailed data required for the development of the computer model are identified by the conceptual model. Until the conceptual model is defined the data required for the computer model are not known. It therefore makes no sense to start a detailed data collection exercise. It is for this reason that data collection and analysis is placed last in the list of sub-processes above.

The subject of conceptual modelling is looked at in detail in Chapters 5 and 6 and data collection and analysis in Chapter 7.

Model coding

In model coding the conceptual model is converted into a computer model. Here, coding is defined in its most general sense and does not strictly mean computer programming. Instead it simply refers to the development of the model on a computer. As discussed in Section 3.3, the model may be coded using a spreadsheet, specialist simulation software or a programming language.

The assumption here is that the simulation is built and performed on a computer. It is noted in Section 1.2 that other forms of simulation exist, especially physical simulations. If such a model is to be developed, the process described in this chapter would be similar with the exception of model coding. This could be referred to as model building and the term computer model replaced with the more general term operational model.

Experimentation

Once developed, experiments are performed with the simulation model in order to obtain a better understanding of the real world and/or to find solutions to real world problems. This is a process of "what-if" analysis, that is, making changes to the model's inputs, running the model, inspecting the results, learning from the results, making changes to the inputs and so on (Figure 4.2). For instance, in order to determine the number of checkout desks required in a supermarket, the simulation would be run with a particular number of desks and the results inspected. Based on the results, the number of checkout desks would be

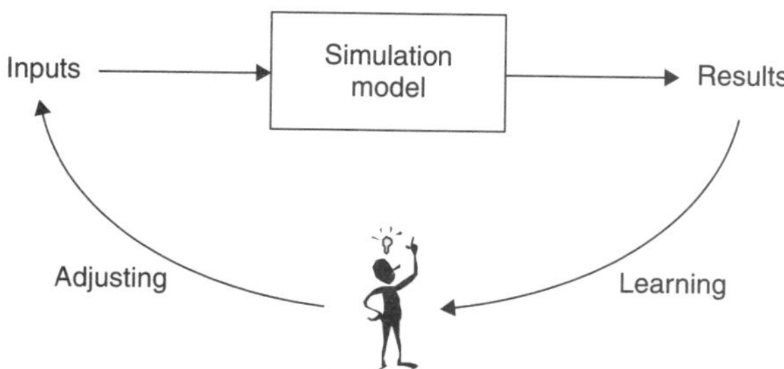

Figure 4.2 "What-if" Analysis with Simulation.

adjusted (more or less) and the model run again. This process would continue until it is felt that sufficient has been learnt about the effect of checkout desks on customer service, or the number of desks required to achieve a particular level of service has been determined.

The outcome of the experimentation process is described as solutions and/or understanding in Figure 4.1. This is because simulation models are not always developed with the aim of obtaining concrete solutions. They can also be used to help develop a better understanding of the real world. Indeed, even when the aim of a model is to provide concrete solutions, very often there is a great deal of wider learning that is obtained just from the process of modelling (Section 1.3.2).

The key issues when performing simulation experiments are:

- Obtaining sufficiently accurate results
- Performing a thorough search of potential solutions (searching the solution space)
- Testing the robustness of the solution (sensitivity analysis)

These issues are discussed in Chapters 9 and 10.

Implementation

Implementation can be thought of in three ways. First, it is implementing the findings from a simulation study in the real world. Where the simulation study has identified a particular solution to the real world problem, then implementation is a case of putting this solution into practice. For instance, the study might have identified the need for a specific number of checkout desks in a supermarket.

A second interpretation of implementation is implementing the model rather than the findings. A model might be developed to help plan weekly production schedules. By running alternative production schedules through the model at the beginning of a week, the best schedule may be selected. In this case, the model needs to be handed over to the organization, staff trained and supported, and the effectiveness of the model continuously monitored.

The third interpretation is implementation as learning. Where the study has led to an improved understanding, implementation is less explicit, but should be apparent in future decision-making. For example, if a supermarket manager has a better understanding of the effect of checkout desks on customer service, he may be more responsive to moving staff to checkout duty when queues increase.

These forms of implementation are not mutually exclusive and a simulation study might result in two or even three of these types. Chapter 11 discusses the subject of implementation in more detail.

4.2.1 Simulation modelling is not linear

The description above implies that simulation modelling is a linear process. First the modeller develops a complete conceptual model. Then he/she moves on to develop the computer model, after which experimentation begins. Only once experimentation is complete are the findings implemented. This is certainly not the case. Simulation modelling involves both repetition and iteration.

The processes in a simulation study may be repeated a number of times in order to obtain the desired improvement in the real world. For example, experimentation with a simulation model leads to a recommended number of checkout desks in a supermarket, but it also identifies the need to set up appropriate staff rosters. As a result, the simulation process is repeated, changing the conceptual model to include staff rosters, adding this to the model code, experimenting with alternative rosters and implementing the findings. Because of the repetitive nature of simulation studies, Figure 4.1 is drawn as a circle.

More importantly, simulation modelling involves iteration. The movement through the processes in a simulation study is not always clock-wise. It is for this reason that the arrows in Figure 4.1 are two-way. For instance, the modeller often starts with only a partial understanding of the real world problem. Based upon this understanding, a conceptual model is developed and a computer model coded. On showing the computer model to the problem owners, shortcomings in the model are identified and so revisions are made to the conceptual model. Alternatively, experimentation leads to an improved understanding of the real world problem and it is realized that the cause of the problem is different from that originally envisaged. As a result, the conceptual model is updated and the model re-coded before experimentation continues. Although the movement through the process is not always clockwise, the general sense of direction is from conceptual modelling towards implementation.

This iteration is also true of the sub-processes in a simulation study. For example, in conceptual modelling, a lack of available data may lead to the redesign of the model, engineering out the need for that data.

Willemain (1995) performed a study in which he observed expert modellers at work. He was able to analyse their modelling process by getting them to talk out loud what they were thinking about while developing models. Analysis of their thoughts showed a high level of iteration in the modelling process. He concluded that a modeller's thinking frequently moves between the various modelling processes, such as those identified in Figure 4.1.

Having highlighted the non-linearity of a simulation study, the rest of this book appears to treat it in a linear fashion by describing each process (and sub-process) in turn, starting with conceptual modelling. This apparent dichotomy is the result of the need to provide a clear explanation of the processes involved in simulation model development and use. To try and describe simulation modelling without imposing an apparent order would simply confuse the reader. It is important, however, that throughout the ensuing explanation, the non-linearity of the simulation process is borne in mind.

4.2.2 Something is missing!

The observant may notice that there is no mention of model testing in Figure 4.1 or in the description above. This is deliberate, since model testing (or verification and validation) is not a single process within simulation modelling, but a continuous one that is performed throughout model development and use. As such, diagrams and explanations that imply that verification and validation are a specific stage in a simulation study are misleading. There is a detailed discussion on simulation verification and validation, and how it fits into the process of performing a simulation study, in Chapter 12.

4.3 Simulation Project Time-Scales

It is difficult to give a specific estimate of the length of a typical simulation project. At one simulation user group I attended, an automotive engineer explained how he saved his company $150,000 in a Friday afternoon, by modelling a conveyor system and proposing a redesign. At the other extreme, those developing military simulations for modelling, say, military campaigns, talk in terms of years of development time. They also expect those models to be used for many years to come.

Cochran *et al.* (1995) surveyed simulation users in industrial settings. Based on the reported average time for a project (Figure 4.3), the results show a wide range of time-scales from less than a week to more than 6 months in duration. They conclude that a typical project takes between 1 and 3 months to complete. Anecdotal evidence would seem to concur with this conclusion.

Very often the time-scale for a simulation study is determined by the time that is available. If the organization needs a result within 2 months, then that dictates the maximum length of the simulation project. The modeller must design the model such that it is possible to develop and use it within that time-scale. Indeed, organizational deadlines mean that available time often dictates model design rather than model design dictating the time-scale (Law 1993).

A further question is what proportion of time is devoted to each phase in a simulation study. This obviously depends on the nature of the study. In particular, experimentation may require only a small proportion of the time if there are only a limited number of alternatives to consider. On the other hand, it may require a large amount of effort if many scenarios are under consideration (Section 10.2.2). As a rough estimate it is useful to think in terms of a one third split between conceptual modelling (including data collection and analysis), model coding and experimentation, bearing in mind that each of these processes is regularly revisited during the life of a project. In stating this, the need for verification and validation is included as part of the time devoted to each process. Model coding, therefore,

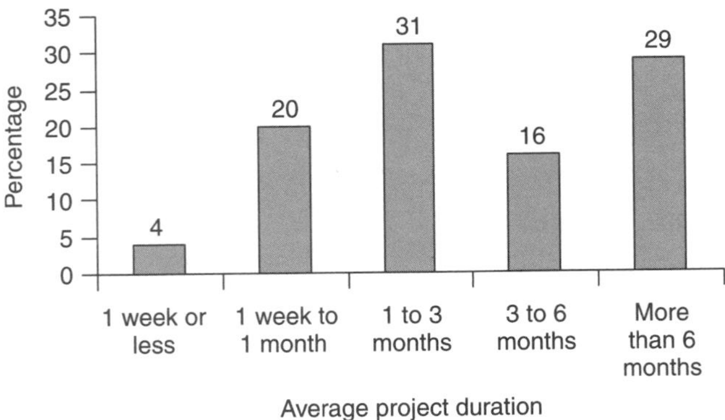

Figure 4.3 Average Time for Simulation Studies in Industrial Settings (*Source*: Cochran *et al.* 1995).

may be as little as 20% of the total time required for the simulation project. Implementation is not included in this split because it is often treated as a separate project that stems from the simulation study.

A common error in estimating the duration of a simulation study is to concentrate solely on the model coding phase. As a result, not enough time is devoted to planning the model and obtaining and analysing the data. Experimentation also becomes something of an afterthought, rushed at the end of the study without obtaining the maximum benefit from the model.

4.4 The Simulation Project Team

Simulation studies are not the effort of an individual modeller, but rely upon teamwork. Ormerod (2001) identifies the following roles in a typical operational research intervention:

- *The doers*: the interveners
- *The done for*: the clients
- *The done with*: project team members
- *The done to*: those interviewed
- *The done without*: members of the organization and society who are not involved in the project, but are affected by it

Translating this into the specific context of a simulation study, a variety of roles are outlined in Table 4.1. It is important to note that these are roles rather than individuals. In other words, a person may take on more than one role, or many people may be required to share a single role. For instance, the modeller is often the project manager and the model user, in that he/she performs the experimentation. Sometimes the client and the modeller are the same person, if the client chooses to develop his/her own model. There may, however, be a number of people tasked with being data providers. Note that the model user appears twice in the list, first as a "done for" and second as a "doer". In the early part of the project the model user is effectively a client, since the model is being developed for his/her use. In the latter part he/she turns doer, using the model to provide information to the organization. All this means that the simulation project team may consist of anything from one person, playing many roles, to a larger group of up to 10 or more, playing single roles. The exact make-up of the project team depends on the nature and scale of the simulation project being performed.

The first three categories have direct involvement in the project team, while the latter two have little or no involvement. A wide group of people may need to be interviewed in order to obtain information about the system being modelled, but they do not need to have direct involvement in the simulation project. There may be a great many beneficiaries of the project, some of whom are even unaware of its existence. Customers in a bank are probably not aware that a simulation model has been developed to improve the level of service offered. They are, nevertheless, beneficiaries.

Table 4.1 Roles in a Simulation Study.

Doers	Project manager	Responsible for managing the process; may not have specific modelling skills
	Modeller	Develops the model (conceptual and computer)
	Model user (in later stages)	Experiments with the model to obtain understanding and look for solutions to the real world problem
Done for	Clients	The problem owner and recipient of the results; directly or indirectly funds the work
	Model user (in early stages)	Recipient of the model
Done with	Data providers	Subject matter experts who are able to provide data and information for the project
	Modelling supporter	A third party expert (software vendor, consultant or in-house expert) provides software support and/or modelling expertise
Done to	Those interviewed for information	A wide group of people from whom information is obtained
Done without	Management, staff, customers	Beneficiaries of the project, but not involved; in some cases they are not aware of the project

It is important that the simulation project team meet on a regular basis. It is not unusual to hold weekly meetings. Outside of this, there are likely to be many formal and informal smaller group meetings. Although meetings are typically held face-to-face, over the telephone or via email, modern technology is making other methods of communication available to us. Video conferencing, net conferencing and chat rooms all provide interactive environments that may be more effective than telephone and email communications, and could remove the need (at least in part) for travel to face-to-face meetings. Taylor *et al.* (2002) explore the use of net conferencing during simulation studies.

Note that these roles do not just require technical skills. Project management and socio-political skills are also needed to a greater or lesser degree depending upon the role being taken (Ormerod 1996). There is, for instance, a need for skills in negotiation, consensus building and reflection among others.

4.5 Hardware and Software Requirements

There are few software applications that require the computing power necessary for simulation. A large simulation model may take a number of hours to run and of course many runs may be required for thorough experimentation. Therefore, any improvement in computing power is helpful. Even for relatively small models, the run-time is normally counted in minutes and not seconds. As a result, the general advice about computer hardware for simulation is the faster the better and plenty of memory is helpful too. It is best to use the most recent computer available.

Beyond the simulation software (Chapter 3) there is a range of other packages that may be useful during a simulation study. Spreadsheets and databases are particularly useful for storing, retrieving and analysing sets of data. Statistical packages may be useful for working through more complex analyses. There are also some specialist packages for simulation analysis, for instance, ExpertFit (www: Averill M. Law & Associates) and Stat::Fit (www: Geer Mountain Software) for fitting distributions to empirical data (Section 7.5.2). Simulation software vendors often sell peripheral software for their packages such as output analysers, optimizers and powerful animation generators.

Portability is an important issue in considering hardware and software requirements. It is likely that the simulation model needs to be demonstrated at various locations. Obviously laptop computers provide powerful and portable hardware. These days, portability is more likely to be restricted by the software. Many organizations purchase network licences, which is very efficient in terms of gaining maximum use of the available licences. The downside is that unless the modeller is able to log-in to the network, the software is not portable. Improvements in the distribution of software over the world wide web are likely to overcome this issue, but in the meantime it might be preferable to have at least some individual licences.

4.6 Project Costs

Most simulation software is not cheap and most simulation projects take a few weeks to complete. As a result, simulation is certainly not cheap. This of course must be balanced against the benefits that can be gained from the use of simulation that are often an order of magnitude greater than the cost. The following costs may fall into the budget for a simulation study (approximate costs are in brackets):

- Simulation software purchase ($500–$20,000)
- Simulation software maintenance (5–20% of purchase cost)
- Hardware purchase ($1000–$2000)
- Hardware maintenance (5–20% of purchase cost)
- Simulation software training (free–$2000 per person)
- Training in simulation modelling ($1000–$2500 per person)
- Person time: modelling, data collection, experimentation, project management, meetings (up to $2000 per day)
- Consultancy support (up to $2000 per day)

Training in simulation modelling is separated from simulation software training because simulation vendors only tend to offer the latter. The wider skills required for simulation modelling need to be obtained from elsewhere. It is these skills that this book tries to develop. The last category refers to the use of a modelling supporter.

Organizations need to consider the advantages and disadvantages of employing external consultants over developing and using in-house expertise. External consultants already have the simulation expertise and so the cost of training is avoided. There may not be a need to purchase the simulation software either, since the consultant should already own a licence. If the organization wishes to have a copy of the model, run-only licences are often available at a lower cost than the full software. These allow the user to run the model and change some input data, but do not allow changes to the model code. It is also likely that an external consultant who is a specialist modeller will be able to complete a simulation study more quickly.

What external consultants may not have is a detailed knowledge of the organization and so time needs to be spent transferring this knowledge. This is unlikely to be required to the same degree with in-house simulation modellers. At an extreme, the client is able to take on the role of the modeller, maximizing the knowledge brought to the modelling work. This is possible because modern simulation software is relatively easy to use. Be wary, however, there is more to simulation than simply using a package and rarely is a simulation model simple. Because the real world is complex, so too are simulation models. If the clients are to develop their own simulation models, they need to develop their skills as simulation modellers as well as users of simulation software.

This dichotomy between transferring modelling knowledge to domain experts or domain knowledge to modelling experts is similar to the issue that faced the authorities in the film "Armageddon". Should they teach astronauts to drill holes in asteroids or oil riggers to fly spaceships? Their choice of the oil riggers seemed more related to the script writers' need to maximize box-office takings than logic!

A second issue with using external consultants is that they are expensive. At least the daily cost suggests this is the case. The daily cost, however, must be weighed against the potential to complete the project more quickly and the saving in training and computing costs. One compromise is to use external consultants for model development, taking the role of modeller, and then for someone in-house to act as model user. Another option is to use a consultant more sparingly as a modelling supporter, providing on-the-job training to a less expert, but cheaper, modeller.

4.7 Project Selection

In many organizations the requirement for simulation modelling is the result of a single problem situation that occurs at a point in time. This is true, even when simulation is well established within an organization. As a result, there is no choice over the subject of a simulation study.

If a choice does exist, then various factors need to be considered. Apart from the obvious need for the work to be feasible, the ratio of potential benefit to cost should be weighed for the different options. It is obviously best to look for projects that give the maximum benefit for the cost, if this can be predicted. Another consideration is the time-scale, particularly if simulation is new to an organization. In general it is not a good idea to perform a large-scale study as an initial project. The first study is often seen as a proving ground and early success is important, particularly to win over the doubters (as inevitably there almost always are). If it is not possible to select a smaller-scale project, then it is useful to break the work into smaller steps, providing a deliverable at each stage. This is a good policy, even when simulation is well established within an organization.

4.8 Conclusion

The key processes in a simulation study are described above along with a series of issues in setting-up and managing such projects. These issues include the time-scales for simulation projects, the members of a simulation project team, the hardware and software requirements, the cost of a project and the selection of an appropriate project. Proper management of a simulation study requires more than just the appropriate technical skills, there is also a need for project management and socio-political skills. It is also emphasized that simulation modelling is not a linear process, but that it involves repetition and iteration of the processes involved. The rest of the book now concentrates on a more detailed description of each of the processes in a simulation study. Although, for the sake of clarity, these are described in a linear fashion, the need for repetition and iteration must be constantly kept in mind.

References

Banks, J., Carson, J.S., Nelson, B.L. and Nicol, D.M. (2001) *Discrete-Event System Simulation*, 3rd edn. Upper Saddle River, NJ: Prentice Hall.

Cochran, J.K., Mackulak, G.T. and Savory, P.A. (1995) "Simulation project characteristics in industrial settings". *Interfaces*, 25(4), 104–113.

Dietz, M. (1992) "Outline of a successful simulation project". *Industrial Engineering*, 24(11), 50–53.

Gogg, T. and Mott, J. (1992) *Improve Quality and Productivity with Simulation*. Palos Verdes Pnsl., CA: JMI Consulting Group.

Hoover, S.V. and Perry, R.F. (1990) *Simulation: A Problem-Solving Approach*. Reading, MA: Addison-Wesley.

Landry, M., Malouin, J.L. and Oral, M. (1983) "Model validation in operations research". *European Journal of Operational Research*, 14(3), 207–220.

Law A.M. (1993) "A forum on crucial issues in the simulation modeling". *Industrial Engineering*, 25(5), 32–36.

Law, A.M. and Kelton, W.D. (2000) *Simulation Modeling and Analysis*, 2nd edn. New York, McGraw-Hill.

Musselman, K.J. (1992) "Conducting a successful simulation project". *Proceedings of the 1992 Winter Simulation Conference* (Swain, J.J., Goldsman, D., Crain, R.C. and Wilson, J.R., eds), Piscataway, NJ: IEEE, pp. 115–121.

Nordgren, W.B. (1995) "Steps for proper simulation project management". *Proceedings of the 1995 Winter Simulation Conference* (Alexopoulos, C., Kang, K., Lilegdon, W.R. and Goldsman, D., eds). Piscataway, NJ: IEEE, pp. 68–73.

Ormerod, R.J. (1996) "On the nature of OR – entering the fray". *Journal of the Operational Research Society*, 47(1), 1–17.

Ormerod, R.J. (2001) "Viewpoint: the success and failure of methodologies – a comment on Connell" (2001): evaluating soft OR". *Journal of the Operational Research Society*, 52(10), 1176–1179.

Shannon, R.E. (1975) *Systems Simulation: The Art and Science*. Englewood Cliffs, NJ: Prentice-Hall.

Shannon, R.E. (1998) "Introduction to the art and science of simulation". *Proceedings of the 1998 Winter Simulation Conference* (Medeiros, D.J., Watson, E.F., Carson, J.S. and Manivannan, M.S., eds), Piscataway, NJ: IEEE, pp. 7–14.

Szymankiewicz, J., McDonald, J. and Turner, K. (1988) *Solving Business Problems by Simulation*. Maidenhead, UK: McGraw-Hill.

Taylor, S.J.E., Hlupic, V., Robinson, S. and Ladbrook, J. (2002) "GROUPSIM: Investigating issues in collaborative simulation modelling". *Operational Research Society Simulation Workshop 2002*. Operational Research Society, Birmingham, UK, pp. 11–18.

Ulgen, O. (1991) "Proper management techniques are keys to a successful simulation project". *Industrial Engineering*, 23(8), 37–41.

Willemain, T.R. (1995) "Model formulation: what experts think about and when". *Operations Research*, 43(6), 916–932.

Internet addresses

Averill M. Law & Associates, Inc.: ExpertFit, www.averill-law.com (July 2003)
Geer Mountain Software Corp.: Stat::Fit, www.geerms.com (July 2003)

Conceptual Modelling 5

5.1 Introduction

A simulation of a fast-food restaurant could take many forms. At the simplest level the model might include only the queues and service desks. The model, however, could be expanded to include the tables and seating area, the kitchen, the supply of raw materials, the drive thru, the car park and so on. There is also a need to consider the level of detail at which each component is to be modelled. The service desks, for instance, could be modelled as a fixed time or a statistical distribution. At a greater level of detail the process could be modelled as a series of sub-steps (take order, collect food, take money, give change, etc.) and process failures and interruptions could be modelled. The modeller, along with the clients, must determine the appropriate scope and level of detail to model, a process known as conceptual modelling or designing the model.

The purpose of this and the next chapter is to describe the requirements for conceptual modelling and to describe how a simulation modeller might go about designing the conceptual model. In this chapter the importance of conceptual modelling is emphasized before defining the term conceptual model more precisely. The requirements of a conceptual model are then described. Finally, the practical issue of how to communicate the conceptual model to all members of the simulation project team is discussed. In the next chapter, the question of how to design the conceptual model is covered.

5.2 Conceptual Modelling: Important but Little Understood

Conceptual modelling is almost certainly the most important aspect of the simulation modelling process (Law 1991). The model design impacts all aspects of the study, in particular the data requirements, the speed with which the model can be developed, the validity of the model, the speed of experimentation and the confidence that is placed in the model results. A well designed model significantly enhances the possibility that a simulation study will meet its objectives within the required time-scale. What sets truly successful modellers apart is their effectiveness in conceptual modelling (Ward 1989).

It is often said of simulation studies that 50% of the benefit is obtained just from the development of the conceptual model. The modeller needs to develop a thorough understanding of the operations system in order to design an appropriate model. In doing so, he/she asks questions and seeks for information that often have not previously been considered. In this case, the requirement to design a simulation model becomes a framework for system investigation that is extremely useful in its own right. Indeed, Shannon (1975) goes so far as to say that effective conceptual modelling may lead to the identification of a suitable solution without the need for any further simulation work.

Against this claim of importance, some might argue that the emergence of modern simulation software has reduced, or even removed, the need for conceptual modelling. After all, the modeller can now move straight from developing an understanding of the real world problem to creating a computer model. On the surface this argument has some credence, but what it ignores is that the modeller still has to make decisions about the content and assumptions of the model. What modern simulation software does provide is an environment for more rapid model development, making prototyping more feasible and enabling a greater level of iteration between conceptual modelling and computer modelling. The software does not, however, reduce the level of decision-making about the model design.

On the contrary, it could be argued that the power and memory of modern hardware and the potential for distributed software has increased the need for conceptual modelling. Both Salt (1993) and Chwif *et al.* (2000) bemoan the increasing complexity of simulation models and the problems associated with them. Among the many reasons they cite for this is the "possibility" factor. People build more complex models because the hardware and software enables them to. Although this extends the utility of simulation to problems that previously could not have been tackled, it is also likely that models are being developed that are far more complex than they need be. In this sense there are certain advantages in having only limited computing capacity; it forces the modeller to design the model carefully! As a result of the extended possibilities, careful model design is probably increasing in importance.

Having argued that conceptual modelling is of utmost importance, it must also be recognized that it is probably the least understood aspect of simulation modelling. There is surprisingly little written on the subject. It is difficult to find a book that devotes more than a handful of pages to the design of the conceptual model. Neither are there a plethora of research papers, with only a handful of well regarded papers over the last four decades. A search through the academic tracks at the 2001 Winter Simulation Conference (Peters *et al.* 2001), the main international conference on discrete-event simulation, reveals a host of papers on other aspects of simulation modelling. There is, however, only one paper that gives space to the subject of conceptual modelling, and that is very limited (Law and McComas, 2001). It would be unreasonable not to note that the subject is briefly mentioned in two other papers!

The main reason for this lack of attention is no doubt that conceptual modelling is more of an "art" than a "science" and therefore it is difficult to define methods and procedures.

As a result of the dearth of advice on the subject, the art of conceptual modelling is largely learnt by experience. This is not a satisfactory situation for such an important aspect of the simulation modelling process. In order to address this issue, this and the next chapter attempt to provide specific advice on how to develop a conceptual model. This is done by looking at the subject from various angles. This chapter introduces the basic concepts of conceptual modelling. First, the meaning of conceptual modelling is more precisely defined. Then the requirements of a conceptual model are discussed. The chapter concludes by discussing the reporting and communication of the conceptual model. Chapter 6 goes on to discuss the actual process of conceptual modelling and how the conceptual model is designed. These ideas are derived from the limited literature that is available on the subject and by reflecting upon personal experience in conceptual modelling.

5.3 What is a Conceptual Model?

Zeigler (1976) sheds some light on the definition of a conceptual model by distinguishing between four terms: the *real system* is that which the simulation model is to represent. The *experimental frame* is the limited set of circumstances under which the real system has been observed, in other words, there is not a complete understanding of the real system. The *base model* is capable of accounting for the complete behaviour of the real system. Since this model is very complex it cannot be fully known. Meanwhile, in the *lumped model* the components of the system are lumped together and the interconnections are simplified. The structure of this model is fully known to the modeller. In our terms, the lumped model and conceptual model can be considered equivalent.

This definition, however, provides little more than a sense that the conceptual model is a simplified representation of the real system. A more descriptive definition of a conceptual model is as follows:

The conceptual model is a non-software specific description of the simulation model that is to be developed, describing the objectives, inputs, outputs, content, assumptions and simplifications of the model.

There are two key features of this definition. First, it specifically identifies the independence of the conceptual model from the software in which the simulation is to be developed. Indeed, in an ideal world the software should be selected on the basis of the understanding of the conceptual model. Since the world is less than ideal, it is often the case that the conceptual model is designed around the software that is available to the modeller. Indeed, because the processes in a simulation study are performed iteratively, there is an interplay between the computer model as it is being coded and the conceptual model, with constant adjustments to both.

The second feature is that the definition outlines the key components of the conceptual model, which are as follows:

- *Objectives*: the purpose of the model and modelling project.
- *Inputs*: those elements of the model that can be altered to effect an improvement in, or better understanding of, the real world; otherwise known as the experimental factors.

- *Outputs*: report the results from simulation runs.
- *Content*: the components that are represented in the model and their interconnections.
- *Assumptions* made either when there are uncertainties or beliefs about the real world being modelled.
- *Simplifications* incorporated in the model to enable more rapid model development and use (Section 6.3).

Assumptions and simplifications are identified as separate facets. Assumptions are ways of incorporating uncertainties and beliefs about the real world into the model. Simplifications are ways of reducing the complexity of the model. As such, assumptions are a facet of limited knowledge or presumptions, while simplifications are a facet of the desire to create simple models.

The content of the model should be described in terms of two dimensions (Robinson 1994):

- *The scope of the model*: the model boundary or the breadth of the real system that is to be included in the model.
- *The level of detail*: the detail to be included for each component in the model's scope.

The purpose of the conceptual model is to set out the basis on which the computer based simulation (computer model) is to be developed. It is in effect a functional specification of the computer software. For many modellers there is a temptation to start coding the computer model as soon as possible. Without due attention to the development of the conceptual model, however, this can lead to a model that does not achieve what is required and, at the extreme, the model may have to be completely rewritten, wasting significant amounts of time.

5.4 Requirements of the Conceptual Model

In designing a conceptual model it is useful to have a set of requirements in mind. In this way the model can be designed so as to meet these requirements. So what are the requirements for an effective conceptual model? This question is first answered by describing four main requirements after which the overarching need to keep the model as simple as possible is discussed.

5.4.1 Four requirements of a conceptual model

Willemain (1994) lists five qualities of an effective model: validity, usability, value to client, feasibility and aptness for clients' problem. Meanwhile, Brooks and Tobias (1996) identify 11 performance criteria for a good model. Based on these lists, here it is proposed that there are four main requirements of a conceptual model: validity, credibility, utility and feasibility.

As is discussed in Section 12.2, a valid model is one that is sufficiently accurate for the purpose at hand. However, since the notion of accuracy is of little meaning for a model that has no numeric output, conceptual model validity might be defined more precisely as:

A perception, on behalf of the modeller, that the conceptual model will lead to a computer model that is sufficiently accurate for the purpose at hand.

Underlying this notion is the question of whether the model is right. Note that this definition places conceptual model validity as a perception of the modeller. It also maintains the notion that a model is built for a specific purpose, which is common to most definitions of validity. The subject of validity is discussed in more detail in Chapter 12.

Credibility is similar to validity, but is taken from the perspective of the clients rather than the modeller. The credibility of the conceptual model is therefore defined as:

A perception, on behalf of the clients, that the conceptual model will lead to a computer model that is sufficiently accurate for the purpose at hand.

The third concept, *utility*, is defined as:

A perception, on behalf of the modeller and the clients, that the conceptual model will lead to a computer model that is useful as an aid to decision-making within the specified context.

Whereas the definitions of validity and credibility are specific to the modeller and the clients respectively, utility is seen as a joint agreement about the usefulness of the model. The concept of utility, as defined here, moves away from simply asking if the model is sufficiently accurate, to whether it is useful. Within any context a range of models could be designed, all of which might be sufficiently accurate for the purpose at hand. As such, all these models would be valid and credible. However, if a proposed model is large and cumbersome, albeit sufficiently accurate, it may have limited utility. Indeed, a less accurate (but still sufficiently accurate), more flexible model that runs faster may have greater utility by enabling a wider range of experimentation within a time-frame.

The final requirement, *feasibility*, is defined as follows:

A perception, on behalf of the modeller and the clients, that the conceptual model can be developed into a computer model.

Various factors may make a model infeasible. For instance, it might not be possible to build the proposed model within the required time-scale, the data requirements of the model may be too onerous, or there is insufficient knowledge of the real system to develop the proposed model. Whichever, it is important that the conceptual model can be developed into a computer model.

A final point to note is that these four concepts are not mutually exclusive. A modeller's perception of a model's accuracy is likely to be highly correlated with the clients' perceptions of the same. Nor is an infeasible model a useful model. It is useful, however, to separate these concepts, so a modeller can be cognizant of them when designing the conceptual model.

5.4.2 Keep the model simple

Overarching all of the requirements described above is the need to avoid the development of an over-complex model. In general the aim should be to: *keep the model as simple as possible to meet the objectives of the simulation study*. Simple models have a number of advantages. They can be developed faster, are more flexible, require less data, run faster, and it is easier to interpret the results since the structure of the model is better understood (Innis and Rexstad 1983; Ward 1989; Salt 1993; Chwif *et al.* 2000). As the complexity increases these advantages are lost.

Keeping models simple is at the heart of good modelling practice. This does not mean that complex models should never be developed, they are sometimes necessary to achieve the objectives of the study. There is, however, a tendency to try and model every aspect of a system when a simpler, more focused model would achieve the modelling objectives with far less effort.

Robinson (1994) demonstrates the need for simplicity with the graph in Figure 5.1. This shows the model accuracy gained from increasing levels of complexity (scope and level of detail). It shows a typical 80/20 rule, that is, 80% of the accuracy is gained from only 20% of the complexity (point *x*). Beyond this, there are diminishing returns from increasing levels of complexity. It is impossible to create a model that is 100% accurate, since it is not possible to capture every aspect of the real world in a model. Indeed, it is argued that increasing the complexity too far may lead to a less accurate model, since the data and information are not available to support the detail being modelled. For instance, it is unlikely that we could accurately model the exact behaviour of individuals in our fast-food restaurant example, and attempts to do so, beyond very simple rules, may lead to a less accurate result. Although this graph is not based on empirical data, it is useful for illustrating the need for simplicity.

In a discussion on the subject of simplicity, Ward (1989) makes the useful distinction between constructive simplicity and transparency. Transparency is an attribute of the client (how well he/she understands the model) while constructive simplicity is an attribute of the model itself (the simplicity of the model). The modeller must not only consider simplicity, but also transparency in designing a model. Since transparency is an attribute of the client, it is dependent on the client's knowledge and skill. In other words, a model that is transparent

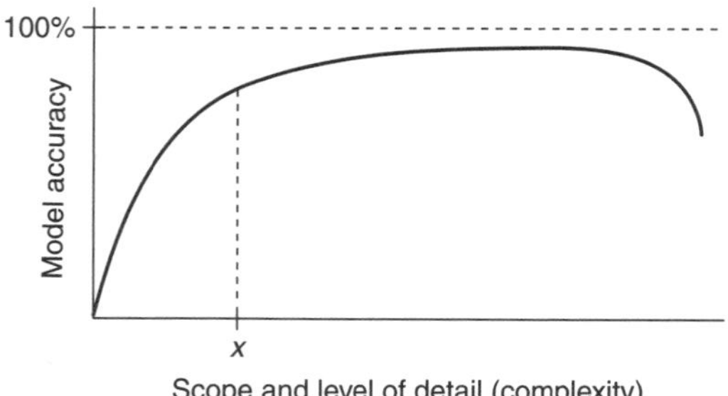

Figure 5.1 Simulation Model Complexity and Accuracy. (Based on Robinson 1994; Reprinted with the Permission of the Institute of Industrial Engineers, 3577 Parkway Lane, Suite 200, Norcross, GA 30092, 770-449-0461. Copyright © 1994.)

to one client may not be to another. The modeller must, therefore, design the model with the needs of the particular client in mind. This is necessary to develop the credibility of the model as discussed in Section 5.4.1, since a model that is not transparent to the client is unlikely to have credibility.

Such exhortations highlight the importance of developing simple models. The requirements stated in the previous section give the modeller a guide in determining whether a conceptual model is appropriate. Neither describes how a modeller might go about deciding what to include and what to exclude from a model. This is the subject of the next chapter. The next chapter also includes a discussion on some useful methods of simplification (Section 6.3).

5.5 Communicating the Conceptual Model

In order to determine whether the conceptual model meets the four requirements set out in Section 5.4.1, it is important that there is a shared understanding of the modelling context (real world) and model design between the modeller and clients (as well as the other roles in the simulation study). As such, there needs to be a mechanism for communicating the conceptual model. This is one of the roles of a project specification.

5.5.1 Simulation project specification

The output from conceptual modelling should be described in a project specification along with details of how the simulation study is to be managed. In this way a shared understanding of the conceptual model and the simulation study can be developed between all project team members. Indeed, the project specification acts as the primary means for validating the conceptual model (Section 12.4.1). It also provides a reference point for developing and verifying the computer model, performing appropriate experiments and reviewing the success of the simulation study.

Depending on the nature of the project and the relationship between the clients and modeller, the specification should describe the majority, if not all, of the following:

- Background to the problem situation (Section 6.2.1).
- Objectives of the simulation study (Section 6.2.2).
- Expected benefits (Section 1.3.2).
- The conceptual model: inputs, outputs, content (scope and level of detail), assumptions and simplifications (Chapter 6).
- Experimentation: scenarios to be considered (Chapter 10).
- Data requirements: data required, when required, responsibility for collection (Section 7.2).
- Time-scale and milestones (Section 4.3).
- Estimated cost (Section 4.6).

In general the specification takes the form of a written document that can be circulated to all involved in the simulation study. It is best to keep the document fairly short, probably not more than 10 pages, to ensure that it is read and feedback is obtained. Of course there are occasions when a larger specification is required, as indeed there are times when a brief verbal description will suffice. This all depends on the size and complexity of the model and the formality of the process required.

It is vital that the modeller obtains feedback so he/she is able to judge the validity, credibility, utility and feasibility of the proposed model. There should also be some discussion about the management of the project, for instance, the collection of data, time-scales and costs. To aid this process, it may be useful formally to present the project specification to the simulation project team and to obtain immediate feedback. All feedback should be dealt with appropriately. If the conceptual model is challenged then it should either be changed in line with the feedback, or the modeller should take time to justify the reasoning behind the conceptual model. This is particularly necessary when assumptions and simplifications are questioned. The modeller must decide to change the model or justify the assumption or simplification. The judgement as to which depends on the extent to which a change versus a justification affects the validity, credibility, utility and feasibility of the model.

The iterative nature of simulation studies is discussed in Section 4.2.1. Because the process is iterative, it should not be expected that once model coding commences the specification remains unchanged. There are four main reasons why it should be expected that the specification will change during a simulation study:

- Omissions in the original specification.
- Changes in the real world.
- An increased understanding of simulation on behalf of the clients.
- The identification of new problems through the development and use of the simulation model.

Effective conceptual modelling, communication and feedback should limit the first cause of change. Changes to the real world inevitably happen, for instance, a change to the design of a manufacturing system that may be on a small scale (e.g. an additional machine) or on a larger scale (e.g. a complete redesign). The last two reasons for change are both positive aspects of simulation modelling and should be encouraged.

Because things change, it is important that a mechanism is put in place for handling these changes. If the model is simply updated *ad hoc*, without any proper reporting, then the specification soon becomes outdated and there is no audit trail of model alterations. To maintain a record of changes, it is useful to have a "specification change form" that is used every time an alteration is put forward. This can be circulated to ensure all are informed and agree to the change.

Of course, if the conceptual model is continuously changing, it may become impossible to complete the model development and experimentation. It is useful, therefore, to reach a point where it is agreed that the specification is frozen. From this point on, all change issues are logged, but unless the change is particularly significant, the conceptual model is not altered. Once the simulation is complete and the results have been reported, a further repetition of the simulation process may be carried out in which the logged changes are included in the model. The need for this depends on whether the changes are judged to be of sufficient significance to warrant further modelling.

5.5.2 Representing the conceptual model

As part of the project specification it is important to have a means for representing the content of the conceptual model. There are four main methods of representation in common use:

- Component list
- Process flow diagram
- Logic flow diagram
- Activity cycle diagram

Of course, more than one of these methods may be used to give a different view of the same conceptual model. There are also some other methods of conceptual model representation, for instance, Petri nets (Torn 1981), event graphs (Som and Sargent 1989) and condition specification (Overstreet and Nance 1985). UML (the unified modeling language) is currently of interest as a means for representing a conceptual model (Richter and März 2000). Meanwhile, Pooley (1991) gives an overview of diagramming techniques that might support conceptual modelling.

It is not the intention to provide detailed descriptions of these model representation methods here. However, an illustration of each of the methods is provided using the simple example of a single server queue, that is, customers arriving, queuing and being served by one server. Where possible, references are provided for those that wish to investigate the representation methods further.

Component list

This provides a list of the components in the model with some description of the detail included for each. Table 5.1 provides an example for the single server queue. Another example can be found in Section 6.2.4. Although this approach is very simple, it does not provide a visual representation of the conceptual model and it is difficult to capture complex logic and the process flow.

Table 5.1 Component List for Single Server Queue.

Component	Detail
Customers	Time between arrivals (distribution)
Queue	Capacity
Service desk	Service time (distribution)

Process flow diagram (process map)

In this approach the conceptual model is represented as a process flow or process map, showing each component of the system in a sequence and including some description of the model detail. A process might be shown as a box and a queue as a circle. Figure 5.2 is an example of a process flow diagram for the single server queue. In this diagram the detail of the components is denoted in brackets.

This is a fairly simple approach and the visual representation is useful for showing the process flow. Since many simulation packages use a similar representation, this approach is beneficial. It is still difficult, however, to capture more complex logic. Software exists specifically for process mapping, for instance, ARIS (Davis 2001).

Logic flow diagram

Logic flow diagrams use standard flow diagram symbols to represent the logic of the model rather than the process flow. Figure 5.3 shows an example for the single server queue. These diagrams are good for capturing logic and the nomenclature is likely to be familiar to the user. The process flow is not always obvious, however, and these diagrams can quickly become large, complex and cumbersome for models of any reasonable scale. Software such as Visio (www: Microsoft Visio) and Flowcharter (www: iGrafx Flowcharter) support flow diagramming.

Activity cycle diagram

Activity cycle diagrams are used as a specific means for representing discrete-event simulation models (Hills 1971). Figure 5.4 shows an example for the single server queue. Circles represent dead states, where an item waits for something to happen. Active states, represented by rectangles, are where an item is acted upon. This normally entails a time to process the item before passing it on to the next state. In general, active and dead states alternate. A dead state of "outside" the model is included in Figure 5.4 in order to create a complete activity cycle, that is, customers come from and are returned to "outside".

Activity cycle diagrams sit somewhere between process flow diagrams and logic flow diagrams in that they describe, in part, the logic of a model while also giving a visual representation. They can quickly become very complex, however, for models that are not moderate in scale. They provide a convenient means for identifying the events in a simulation (Section 2.2.2) and so their main use has been to act as a basis for programming

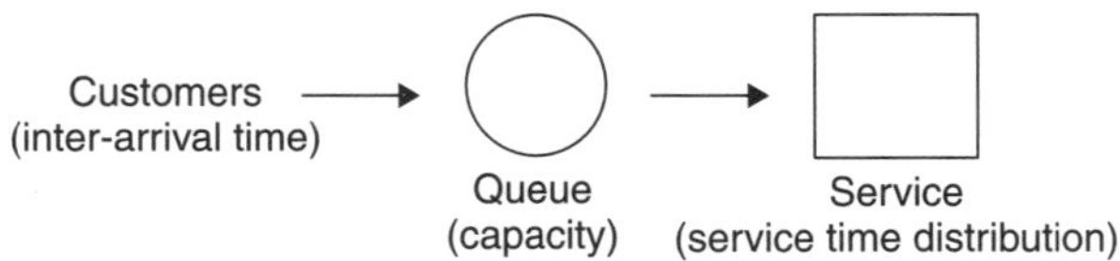

Figure 5.2 Process Flow Diagram for Single Server Queue.

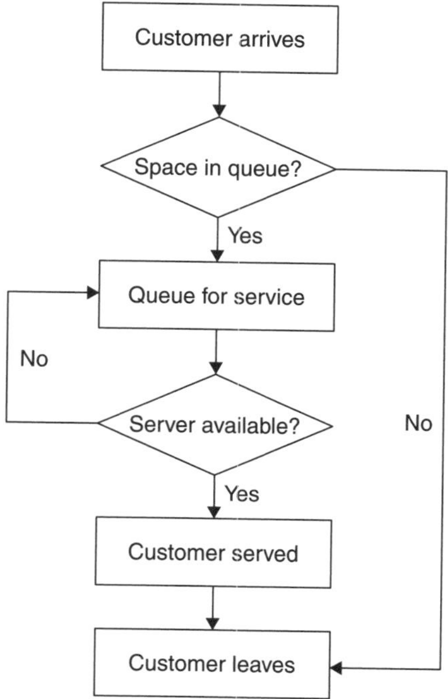

Figure 5.3 Logic Flow Diagram for Single Server Queue.

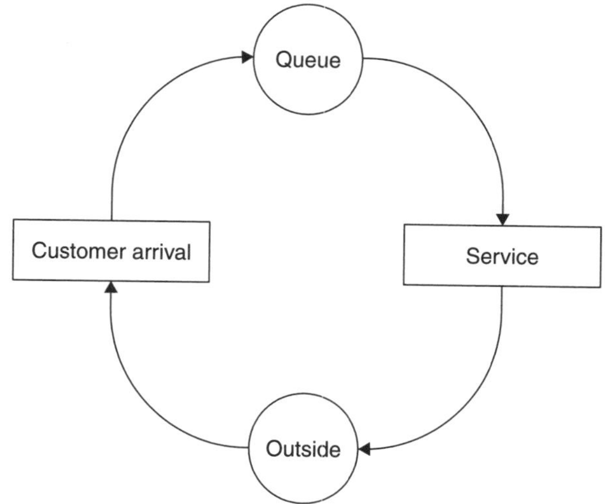

Figure 5.4 Activity Cycle Diagram for Single Server Queue.

simulation models. As a result, they are probably less useful if a simulation package is to be employed. For a more detailed description of activity cycle diagrams see Pidd (1998).

5.6 Conclusion

Conceptual modelling is almost certainly the most important aspect of a simulation study. It is vital that an appropriate model is designed in order for the rest of the simulation study to succeed. Unfortunately, conceptual modelling is also the least understood aspect of simulation modelling. This chapter addresses the issue by providing a definition for a conceptual model and describing the requirements of a conceptual model, namely, validity, credibility, utility and feasibility. It is important to design a model that is as simple as possible, while ensuring that it can meet the objectives of the study. The use of a project specification for communicating the conceptual model and methods of representing the model are also described. Now our attention turns to the process of designing the conceptual model.

Exercise

E5.1 Section 5.5.2 introduces various methods for representing a conceptual model. Investigate these methods in more depth, identifying the strengths and weaknesses of the various approaches. Use the references provided in Section 5.5.2 as a starting point.

References

Brooks, R.J. and Tobias, A.M. (1996) "Choosing the best model: level of detail, complexity and model performance". *Mathematical and Computer Modelling*, 24(4), 1–14.

Chwif, L., Barretto, M.R.P. and Paul, R.J. (2000) "On simulation model complexity". *Proceedings of the 2000 Winter Simulation Conference* (Joines, J.A., Barton, R.R., Kang, K. and Fishwick, P.A., eds). Piscataway, NJ: IEEE: pp. 449–455.

Davis, R. (2001) *Business Process Modelling with ARIS: A Practical Guide*. Berlin, Germany: Springer-Verlag.

Hills, P.R. (1971) *HOCUS*. Egham, Surrey, UK: P-E Group.

Innis, G. and Rexstad, E. (1983) "Simulation model simplification techniques". *Simulation*, 41(1), 7–15.

Law, A.M. (1991) "Simulation model's level of detail determines effectiveness". *Industrial Engineering*, 23(10), 16–18.

Law, A.M. and McComas, M.G. (2001) "How to build valid and credible simulation models". *Proceedings of the 2001 Winter Simulation Conference* (Peters, B.A., Smith, J.S., Medeiros, D.J. and Rohrer, M.W., eds). Piscataway, NJ: IEEE. pp. 22–29.

Overstreet, M.C. and Nance, R.E. (1985) "A specification language to assist in analysis of discrete event simulation models". *Communications of the ACM*, 28(2), 190–201.

Peters, B.A., Smith, J.S., Medeiros, D.J. and Rohrer, M.W. (2001) *Proceedings of the 2001 Winter Simulation Conference*. Piscataway, NJ: IEEE.

Pidd, M. (1998) *Computer Simulation in Management Science*, 4th edn. Chichester, UK: Wiley.

Pooley, R.J. (1991) "Towards a standard for hierarchical process oriented discrete event diagrams". *Transactions of the Society for Computer Simulation*, 8(1), 1–41.

Richter, H. and März, L. (2000). "Toward a standard process: the use of UML for designing simulation models". *Proceedings of the 2000 Winter Simulation Conference* (Joines, J.A, Barton, R.R., Kang, K. and Fishwick, P.A., eds). Piscataway, NJ: IEEE, pp. 394–398.

Robinson, S. (1994) "Simulation projects: building the right conceptual model". *Industrial Engineering*, 26(9), 34–36.

Salt, J. (1993) "Simulation should be easy and fun". *Proceedings of the 1993 Winter Simulation Conference* (Evans, G.W., Mollaghasemi, M., Russell, E.C. and Biles, W.E., eds). Piscataway, NJ: IEEE, pp. 1–5.

Shannon, R.E. (1975) *Systems Simulation: the Art and Science*. Englewood Cliffs, NJ: Prentice-Hall.

Som, T.K. and Sargent, R.G. (1989) "A formal development of event graphs as an aid to structured and efficient simulation programs". *ORSA Journal on Computing*, 1(2), 107–125.

Torn, A.A. (1981) "Simulation graphs: a general tool for modeling simulation designs". *Simulation*, 37(6), 187–194.

Ward, S.C. (1989) "Arguments for constructively simple models". *Journal of the Operational Research Society*, 40(2), 141–153.

Willemain, T.R. (1994) "Insights on modeling from a dozen experts". *Operations Research*, 42(2), 213–222.

Zeigler, B.P. (1976) *Theory of Modelling and Simulation*. Chichester, UK: Wiley.

Internet addresses

Microsoft Visio: http://www.microsoft.com/office/visio/default.asp (July 2003)
iGrafx Flowcharter: http://www.igrafx.com/products/flowcharter/ (July 2003)

DEVELOPING THE CONCEPTUAL MODEL

6

6.1 Introduction

The previous chapter provided a grounding in the basic concepts behind conceptual modelling, in particular, the definition of, and requirements for, a conceptual model. What it did not answer was the question of how to develop a conceptual model. This is the subject of this chapter. The question is answered from two perspectives. First, a framework for developing a conceptual model is described. Secondly, some methods of model simplification are discussed. This first perspective starts from the standpoint that the modeller has a blank sheet of paper. The second perspective assumes that the modeller has a model design and is looking for ways to improve it.

6.2 A Framework for Conceptual Modelling

In general the process of designing a conceptual model is seen very much as an art. As such there is very little guidance available. The most useful guidance probably comes from those who have offered a set of modelling principles (Morris 1967; Powell 1995; Pidd 1999). These range from the socio-political, such as regular contact with subject matter experts, to the more technical, such as developing prototype models along the way. Although these principles are useful for giving some guide to conceptual model design, they do not answer the question of how to develop the conceptual model.

Figure 6.1 provides an outline of a framework for conceptual modelling. The purpose of this framework is to provide a modeller with an understanding of how to develop a conceptual model. The framework consists of four key elements:

- Develop an understanding of the problem situation
- Determine the modelling objectives
- Design the conceptual model: inputs and outputs
- Design the conceptual model: the model content

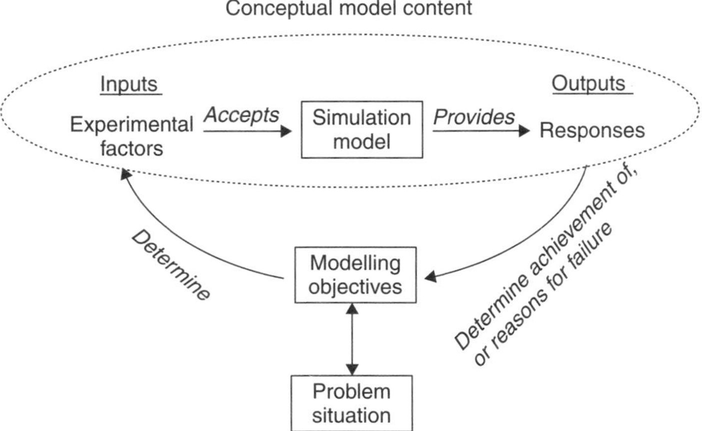

Figure 6.1 A Framework for Conceptual Modelling.

Starting with an understanding of the problem situation, a set of modelling objectives are determined. These objectives then drive the derivation of the conceptual model, first by defining the inputs and outputs, and then by defining the content of the model itself. These elements are described in detail below.

Before going on to detailed descriptions, it is worth remembering that in the same way that the process of performing a simulation study is iterative, so too is conceptual modelling. There is likely to be a great deal of iteration between the elements in the conceptual modelling framework, as well as with the other processes in a simulation study. Some of the reasons for this iteration are discussed in the description that follows.

In order to illustrate the framework an example of modelling a fast-food restaurant is used. This context has been chosen since it is familiar to the majority of readers. Further to this, there are two mini case studies at the end of the book, Wardeon Cinema (Appendix 1) and Panorama Televisions (Appendix 2). These provide an example of a simulation of a service operation and a manufacturing operation respectively. They illustrate the modelling principles described in this book, including the conceptual modelling framework. The case studies are referred to throughout the rest of the book and it is suggested that the reader follow these as a means of seeing how the modelling principles are applied.

6.2.1 Developing an understanding of the problem situation

It is obviously necessary for the modeller to develop a good understanding of the problem situation if he/she is to develop a model that adequately describes the real world. The approach to this process depends in large measure on the extent to which the clients understand, and are able to explain, the problem situation.

In many circumstances the clients will be able to provide such an explanation, for instance, by describing the operation of the (proposed) real world system that is at the heart of the problem situation. The accuracy of the description, however, may be dubious.

One issue is that the clients may not have a good understanding of the cause and effect relationships within the problem situation. For instance, in a recent modelling study of a telephone helpline, the belief was that the support function was understaffed (cause) which resulted in poor customer service (effect). Although the effect was correctly identified (and was in fact the reason why the study was performed), it transpired that increasing staff resources provided almost no benefit in terms of improved customer service. What was required was a change to the business process.

Another problem for the modeller is that the clients almost certainly have different world views or Weltanschauungen (Checkland 1981). In a recent study of maintenance operations, it seems as though there were as many different descriptions of how the maintenance engineers go about their tasks as people who were interviewed. This should be no surprise, especially when dealing with human activity systems in which the vagaries of human behaviour and decision-making impact on the performance of the system.

What becomes apparent is that, although on the face of it the modeller's role is to learn from the clients in order to develop an understanding of the problem situation, the modeller in actual fact has to play a much more active role. Providing the right prompts and speaking with the right people is vital to developing this understanding. The modeller should also be willing to suggest alternative versions of the events in order to facilitate new ways of perceiving the problem situation. Such discussions might be carried out face-to-face in meetings and workshops, or remotely by telephone or email, for example.

When the clients have a reasonable grasp of the problem situation then discussion and careful note-taking should suffice. In addition, it is important that the modeller confirms his/her understanding by providing descriptions of the problem situation for the clients. This acts as a means of validating the conceptual model as it is developed (Section 12.4.1). If the clients have a poor grasp of the problem situation, then more formal problem structuring methods may prove useful, for instance, soft systems methodology (Checkland 1981), cognitive mapping (Eden and Ackermann 2001) and causal loop diagrams (Sterman 2000). Balci and Nance (1985) describe a methodology for problem formulation in simulation modelling that includes developing an understanding of the problem situation, as well as objective setting and verification of the formulated problem. Lehaney and Paul (1996) describe the use of soft systems methodology for structuring a problem before going on to develop a simulation.

It is during the process of understanding the problem situation that areas where there is limited knowledge of the operations system are likely to be identified. It is about these areas that assumptions have to be made. These should be documented and recorded in the project specification (Section 5.5.1). For the reasons stated below, areas of limited knowledge continue to be identified as a simulation study progresses. This means that new assumptions need to be made and then added to the project specification.

The problem situation, and the understanding of it, should not be seen as static. Both will change as the simulation study progresses, the simulation itself being one of the catalysts for this change. A simulation model and the information required to develop it almost always act as a focus for clarifying and developing a deeper understanding of the real world system that is being modelled. This acts to increase the level of iteration between modelling processes across a simulation study, with adjustments to the conceptual model

Table 6.1 Fast-Food Restaurant Illustration: The Problem Situation.

A fast-food restaurant is experiencing problems with one of the branches in its network. Customers regularly complain about the length of time they have to queue at the service counters. It is apparent that this is not the result of shortages in food, but a shortage of service personnel.

being required, even at the point when the model is being used for experimentation, as new facets of the problem situation emerge.

As stated earlier, the conceptual modelling framework is illustrated with an example of a fast-food restaurant. Table 6.1 describes the problem situation at the restaurant.

6.2.2 Determining the modelling objectives

The modelling objectives are central to the modelling process. They are the means by which the nature of the model is determined, the reference point for model validation, the guide for experimentation, and one of the metrics by which the success of the study is judged. Later it is shown how the objectives can be used to help design the conceptual model (Section 6.2.3).

A model has little intrinsic value unless it is used to aid decision-making, and so the purpose of a modelling study is not the development of the model itself. If it were, then having developed the model, the objective would have been met and the study would be complete. The logical conclusion to this process is the existence of models that have never served any useful purpose, or models that are looking for a problem to solve. There are exceptions to this rule of course. For instance, a generic model of a hospital emergency unit may be developed with a view to selling the model to numerous hospitals. On the surface, the purpose of the original modelling project is the development of a model. Underlying this, however, the model developers must have in mind some purpose for the model, for instance, to determine resource requirements. Indeed, many military models are apparently developed in this fashion. A model is developed and then an application for the model is sought. In this paradigm, the model needs to be assessed whenever a new purpose is found (Gass 1977).

In forming the objectives, a useful question to ask is "by the end of this study what do you hope to *achieve*?" Beyond this, three aspects should be considered. First, what is it that the clients wish to achieve? Typically this involves increasing throughput, reducing cost or improving customer service (often measured by some queuing metric). Improving the clients' understanding of the real world system, or reducing the risk of an investment are also valid objectives, albeit that they are less quantifiable.

Secondly, what level of *performance* is required? To state that the objective is to increase throughput is insufficient. By how much should the throughput be increased? Whenever it is possible, targets of performance for each objective should be sought. These might be expressed as straightforward targets (e.g. increase/reduce by a percentage or absolute amount) or the need to optimize (i.e. maximize or minimize) some measure. This can only be done when the objective can be quantified. To try and express performance levels for improved understanding is probably meaningless.

Finally, what *constraints* must the clients (or modeller) work within? Often there is a limited budget or a limited number of approaches available for achieving the objectives. For instance, the clients may only be willing to consider changes in production scheduling to gain throughput improvements, while ruling out the purchase of additional equipment.

It must be recognized that the clients may not be able to give a complete set of objectives, for the same reasons as their understanding of the problem situation may be incomplete. Further to this, the clients may have a limited, and possibly misconceived, understanding of what a simulation model can do for them, particularly if they have not been involved in simulation studies previously. Therefore, it is important that the modeller is willing to suggest additional objectives as well as to redefine and eliminate the objectives suggested by the clients. The modeller should also educate the clients, explaining how simulation might act as an aid. One means for achieving this is for the modeller to demonstrate one or more models of similar problem situations, and to provide descriptions of the modelling work that underlay them. In this way the clients will obtain a better understanding of how simulation can, and cannot, help. Objective setting should involve the clients in learning about simulation and its potential, as much as the modeller in learning about the problem situation. In this way the modeller is able to manage the expectations of the clients, aiming to set them at a realistic level. Unfulfilled expectations are a major source of dissatisfaction among clients in simulation modelling work (Robinson and Pidd 1998; Robinson 1998).

Since the problem situation and the understanding of it can change, so too can the objectives. They are by no means static. Added to this, as the clients' understanding of the potential of simulation improves, as it inevitably does during the course of the study, their requirements and expectations will also change. Consequently the iteration between the modelling processes is further increased, with changes in objectives affecting the design of the model, the experimentation and the outcomes of the project. It is for this reason that there is a two-way arrow between the "problem situation" and the "modelling objectives" in Figure 6.1.

The modelling objective for the fast-food restaurant example is given in Table 6.2.

General project objectives

In designing a simulation model the modelling objectives are not the only concern. The modeller should also be aware of some more general project objectives. Time-scale is particularly important. If there is only a limited time available for the project, then the modeller may be forced into a more conservative model design. This helps reduce model development time and quicken its run-speed, reducing the time required for experimentation.

Table 6.2 Fast-Food Restaurant Illustration: Modelling Objectives.

The number of service staff required during each period of the day to ensure that 95% of customers queue for less than 3 minutes for service. Due to space constraints, a maximum of six service staff can be employed at any one time.

The modeller should also clarify the nature of the model required by the clients, specifically in terms of the *visual display* and the *type of model use*. What level of visual display is needed? Is a simple schematic sufficient, or is a 3D view required? Do the clients wish to use the model themselves? If so, what data input and results viewing facilities do they require? What level of interactive capability is necessary to enable appropriate experimentation? All these issues have an impact on the design of the simulation model.

6.2.3 Designing the conceptual model: the inputs and outputs

The first stage of conceptual model design does not involve the details of the model itself, but the model's inputs and outputs, depicted as the experimental factors and responses in Figure 6.1. It is much easier to start by giving consideration to these, than to the content of the model. Indeed, it should be a fairly straightforward task to move from the modelling objectives to the experimental factors. In effect, these are the means by which it is proposed that the objectives are to be achieved. These means might be reflected in the statement of the objectives themselves, for instance, "to obtain a 10% improvement in customer service by developing effective *staff rosters*", or "to increase throughput . . . by changing the *production schedule*". Alternatively, the experimental factors may be less explicit, but can be obtained by simply asking the clients how they intend to bring about the improvement in the operation of the real world system. The modeller should also provide input to this discussion based on his/her knowledge of simulation. Altogether, this might lead to a substantial list of factors. Note that the experimental factors may be qualitative (e.g. changes to rules or the model structure) as well as quantitative.

Although the clients would often have control over the experimental factors in the real world, it is sometimes useful to experiment with factors over which they have little or no control (e.g. the arrival rate of customers). By experimenting with such factors a greater understanding of the real system can be obtained. This, after all, is a key benefit of simulation.

Where possible, it is useful to determine the range over which the experimental factors are to be varied. This can be achieved through discussion between the modeller and the clients. If the size of a storage area is being experimented with, what is the maximum size that could/would be considered? If the number of staff on a shift is being investigated, what is the minimum and maximum number possible? The simulation model can then be designed to enable this range of data input. On some occasions this helps to avoid an over-complex model design that provides for a much wider range of data input than is necessary.

There should also be some discussion on the method of data entry for the experimental factors. This might be direct into the model code, through a set of menus, through a data file or via third party software such as a spreadsheet. In large measure this depends upon the intended users of the model and their familiarity with computer software. This decision relates to the general project objectives discussed above.

Similarly, the identification of the responses required from the model should not provide a major challenge. The responses have two purposes. The first is to identify whether the objectives have been achieved. For example, if the objective is to increase throughput by a certain amount, then it is obvious that the model needs to report the throughput. The second purpose of the responses is to point to the reasons why the objectives are not being achieved. Taking the throughput example, this might require reports on machine and resource utilization and buffer/work-in-progress levels at various points in the model. By inspecting these reports, the user should be able to identify potential bottlenecks, and look for solutions.

Another issue to be considered is how the information is reported, for instance, as numerical data (mean, maximum, minimum, standard deviation) or graphical data (time-series, histograms, Gantt charts, pie charts). For an interesting discussion on the presentation of data, and the relative merits of numerical and graphical reports, see Ehrenberg (1999). Appendix 3 provides a description of various numerical and graphical reporting methods, as well as a discussion on the advantages and disadvantages of each. The identification of suitable responses and methods of reporting should be determined by close consultation between the simulation modeller and the clients, both bringing their respective expertise to bear. The nature of the reports depends upon the requirements for visual and interactive features in the model, as outlined in the discussion on general project objectives above.

Table 6.3 shows the relevant experimental factors and responses for the fast-food restaurant example.

As with all aspects of the modelling process, both the experimental factors and responses will change as the project progresses. It may be realized, for instance, that changing the staff rosters is not effective in improving customer service, but that changing the business process is. As experimentation progresses, the need to inspect reports on the level of rework to understand the restrictions in throughput may become apparent. The experimental factors and responses may also change as a result of changes to the problem situation, the understanding of the problem situation, or the modelling objectives.

It should be apparent from the description above that the modelling objectives are central to the conceptual modelling framework described here. It is for this reason that determining the modelling objectives is described as part of the conceptual modelling process. Since the understanding of the problem situation is central to the formation of the modelling objectives, it is also considered to be part of the conceptual modelling process.

6.2.4 Designing the conceptual model: the model content

Having identified the model's inputs and outputs, the modeller can identify the content of the model itself. Although this book is about simulation modelling, the need to consider

Table 6.3 Fast-Food Restaurant Illustration: Experimental Factors and Responses.

Experimental Factors
- Staff rosters (total number of staff at each hour of the day)

Responses (to determine achievement of objectives)
- Percentage of customers queuing for less than 3 minutes

Responses (to identify reasons for failure to meet objectives)
- Histogram of waiting time for each customer in the queues, mean, standard deviation, minimum and maximum
- Time-series of mean queue size by hour
- Staff utilization (cumulative percentage)

the appropriate modelling approach should not be forgotten at this point. In designing the content of the model, and indeed before this point is reached, the modeller should consider whether simulation is the most suitable approach. This is particularly pertinent because simulation is among the most arduous modelling approaches, and so alternatives should be used whenever possible (Section 1.3.2).

Assuming that simulation is deemed to be the right approach, the starting point in designing the model content is to recognize that the model must be able to accept the experimental factors and to provide the required responses. In this respect, the experimental factors and responses provide the basis of what the model needs to include. Taking the example of staff rosters, it is immediately obvious that the model must represent these. The model must then provide the relevant reports, for instance, waiting time. Therefore, the model must include the queues.

Having identified the immediate entry point of the experimental factors, and exit point of the responses, the modeller must then identify the key interconnections between these and the other components of the real world. It is only those interconnections that are judged to be important, with respect to correctly interpreting the experimental factors and providing accurate values for the responses that need to be included in the model. It is probably useful first to think in terms of the scope and then the level of detail.

The scope of the model must be sufficient to provide a link between the experimental factors and the responses. For instance, a model that looks at the throughput (response) resulting from a particular production schedule (experimental factor) needs to include at least all the critical processes within the manufacturing flow from entry of the schedule to creation of the finished items. The scope must also include any processes that interconnect with this flow such that they have a significant impact on the responses, the meaning of significant being defined by the level of model accuracy required. For instance, the manufacturing model must include any processes that interconnect with the production flow and have a significant impact on the throughput. If the supply of raw materials has only a small impact on the throughput, because material shortages are rare, then it is probably unnecessary to model them. If a high level of model accuracy is needed, however, then it is more likely that the supply of raw materials (or at least the shortage of raw materials) needs to be modelled.

The level of detail must be such that it represents the components defined within the scope and their interconnection with the other components of the model with sufficient accuracy. This again can be considered with respect to the impact on the model's responses. For example, considering a single machine on a manufacturing line, the cycle time and breakdowns are very likely to have a significant impact on throughput. Machine changeovers probably have sufficient impact to make them worth modelling. Beyond this, the small variations in the machine cycle, the type of machine failure, etc., are probably of little importance to accurately predicting throughput, and so can be excluded from the model.

Prototyping is a powerful method in helping to form a decision about the scope and level of detail to include in a model (Powell 1995; Pidd 1999). The modeller develops simple computer models, gradually increasing the scope and level of detail. The intention is to throw these models away and not to use them for formal analysis, although they can often provide useful insights for the clients. Their primary purpose is to provide an insight into the key variables and interconnections in order to help with the design of the conceptual model.

In designing the simulation, the modeller must keep in mind the general project objectives (Section 6.2.2). If the requirement is for a complex visual display, then additional detail may need to be added to the model. If the time-scale is limited, then the scope and level of detail in the model may need to be reduced, possibly compromising on accuracy.

It is also important to keep a record of any assumptions that are made during the design of the model content. They need to be presented to all involved in the simulation study to ensure that everyone understands and is comfortable with the assumptions that are being made. Any simplifications should be noted and explained as well. Methods of simplification are discussed in Section 6.3.

Table 6.4 shows the proposed scope of the fast-food restaurant model, with a justification for what is to be included and excluded. Table 6.5 provides similar information for the level of detail. These tables represent the conceptual model as a component list as described in Section 5.5.2.

Throughout the development of the conceptual model, the modeller should look for opportunities to simplify the model. This is the subject of the next section.

6.2.5 The role of data in conceptual modelling

In Section 7.2 the types of data required in a simulation study are discussed. Preliminary or contextual data are required for developing an understanding of the problem situation and so are central to the development of conceptual modelling. Meanwhile, data for model realization (developing the computer model) are not required for conceptual modelling, but are identified by the conceptual model.

In a perfect world, where accurate data for any part of a process could easily be obtained, the conceptual model would be designed without consideration for whether the data can be gathered. The world, of course, is less than perfect! Not all data are readily available

Table 6.4 Fast-Food Restaurant Illustration: Model Scope.

Component	Include/exclude	Justification
Customers	Include	Flow through the service process
Staff – Service	Include	Experimental factor, required for staff utilization response
– Food preparation	Exclude	Material shortages are not significant
– Cleaning	Exclude	Do not interconnect with speed of service
Queues at service counters	Include	Required for waiting time and queue size response
Tables	Exclude	Not related to waiting for food
Kitchen	Exclude	Material shortages are not significant

Table 6.5 Fast-Food Restaurant Illustration: Model Level of Detail.

Component	Detail	Include/exclude	Comment
Customers	Customer inter-arrival times	Include	Modelled as a distribution
	Size of customer order	Exclude	Represented in service time
Service staff	Service time	Include	Modelled as a distribution, taking account of variability in performance and size of order
	Staff rosters	Include	Experimental factor
	Absenteeism	Exclude	Not explicitly modelled, but could be represented by perturbations to the staff rosters
Queues	Queuing	Include	Required for waiting time and queue size response
	Capacity	Exclude	Assume no effective limit
	Queue behaviour (jockey, balk, leave)	Exclude (except assume join shortest queue)	Behaviour not well understood. Results will show imbalance of arrival and service rates (see Section 6.3.5)

or indeed collectable, and sometimes it is impossible to obtain adequate data, making the proposed conceptual model problematic. This leaves the modeller with two options. One is to redesign the conceptual model in such a way as to engineer out the need for troublesome data. The other is to resist changing the conceptual model and to handle the data in other ways. Methods for dealing with unavailable data are discussed in Section 7.3. In practice, the modeller probably uses a mixture of the two approaches. As such, the conceptual model defines the data that are required, while the data that are available, or collectable, affect the design of the conceptual model. This serves to increase the level of iteration required in the modelling process, as the modeller must move between consideration for the design of the model and the availability of data.

6.2.6 Summary of the conceptual modelling framework

The framework described above consists of four key stages: developing an understanding of the problem situation, determining the modelling objectives, determining the model inputs and outputs, and designing the model content. It is also necessary to consider whether simulation is the most appropriate modelling approach as part of the conceptual modelling process. The aim of the framework is to provide the modeller with some guidance over how to design the conceptual model. Throughout the design process the modeller must be cognizant of the four requirements of a conceptual model described in the previous chapter (Section 5.4.1): validity, credibility, utility and feasibility. The aim should also be to develop a model that is as simple as possible for the purpose at hand (Section 5.4.2).

The level of iteration required in the development of the conceptual model should be stressed. It is not a case of providing a design and then going ahead and developing the computer model. Many iterations of conceptual model design and client interaction are required. Frequent iterations between model coding, experimentation and model design are also necessary. An important task of the modeller is to plan for change. By developing flexibility into the model it should be possible relatively easily to incorporate changes to the experimental factors, the responses and the content of the model itself. If one thing can be counted upon, it is that the conceptual model will change as the simulation study progresses.

6.3 Methods of Model Simplification

Apart from having a framework for conceptual modelling, it is also useful for the modeller to have some methods of model simplification at his/her disposal. As discussed in Section 5.3, simplifications are not assumptions about the real world, but they are ways of reducing the complexity of a model. Model simplification involves reducing the scope and level of detail in a conceptual model either by:

- removing components and interconnections that have little effect on model accuracy

or by:

- representing more simply components and interconnections while maintaining a satisfactory level of model accuracy.

This can either be achieved by identifying opportunities for simplification during conceptual modelling or once the conceptual model is complete and beyond, for instance, during model coding. The main purpose of simplification is to increase the utility of a model while not significantly affecting its validity or credibility. In general, simplification enables more rapid model development and use (Section 5.4.2). Simplification may be necessary if the original model design is deemed infeasible, for instance, because required data are not available.

There are a number of discussions on methods of model simplification. Morris (1967) and Courtois (1985) both discuss methods that are applicable in the general context of modelling. Zeigler (1976), Innis and Rexstad (1983), Yin and Zhou (1989) and Robinson (1994) all discuss the simplification of simulation models. In this section a number of useful methods of simulation model simplification are described.

Before describing some methods of model simplification, it is worth noting that one of the most effective approaches for simplifying a model is, in fact, to start with the simplest model possible and gradually to add to its scope and level of detail (Pidd 1999). Once a point is reached at which the study's objectives can be addressed by the model, then no further detail should be added. Finding an appropriate point at which to stop, however, requires careful attention and discipline on the part of the modeller. The framework described earlier in this chapter should aid this process.

6.3.1 Aggregation of model components

Aggregation of model components provides a means for reducing the level of detail. Two specific approaches are described here: black-box modelling and grouping entities.

Black-box modelling

In black-box modelling a section of an operation is represented as a time delay. Model entities that represent parts, people, information and such like enter the black-box and leave at some later time. This approach can be used for modelling anything from a group of machines or service desks to a complete factory or service operation. I have developed a model of a complete manufacturing supply chain as a series of interconnected plants, each modelled as a black-box.

Figure 6.2 illustrates the approach. As an entity X_i enters the black-box, the time at which it is due to leave, t_i, is calculated. When the simulation reaches time t_i, the entity leaves the box. The time an entity spends in the box can of course be sampled from a distribution. The approach can also be extended to account for re-sequencing of entities (e.g. re-work), stoppages and shifts by manipulating the values of t_i for each entity in the box.

Grouping entities

Instead of modelling individual items as they move through a system, a simulation entity can represent a group of items. This is particularly useful when there is a high volume of items moving through a system, for example, a confectionery wrapping process in which hundreds of chocolate bars are wrapped each minute. To model each chocolate bar individually would lead to hundreds of events per simulated minute, which would have a detrimental effect on simulation run-speed. It is beneficial in this case for an entity to represent, say, 100 chocolate bars.

The approach can easily be adapted to model situations where the number of items represented by an entity changes as the entity moves through the model. For example, a certain number of chocolate bars are rejected (or eaten!) at an inspection area. This can be modelled by holding as an attribute of the entity the number of chocolate bars it represents. The attribute value can then be adjusted as the entity moves through the model.

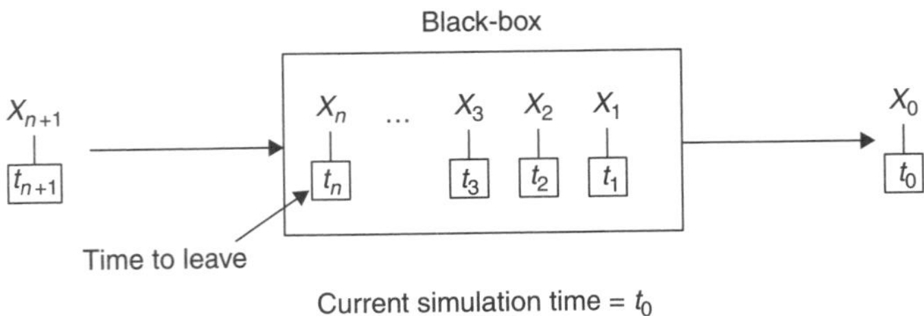

Figure 6.2 Black-Box Modelling. (Robinson 1994; Reprinted with Permission of the Institute of Industrial Engineers, 3577 Parkway Lane, Suite 200, Norcross, GA 30092, 770-449-0461. Copyright © 1994.)

6.3.2 Excluding components and details

On occasions it is not necessary to include some components in a simulation because their omission has little effect on the accuracy of the model. This is a form of scope reduction.

Resources required for a process to take place need not be modelled if it can be assumed that the resource is always, or almost always, available to perform that task. In this case it is only necessary to model the process. For instance, an operator who is dedicated to a task on a manufacturing line need not be modelled explicitly.

The modelling of machine repairs provides a very specific example of model simplification, in this case driven by the availability of appropriate data. If the resources required for repair (normally maintenance operators and possibly some equipment) are to be modelled explicitly, then it is necessary to have data on actual repair times. However, many organizations only collect data on machine down times, that is, the total time the machine is down including the time for the resources to be made available. If down time data are being modelled, then the resources should not be explicitly included in the simulation, otherwise a form of double counting is taking place.

Some details may be excluded from a model because they, too, are deemed to have little impact on model accuracy. An example would be the modelling of shift patterns. These only need to be modelled if:

- Different areas work to different shifts.
- The availability of labour, process speed or process rules vary between shifts.
- Operations continue outside of shifts, for instance, machine repair.
- Shifts need to be modelled to give the simulation credibility.

Otherwise, it is unnecessary to model the dead time between shifts.

6.3.3 Replacing components with random variables

Rather than model a component or group of components in detail it may be possible to represent them as a set of random variables, sampled from some distributions. For instance, modelling transportation systems such as fork-lift trucks, automatic guided vehicles, heavy goods vehicles or trains can be complex. Depending on the context, allowance needs to be made for breakdowns, punctures, traffic congestion, weather conditions, turnaround times and driver shifts.

As part of a model that represented two sites, I was tasked with modelling the delivery of goods between the two locations. Having spent some time understanding the complexities of the delivery process and everything that could go wrong, it was apparent that a complete representation would require a complex model. The solution was to ask the question: how many deliveries are made each day and what is the typical movement time? It was then possible to represent the complete delivery system as three random variables: the number of deliveries per day, the departure times and the arrival times. This was a much simpler model to develop and to manipulate during experimentation.

6.3.4 Excluding infrequent events

Some events only affect an operations system on an infrequent basis. A warehouse crane may only break down once every 2 years. Hospitals do not often have to deal with major disasters. It is probably best to exclude the possibility of such events occurring during a simulation run so as to investigate the operations system under normal working conditions. The effect of such events can always be investigated by performing specific runs in which the event is forced on the model (e.g. a crane breakdown or a flood of patients into an emergency department).

6.3.5 Reducing the rule set

Rules are used in simulation models to determine routes, processing times, schedules, allocation of resources and such like. A model can be simplified by reducing the rule set, while maintaining a sufficient level of accuracy. In many cases, 80% of circumstances are covered by 20% of the rule set, for instance, routing decisions for automatic guided vehicles. Judgement is required as to whether it is worth modelling the other 80% of the rule set for a small improvement in model accuracy.

One specific difficulty in simulation modelling is representing human interaction with an operations system. For instance, it is very difficult to know how people behave when queuing in a service system. How does a person determine which queue to join in a supermarket? When does a person decide to jump from one queue to another? When would someone decide to leave a queue? In what circumstances would a person decide not to join a queue? Because such decisions are dependent on the individual, it is practically impossible to devise a valid rule set for all people in all situations. Therefore, normal practice is to use a simplified set of rules, for instance, customers choose the shortest queue or they will not join a queue if there are more than five people in it.

An extreme, but nevertheless useful, approach is to dispense with the rule set altogether. In the service system example above the simulation could make no assumptions about queuing behaviour beyond perhaps assuming people join the shortest queue. This would mean that if there is an imbalance between service rate and arrival rate the queues would become very large. Albeit unrealistic, this provides the model user with useful information, that is, the system is not balanced and custom is likely to be lost unless the service rate can be increased.

6.3.6 Splitting models

Rather than build one large model, it can be beneficial to split the model into two or more parts. A simple way of achieving this is to split the models such that the output of one sub-model (model A) is the input to another (model B), see Figure 6.3. As model A runs, data concerning the output from the model, such as output time and any entity attributes, can be written to a data file. Model B is then run and the data read such that the entities are recreated in model B at the appropriate time.

The advantage of splitting models is that the individual models run faster. It is also quite probable that a single run of all the sub-models is quicker than one run of a combined

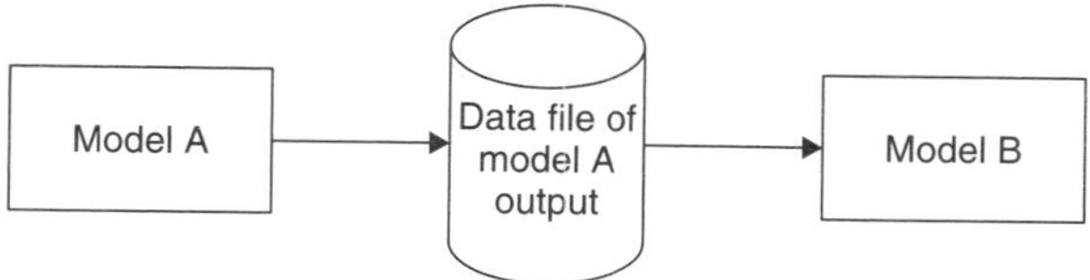

Figure 6.3 Splitting Models. (Robinson 1994; Reprinted with Permission of the Institute of Industrial Engineers, 3577 Parkway Lane, Suite 200, Norcross, GA 30092, 770-449-0461. Copyright © 1994.)

model because of reduced processing at the C-phase; assuming the three-phase method is being employed (Section 2.2.2). This is a result of there being fewer conditional events in each sub-model. In a combined model, every C-event would need to be checked whenever an event occurs somewhere in the model, leading to a lot of redundant processing. Another advantage of splitting models is that it is possible to speed development time by having separate modellers develop each model in parallel.

Where splitting models is not so successful is when there is feedback between the models. For instance, if model B cannot receive entities, because the first buffer is full, then it is not possible to stop model A outputting that entity, although in practice this is what would happen. It is best, therefore, to split models at a point where there is minimal feedback, for instance, where there is a large buffer.

There is much interest in running simulations in parallel on separate computers, with the aim of gaining run-speed advantages. If split models are run in parallel, then it should be possible to model feedback effects and so overcome the difficulty described above. At present, however, there are a number of obstacles to the use of parallel computing for simulation, not least developing efficient mechanisms for synchronizing the models as they run.

6.3.7 What is a good simplification?

Although model simplifications are beneficial, a poor choice of simplification, or over-simplifying a model, may seriously affect the accuracy of the simulation. A good simplification is one that brings the benefits of faster model development and run-speed (utility), while maintaining a sufficient level of accuracy (validity). How can a modeller determine whether a simplification is good or not? There are two broad approaches.

The first is to use judgement in deciding whether a simplification is likely to have a significant effect on model accuracy. This should be determined by discussion between the modeller, client and other members of the simulation project team. The project specification (Section 5.5.1) is a useful mechanism for explaining and discussing the efficacy of proposed simplifications. Of course, this approach provides no certainty over whether a simplification is appropriate or not. An expert modeller is likely to have much experience in applying model simplifications and it may be useful to seek advice from such people before employing a particular simplification.

The second approach is to test the simplification in the computer model; a form of prototyping. The modeller develops two computer models, one with and one without the simplification. It is then possible to compare the results from the two models to see the effect on accuracy. This, of course, provides much greater certainty over the appropriateness of a simplification, but the advantage of faster model development is lost.

Apart from maintaining a sufficient level of accuracy (validity), a good simplification should not compromise credibility either. Over-simplification can make a model less transparent, reducing its credibility. Take, for example, the use of black-box modelling. Although a black-box may provide a sufficiently accurate representation of part of an operations system, the details of the representation are not transparent. For some clients this may be satisfactory, but for others it may be necessary to provide a more detailed representation to give the model credibility. It is sometimes necessary to include a greater scope and level of detail than is required to assure the accuracy of the model, in order to assure the model's credibility. A poor simplification is one that causes a client to lose confidence in a model. Indeed, there are occasions when it is necessary to reverse the concept of simplification and actually increase the complexity (scope and level of detail) of the model, simply to satisfy the requirement for credibility.

6.4 Conclusion

The issue of how to develop a conceptual model is discussed from two standpoints: first, by presenting a framework for conceptual modelling, enabling a modeller to design a conceptual model from scratch; secondly, by describing a number of methods for simplifying an existing conceptual model. The framework is illustrated with reference to an example of a fast-food restaurant. The framework and methods of simplification are further illustrated by the mini case studies at the end of the book, Wardeon Cinema (Appendix 1, Section A1.2) and Panorama Televisions (Appendix 2, Section A2.2).

A final issue that has not been discussed is the validation of the conceptual model. This is covered in Section 12.4.1 as part of a more general discussion on the verification and validation of simulation models.

Exercises

E6.1 A bank is planning its requirements for ATMs (automated teller machines) in a new branch. There are spaces for up to six ATMs, not all of which have to be used. Three types of ATM can be purchased: general ATMs (giving cash, balances, mini statements and PIN change facilities), ATMs for paying money into accounts and ATMs that provide full account statements. The bank has a policy that customers should not wait for more than 5 minutes in the majority of cases (generally interpreted as 99%).

Develop a conceptual model for this problem outlining the objectives, experimental factors and responses, model scope and level of detail, and assumptions and simplifications.

E6.2 Take a typical operations system, preferably one that can be observed (e.g. a supermarket or airport), and identify in broad terms at least three conceptual models that could be developed of the system. For each model identify the objectives and model content.

E6.3 Obtain and read some simulation case studies (see Exercise E1.3 in Chapter 1 for potential sources). Identify the objectives of the simulation study, the experimental factors and responses, and any assumptions and simplifications that were made. As far as possible try to identify the scope and level of detail modelled. Can you identify any means for improving upon the simulation model that was developed (e.g. more or less detail, different assumptions)?

E6.4 For each of the following situations identify a method of simplification that could be employed in a simulation model of the system:

a) A factory that produces a range of products: 80% of orders are for two product types, 18% for five product types and the remaining 2% for 17 product types.
b) A bottling plant that fills, caps and labels bottles at a rate of five bottles a second.
c) An automotive final assembly line that is experiencing problems with the supply of seven key components (out of hundreds that are supplied to the line). The company wishes to investigate the inventory policy for these components.
d) Modelling weather conditions at a port.
e) A supply chain for the manufacture, warehousing, distribution and retailing of wooden doors.
f) A model representing the splitting of trains as they arrive at a rail yard and the forming of trains ready for departure.
g) A ceramics factory in which crockery is processed by pallet loads through the glazing and firing processes.

E6.5 Design a conceptual model for the Wardeon Cinema case described in Appendix 1 (Section A1.2.1). Identify the modelling objectives, model inputs and outputs, model content and any assumptions and simplifications.

E6.6 Design a conceptual model for the Panorama Televisions case described in Appendix 2 (Section A2.2.1). Identify the modelling objectives, model inputs and outputs, model content and any assumptions and simplifications.

References

Balci, O. and Nance, R.E. (1985) "Formulated problem verification as an explicit requirement of model credibility". *Simulation*, 45(2), 76–86.

Checkland, P.B. (1981) *Systems Thinking, Systems Practice*. Chichester, UK: Wiley.

Courtois, P.J. (1985) "On time and space decomposition of complex structures". *Communications of the* ACM, 28(6), 590–603.

Eden, C. and Ackermann, F. (2001) "SODA–the principles". In *Rational Analysis for a Problematic World Revisited*, 2nd edn. (Rosenhead, J.V. and Mingers, J., eds), Chichester, UK: Wiley, pp. 21–41.

Ehrenberg, A. (1999) "What we can and cannot get from graphs, and why". *Journal of Targeting, Measurement and Analysis for Marketing*, 8(2), 113–134.

Gass, S.I. (1977) "Evaluation of complex models". *Computers and Operations Research*, 4, 27–35.

Innis, G. and Rexstad, E. (1983) "Simulation model simplification techniques". *Simulation*, 41(1), 7–15.

Lehaney, B. and Paul, R.J. (1996) "The use of soft systems methodology in the development of a simulation of out-patient services at Watford General Hospital". *Journal of the Operational Research Society*, 47(7), 864–870.

Morris, W.T. (1967) "On the art of modeling". *Management Science*, 13(12), B707–717.

Pidd, M. (1999) "Just modeling through: a rough guide to modeling". *Interfaces*, 29(2), 118–132.

Powell. S.G. (1995) "Six key modeling heuristics". *Interfaces*, 25(4), 114–125.

Robinson, S. (1994) "Simulation projects: building the right conceptual model". *Industrial Engineering*, 26(9), 34–36.

Robinson, S. (1998) "Measuring service quality in the process of delivering a simulation study: the customer's perspective". *International Transactions in Operational Research*, 5(5), 357–374.

Robinson, S. and Pidd, M. (1998) "Provider and customer expectations of successful simulation projects". *Journal of the Operational Research Society*, 49(3), 200–209.

Sterman, J.D. (2000) *Business Dynamics: Systems Thinking and Modeling for a Complex World*. New York: Irwin/McGraw-Hill.

Yin, H.Y. and Zhou, Z.N. (1989) "Simplification techniques of simulation models". *Proceedings of Beijing International Conference on System Simulation and Scientific Computing*, Chinese Association for System Simulation, Beijing pp. 782–786.

Zeigler, B.P. (1976) *Theory of Modelling and Simulation*. Chichester, UK: Wiley.

DATA COLLECTION AND ANALYSIS

7

7.1 Introduction

Data are of course central to the development and use of simulation models. Much effort may go into the design of the conceptual model and into the coding of the computer model. However, if the data that are used to design and populate the model are inaccurate then the results from the model will also be inaccurate.

In this chapter a number of issues surrounding the collection and analysis of data are discussed. First, the discussion focuses on identifying the data requirements. Attention then turns to obtaining the data and in particular how inaccurate data and data that are not available should be dealt with. One of the main reasons for using a simulation model is the ability to model variability (Section 1.3.1). Four methods for modelling variability are described: traces, empirical distributions, statistical distributions and bootstrapping. The advantages and disadvantages of each as well as some further issues in modelling variability are also discussed. The chapter concludes with a discussion on the selection of appropriate statistical distributions.

Data, otherwise known as input modelling, is a subject that can be described very much from a statistical perspective. Much research in the area rightly adopts this approach. The purpose of this chapter, however, is to focus on the practical issues and, as such, the statistical content is kept to a minimum.

7.2 Data Requirements

Generally the word data is taken to mean quantitative data, or numbers. Certainly numeric data are very important in simulation modelling and in some cases large quantities of such data are required. Data are needed on cycle (service) times, breakdown frequencies, arrival patterns and so on. The concentration on quantitative data, however, ignores the importance of qualitative data as well. In general terms these are non-numeric facts and beliefs about a system that are expressed in pictures or words. For instance, many manufacturing based simulation studies rely on computer aided design (CAD) drawings of the layout (a picture) to define the nature of the process. Many of the decision rules used to control elements of a system, for instance, routing of automatic guided vehicles (AGVs) or the queuing behaviour of customers, are expressed in words. In this chapter, and elsewhere in the book, the word data refers to both quantitative and qualitative data, albeit that much of the discussion focuses on the collection and particularly analysis of quantitative data.

It is also worth noting that there is a difference between data and information. Information is typically viewed as data with interpretation, in other words data that have been analysed for some purpose. A simulation modeller may be given raw data or data that have been interpreted in some fashion (information). Take, for instance, the information obtained from a time study. *Data* on the time required to perform certain tasks are aggregated to provide *information* on a standard time to perform an activity. The standard time includes various allowances for breaks, skill level and process inefficiency. The modeller must decide whether he/she needs access to the underlying data or whether the information is adequate for the purpose of the simulation study. As well as being given data and information, the modeller often needs to analyse data to provide information useful to the simulation. An example is fitting statistical distributions (Section 7.5.2).

In simulation, as in any modelling exercise, data requirements can be split into three types (Pidd 2003). The first is preliminary or contextual data. In order for the modeller and clients to develop a thorough understanding of the problem situation some data needs to be available, for instance, a layout diagram, basic data on process capability and beliefs about the cause of problems that are being experienced. At this stage large data collection exercises should be avoided if possible, since the data are only required for developing an understanding and are generally not needed for detailed analysis. These data are very much part of the conceptual modelling process because they are necessary for the development of the conceptual model.

The second data required are data for model realization, that is, developing the computer model. In moving from the conceptual model to a computer model many data are required, for example, detailed data on cycle times and breakdowns, customer arrival patterns and descriptions of customer types, and scheduling and processing rules. It may be necessary to carry out a detailed collection exercise to obtain these data. These data are directly identified from the conceptual model, since this describes all the components of the model and the detail associated with them. As such, identification of the data required for model realization is an output of the conceptual modelling process.

Finally, data are required for model validation. It is important to ensure that each part of the model, as well as the model as a whole, is representing the real world system with sufficient accuracy. Assuming that the real world system exists, then the obvious way to do this is to compare the model results with data from the real system. Model validation is discussed in Chapter 12.

In large measure this chapter concentrates on the data required for model realization and more on quantitative rather than qualitative data. Many of the principles, however, can be applied to all the types of data.

7.3 Obtaining Data

Having identified the data requirements the data must be obtained. Some data are immediately available, others need to be collected. Table 7.1 describes three types of data that might be encountered.

Category A data are available either because they are known or because they have been collected previously. For instance, the physical layout of a manufacturing plant and the cycle times of the machines are often known. On occasions data have been collected for some other purpose and prove suitable for the simulation model. For example, data may have been collected on service times and arrival rates in a bank for a survey of staffing levels. There are a growing number of electronic monitoring systems in use that automatically collect data on the operation of a system. With category A data it is important to ensure that the data are accurate and in the right format for the simulation model, a subject that is discussed below.

Category B data need to be collected. Data that fall into this category often include service times, arrival patterns, machine failure rates and repair times, and the nature of human decision-making. The collection of these data might be a case of putting a data collection exercise in place by either getting people or electronic systems to monitor the operation. It might require interviews with subject matter experts such as staff, equipment suppliers and possibly customers. Although the modeller might become directly involved in the collection of data, if it is going to be a lengthy exercise then it is often more efficient to have people dedicated to the task. In Section 4.4 these people are referred to as data providers. In collecting category B data it is important to ensure that the data obtained are both accurate and in the right format. These issues are discussed in the next sub-sections.

Category C data are not available and cannot be collected. These often occur because the real world system does not yet exist, making it impossible to observe it in operation. Time availability is another factor, both in terms of person-time and in terms of elapsed time available to collect meaningful data. Say, for instance, data are not available on the repair time for a machine. Assuming the physical system is in existence, it is obviously possible to observe the machine and record the repair time when it fails. If, however, the machine only fails on average once a week and the simulation study must be complete in 6 weeks, there is only time to observe about six machine failures. This is unlikely to yield a meaningful distribution of repair times. In this case, the limited time available for the project moves data that would otherwise be in category B into category C. Data on machine failures often fall into category C. In service operations demand data are rarely available, instead data are collected on transactions, ignoring the demand lost because customers felt

Table 7.1 Categories of Data Availability and Collectability.

Category A	Available
Category B	Not available but collectable
Category C	Not available and not collectable

the queue was too long. Unfortunately category C data are not uncommon. Almost every simulation study in which I have been involved has included some category C data. As a result it is important to have some means for dealing with these data, as well as data that are available, but are inaccurate.

7.3.1 Dealing with unobtainable (category C) data

There are two main ways of dealing with category C data. The first is to estimate the data and the second is to treat the data as an experimental factor rather than a fixed parameter.

The data may be estimated from various sources. It may be possible to obtain surrogate data from a similar system in the same, or even another, organization. For some processes standardized data exist. Tables, known as predetermined motion time systems, giving standard times for performing manual tasks have been devised and can be used to determine a total time for an activity (Wild 2002). Discussion with subject matter experts, such as staff and equipment suppliers, might provide reasonable estimates. Ultimately, it might come down to making an intelligent guess.

The presence of estimated data in a simulation leaves some uncertainty about the validity of the model and will no doubt reduce its credibility. It is difficult to imagine an organization setting out on a major investment programme based on a set of results obtained from estimates or even guesswork. Nor should it be expected to. This can be addressed in a number of ways. First, it is important that when estimates have been made these are clearly identified in the list of assumptions (Section 5.3). Secondly, as part of the experimentation stage of the study, some sensitivity analysis should be performed on these data (Section 10.6). In this way the sensitivity of the results to changes in the estimated data can be identified. It may be that the results are not sensitive, in which case there need be little concern over the accuracy of the estimates. If, however, the results are sensitive, it is important to identify the effect of potential inaccuracies, so the clients have the necessary information on which to base their decisions. Finally, aim to improve the estimates as the project progresses, particularly if the results are very sensitive to the data. Some data collection may be possible during the life-cycle of the project. Consideration should also be given to returning to the model later when more accurate estimates have been obtained or it has been possible to collect the data. Hartley (2002) describes a simulation study based on estimated data and the use of sensitivity analysis.

Another approach for dealing with category C data is to treat the data as an experimental factor. Instead of asking what the data are, the issue is turned around and the question is asked: what do the data need to be? For example, I was modelling a manufacturing plant for which we only had poor data on machine failures. There was no means for improving these estimates since the plant was not in operation. The problem was resolved by recognizing that the organization had some control over the number and length of machine breakdowns. Therefore, the question was asked: what level of machine failures needs to be achieved to meet target throughput? The machine failures were treated as an experimental factor. Having identified the required level, discussions were held as to how this level might be achieved by looking at policies for preventative maintenance and for repairing machines quickly when they did fail. Of course, the approach of treating category C data as an experimental factor can only be applied when there is some control over the data in question.

The approaches for dealing with category C data described above seem to suffice in most circumstances. Ultimately, if the data cannot be obtained and these approaches do not suffice there are three further options. One is to revise the conceptual model so the need for the data is engineered out of the model. This is not always possible. The second is to change the modelling objectives so the data are no longer needed. Of course, if the objective in question is critical, this is not a satisfactory solution. The third is to abandon the simulation study altogether, but then the organization is potentially left to make decisions in the absence of any information.

7.3.2 Data accuracy

Albeit that data may be available (category A), it does not follow that they are necessarily accurate. The source of the data should be investigated. Is it likely that there are errors due to the nature of the data collection exercise? For what purpose were the data collected? If it is very different from the intended use in the model, are the data still usable? Draw a graph of the data and look for unusual patterns or outliers. Remember, in many cases the data are just a sample of historic events. Also, the past is not necessarily a good indication of the future. For example, the pattern of breakdowns may not continue to follow historic patterns as preventative maintenance procedures are changed to address the main causes of failure. These are all issues of data validation, discussed in Section 12.4.2.

If the data are considered to be too inaccurate for the simulation model, then an alternative source could be sought. If this is not available, then expert judgement and analysis might be used to determine the more likely values of the data. For instance, the data might be cleaned by removing outliers and obvious errors. If none of these suffice, then the data could be treated as category C.

When collecting data (category B) it is important to ensure that the data are as accurate as possible. Data collection exercises should be devised to ensure that the sample size is adequate and as far as possible recording errors are avoided. If staff are tasked with collecting data, do they have a vested interest in exaggerating or underestimating the data? What mechanisms can be put in place to monitor and avoid inaccuracies creeping into the data collection? For critical data it might be useful to have two sets of observations that can be cross-checked. In all this, the trade-off between the cost and time of collecting data versus the level of accuracy required for the simulation should be borne in mind.

7.3.3 Data format

Data need not just be accurate, they also need to be in the right format for the simulation. Time study data are aggregated to determine standard times for activities. In a simulation the individual elements (e.g. breaks and process inefficiencies) are modelled separately. As a result, standard time information is not always useful (in the right format) for a simulation model.

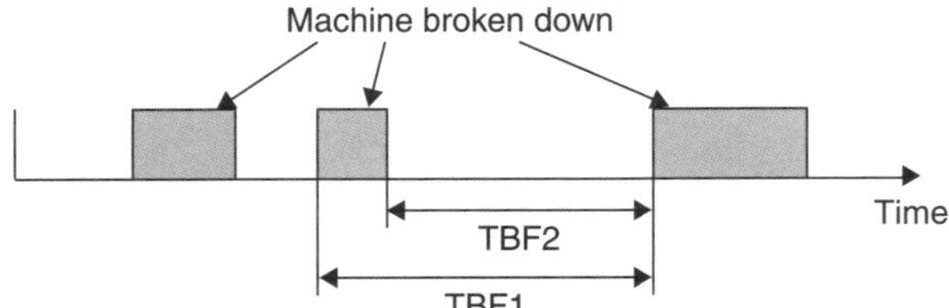

Figure 7.1 Interpretation of Time between Failure.

It is important that the modeller fully understands how the computer model, particularly the underlying software, interpret the data that are input. One example of this is the interpretation of time between failure (Figure 7.1). One interpretation is that time between failure is the time from the start of one breakdown to the start of the next (TBF1). The other is that time between failure is taken from the end of one breakdown to the start of the next (TBF2). Using the wrong interpretation for these data would yield a very different result from that intended.

Obviously the modeller needs to know the format of the data that are being supplied or collected and to ensure that these are appropriate for the simulation model. If they are not, then the data should be treated as inaccurate and actions taken to improve the data or find an alternative source. The last resort is to treat the data as category C.

7.4 Representing Unpredictable Variability

Section 1.3 shows that modelling variability, especially unpredictable (or random) variability, is at the heart of simulation modelling. Many aspects of an operations system are subject to such variability, for instance, customer arrivals, service and processing times and routing decisions. Section 2.3 describes the use of random numbers as a basis for representing variability and gives an overview of how they are used to sample from empirical and statistical distributions. These sections outline the motivation and the underlying theory for modelling variability. When it comes to designing the simulation, the modeller must determine how to represent the variability that is present in each part of the model. There are basically three options available: traces, empirical distributions and statistical distributions. These approaches are described below as well as the advantages and disadvantages of each (Section 7.4.4). A fourth option for modelling unpredictable variability, known as bootstrapping, also attracts some interest and is briefly described in Section 7.4.5. Finally, there is a discussion on some further issues in modelling variability.

7.4.1 Traces

A trace is a stream of data that describes a sequence of events. Typically it holds data about the time at which the events occur. It may also hold additional data about the events such as the type of part to be processed (part arrival event) or the nature of the fault (machine breakdown event). The trace is read by the simulation as it runs and the events are recreated in the model as described by the trace. The data are normally held in a data file or a spreadsheet.

Traces are normally obtained by collecting data from the real system. Automatic monitoring systems often collect detailed data about system events and so they are a common source of trace data. For instance, in a call centre the call handling system collects data on call arrivals, call routes and call durations. Factory monitoring systems collect data on machine failures, down times and fault types. Table 7.2 is an example of a trace showing the time calls arrived at a call centre and the nature of the call.

7.4.2 Empirical distributions

An empirical distribution shows the frequency with which data values, or ranges of data values, occur and are represented by histograms or frequency charts. They are normally based on historic data. Indeed, empirical distributions can be formed by summarizing the data in a trace. As the simulation runs, values are sampled from empirical distributions by using random numbers as described in Section 2.3. Most simulation software enable the user directly to enter empirical distribution data. The sampling process is then hidden from the user except for, in some cases, the need to specify a pseudo random number stream (Section 2.3.5). An example of an empirical distribution is given in Figure 7.2 showing the inter-arrival time of calls at a call centre. Note that it is more common to think in terms of time between arrivals (inter-arrivals times) than arrival rates in simulation, since the interest is in modelling the specific point at which an arrival event occurs.

If the empirical distribution represents ranges of data values, as in Figure 7.2, then it should be treated as a continuous distribution so values can be sampled anywhere in the

Table 7.2 Example of a Trace: Call Arrivals at a Call Centre.

Call arrival time (minutes)	Call type
0.09	1
0.54	1
0.99	3
1.01	2
1.25	1
1.92	2
2.14	2
2.92	3
3.66	3
5.46	2
.	.
.	.
.	.

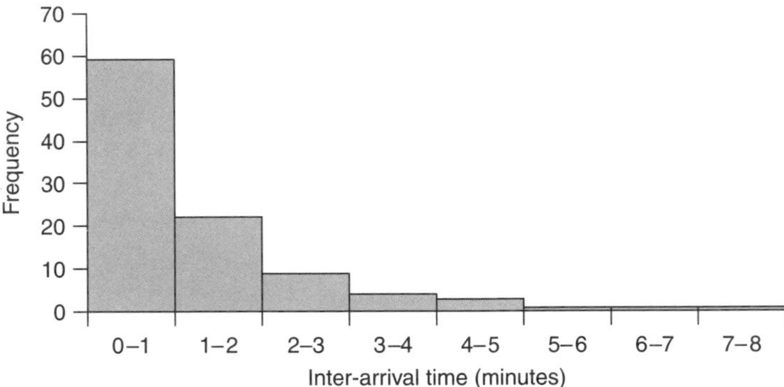

Figure 7.2 Example of an Empirical Distribution: Call Arrivals at a Call Centre.

range. The process for sampling continuous values is described in Section 2.3.3. If the data are not in ranges, for instance, the distribution describes a fault type on a machine, then the distribution is discrete and should be specified as such. Most simulation software give the option to define an empirical distribution as either continuous or discrete.

7.4.3 Statistical distributions

Statistical distributions are defined by some mathematical function or probability density function (PDF). There are many standard statistical distributions available to the simulation modeller. Perhaps the best known is the normal distribution that is specified by two parameters: *mean* (its location) and *standard deviation* (its spread). The PDF for a normal distribution with a mean of two and standard deviation of one is shown in Figure 7.3. For a given range of values of x, the area under the curve gives the probability of obtaining that range of values. So for the normal distribution the most likely values of x occur around the mean, with the least likely values to the far right-hand and left-hand sides of the distribution.

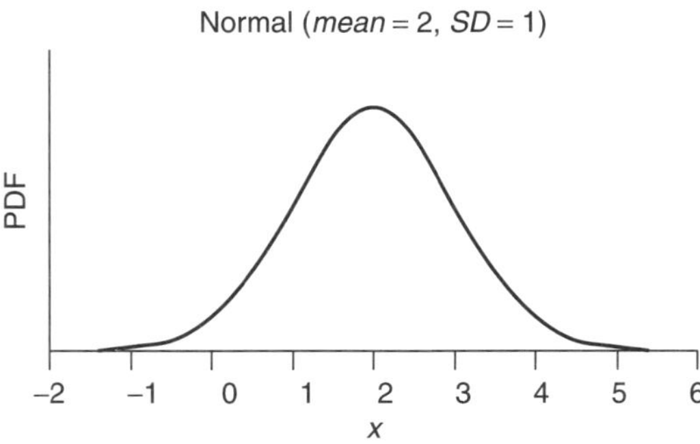

Figure 7.3 The Normal Distribution.

Although familiar, the normal distribution only has limited application in simulation modelling. It can be used, for instance, to model errors in weight or dimension that occur in manufacturing components. One problem with the normal distribution is that it can easily generate negative values, especially if the standard deviation is relatively large in comparison to the mean. This is completely invalid if, say, the distribution is being used to sample the time required for an activity.

It is obvious from an inspection of Figure 7.2 that the inter-arrival time data are not normally distributed. Some other distribution needs to be used. Appendix 4 provides descriptions of a variety of distributions that can be used in developing simulation models. Here, some of the most useful distributions are described. They are split into three types:

- *Continuous distributions*: for sampling data that can take any value across a range.
- *Discrete distributions*: for sampling data that can take only specific values across a range, for instance, only integer or non-numeric values.
- *Approximate distributions*: used in the absence of data.

The process for sampling values from statistical distributions is outlined in Section 2.3.4. Most simulation software, however, provide functions for sampling from these distributions, so the users need only concern themselves with entering the correct parameters.

Continuous distributions

The normal distribution is an example of a continuous distribution. Two other continuous distributions, which are commonly used in simulation models, are the negative exponential (Figure 7.4) and Erlang (Figure 7.5) distributions. The negative exponential (or just exponential) distribution has only one parameter, the *mean*. It is derived from the characteristics of purely random arrival processes. As a result, it is used to sample time between events, such as the inter-arrival time of customers and the time between failure of machines. Note that there is a close relationship between the negative exponential distribution and the Poisson

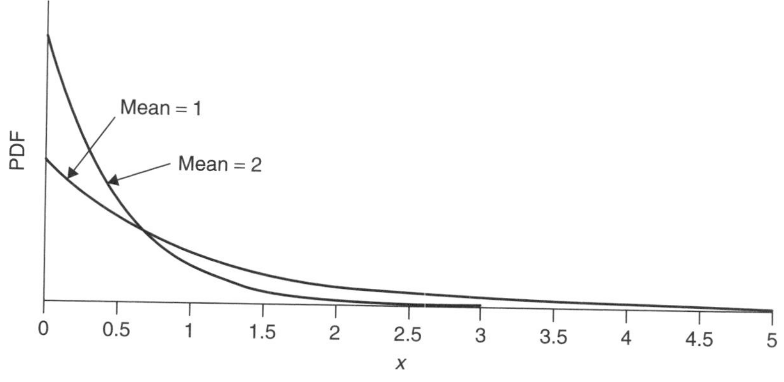

Figure 7.4 Negative Exponential Distribution.

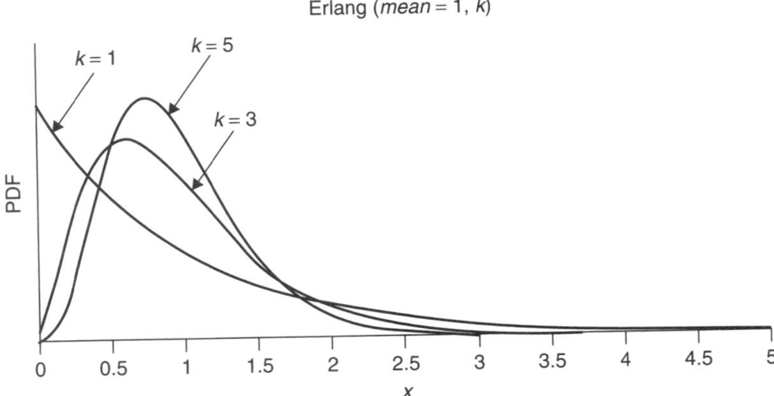

Figure 7.5 Erlang Distribution.

distribution, which can be used to sample the number of events in an interval of time (see later in this section). The negative exponential distribution gives a high probability of sampling values of x close to zero and a low probability of sampling higher values. When modelling inter-arrival times this implies that the majority of arrivals occur quite close together with occasional long gaps. Note that the empirical distribution in Figure 7.2 is very close in shape to the negative exponential distribution.

Another use for the negative exponential distribution is to represent the time to complete a task, for instance, the time to serve a customer or repair a machine. In this context it suffers from the limitation that it is possible to get near zero times which in most situations is not realistic.

The Erlang distribution (Figure 7.5) is named after Agner Erlang, a Danish mathematician, and is based on his observations of queuing in telephone systems. It has two parameters, the *mean* and a positive integer k. The value of k determines the skew of the distribution, that is, the length of the tail to the right. If k is one, the Erlang distribution is the same as a negative exponential distribution with an equivalent mean. As the value of k increases the skew reduces and the hump of the distribution moves towards the centre. Typically values of k between two and five are used.

The Erlang distribution is used to represent the time to complete a task. For values of k greater than one it overcomes the limitation of the negative exponential distribution by giving a very low probability of near zero times. It is also used for modelling inter-arrival times, particularly if the arrivals cannot occur in very close succession, such as the arrival of ships into a harbour. It should be noted that the Erlang distribution is a special case of the gamma distribution described in Appendix 4.

Discrete distributions

The binomial distribution describes the number of successes, or failures, in a specified number of trials. It can be used, for instance, to model the number of defects in a batch of items. The distribution has two parameters, the number of *trials* and the *probability* of success.

The binomial distribution can be explained with reference to an everyday example. We know that if someone rolls a die there is 1/6 chance of getting the number six. We also know, however, that if the die is rolled 60 times that person will not necessarily get 10 sixes. There might be anywhere between zero and 60 sixes, although the number is most likely to be somewhere close to 10. The person has carried out 60 trials, each one with a 1/6 probability of success (here defined as getting a six). The binomial distribution in Figure 7.6 shows the probability of obtaining different numbers of sixes from those 60 trials. Note that 10 sixes has the highest probability.

The Poisson distribution (Figure 7.7) is a second type of discrete distribution. It is used to represent the number of events that occur in an interval of time, for instance, total customer arrivals in an hour. It can also be used to sample the number of items in a batch of random size, for example, the number of boxes on a pallet. It is defined by one parameter, the *mean*. The Poisson distribution is closely related to the negative exponential distribution in that it can be used to represent arrival rates (λ), whereas the negative exponential distribution is used to represent inter-arrival times ($1/\lambda$).

Approximate distributions

Approximate distributions are not based on strong theoretical underpinnings, but they provide a useful approximation in the absence of data. As such they are useful in providing a first pass distribution, particularly when dealing with category C data.

The simplest form of approximate distribution is the uniform distribution, which can either be discrete or continuous (Figure 7.8 (a) and (b) respectively). This distribution is

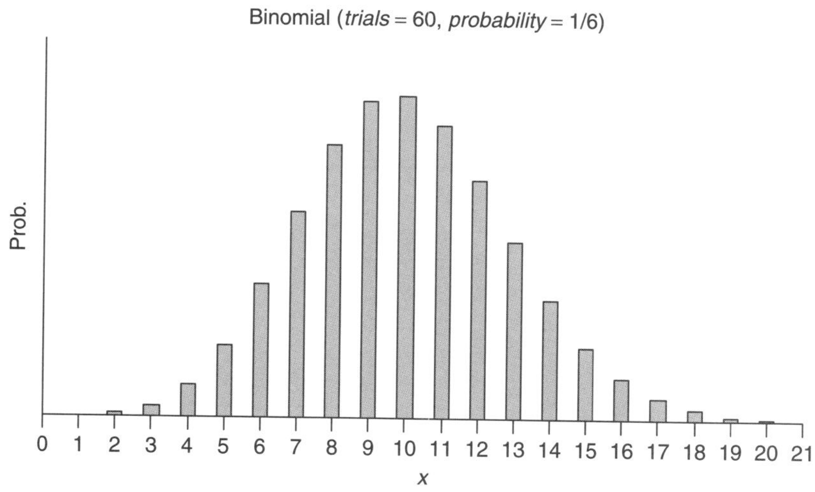

Figure 7.6 Binomial Distribution.

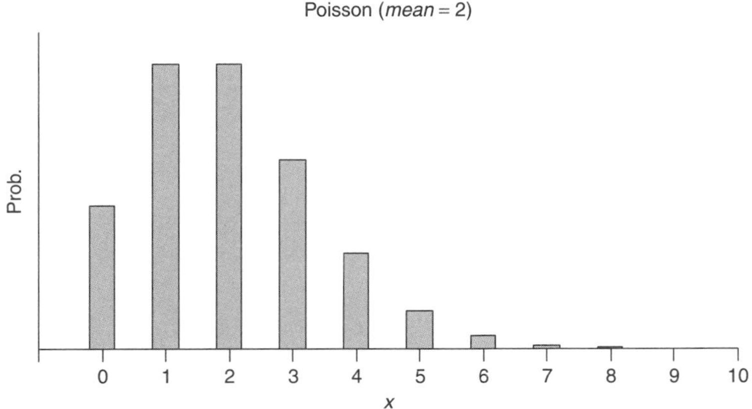

Figure 7.7 Poisson Distribution.

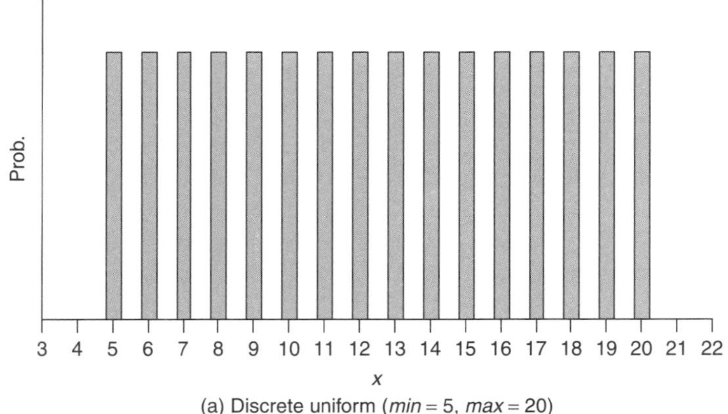

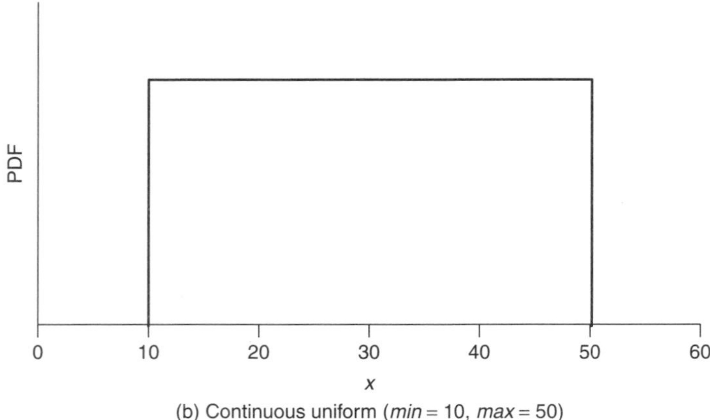

Figure 7.8 Uniform Distribution.

useful when all that is known is the likely minimum and maximum of a value. It might be that little is known about the size of orders that are received by a warehouse, except for the potential range, smallest to largest. A discrete uniform distribution could provide a useful approximation, at least until more data come to light. The time to perform a task may not be known, but a maximum and minimum might be estimated and a continuous uniform distribution applied.

The triangular distribution (Figure 7.9) provides a slightly more sophisticated approximation than the uniform distribution by including a third parameter, the *mode*, or most likely value. The triangular shape can be quite similar to the shape of an Erlang distribution. As such, the triangular distribution can be used, among other things, as an approximation for task times and possibly inter-arrival times. It is important to note that, depending on the parameters, the mean of the triangular distribution can be quite different from the mode (see Appendix 4 for calculation of the mean). Care must be taken when asking for the average so it is clear that the modal average is required and not the mean.

A more detailed list of distributions and their applications is provided in Appendix 4.

7.4.4 Traces versus empirical distributions versus statistical distributions

Which of the three approaches for modelling unpredictable variability should be preferred? Each approach has its advantages and disadvantages.

Traces enable a simulation to represent historic events in the real system exactly as they occurred. This is particularly beneficial for validating a model since it is possible to recreate historic events and see if the simulation results are close to the performance measures obtained from the real system when those events occurred. Traces may also help to improve the credibility of a model, since the clients can see patterns they recognize occurring in the model and the approach is more transparent than using random numbers to sample from distributions.

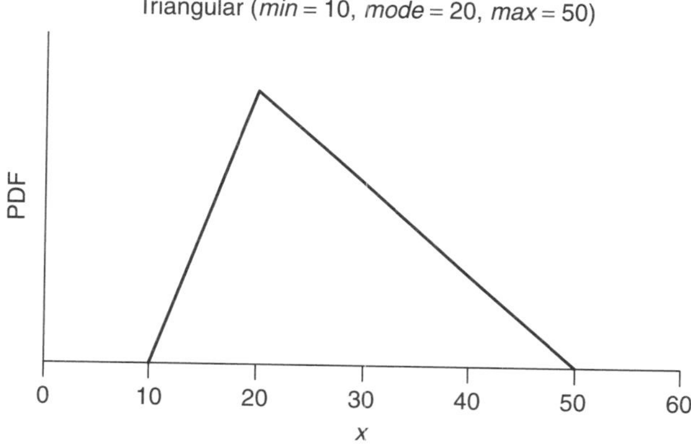

Figure 7.9 Triangular Distribution.

Traces have a number of disadvantages, however. There is the obvious need for the real system to exist and for the necessary data to have been collected from that system. Of course, many simulations are developed to model proposed systems. Even if the real system does exist, as shown in Section 7.3, the necessary data may not be available or even collectable. If a simulation involves many sources of unpredictable variability, and each is to be represented by a trace, then the approach may require not insubstantial amounts of computer memory. From a more theoretical perspective, a trace restricts the model to one sequence of events and so prevents the use of multiple replications (Section 9.6.1) or sensitivity analysis (Section 10.6), that is, unless multiple traces are available. The variability in the model is also restricted to the range and sequence encountered in the trace. In practice the range of variability may be much greater.

The use of empirical distributions overcomes some of the shortcomings of a trace. It does not use up large quantities of computer memory. Because a sampling process is employed, based on the use of random numbers, it is possible to change the stream of random numbers and alter the pattern of variability in the model (Section 2.3.5). This is an important advantage and is the basis for performing multiple replications (Section 9.6.1).

On the downside, the range of variability is still restricted to that observed in historic events. It is also difficult to perform sensitivity analysis with an empirical distribution, except for individually altering frequencies and cell ranges. There is still a need to obtain data from the real system, if it exists. The possibility of directly comparing model and real world results to validate the model is lost. Although the distributions themselves are probably transparent to a non-expert, the underlying sampling approach may not be. This could reduce the credibility of models employing empirical distributions over those employing traces.

Statistical distributions maintain some of the advantages of empirical distributions, namely, the limited use of computer memory and the ability to change the random streams and so perform multiple replications. Further to this, sensitivity analysis can be performed quite easily with statistical distributions. All that is required is a change to the distributions' parameters, and on some occasions the distribution type. Nor is there a specific need to have data from the real system, since the parameters can be estimated. Of course, real data are still preferred if they are available.

The range of variability is not restricted to that encountered in historic events. The use of a statistical distribution is an attempt to represent the population distribution rather than just a sample as given by an empirical distribution or trace. As a result, the statistical distribution should give the full range of variability that might occur in practice. However, since the population distribution is rarely known, it is not possible to determine exactly its shape or parameters. Therefore, the assumption that a statistical distribution gives the correct range of variability depends upon how good an approximation it is to the population distribution.

Another problem with the range of variability is that many statistical distributions have long tails and so there are occasions on which extreme values might be sampled. For instance, an extremely long repair time could be sampled from an Erlang distribution, or a negative value from a normal distribution. This could significantly affect the results of a simulation run or, in the case of negative times, be completely invalid. This can be guarded against by checking for such events or by truncating the distribution, that is, setting an upper (or lower) limit on the values that can be sampled.

On the downside, the possibility of direct comparison to historic results is not available and statistical distributions are probably the least transparent approach for the clients, potentially reducing the credibility of the model. Finally, some data cannot be represented, or at least easily so, by a statistical distribution. For instance, some empirical data are discontinuous so they do not have a smooth shape (Figure 7.10a). Other data have two peaks (bimodal distributions) or more (Figure 7.10b). Although there are procedures for fitting distributions to such data, they are quite complex and they are not always successful.

Returning to the question at the start of this section, as a general rule, statistical distributions are the preferred approach. They have important advantages over both empirical distributions and traces. That said, this does not mean that the other approaches should be completely discounted. It may not be possible to find an appropriate statistical distribution and so an empirical distribution is the only reasonable choice. There may be an over-riding need to stay close to historic events, particularly for the purposes of model validation and model credibility, in which case a trace might be used. Of course a trace might be used for validating a model and then a statistical distribution used in its place

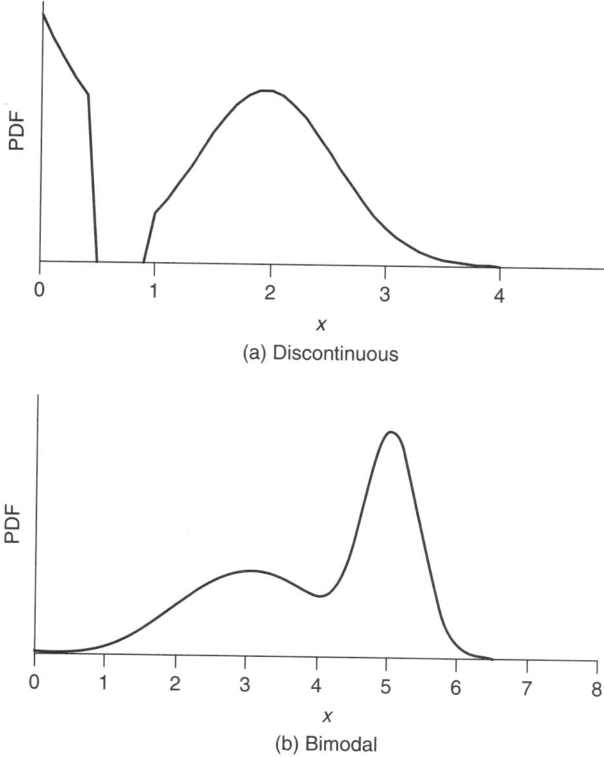

Figure 7.10 Discontinuous and Bimodal Distributions.

afterwards. Ultimately, the nature of the data available and the purpose of the modelling effort determine the appropriate method of representing unpredictable variability. For further discussion on this topic see Law and Kelton (2000) and Biller and Nelson (2002).

7.4.5 Bootstrapping

There is some interest in a fourth approach for modelling unpredictable variability known as bootstrapping. Rather than fit a distribution to the data or summarize the data in an empirical distribution, data are simply re-sampled at random with replacement (as with the top hat method described in Section 2.3.1) from the original trace. Table 7.3 shows two bootstrap samples from the trace data given in Table 7.2. Note that because the data are re-sampled at random with replacement, a value may appear more or fewer times than it did in the original trace.

Bootstrapping is particularly useful when there is only a small sample of data available. In effect, it is a way of extending the use of traces. It does, of course, have the limitation that data outside the range found in the trace cannot be sampled. Demirel and Willemain (2002) discuss the use of bootstrap methods for generating input data in simulations.

Bootstrapping has a wider application in simulation than just representing unpredictable variation in the inputs to a model. It is also useful in the analysis of simulation output and in model validation. For a more wide-ranging discussion on bootstrapping in simulation see Kleijnen *et al.* (2001), Cheng (2001) and Barton and Schruben (2001). More general discussions on bootstrapping can be found in Hjorth (1993) and Chernick (1999).

7.4.6 Further issues in representing unpredictable variability: correlation and non-stationary data

Biller and Nelson (2002) highlight the problem of dependency, or correlation, in input data. This can come in the forms of dependency over time or dependency at a point in

Table 7.3 Bootstrap Samples from Trace Data.

Original Data			
Call arrival time (min)	Call inter-arrival time (min)	Bootstrap 1: inter-arrival time	Bootstrap 2: inter-arrival time
0.09	0.09	0.67	0.02
0.54	0.45	1.80	0.09
0.99	0.45	0.02	0.45
1.01	0.02	0.09	0.24
1.25	0.24	0.45	0.78
1.92	0.67	0.67	1.80
2.14	0.22	0.74	0.45
2.92	0.78	0.74	0.22
3.66	0.74	0.78	0.67
5.46	1.80	0.24	0.45

time. Take, for instance, the orders received at a distribution centre from a retail outlet. A large order one week causes the retailer to overstock and so the following week a smaller order is received. There is time-series dependence in the orders.

Alternatively there can be dependence at a point in time. We may want to model the equipment customers will use on a visit to a gymnasium. The probability of using a particular piece of equipment, say a running machine, depends on the type of customer, their sex, age and fitness. Of course, these two types of dependency might also be combined. In the gymnasium example, the type of equipment a customer uses also depends on the previous equipment they have used during the session.

Such dependencies should not be ignored and require careful modelling. Perhaps the simplest approach is to use a series of conditional probability distributions. In the gymnasium example this would entail having different probability distributions for different customer types. This could be combined with some history of previous equipment use, to create a time-series dependence as well. However, this could quickly become very complex with many levels of condition and alternative distributions. More complex procedures exist for generating correlated input data. For those wishing to investigate such procedures, Law and Kelton (2000) provide a useful introduction. Deler and Nelson (2001) discuss methods for dealing with time-series dependence. Unfortunately, simulation software give little specific help in dealing with correlated input data.

Another problem occurs when distributions change over time, otherwise referred to as non-stationary input data. The most commonly found example of this is in modelling arrivals. Customers do not arrive at a steady rate throughout a day or week. For many service organizations lunch times and early evenings are the busiest periods. Although one distribution, say a negative exponential, may be able to explain the nature of arrivals at any point in the day, the parameters of that distribution are changing throughout the day. In the case of a negative exponential distribution the mean inter-arrival time is lower in busier periods.

Simply changing the mean of the distribution is not appropriate. If, for example, the arrivals are moving from a quiet period to a busy period, a sample might be taken just before the end of the quiet period that implies there will be a long gap before the next arrival. It is then some time into the busy period before the next arrival occurs and more frequent arrivals are sampled. This leads to an inaccuracy in the model. A useful procedure for dealing with this issue is thinning (Lewis and Shedler 1979). The mean arrival rate is set to the maximum (minimum mean inter-arrival time) that will occur during the simulation run. In quieter periods a proportion of the arrivals are thrown away, ensuring that the mean is effectively correct. Note that some simulation software provide automatic procedures for modelling non-stationary arrivals.

7.5 Selecting Statistical Distributions

The simulation modeller, in co-operation with the rest of the simulation modelling team, must decide which statistical distributions are most appropriate for the model that is being developed. Distributions can be selected either from known properties of the process being modelled, or by fitting a distribution to empirical data. Both approaches are now described.

7.5.1 Selecting distributions from known properties of the process

It is often possible to select an appropriate distribution by considering the properties of the process being modelled. If customer arrivals at a bank are being modelled, then it is probably reasonable to assume that those arrivals are at random, and so a negative exponential distribution can be used. Erlang, gamma and lognormal distributions are known to represent the properties of a service process. The gamma distribution provides a greater range of shapes than the Erlang. The lognormal distribution can have a greater peak (probability) around the modal average than the Erlang or the gamma distributions. If time between failure is being modelled, then it is probably reasonable to assume a Weibull distribution. All these uses for distributions are given in Appendix 4.

The advantage of selecting a distribution from the properties of the process is that only the parameters of the distribution need to be determined and detailed data do not need to be collected. For instance, for the negative exponential distribution, just the mean inter-arrival time is needed. Rather than measure the inter-arrival time between every customer, it is easier to count the number of customers that arrive in a period of time to determine the mean arrival rate. The mean inter-arrival time is then simply the reciprocal of the mean arrival rate.

When data cannot be obtained then there is no choice but to select distributions on the known properties of the process. In this case the parameters must be estimated. For mean values and even standard deviations this may be reasonably straightforward, but for other parameters such as skew and shape, this is more difficult. For data that are non-stationary (Section 7.4.6), it may not be a straightforward task to estimate how the parameters of the distribution change through time. Creating a spreadsheet model that shows the effect of different parameters on the location, spread and shape of a distribution may be useful in aiding the selection of appropriate parameters (a spreadsheet that displays distribution shapes, Distributions.xls, is provided on the web site www.wileyeurope.com/go/robinson). It is important that all assumptions are clearly stated in the description of the conceptual model.

7.5.2 Fitting statistical distributions to empirical data

When empirical data are available then it is often possible to fit a statistical distribution to those data. This process consists of three stages:

- Select a statistical distribution.
- Determine the parameters.
- Test the goodness-of-fit.

It is not a case of selecting a single distribution or set of parameters, but a series of distributions should be tried with different parameter values. In other words, there should be a number of iterations through these stages. The following example is used to illustrate each stage in fitting a distribution:

Data have been collected on the repair time of a machine. In total, 100 observation have been made and recorded in the histogram shown in Figure 7.11.

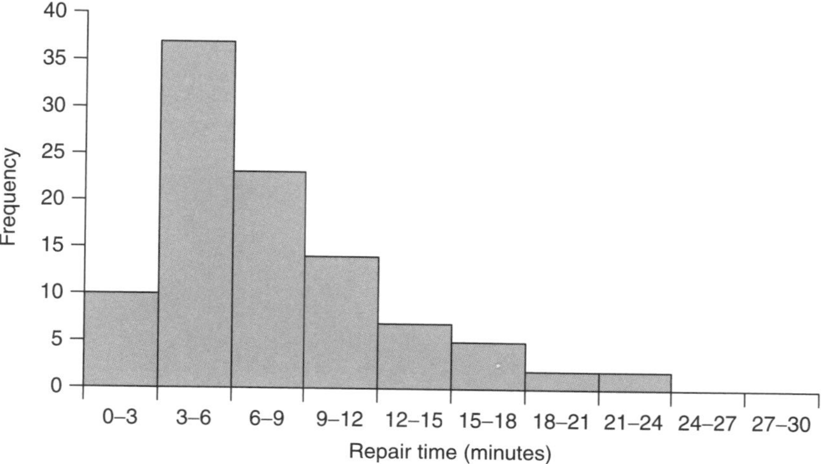

Figure 7.11 **Distribution Fitting Example: Repair Time Data.**

Select a statistical distribution

An appropriate distribution can be selected in two ways. First, inspect the data. A histogram is a particularly useful representation for helping with this since it shows the shape of the distribution of the empirical data. Second, a distribution can be selected based on the known properties of the process in a similar fashion to that described in Section 7.5.1 above. It is best to use both these approaches to ensure that they are in agreement.

In our example the histogram in Figure 7.11 suggests the shape is Erlang or gamma, or possibly some similar distribution such as lognormal or Weibull. All of these can be used to represent the time to complete a task, which is appropriate for this situation. As a first try, we shall try and fit an Erlang distribution to the data.

Determine the parameters

Having selected what is believed to be an appropriate distribution, the next step is to determine the parameters of that distribution. For the Erlang distribution this requires an estimate of the mean and the k parameter.

The mean can be calculated from the histogram data, as shown in Table 7.4. This is an estimate based on the data summarized in the histogram. A better estimate can be obtained if the underlying data are available by summing the data and dividing by the number of observations. Of course, both are estimates of the population mean based on the sample of data obtained.

There is no means for estimating the k parameter. The only approach available is trial and error. In this case, the distribution seems to be skewed to the right and the hump is near to the left. As a result, low values of k will be tried (one, three and five), although it seems unlikely that one will suffice since the hump is not completely to the left.

Table 7.4 Distribution Fitting Example: Calculation of the Mean.

Repair time range (minutes)	(a) Frequency	(b) Range mid-point	(a) × (b)
0–3	10	1.5	15
3–6	37	4.5	166.5
6–9	23	7.5	172.5
9–12	14	10.5	147
12–15	7	13.5	94.5
15–18	5	16.5	82.5
18–21	2	19.5	39
21–24	2	22.5	45
24–27	0	25.5	0
27–30	0	28.5	0
Total	100		762
Estimated mean = 762/100 = 7.62 minutes			

Test the goodness-of-fit

The goodness-of-fit can be tested both graphically and using statistical tests. The simplest graphical approach is to compare the histogram of the empirical data with a histogram of the proposed distribution. The latter can be created by taking many samples (say 10,000 or more) from the proposed distribution and placing them in the same cell ranges used for the histogram of the empirical data. These samples can be generated using the distribution functions in the simulation software, or for some distributions, using similar functions that are available in a spreadsheet. Because this in itself is a sampling procedure it will not be completely accurate, but as long as a large number of samples is taken it should suffice.

A more accurate approach is to calculate the frequencies from the cumulative distribution functions for the proposed distributions. This will provide an exact value for the percentage of observations that should fall in each cell range. Again, spreadsheets often have cumulative distribution functions for many of the distributions that are commonly used in simulation models.

Table 7.5 shows the expected frequencies, as a percentage, for the three Erlang distributions being considered (these have been derived from the "GAMMADIST" function in Excel). It also shows the frequencies, normalized as a percentage, for the empirical (observed) data. Figure 7.12 uses histograms to compare the empirical data with the three distributions proposed. Inspection of the histograms suggests that the Erlang (7.62, 3) is the best fit. In the first graph the hump of the fitted distribution is too far to the left and the tail too long. In the third graph, the hump is too far to the right and the tail a little short. Although not a perfect fit, the second graph seems reasonable. Of course, an alternative distribution could be tried.

The problem with inspecting histograms is that the shape of the distributions can be quite different depending on the cell ranges chosen. This can easily lead to erroneous

Table 7.5 Distribution Fitting Example: Expected and Observed Frequencies.

	Frequency (percentage)			
Repair time range (minutes)	Erlang (7.62, 1)	Erlang (7.62, 3)	Erlang (7.62, 5)	Empirical
0–3	32.54	11.64	4.99	10.00
3–6	21.95	30.39	30.90	37.00
6–9	14.81	26.67	34.32	23.00
9–12	9.99	16.30	19.08	14.00
12–15	6.74	8.35	7.47	7.00
15–18	4.55	3.86	2.37	5.00
18–21	3.07	1.66	0.65	2.00
21–24	2.07	0.68	0.16	2.00
24–27	1.40	0.27	0.04	0.00
27–30	0.94	0.10	0.01	0.00
>30	1.95	0.06	0.00	0.00
Total	100.00	100.00	100.00	100.00

conclusions. It is a good idea, therefore, to try a number of cell widths to ensure that the correct conclusion is reached. Another problem with inspecting histograms occurs if only a small amount of data is available, say less than 30 samples. In this case the shape of the histogram is unlikely to be smooth.

Graphical approaches based on cumulative probabilities overcome both of these problems. One such approach is the probability–probability plot, or P–P plot. This is a graph on which the expected cumulative probability of the proposed distribution is plotted against the observed cumulative probability of the empirical distribution. The cumulative probabilities for the three Erlang distributions and the empirical distribution are shown in Table 7.6. Figure 7.13 shows the resulting P–P plots. The dashed line has an intercept of zero and a slope of 1, in other words, it signifies the line expected if the proposed distribution fits the empirical data exactly.

Of the three P–P plots, the middle one shows the best fit, that is, least divergence from the dashed line. Certainly the first plot shows quite a poor fit. The third plot is an improvement, but it is not as close as the first. It would seem that the Erlang (7.62, 3) is the best fit.

Another graphical approach based on cumulative probabilities is the quantile–quantile plot, or Q–Q plot. Descriptions of these can be found in Law and Kelton (2000) and Banks *et al.* (2001). Their main advantage over P–P plots is that they show discrepancies at either end of the distribution more clearly. P–P plots give a clearer picture of differences around the middle of a distribution.

Graphical approaches give a good guide as to the goodness-of-fit and certainly enable a modeller to weed out poor candidates. Following on from a graphical analysis it is possible to perform statistical tests to determine how closely a distribution fits the empirical data. The chi-square test is probably the best known goodness-of-fit test. The test is based on the

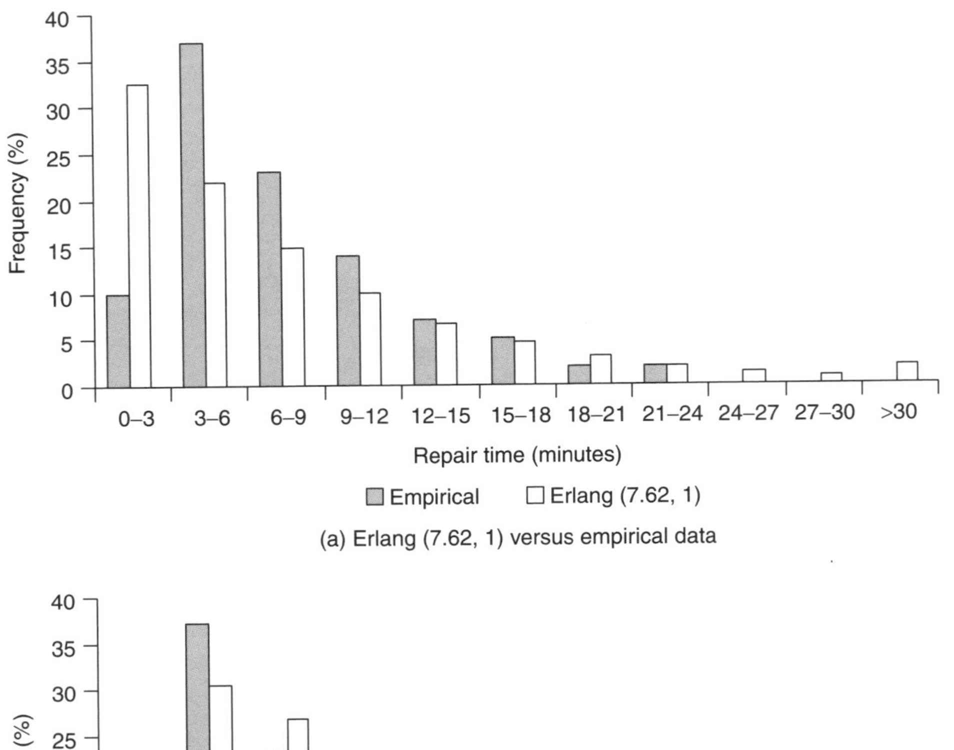

(a) Erlang (7.62, 1) versus empirical data

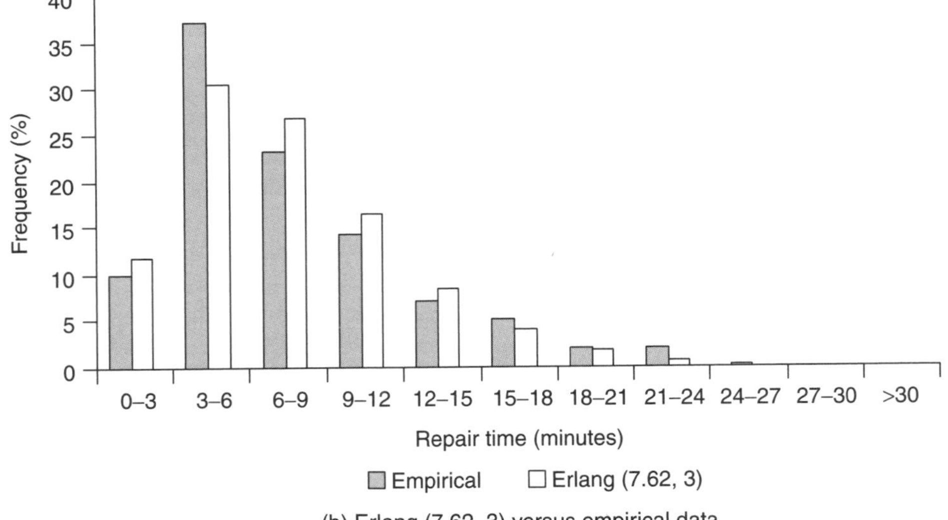

(b) Erlang (7.62, 3) versus empirical data

Figure 7.12 Distribution Fitting Example: Histogram Comparison of Expected and Observed Frequencies.

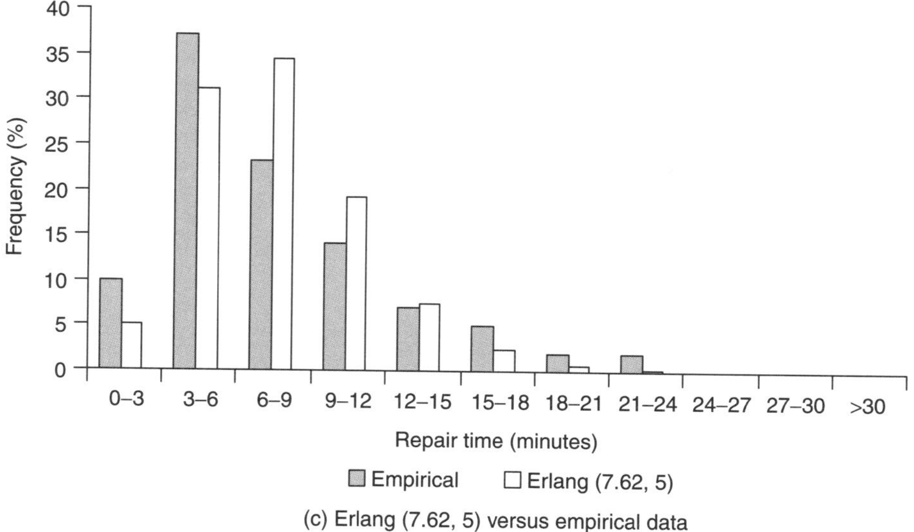

(c) Erlang (7.62, 5) versus empirical data

Figure 7.12 ***(continued).***

calculation of the chi-square value as follows:

$$\chi^2 = \sum_{i=1}^{k} \frac{(O_i - E_i)^2}{E_i}$$

where:

χ^2 = chi-square value
O_i = observed frequency in ith range (empirical distribution)
E_i = expected frequency in ith range (proposed distribution)
k = total number of ranges

Table 7.7 shows the results of this calculation for the repair time example. Note that the ranges above 18 have been added together since the chi-square test is not reliable when the frequencies in any cell are too small (much below five).

Two other factors need to be determined to carry out the test: the *level of significance* and the *degrees of freedom*. The meaning of these terms is not explained here but can be found in most statistical textbooks. Typically, 5% is used for the level of significance. The number of degrees of freedom is calculated as follows:

$$\textit{Degrees of freedom} = \textit{Number of cell ranges} - \textit{Number of estimated parameters} - 1$$

In the repair time example the number of ranges is seven and two parameters have been estimated, the distribution mean and k. There are, therefore, four degrees of freedom.

To complete the test, the chi-square value is compared with a critical value, which can be read from chi-square tables (Appendix 5) or generated in a spreadsheet using the appropriate function ('CHIINV' in Excel). The critical value is obtained for the correct

Table 7.6 **Distribution Fitting Example: Expected and Observed Cumulative Frequencies.**

Repair time range (minutes)	Cumulative probability: Erlang (7.62, 1)	Erlang (7.62, 3)	Erlang (7.62, 5)	Empirical
0–3	0.33	0.12	0.05	0.10
3–6	0.54	0.42	0.36	0.47
6–9	0.69	0.69	0.70	0.70
9–12	0.79	0.85	0.89	0.84
12–15	0.86	0.93	0.97	0.91
15–18	0.91	0.97	0.99	0.96
18–21	0.94	0.99	1.00	0.98
21–24	0.96	1.00	1.00	1.00
24–27	0.97	1.00	1.00	1.00
27–30	0.98	1.00	1.00	1.00
>30	1.00	1.00	1.00	1.00

level of significance and the number of degrees of freedom. In the example it is 11.07. If the chi-square value is less than the critical value then the hypothesis is accepted and the proposed distribution cannot be rejected as a good fit. If the chi-square value is more than the critical value then the hypothesis and the proposed distribution are rejected. The results for the example are shown in Table 7.8. The Erlang (7.62, 3) is the only one to pass the test and therefore it seems to be the most appropriate.

The advantage of the chi-square test is that it can be applied to any distribution. It suffers, however, from a similar disadvantage to the histogram inspection method, in that the use of different cell ranges can lead to quite different results. There is also an absence of guidance on how to choose cell widths. Other tests exist which overcome this problem, for

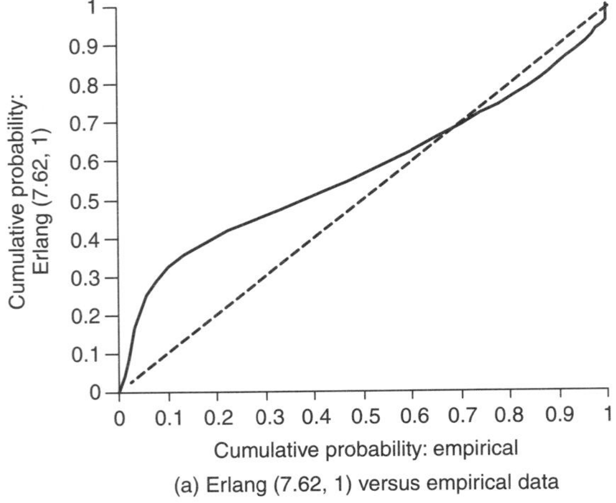

(a) Erlang (7.62, 1) versus empirical data

Figure 7.13 Distribution Fitting Example: Probability–Probability Plots.

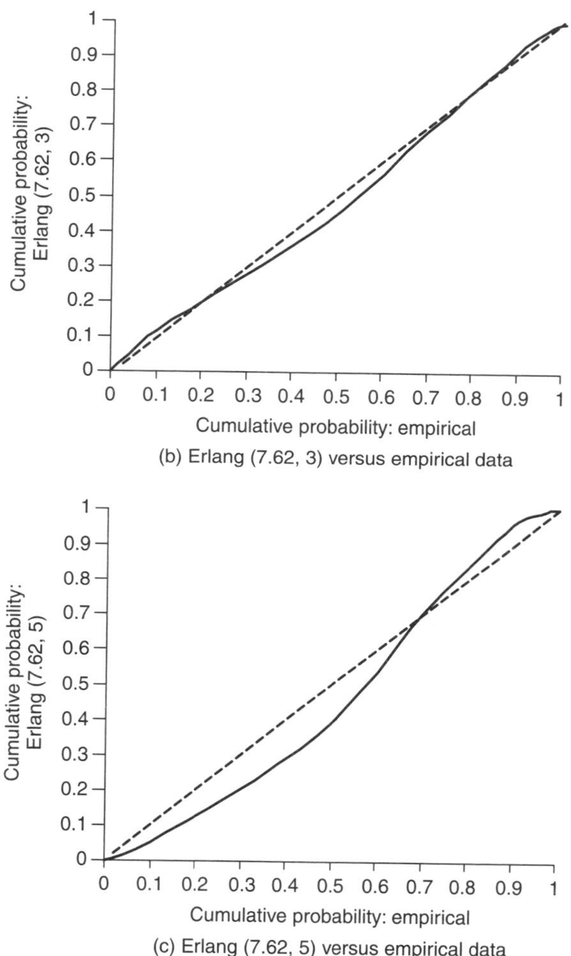

Figure 7.13 ***(continued).***

instance, the Kolmogorov–Smirnov test, but these cannot be applied to such a wide range of distributions. For further details on the chi-square test and other goodness-of-fit tests, see Law and Kelton (2000) and Banks *et al.* (2001).

Conclusion to distribution fitting example

Three tests have been performed on the repair time data. Each test has reached the same conclusion, that is, the Erlang (7.62, 3) provides the best fit. This does not, however, mean that we should simply accept this distribution as being correct. We should try other parameter values, particularly trying k values of two and four. It is also worth trying other types of distribution, for instance, a lognormal.

Table 7.7 Distribution Fitting Example: Calculation of Chi-Square Value.

	$(O_i - E_i)^2/E_i$		
Repair time range (minutes)	Erlang (7.62, 1)	Erlang (7.62, 3)	Erlang (7.62, 5)
0–3	15.62	0.23	5.04
3–6	10.31	1.44	1.20
6–9	4.53	0.51	3.74
9–12	1.61	0.33	1.35
12–15	0.01	0.22	0.03
15–18	0.05	0.34	2.92
>18	3.12	0.54	11.32
Chi-square value	35.25	3.60	25.61

Table 7.8 Distribution Fitting Example: Results of the Chi-Square Test.

Proposed distribution	Chi-square value	Critical value	Accept/ reject
Erlang (7.62, 1)	35.25	9.49	Reject
Erlang (7.62, 3)	3.60	9.49	Accept
Erlang (7.62, 5)	25.61	9.49	Reject

Issues in distribution fitting

An important issue to consider is the difference between the best fit and the best distribution. By continuing to change parameters and distribution types it is probably possible to obtain a better fit, but this does not mean that the best distribution has been found. The modeller must not blindly accept the best statistic, but must also apply his/her knowledge of the process. If the best fit distribution makes little sense in the context in which it is to be used, then it is better to use a less well fitting but logically more appropriate distribution. For instance, a normal distribution might give the best fit when applied to service time data in a bank. If, however, there is little reason to suspect that the service times are normally distributed, then this distribution should be rejected.

It must not be forgotten that the empirical data are just a sample. The shape and parameters that are estimated from the data, such as the mean, are just estimates. In such circumstances it is never possible to say with certainty that the correct statistical distribution has been found. When we select a statistical distribution we are making an assumption about the nature of the population distribution based on what is often quite a small sample. Such assumptions should be added to the description of the conceptual model.

Distribution fitting software

The description above shows that effective distribution fitting may involve many iterations with different distribution types and parameter values. For each, a series of graphs and statistical tests can be performed. If performed manually, this process can take up a great deal of time. Thankfully, there are a number of software packages that automate this process, most notably ExpertFit (www: Averill M. Law & Associates) and Stat::Fit (www: Geer Mountain Software). The user need only enter the empirical data and the software automatically generates graphical and statistical reports, recommending the best fitting distributions.

7.6 Conclusion

The discussion above centres on various issues surrounding the collection and use of data in simulation models. Specifically the identification of the data requirements, obtaining data and dealing with unobtainable and inaccurate data. Four methods of representing unpredictable variability are identified: traces, empirical distributions, statistical distributions and bootstrapping. The advantages and disadvantages of each are discussed. Issues related to correlated data and non-stationary data are also outlined. Finally, methods for selecting appropriate statistical distributions are described. Appendix 4 provides a more thorough list of statistical distributions that might be used in simulation modelling. Details of the data that are required for the Wardeon Cinema and Panorama Televisions case studies are provided in Appendix 1 (Section A1.3) and Appendix 2 (Section A2.3) respectively.

Exercises

E7.1 A simulation model is being developed of the check-in area at an airport. Different airlines follow slightly different procedures and within airlines the staff have quite different levels of experience. Discuss the problems that might be encountered in collecting data on check-in times.

E7.2 Which statistical distributions would be most appropriate for modelling the following processes?

- *Process 1*: the weight of a bottle leaving a filling process
- *Process 2*: the time between failure of a machine
- *Process 3*: the check-in time at an airport
- *Process 4*: the number of orders for a product received at a warehouse from a retail outlet

E7.3 Table 7.9 provides 100 values collected from the four processes listed in exercise E7.2. The mean and standard deviation of the data are also calculated. Fit statistical distributions to the data for each of the processes. Note: these data are available in a spreadsheet (Exercise7.xls) on the web site (www.wileyeurope.com/go/robinson).

Table 7.9 Data Collected from Four Processes.

Observation	Process 1	Process 2	Process 3	Process 4
1	9.91	9.21755	2.65	5
2	9.53	142.887	3.40	8
3	9.99	32.0088	2.64	6
4	10.04	75.3285	3.38	8
5	10.53	49.1267	2.36	3
6	10.26	175.021	5.19	2
7	9.88	71.0796	1.64	2
8	9.13	281.486	3.06	9
9	10.46	111.284	1.69	5
10	10.11	106.306	3.54	5
11	9.72	2.84187	2.15	3
12	10.67	81.3795	2.13	6
13	11.06	73.582	2.23	6
14	10.07	35.6692	1.78	3
15	9.67	57.6838	1.15	4
16	10.24	45.8048	2.17	5
17	9.24	24.2765	2.35	8
18	11.00	274.122	1.80	9
19	10.52	2.24356	1.00	4
20	10.40	143.062	1.49	5
21	10.58	108.228	2.04	8
22	10.32	104.382	2.08	5
23	9.30	96.5035	1.20	7
24	10.20	43.0083	1.59	4
25	10.13	40.149	1.60	5
26	10.71	352.755	2.01	4
27	9.61	392.27	1.30	5
28	10.56	176.637	1.95	3
29	10.25	215.806	2.36	5
30	10.33	71.1458	2.31	4
31	10.14	6.60153	2.23	5
32	9.66	230.495	1.80	2
33	10.99	33.5363	2.31	5
34	10.72	42.5306	3.55	7
35	9.74	110.969	1.90	8
36	10.97	235.793	2.25	7
37	11.29	115.948	3.21	6
38	9.55	405.556	2.08	2
39	10.18	20.1971	2.28	6
40	11.52	11.3048	1.16	7
41	10.71	353.97	1.06	8
42	10.85	96.9523	0.87	6
43	9.61	69.7782	3.14	5
44	10.30	515.399	1.19	5

Table 7.9 (*continued*)

Observation	Process 1	Process 2	Process 3	Process 4
45	9.64	600.295	0.92	12
46	9.30	398.934	2.47	4
47	9.47	503.44	1.29	5
48	10.12	11.1054	0.76	6
49	9.24	3.57827	3.13	4
50	9.87	289.247	2.47	9
51	9.86	6.68169	1.00	7
52	10.44	24.4547	1.84	8
53	10.03	123.56	2.99	3
54	10.32	46.0386	2.86	6
55	10.99	524.57	4.48	1
56	10.02	63.9097	4.16	5
57	10.35	8.00313	2.74	4
58	10.42	24.1011	4.68	5
59	9.46	20.4822	3.03	2
60	10.21	45.088	2.64	3
61	9.74	147.438	1.67	1
62	8.77	85.8522	2.91	5
63	10.11	136.507	1.51	3
64	10.54	35.2654	2.91	4
65	9.82	241.444	3.53	3
66	9.28	4.15181	4.78	3
67	9.60	109.756	3.31	7
68	10.39	3.45408	2.26	4
69	9.87	48.5153	2.53	4
70	10.98	131.61	1.42	5
71	10.39	160.766	2.93	9
72	9.31	30.2505	1.03	5
73	10.27	131.609	2.26	4
74	10.28	159.829	1.97	5
75	10.49	157.356	2.68	7
76	9.37	121.353	5.09	6
77	9.39	143.064	0.30	7
78	9.75	109.298	2.26	4
79	9.85	531.32	1.47	2
80	10.28	53.4291	3.09	3
81	10.33	45.0377	3.79	6
82	9.13	89.1195	1.79	2
83	9.99	51.2836	2.41	9
84	10.27	6.98948	1.95	4
85	9.74	120.514	2.08	5
86	10.71	263.818	1.54	8
87	9.88	273.378	0.76	6

(*continued overleaf*)

Table 7.9 *(continued)*

Observation	Process 1	Process 2	Process 3	Process 4
88	10.29	87.814	2.81	5
89	9.88	274.103	1.36	3
90	10.36	1509.39	2.52	7
91	9.92	523.546	1.06	5
92	10.23	33.194	2.04	8
93	10.10	423.614	0.98	2
94	9.93	121.732	2.04	4
95	10.62	81.2766	0.93	5
96	10.56	16.2324	1.96	7
97	9.86	61.1575	1.42	3
98	9.72	77.974	1.62	4
99	9.77	278.813	1.18	6
100	10.68	121.635	3.77	7
Mean	10.11	153.41	2.25	5.16
St. dev.	0.52	197.67	1.00	2.09

E7.4 Use the Distributions.xls spreadsheet (see the web site www.wileyeurope.com/go/robinson) to investigate the effect of changing distribution parameters on the shape, mean and standard deviation of the distributions.

E7.5 Identify the data requirements for the bank model described in Exercise E6.1 (Chapter 6).

E7.6 Identify the data requirements for the Wardeon Cinema case described in Appendix 1 (Section A1.2.1).

E7.7 Identify the data requirements for the Panorama Televisions case described in Appendix 2 (Section A2.2.1).

References

Banks, J., Carson, J.S., Nelson, B.L. and Nicol, D.M. (2001) *Discrete-Event System Simulation*, 3rd edn. Upper Saddle River, NJ: Prentice Hall.

Barton, R.R. and Schruben, L.W. (2001) "Resampling methods for input modeling". *Proceedings of the 2001 Winter Simulation Conference* (Peters, B.A., Smith, J.S., Medeiros, D.J. and Rohrer, M.W., eds). Piscataway, NJ: IEEE, pp. 372–378.

Biller, B. and Nelson, B.L. (2002) "Answers to the top ten input modeling questions". *Proceedings of the 2002 Winter Simulation Conference* (Yucesan, E., Chen, C.-H., Snowden, S.L. and Charnes, J.M., eds). Piscataway, NJ: IEEE, pp. 35–40.

Cheng, R.C.H. (2001) "Analysis of simulation experiments by bootstrap resampling". *Proceedings of the 2001 Winter Simulation Conference* (Peters, B.A., Smith, J.S., Medeiros, D.J. and Rohrer, M.W., eds). Piscataway, NJ: IEEE, pp. 179–186.

Chernick, M.R. (1999). *Bootstrap Methods: A Practitioners Guide*. New York: Wiley.

Deler, B. and Nelson, B.L. (2001) "Modeling and generating multivariate time series with arbitrary marginals and autocorrelation structures". *Proceedings of the 2001 Winter Simulation Conference* (Peters, B.A., Smith, J.S., Medeiros, D.J. and Rohrer, M.W., eds). Piscataway, NJ: IEEE, pp. 275–282.

Demirel, O.F. and Willemain, T.R. (2002) "Generation of simulation input scenarios using bootstrap methods". *Journal of the Operational Research Society*, 53(1), 69–78.

Hartley III, D.S. (2002) "Simulating without data". *Proceedings of the 2002 Winter Simulation Conference* (Yucesan, E., Chen, C.-H., Snowden, S.L. and Charnes, J.M., eds). Piscataway, NJ: IEEE, pp. 975–980.

Hjorth, J.S.U. (1993) *Computer Intensive Statistical Methods: Validation, Model Selection and Bootstrap*. London: Chapman & Hall.

Kleijnen, J.P.C., Cheng, R.C.H. and Bettonvil, B. (2001) "Validation of trace-driven simulation models: Bootstrap methods". *Management Science*, 47(11), 1533–1538.

Law, A.M. and Kelton, W.D. (2000) *Simulation Modeling and Analysis*, 3rd edn. New York: McGraw-Hill.

Lewis, P.A.W. and Shedler, G.S. (1979) "Simulation of nonhomogeneous Poisson process by thinning". *Naval Research Logistics Quarterly*, 26, 403–413.

Pidd, M. (2003). *Tools for Thinking: Modelling in Management Science*, 2nd edn. Chichester, UK: Wiley.

Wild, R. (2002) *Operations Management*, 6th edn. London: Continuum.

Internet addresses

Averill M. Law & Associates, Inc.: ExpertFit, www.averill-law.com (July 2003)

Geer Mountain Software Corp.: Stat::Fit, www.geerms.com (July 2003)

MODEL CODING

8

8.1 Introduction

Model coding is the second key process in a simulation study, as described in Section 4.2. It involves the conversion of the conceptual model into a computer model. Coding is interpreted in a very general sense, meaning the entering of information into a computer rather than strictly referring to the use of programming constructs. Although the model might be developed using a spreadsheet or programming language, the assumption is that the most likely approach is to use a simulation software package. Despite this focus on simulation software, the principles described below do generally relate to any one of the software types.

This chapter describes the key activities in moving from a conceptual model to a computer model. This involves the development of a model structure, the coding of the model and the documentation of the model. There is also some discussion on the wider documentation of the simulation project. A final important activity, related to model coding, is the testing of the model. This subject, however, is left until Chapter 12 as part of a wider discussion on verification and validation.

8.2 Structuring the Model

Before a line of code is written in the simulation software it is worthwhile spending time away from the computer determining how to structure the model in the chosen software. Rushing to the computer keyboard without first thinking through the model structure can easily lead to code that is inefficient or has to be deleted and rewritten because it is inappropriate. At worst, a complete model, or at least a section of a model, may need to be restarted because the code is poorly designed. Although it takes time to think through the structure of the model before entering the code, this is often time saved because many errors and inefficiencies are avoided.

As a conceptual model is a *non-software* specific description of the simulation model (Section 5.3), so the model structure is a *software* specific description. This is the point at which the modeller considers how the conceptual model might be implemented in the specific software that is to be used for the simulation study. For the first time the modeller starts to think about the constructs of the simulation software and how they relate to the problem being tackled.

In designing the model structure the modeller should have four aims in mind:

- *Speed of coding*: the speed with which the code can be written.
- *Transparency*: the ease with which the code can be understood.
- *Flexibility*: the ease with which the code can be changed.
- *Run-speed*: the speed with which the code will execute.

These are not mutually exclusive, for instance, to enhance transparency it may be necessary to use a more long-winded form of code. The modeller should also have in mind the general project objectives (Section 6.2.2), that is, the level of visual display required and the data input, results viewing and interactive capabilities needed. All these, particularly the visual display, may affect the structure of the model. A more complex visual display often requires additional components and logic.

The model structure is typically a paper-based description of the model, outlining the constructs and logic of the simulation in terms of the software being used. It normally entails some form of schematic outlining the components, variables, attributes and logic of the model. It is not necessary to write out each line of code, but it is useful to describe the code in natural language, for instance, "if call type is A, route to enquiries". The way in which the structure is expressed depends very much on the nature of the software being used. For this reason it is difficult to define a standard format for describing the model. That said there is some scope in using standard notations such as IDEF0 (Icam DEFinition) and UML (the unified modeling language) (Richter and März 2000; Oscarsson and Urenda Moris 2002).

For sections of the model that involve more complex logic, it is often difficult to design the model structure away from the computer, particularly if the modeller is less experienced with the software. In this case it can be useful to develop a prototype of a section of the model in the computer software. In this way the modeller is able rapidly to try alternative coding approaches. The prototype code, if successful, may not have to be thrown away, since some simulation packages allow sections of code to be imported from one model to another.

As with all parts of the simulation modelling process, there is a great deal of iteration both within and between the key processes. As a result, the model structure will change as the project progresses. It is important, therefore, to continue to document changes to the model structure, so the description of the model is always in line with the model code.

8.3 Coding the Model

When developing the computer model itself the modeller should pay attention to three important activities:

- *Coding*: developing the code in the simulation software.
- *Testing*: verifying and white-box validating the model.
- *Documenting*: recording the details of the model.

Rather than develop the complete code, then test and then document, it is best to develop the code in small steps, testing and documenting it at each stage. Such incremental development helps to ensure that the model is more thoroughly tested and documented and that errors are identified early, before they become very difficult to unravel. If these activities are left to the end, they will almost certainly not be performed so thoroughly. Most simulation software support an incremental approach, enabling a small portion of a model to be run and tested without the need for the complete model code.

Verification and white-box validation are discussed in Section 12.4.3. The documentation of the model is discussed below. Meanwhile, two important issues of good practice in model coding are now discussed, that is, separating the data and results from the model content and the use of pseudo random number streams.

Before discussing these issues it should be noted that there is no attempt here to discuss how models should be coded in specific software packages. Software vendors generally provide training courses for this purpose and in some cases tutorial guides. Some books are available that describe how to use a specific software package, for instance, Kelton *et al.* (1998) and Harrell *et al.* (2003).

8.3.1 Separate the data from the code from the results

When developing a spreadsheet, it is good practice to separate the data from the formulae. Rather than hard code a value, it should be placed in a separate cell and referenced by the formulae. In this way the user of the spreadsheet can easily alter the data that drive the model without having to look through the formulae to see where the data might be located. It also means that all the data can be placed in one area of the spreadsheet, again making it easier to maintain and use the model.

In the same way, it is good practice in simulation modelling to separate the data and the results from the model code. A typical structure is shown in Figure 8.1. Here the general model data and experimental factors are placed in separate locations. This has the advantage that the users need only access the experimental factors and do not have to concern themselves to the same degree with the general model data. Similarly, they are able to access the results without needing a detailed knowledge of the simulation code or the proprietary software.

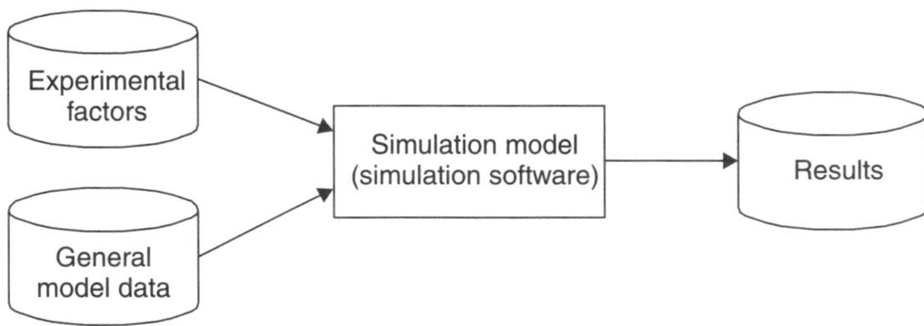

Figure 8.1 Separate the Data from the Code from the Results.

The data, experimental factors and results are normally held in a spreadsheet, a database or a data file (text format). Spreadsheets, and perhaps to a lesser extent databases, have the obvious advantage of familiarity and the ability to perform further analyses, particularly on the results. It is also possible to use the facilities of the spreadsheet or database to improve the presentation of the data and the results. Most simulation software provide facilities for reading from and writing to data files. Many provide facilities for direct linking to spreadsheets and databases.

There are various advantages of separating the data from the model from the results:

- *Familiarity*: users do not need extensive training in the data input and results generation software.
- *Ease of use*: in-depth understanding of the simulation code and simulation software is not required.
- *Presentation*: ability to use specialist software (e.g. spreadsheet) for presenting the data and the results.
- *Further analysis*: ability to use specialist software facilities for further analysis of the data and the results.
- *Version control*: provides a mechanism for maintaining a record of all experimental scenarios by holding separate versions of the experimental factors file and the results file.

The main disadvantage is that the development time is likely to be greater. In most cases this is more than compensated for by the advantages above, particularly as the changes required during experimentation should be made more quickly. The case where it may not be worth investing the extra development time is if the model is to be used only by the modeller and if only a few experiments are to be performed before the model becomes redundant (Section 13.2).

8.3.2 Use of pseudo random number streams

Section 2.3.5 describes how random numbers are generated on a computer. The concept of a pseudo random number stream is also introduced. This is a stream of random numbers whose sequence can be replicated exactly because the stream always starts from the same seed. As a consequence, if a simulation run is repeated, despite there being random elements in the model, the same result will be obtained.

Most, but not all, simulation packages allow the user to specify the pseudo random number stream that is to be used for each part of the model involving random sampling. The question is, which streams should be selected? At one level the answer is any stream, since all of them provide a sequence of random numbers. This does assume that all the streams genuinely appear random. Perhaps this should not be taken for granted without testing the streams that are generated by the software. For more details on the testing of random number streams see Kleijnen and van Groenendaal (1992), Pidd (1998) and Law and Kelton (2000).

At a second level, however, the answer to the question is that a different stream should be used on each occasion. Put another way, a pseudo random number stream should be referenced only once in a model. The reason for this is to ensure consistency in the random sampling when making changes to the model during experimentation. This is best explained with an example.

Say, for instance, that a model is being developed of a service process. Customers arrive, queue and are then served at one of three service points. For simplicity it is assumed that the customers are directed to the service points in strict rotation, so:

- customer 1 is served at service point 1
- customer 2 is served at service point 2
- customer 3 is served at service point 3
- customer 4 is served at service point 1
- customer 5 is served at service point 2 and so on.

The service time is distributed negative exponentially with a mean of 5 minutes. Table 8.1 provides a sequence of random numbers (a pseudo random number stream) and the associated samples from the negative exponential distribution, calculated as:

$$x = \frac{-1}{\lambda} \log_e(1 - u)$$

where:

x = random sample
$1/\lambda$ = mean inter-arrival time (λ = mean arrival rate)
u = random number, $0 <= u < 1$

Table 8.1 Pseudo Random Number Stream and Negative Exponential (mean = 5) Samples.

Sample number	Random number stream	Negative exponential (mean = 5)
1	0.367733	2.29
2	0.582229	4.36
3	0.283212	1.66
4	0.638273	5.08
5	0.685906	5.79
6	0.491007	3.38
7	0.387991	2.46
8	0.675745	5.63
9	0.703629	6.08
10	0.555504	4.05
11	0.813298	8.39
12	0.607994	4.68
.	.	.
.	.	.
.	.	.

Suppose that instead of using different streams of random numbers for each of the service points we break our rule and use the same stream for each (the stream in Table 8.1). The resulting service times at each service point are shown in Table 8.2.

A second experiment is run, but this time with only two service points. The resulting service times are shown in Table 8.3. What can be seen is that not only has the number of service points changed between the two simulation runs, but also the service times sampled at each service point. In other words, the random sampling has not been replicated exactly from one experiment to another. Therefore, the results of the two experiments cannot be compared directly, at least in terms of the effect of a change in the number of service points. This problem would not have occurred, however, had different pseudo random number streams been used to sample service times at each of the service points. The removal of service point 3 would not have affected the service times sampled at service points 1 and 2. As a result, any difference in the results from the two experiments could be attributed purely to the change in the number of service points.

Table 8.2 Service Times at the Three Service Points Assuming the same Stream of Random Numbers is used for Sampling Times at Each.

	Service time (min)		
Service number	Service point 1	Service point 2	Service point 3
1	2.29	4.36	1.66
2	5.08	5.79	3.38
3	2.46	5.63	6.08
4	4.05	8.39	4.68
.	.	.	.
.	.	.	.
.	.	.	.

Table 8.3 Service Times at Two Service Points Assuming the same Stream of Random Numbers is used for Sampling Times at Each.

	Service time (minutes)	
Service number	Service point 1	Service point 2
1	2.29	4.36
2	1.66	5.08
3	5.79	3.38
4	2.46	5.63
.	.	.
.	.	.
.	.	.

The use of different streams of random numbers for each part of a model that involves random sampling is known as the use of *common random numbers*. This is part of a much wider body of theory on variance reduction techniques that is briefly discussed in Section 9.6.2. There is some further discussion on the use of common random numbers when comparing the results from simulation experiments in Section 10.4.

A word of caution must be given, however, on the use of common random numbers. Although the approach can be shown to work in certain cases, such as the one described above, there is no guarantee that it will always perform as desired. In very complex models, with many interactions, it is not difficult to envisage a situation where changing, removing or adding an element would have knock-on effects that meant the random sampling in other parts of the model is perturbed despite the use of common random numbers. Further to this, most simulation software do not give the modeller control over the use of pseudo random number streams beyond specifying which streams are to be employed. It may, therefore, be difficult to gain the synchronization in random number usage required for maintaining common random numbers between simulation experiments. For a more detailed discussion on common random numbers and its applicability, see Law and Kelton (2000).

8.4 Documenting the Model and the Simulation Project

Documentation is generally seen as a vital part of simulation modelling. Oscarsson and Urenda Moris (2002) quote typical figures for the cost of documentation in software development of around 20 to 30% of the total development costs, suggesting that a similar level of effort should be put into documenting simulation models. Despite this, most simulation models are very poorly documented and it is hard to find any significant discussion on the topic. Gass (1984) is one of the few examples.

There are a number of motivations for documenting a simulation model. First, it is important for the modeller to be able to remember what has been done. Beyond this, further development of a model may need to be carried out by someone other than the original modeller because, for instance, the personnel change. The new modeller needs to be able to understand what has been done. It may be that a model, or a component of a model, is to be reused in another application. Without proper documentation it is difficult for someone to assess whether the model or component is appropriate for the new circumstance.

Outside of model development, model documentation is important for the clients and users of the simulation, so they are able to understand the inner workings of the model when experimenting with it and when interpreting the results. Suitable documentation should mean that a detailed knowledge of the simulation software and model code is not required. Documentation will also help to improve the credibility of a model. Finally, documentation is vital for model verification and validation (Chapter 12), particularly if the model is to be the subject of an external review (Kleijnen 1995).

Of course the prime demotivation for documenting a model properly is the cost and time involved, nor does it seem to be constructive in the same manner as, say, model coding.

In simulation studies three types of documentation are required: model documentation, project documentation and user documentation. The following are useful forms of model documentation:

- The conceptual model (Section 5.5.2)
- A list of model assumptions and simplifications (Section 5.3)
- The model structure (Section 8.2)
- The input data and experimental factors: including interpretation and sources of data (Chapter 7)
- The results format: interpretation of results (Section 6.2.3)
- Using meaningful names for components, variables and attributes.
- Comments and notes in the code
- The visual display of the model

Some of this is held externally to the model code, while some is included as part of the code, particularly the last three items. If the data and the results are held separately from the model code then this provides a natural place for documenting their meaning and the sources of the data. Note that many of the items listed above have already been generated by the work undertaken during conceptual modelling, data collection and analysis, and model structuring.

The project documentation may include:

- The project specification (Section 5.5.1)
- Minutes of meetings
- Verification and validation performed (Chapter 12)
- Experimental scenarios run (Chapter 10)
- Results of experiments (associated with each scenario) (Chapter 10)
- Final report (Section 11.2.1)
- Project review (Section 11.3.3)

It is good practice to keep a record of all the experimental scenarios run and of the results associated with them. Again, the separation of the experimental factors and the results from the model code aids this process, since this information can be stored in a series of appropriately named files. Ulgen (1991) describes how the Production Modeling Corporation ensure simulation projects are properly managed by defining various documents that must be generated at each stage.

The final form of documentation is for the users of a model. This is only required if the model is to be handed over to a user for experimentation. Such documentation should include:

- The project specification: providing background to the project and the conceptual model.
- Input data: interpretation and sources of data.
- Experimental factors: their meaning, range and how to change them.
- Guide to running the model.
- Results: accessing and interpreting results.

Much of this can be extracted from the model and project documentation.

The lists above are only a guide to the documents that might be required for documenting the model and the project, and providing help for the users of a model. It is not always necessary to document a model to this extent. In Section 13.2 different model types are described. If a model is to be thrown away after use then the need for model documentation is much reduced. It merely needs to be enough for the lifetime of the simulation project, providing the modeller with a record of the model and giving the clients and users sufficient confidence in the work. The shorter the lifetime of the model, the lower the documentation requirement is likely to be.

On the other hand, if the model is to be used in on-going work or it is a generic model, then the documentation requirement is greater. Similarly, if the model is for reuse either as a whole or as model components, then there needs to be a higher level of documentation. One problem is that a simulation that starts life as a throwaway model may become a model that has a longer term use in one form or another. It is, therefore, difficult to predict the level of documentation required.

Finally, Oscarsson and Urenda Moris (2002) note that different levels of documentation are required for different audiences. This can be seen in terms of the simulation study roles defined in Section 4.4. For instance, the modeller obviously requires in-depth model documentation, while the clients are more interested in the project documentation. A wider group of managers are probably only interested in the outcomes of the project, that is, the key results, conclusions and recommendations.

8.5 Conclusion

Model coding involves the development of a model structure, the development of the model code and the documenting of the model. In this chapter various issues that should be attended to during model coding are highlighted.

- It is important to structure the model, converting the conceptual model to a software specific description, before running ahead to model coding.
- The model code should be developed in small steps, documenting and testing the code at each stage.
- It is useful to separate the data, experimental factors and results from the code of the model.
- It is recommended that separate streams of pseudo random numbers are used for each part of the model that requires random sampling (common random numbers).
- Three types of documentation are required: model documentation, project documentation and user documentation. The level of documentation required depends upon the nature of the simulation model and the intended reader.

Model testing (verification and validation) is also an important activity that is carried out during model coding, as well as during the other process in a simulation study. This is discussed in Chapter 12 and specifically in relation to model coding in Section 12.4.3.

The reader may choose to develop simulation models for the Wardeon Cinema and Panorama Televisions case studies (Appendix 1 and 2 respectively). Alternatively, versions of the models are available for various simulation packages on the web site (www.wileyeurope.com/go/robinson).

Exercises

E8.1 Develop a computer model for the bank case described in Exercise E6.1 (Chapter 6). First devise the model structure and then develop the model code in the software of your choice. Set up the data so that the mean arrival rate is about 80% of the mean service rate (for the purposes of calculating this percentage both rates should be aggregated across all customer types and service points).

E8.2 Develop a computer model for the Wardeon Cinema case described in Appendix 1 (Section A1.2.1). First devise the model structure and then develop the model code in the software of your choice.

E8.3 Develop a computer model for the Panorama Televisions case described in Appendix 2 (Section A2.2.1). First devise the model structure and then develop the model code in the software of your choice.

References

Gass, S.I. (1984) "Documenting a computer-based model". *Interfaces*, 14(3), 84–93.

Harrell, C.R., Ghosh, B. and Bowden, R. (2003) *Simulation using Promodel*. New York: McGraw-Hill.

Kelton, W.D., Sadowski, R.P. and Sadowski, D.A. (1998) *Simulation with Arena*. New York: McGraw-Hill.

Kleijnen, J.P.C. (1995) "Verification and validation of simulation models". *European Journal of Operational Research*, 82(1), 145–162.

Kleijnen, J.P.C. and van Groenendaal, W. (1992) *Simulation: A Statistical Perspective*. Chichester, UK: Wiley.

Law, A.M. and Kelton, W.D. (2000) *Simulation Modeling and Analysis*, 3rd edn. New York: McGraw-Hill.

Oscarsson, J. and Urenda Moris, M. (2002) "Documentation of discrete event simulation models for manufacturing system life cycle simulation". *Proceedings of the 2002 Winter Simulation Conference* (Yucesan, E., Chen, C.-H., Snowden, S.L., Charnes, J.M., eds). Piscataway, NJ: IEEE, pp. 1073–1078.

Pidd, M. (1998) *Computer Simulation in Management Science*, 4th edn. Chichester, UK: Wiley.

Richter, H. and März, L. (2000) "Toward a standard process: the use of UML for designing simulation models". *Proceedings of the 2000 Winter Simulation Conference* (Joines, J.A, Barton, R.R., Kang, K. and Fishwick, P.A., eds). Piscataway, NJ: IEEE, pp. 394–398.

Ulgen, O. (1991) "Proper management techniques are keys to a successful simulation project". *Industrial Engineering*, 23(8), 37–41.

EXPERIMENTATION: OBTAINING ACCURATE RESULTS

9.1 Introduction

During experimentation the simulation project team aims to obtain a better understanding of the real world system that is being modelled and look for ways to improve that system. If the experimentation is not carried out correctly then the understanding gained may be incorrect and the improvements identified may not lead to the intended outcomes.

There are two key issues in simulation experimentation. The first is to ensure that accurate results on model performance are obtained from the simulation model. This is the subject of this chapter. The second is to ensure that the search for a better understanding and improvements is performed as efficiently and as effectively as possible. This is referred to as searching the solution space and is the subject of the next chapter.

In this chapter, before discussing specific methods for obtaining accurate results on model performance, the nature of simulation models and simulation output are described. This is important because it affects the approaches that need to be taken to obtaining accurate results. The key issues in obtaining accurate results are then explained, namely, dealing with initialization bias and obtaining sufficient output data. Various methods for dealing with these two issues are described (warm-up period, setting initial conditions, multiple replications and long runs). These methods are illustrated by applying them to the output data from a model of a computer user help desk. Throughout the chapter the focus is primarily on practical issues, which in some cases are supported by the use of statistical methods.

9.2 The Nature of Simulation Models and Simulation Output

The nature of a simulation model and its output affects the means by which accurate results are obtained from a model. For the purposes of this discussion it is assumed that the simulation output is stochastic, that is, the model contains random events. Although it is possible to have a simulation model that does not contain any random events, it is not common practice. It is worth noting that for such deterministic models, some of the issues described below still require attention.

9.2.1 Terminating and non-terminating simulations

A simulation model can be classified as one of two types: terminating and non-terminating. For a *terminating* simulation there is a natural end point that determines the length of a run. The end point can be defined in a number of ways, for instance:

- The model reaches an empty condition, e.g. a bank that closes at the end of a day.
- The completion of the time period under investigation, e.g. the end of the busy lunch period in a supermarket.
- The completion of a trace of input data, e.g. the completion of a production schedule.

Meanwhile, a *non-terminating* simulation does not have a natural end point. An example is a model of a production facility that aims to determine its throughput capability. There is no specific reason why a simulation experiment should terminate other than the model user interrupting the run. For non-terminating models the length of a simulation run needs to be determined by the model user.

9.2.2 Transient output

In most cases the output from a terminating simulation is *transient*. Transient output means that the distribution of the output is constantly changing. Take, for instance, a simulation of a bank. One of the responses of interest is the number of customers served in each hour of the day. Figure 9.1 shows a typical profile for a time-series of the number of customers served. Further to this, for any time period the number of customers served is unlikely to be identical on any given day. This is purely as a result of the random variation in the system. The distribution of customers served in the hour 11:00–12:00 is shown by $f(11{:}00–12{:}00)$ in Figure 9.1. This shows that between 11:00 and 12:00 on any day the number of customers served could be between about 60 and about 100. Over many days, the mean number of customers served between 11:00 and 12:00 will be about 80. Similarly, for each hour of the day there is a distribution of the number of customers served. Because the output data are transient, the distribution varies for each hour of the day. In Figure 9.1 this is shown by normal distributions with differing means and standard deviations. Of course, the distributions do not necessarily have to be normal.

9.2.3 Steady-state output

For non-terminating simulations the output often reaches a *steady state*. Steady state does not mean that the output is not varying, but that the output is varying according to some fixed distribution (the steady-state distribution). Take the example of a simulation of a production facility. The throughput varies day-on-day due to breakdowns, changeovers

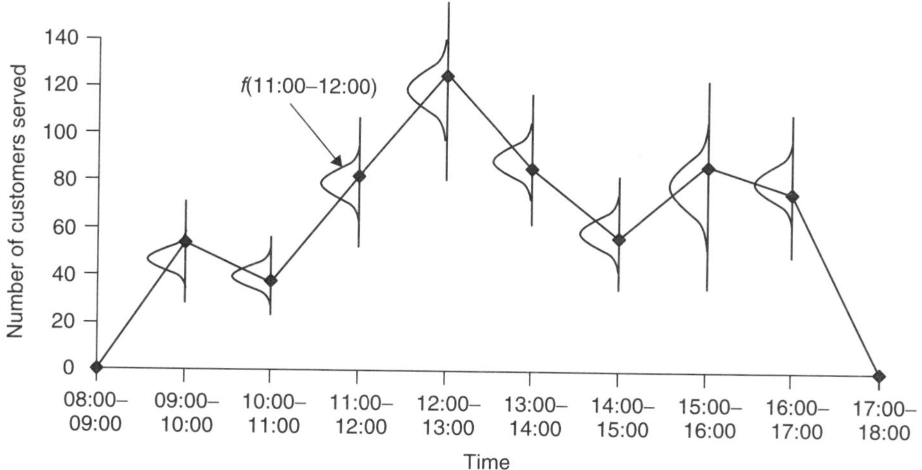

Figure 9.1 Example of Transient Output: Number of Customers Served Hourly in a Bank.

and other interruptions. In the long run, however, the throughput capability (the mean throughput level) remains constant. In steady state the level of variability about that mean also remains constant since the steady-state distribution is constant. Figure 9.2 shows a typical time-series of a response for a non-terminating simulation, in this example showing throughput. From day 10 onwards the throughput is varying around a constant mean according to the steady-state distribution, f(steady state).

It is notable in Figure 9.2 that the model does not start in a steady state. For the first 9 days the response value is much lower which suggests that it is not following the steady-state distribution. What is the reason for this? Think of a typical model of a production facility. At the start of a simulation run there are no parts in the system. As time progresses, parts

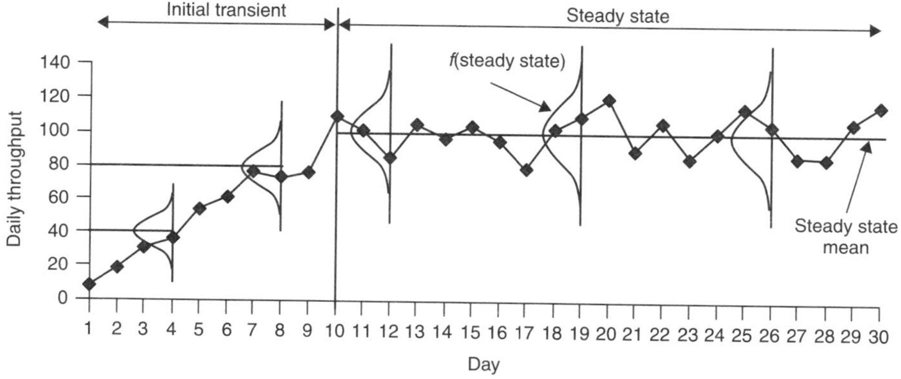

Figure 9.2 Example of Steady-State Output: Daily Throughput from a Production Line.

feed through the system and eventually they begin to be output. As a result the throughput recorded in the model starts at a low level and gradually builds up to its steady-state level. This period in the simulation run is known as the *initial transient* because it occurs at the start of a run (initial) and because the distribution of the output is constantly changing (transient). The output data obtained during the initial transient are obviously unrealistic: most production facilities do not start without any work-in-progress on a Monday morning! The inclusion of such data would bias the results obtain from the simulation (*initialization bias*). Therefore, these data should normally be ignored and only the steady-state data should be accounted for.

Although steady-state output is described with respect to non-terminating simulations, it is possible that a terminating simulation may also reach a steady state, particularly if the termination point implies a long run-length. Similarly, the output from a non-terminating simulation may not reach a steady state.

9.2.4 Other types of output

Transient and steady-state are not the only types of output that occur from simulation models. Law and Kelton (2000) identify a third type, *steady-state cycle*. Think of a simulation of a production facility working two shifts. The night shift has fewer operators and so works at a slower rate, in this circumstance the throughput recorded by the simulation cycles between two steady states. A similar effect might occur in a 24-hour service operation such as a call handling centre for the emergency services. The rate at which calls are received varies with the time of the day. As a result, a simulation response such as calls handled changes as the day progresses. Assuming that the call pattern is similar on each day, the simulation output will cycle through the same series of steady states. Of course the pattern may be more complex, with a day-of-week effect as well. In this case there are two cycles overlaid on one another, a daily and a weekly cycle.

Steady-state-cycle output can be dealt with quite simply by lengthening the observation interval in the time-series to the length of the longest cycle. Rather than recording hourly throughput or throughput by shift in the production example above, the data could be recorded daily. In this way the cycles are subsumed into the longer observation interval and the output analysis can be performed as for steady-state output.

Meanwhile, Robinson *et al.* (2002) describe a fourth output type, *shifting steady-state*. In some models the output shifts from one steady state to another as time progresses. For example, this might be due to changes in product type, number of staff or operating practice, assuming that each of these affects the output response. Unlike the steady-state cycle described above, these shifts do not necessarily occur in a regular or even predictable pattern. The authors also describe a heuristic method for identifying such output behaviour and discuss how the output might be analysed.

9.2.5 Determining the nature of the simulation output

As a general rule, the output from terminating simulations is transient and from non-terminating simulations is steady-state (possibly with a cycle or shifts). This, however, is not always the case. Some further investigation is needed before deciding on the nature of the output.

First, the input data should be inspected. Do they change during a simulation run? For instance, the customer arrival rate might change as the simulation run progresses. If they do not change, then it is probable that the model output is steady-state. If the data change, and the model is terminating, then this is indicative of transient output. If the model is non-terminating, and the data change according to a regular cycle, then this suggests the output is steady-state-cycle.

Secondly, the output data should be investigated, particularly by viewing time-series. If the output is steady-state, then the time-series should reveal a typical initial transient and then steady-state pattern as shown in Figure 9.2. If, however, the output is transient, then the time-series should not settle, as in Figure 9.1. Steady-state cycle output should be reasonably easy to detect, assuming that multiple cycles are not overlaid. Shifts in steady state are not so readily identified by straightforward inspection and require more detailed analysis (Robinson *et al.* 2002).

9.3 Issues in Obtaining Accurate Simulation Results

Before discussing the issues in obtaining accurate simulation results, the key difference between model performance and real system performance needs to be highlighted. This chapter is concerned with obtaining accurate data on the performance of the model. This says nothing about how accurately the model predicts the performance of the real system. This is the concern of model validation (Chapter 12). What is certain, however, is that if the data obtained on the performance of the model are inaccurate, then these data will not provide an accurate prediction of real system performance.

The main aim of simulation output analysis is to obtain an accurate estimate of average (normally the mean) performance, although measures of variability are also important (Section 10.3.2). There are two key issues in assuring the accuracy of the estimates obtained from a simulation model. The first is the removal of any initialization bias, the second is ensuring that enough output data have been obtained from the simulation to obtain an accurate estimate of performance. Both issues, if not properly addressed, can lead to results that are biased and so misleading. Some years ago I performed a series of experiments with a model, each time with a run-length of one week, after allowing for the initialization bias. The run-length was largely dictated by what could be run overnight; at that time a computer with a 25 megahertz processor was considered powerful! The results consistently showed a large shortfall in throughput. Then, during a holiday period, the model was left to run and 26 weeks of output data were obtained. This clearly showed that the first week was an outlier and that the mean throughput was significantly better, albeit still insufficient.

9.3.1 Initialization bias: warm-up and initial conditions

The first issue, the removal of initialization bias, applies to non-terminating simulations and sometimes needs to be addressed for terminating simulations. Many terminating simulations start from, and return to, an empty condition. For instance, most service operations open and close each day with no customers present. There are, however, situations where the empty condition is not a realistic starting point. If a week's production schedule is run through a simulation model, it would be wrong to assume that there is no work-in-progress on Monday morning. We may want to model the lunch period in a bank and it would be incorrect to ignore the customers who are present at the beginning of this period.

There are two ways of handling initialization bias. The first is to run the model for a warm-up period. Basically this entails running the model until it reaches a realistic condition (steady-state for a non-terminating simulation) and only collecting results from the model after this point. The second approach is to set initial conditions in the model. Rather than run the model until it is in a realistic condition, the model is placed in a realistic condition at the start of the run. This often means placing work-in-progress into the model at the beginning of a run, for example, customers or parts. A third option is to use a mix of initial conditions and warm-up. These approaches are discussed in detail in Section 9.5.

9.3.2 Obtaining sufficient output data: long runs and multiple replications

The second issue, ensuring that enough output data have been obtained from the simulation, can be addressed in two ways. The first is to perform a single long run with the model. Obviously this is only an option for a non-terminating simulation, unless perchance the termination point for a terminating simulation is sufficiently far off to collect enough output data. In general, for terminating simulations the only option is to use the second approach, performing multiple replications. A replication is a run of a simulation model that uses specified streams of random numbers, which in turn cause a specific sequence of random events. By changing the random number streams another replication is performed in which the sequence of random events that occur during the model run changes, as do the results obtained. By performing multiple replications and taking the mean of the results, a better estimate of model performance is gained. Performing multiple replications is equivalent to taking multiple samples in statistics. Meanwhile, performing one long run is equivalent to taking one large sample.

As stated above, multiple replications is generally the only approach available for obtaining sufficient output data from terminating simulations. Meanwhile, for non-terminating simulations the model user can use either long runs or multiple replications. These approaches and their relative merits are discussed in detail in Section 9.6.

9.4 An Example Model: Computer User Help Desk

For the purposes of describing the approaches for dealing with initialization bias and ensuring that sufficient output data are obtained, it is useful to refer to an example. Figure 9.3 shows a time-series of output from a simulation of a computer user help desk. This model has been used for a simulation study of a real life help desk.

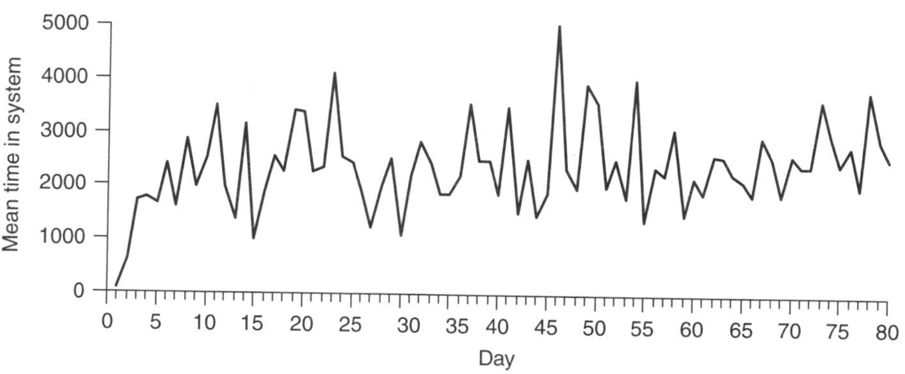

Figure 9.3 Time-Series of Mean Time in the System for User Help Desk Example.

The desk receives telephone call and email enquiries from computer users. The enquiries are received, logged and whenever possible dealt with by the staff on the help desk. A high proportion of the calls require technical expertise or a site visit and so they are passed on to the technical team. Because of a backlog of work it may take hours or even days to bring an enquiry to completion. The time-series in Figure 9.3 shows the mean time that enquiries being completed on each day have spent in the system (in minutes); this is just one of a number of output statistics that may be of interest. It is clear that there is a lot of variability in the time it takes to complete enquiries.

The model is non-terminating and inspection of the time-series strongly suggests that the output is steady-state. The input data do not change during the simulation run, lending further weight to this conclusion. There appears to be some initialization bias since at least the first two observations are low. This is expected as the initial condition of the model is unrealistic; there are no enquiries in the system.

9.5 Dealing with Initialization Bias: Warm-up and Initial Conditions

This section describes two methods for dealing with initialization bias: a warm-up period and setting initial conditions. The third option of using mixed initial conditions and warm-up is also discussed, as well as the advantages and disadvantages of the different methods.

9.5.1 Determining the warm-up period

If a warm-up period is to be employed the key question is what should be the length of the warm-up period? The simple answer is that the warm-up period should be long enough to ensure the model is in a realistic condition. For a non-terminating simulation this normally means that the initial transient has passed and the model output is in steady state. The difficulty in this answer lies in determining whether the model is in a realistic condition.

A host of methods have been proposed for identifying initialization bias and determining the warm-up period. These can be classified into five types.

- *Graphical methods*: involve the visual inspection of time-series of the output data.
- *Heuristics approaches*: apply simple rules with few underlying assumptions.
- *Statistical methods*: rely upon the principles of statistics for determining the warm-up period.
- *Initialization bias tests*: identify whether there is any initialization bias in the data. Strictly these are not methods for identifying the warm-up period, but they can be used in combination with warm-up methods to determine whether they are working effectively.
- *Hybrid methods*: these involve a combination of graphical or heuristic methods with an initialization bias test.

For those that wish to investigate these approaches further, a list of methods and references is provided in Table 9.1. Unfortunately, all of these methods have shortcomings and there does not appear to be one method that can be recommended for all circumstances. Key problems that occur with the methods are overestimating or underestimating the length of the initial transient, relying on very restrictive assumptions and using highly complex statistical procedures.

For our purposes two fairly straightforward graphical methods are described: time-series inspection and Welch's method. Both literature research and anecdotal evidence suggest that these methods are in reasonably common use in practice. Although they are not without their shortcomings, the methods are fairly effective and are certainly better than the other alternative that is commonly used, guesswork!

Time-series inspection

The simplest method for identifying the warm-up period is to inspect a time-series of the simulation output, that is, the key response(s) of the simulation model (Section 6.2.3). The problem with inspecting a time-series of a single run, such as the one in Figure 9.3, is that the data can be very noisy and so it is difficult to spot any initialization bias. It is better, therefore, if a series of replications are run (Section 9.6.1) and the mean averages of those replications for each period are plotted on a time-series. At least five replications should be performed, although more may be required for very noisy data. The more replications that are performed the more the time-series will be smoothed as outliers are subsumed into the calculation of the mean for each period.

Table 9.2 shows the output data (for the first 10 days) obtained from five replications with the user help desk model. It also shows the mean averages of those replications for each period. Those averages are plotted on the time-series in Figure 9.4. Notice how much smoother the time-series is than the one based on only one replication in Figure 9.3.

To determine the warm-up period, the point at which the output appears to settle into a steady state should be identified. That is, the point at which the data are neither consistently higher or lower than their "normal" level and where there is no apparent upward or downward trend in the data. In Figure 9.4 the data appear to settle at day 4. Therefore, a warm-up period of at least 3 days (the first 3 days' data are deleted) is proposed.

Table 9.1 Methods for Determining the Warm-up Period (Robinson 2002).

Category	Method	Reference
Graphical methods	Time-series inspection	See below
	Ensemble average plots	Banks *et al.* (2001)
	Cumulative mean rule	Gordon (1969)
	Deleting the cumulative mean rule	Banks *et al.* (2001)
	CUSUM plots	Nelson (1992)
	Welch's method	Welch (1983)
	Variance plots	Gordon (1969)
	Statistical process control	Robinson (2002)
Heuristics approaches	Schriber's rule	Pawlikowski (1990)
	Conway rule	Gafarian *et al.* (1978)
	Modified Conway rule	Gafarian *et al.* (1978)
	Crossing of the mean rule	Fishman (1973)
	Autocorrelation estimator rule	Fishman (1971)
	Marginal confidence rule	White (1997)
	Goodness of fit	Pawlikowski (1990)
	Relaxation heuristics	Pawlikowski (1990)
	MSER and MSER-5	White and Spratt (2000)
Statistical methods	Kelton and Law regression method	Kelton and Law (1983)
	Randomization tests	Yucesan (1993)
Initialization bias tests	Schruben's maximum test	Schruben (1982)
	Schruben's modified test	Nelson (1992)
	Optimal test	Schruben *et al.* (1983)
	Rank test	Vassilacopoulos (1989)
	The new maximum test	Goldsman *et al.* (1994)
	Batch means test	Goldsman *et al.* (1994)
	Area test	Goldsman *et al.* (1994)
Hybrid methods	Pawlikowski's sequential method	Pawlikowski (1990)
	Scale invariant truncation point method	Jackway and deSilva (1992)

Sometimes it may be necessary to adjust the observation interval in the time-series in order to identify subtle patterns in the data. For instance, the data could be plotted hourly rather than daily. Beyond simply inspecting a time-series, it is also useful to watch the model running (assuming there is a visual display of the simulation). In doing so it may be possible to identify unusual behaviours, such as abnormally high or low levels of work-in-progress in parts of the model. Abnormal behaviour suggests that the model may still be in an initial transient phase.

This very simple method does have some shortcomings. Because it relies upon a subjective assessment, the findings are probably affected by the experience of the user. If the data are

Table 9.2 Results from Five Replications with the User Help Desk Model.

	Mean time in system					
Day	Repl. 1	Repl. 2	Repl. 3	Repl. 4	Repl. 5	Mean
1	93.98	56.88	142.04	110.87	82.32	97.22
2	618.08	501.71	292.19	672.74	135.28	444.00
3	1737.02	1162.92	336.36	1538.36	1291.77	1213.29
4	1769.77	953.53	3895.80	1069.59	3098.86	2157.51
5	1663.22	3006.68	1346.40	2837.09	2118.00	2194.28
6	2425.34	1495.23	2731.65	2855.38	3314.20	2564.36
7	1611.92	1798.13	1922.52	1797.52	3680.18	2162.05
8	2885.21	1185.96	1706.25	1548.68	544.49	1574.12
9	1986.58	3628.20	2958.04	3194.36	4104.93	3174.42
10	2521.63	2122.12	2537.90	2181.94	4068.63	2686.44
.	.	.	.	.	.	.
.	.	.	.	.	.	.
.	.	.	.	.	.	.

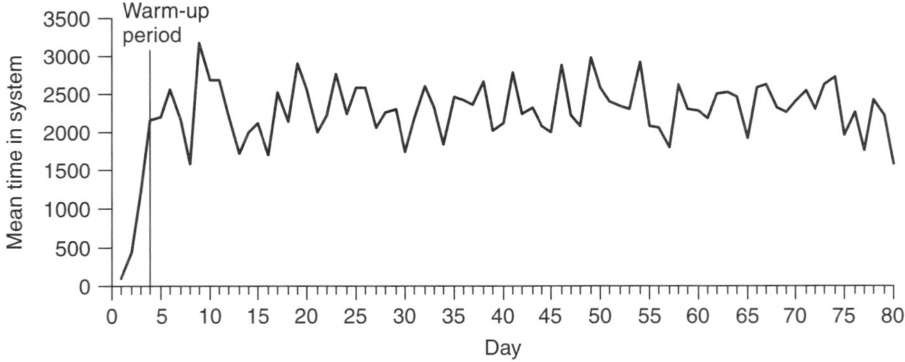

Figure 9.4 Warm-up Period: Time-Series of Mean Result from Five Replications with the User Help Desk Model.

particularly noisy, subtle patterns in the data may go unnoticed. I have seen time-series output that looks as though it is in steady state, but more detailed analysis reveals a trend in the data and that the warm-up period needs to be somewhat longer than originally thought.

Welch's method

Welch (1983) proposes a method based on the calculation and plotting of moving averages. This involves the following steps:

- Perform a series of replications (at least five) to obtain time-series of the output data.
- Calculate the mean of the output data across the replications for each period ($\overline{Y}_i$).
- Calculate a moving average based on a window size w (start with $w = 5$).
- Plot the moving average on a time-series.
- Are the data smooth? If not, increase the size of the window (w) and return to the previous two steps.
- Identify the warm-up period as the point where the time-series becomes flat.

The moving averages are calculated using the following formula:

$$\overline{Y}_i(w) = \begin{cases} \dfrac{\sum_{s=-(i-1)}^{i-1} \overline{Y}_{i+s}}{2i-1} & \text{if } i = 1, \ldots, w \\[2ex] \dfrac{\sum_{s=-w}^{w} \overline{Y}_{i+s}}{2\,w+1} & \text{if } i = w+1, \ldots, m-w \end{cases}$$

where:

$\overline{Y}_i(w)$ = moving average of window size w
$\overline{Y}_i$ = time-series of output data (mean of the replications)
i = period number
m = number of periods in the simulation run

The method is best illustrated with an example. Table 9.3 shows the mean average ($\overline{Y}_i$) of the results obtained from five replications with the user help desk model (as in Table 9.2) and the moving average based on a window size of five. Note that the first five moving averages cannot include the full window of data and so use the top half of the formula above. Figure 9.5 shows a plot of the moving average data.

With a window size of five the moving average line is reasonably smooth. The warm-up period is selected by identifying the point where the line becomes flat, which is at about day 9. This suggests that the first 8 days' data should be deleted from the simulation output and so a warm-up period of at least 8 days is selected.

In using Welch's method the aim should be to select the smallest window size that gives a reasonably smooth line. Although selecting a larger window size will give a smoother line, it also tends to give a more conservative (longer) estimate of the warm-up period. This is wasteful of data and has implications for the run-length (Section 9.6). It is also recommended that the value of w should be no more than a quarter of the total observations in the original time-series. If more observations are required, the simulation model should be run for longer.

Although Welch's method requires the calculation of moving averages, it is relatively simple to use. It has the advantage that the calculation of the moving average smooths out the noise in the data and helps to give a clearer picture of the initial transient. Many authors

Table 9.3 Welch's Method: Calculation of Moving Average (Window = 5).

Day	Mean time in system (mean of five replications)	Data included in the moving average	Moving average ($w = 5$)
1	97.22		97.22
2	444.00	1	584.84
3	1213.29		1221.26
4	2157.51	2	1547.53
5	2194.28		1731.25
6	2564.36	3	1903.62
7	2162.05		2096.58
8	1574.12	4	2212.96
9	3174.42		2285.29
10	2686.44	5	2281.33
11	2672.17		2237.21
12	2219.76	6	2232.31
13	1724.18	7	2229.52
14	2008.91	8	2349.58
15	2113.93	9	2293.24
16	1709.00	10	2230.03
17	2510.45	.	2188.89
18	2131.37	.	2237.11
19	2894.76	.	2284.91
20	2554.64		2336.02
.	.		.
.	.		.
.	.		.

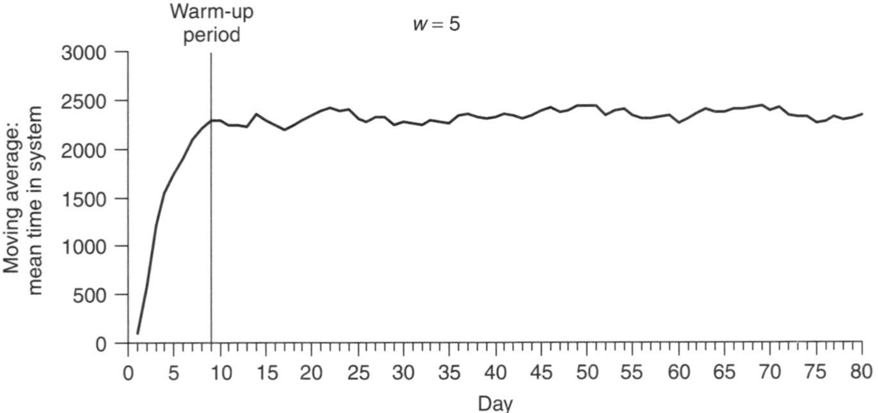

Figure 9.5 Welch's Method: Plot of Moving Average (Window = 5).

recommend the use of Welch's method, for instance, Law and Kelton (2000), Goldsman and Tokol (2000) and Alexopoulos and Seila (2000). It is, however, still a subjective method and the conclusion made no doubt depends on the experience of the user. A particular difficulty is in determining whether the line is 'smooth' and what is the appropriate window size. Finally, since the method is based on cumulative statistics (moving averages), some would argue that it is conservative and tends to overestimate the warm-up period (Gafarian *et al.* 1978; Wilson and Pritsker 1978; Pawlikowski 1990; Roth 1994).

Further issues in determining the warm-up period

Some further issues related to both methods described above need to be mentioned. First, when generating the time-series data the length of the simulation run should be much greater than the anticipated warm-up period. It is important to be sure that the output data have settled into a steady state beyond the warm-up period that is identified.

Secondly, when a model has more than one key response (as defined by the conceptual model, Section 6.2.3), the initial transient should be investigated for each one. The responses may settle to a steady state at different times in the simulation run. The warm-up period should be selected based on the response that takes longest to settle. In the case of the user help desk model, output statistics other than the mean time in the system are likely to be of interest, for instance, the number of completed enquiries and the utilization of staff. Each of these should be investigated for initialization bias.

Finally, in theory the warm-up period should be determined separately for every experimental scenario run with the model. Changes to the experimental factors may lead to quite a different initial transient. In practice, however, such analysis would be too burdensome. As a result, a warm-up period is often selected on the basis of an analysis of the base model alone. If this is the case, it is worth overestimating the warm-up period a little to give a margin of safety. Beyond this, it is worth checking that the warm-up period is still appropriate from time to time, particularly if there are significant revisions to the model. It is also worth checking the warm-up period for the runs from which final results are taken.

An Excel spreadsheet (Warmup.xls) is provided on the web site (www.wileyeurope.com/go/robinson) that implements both the time-series inspection method and Welch's method. The user may enter his/her own data, view a time-series and apply Welch's method with a chosen window size.

The warm-up period and simulation software

Most simulation packages provide a facility for specifying the warm-up period. At the point specified, the results that are automatically collected by the software are reset and the collection of output data starts again. The modeller must be aware that any responses defined outside of those automatically collected by the software also need to be reset. This may require some additional model coding.

9.5.2 Setting initial conditions

As stated in Section 9.3.1, an alternative to using a warm-up period is to set the initial conditions of the model. Typically this means placing work-in-progress, such as parts or customers, into the model at the start of a run.

There are two ways in which appropriate initial conditions can be identified. The first is to observe the real system. In some cases, data on the current state of the real system can be downloaded directly from automatic monitoring systems (this is a necessity if the model is to be used to aid real time decision-making). Obviously this approach can only be used if the real system exists. The second approach is to run the simulation model for a warm-up period and record the status of the model, using this to define the initial condition of the model for future runs.

Apart from defining the work-in-progress in a model, initial conditions can be set for the activities that take place in the model. If customers are only placed in queues at the start of a simulation run then there is an implicit assumption that there are no customers currently being served, that is, no activity is taking place. This is unlikely to be correct. Initial conditions could be set such that customers are placed into the activities as well as the queues and times are sampled to determine when the activities will be complete. A similar approach could be used for parts in machines in a manufacturing model. That said, unless the activity times are long relative to the length of the simulation run, the approximation that all activities start idle is probably reasonable (Law and Kelton 2000). It is often not worth the additional effort in data collection and model coding to include initial conditions for activities.

A third area for which initial conditions can be set is for equipment stoppages (breakdowns and changeovers). If specific initial conditions are not set then the default would effectively be to assume that all activities have just completed a stoppage at the start of the simulation run. The time (or number of operations) until the next stoppage would then be sampled as normal. This is quite unrealistic and so it is probably best avoided. A simple way to set initial conditions in this case is to randomize the time until the first stoppage for each activity. A sample is taken from the distribution normally used to determine time between failure, giving say a time of 123 minutes. A uniform distribution with a minimum of zero and a maximum of 123 is then used to determine the time until the first stoppage. A similar process could be used if the stoppages are based on the number of operations performed rather than time.

9.5.3 Mixed initial conditions and warm-up

In some cases it is useful to use a mix of a warm-up period and initial conditions. The aim is to reduce the length of the warm-up period required. For instance, in a simulation that contains a model of a warehouse (or any large inventory) it would take a long time for the warehouse inventory to grow to a realistic level if no initial condition is set. Therefore, it makes sense to set an initial condition for the inventory. However, unless initial conditions are set for the rest of the model, then a warm-up period is probably still required.

It is recommended that initial conditions are always set for stoppages as described in the last section, otherwise a very long warm-up period may be necessary. Most simulation software automatically set initial conditions for stoppages in one way or another and therefore the user need not be concerned with any additional coding. As a result, it is common practice to use, as a minimum, a mix of initial conditions for stoppages and a warm-up period for work-in-progress and activities.

9.5.4 Initial conditions versus warm-up

Both terminating and non-terminating simulations may start in an unrealistic state and so require initial conditions to be set and/or a warm-up period to be run. For non-terminating simulations the aim is to ensure that the initial transient is removed from the output data. For terminating simulations the aim is to ensure that the results are not biased by an inappropriate starting state. For many simulations of service operations this is a relatively simple matter, since the empty state is a realistic initial condition.

The main advantage of using initial conditions is that it saves time because a warm-up period does not have to be run. This time may become significant if a model needs to be run many times during experimentation. The key problems with setting initial conditions are specifying appropriate conditions and the time required to write the additional code to set those conditions.

Meanwhile, the use of a warm-up period means that time is saved in collecting data about the real system and in model coding. The disadvantages are that more time is required to run the simulation experiments and it can be difficult to determine the length of the warm-up period.

Common practice is to use initial conditions for terminating simulations and a warm-up period for non-terminating simulations, although not exclusively so. The decision on which to use depends very much on the context.

Finally, it should be noted that an alternative to having a warm-up period or initial conditions is simply to employ a very long run-length so the initialization bias becomes of little consequence to the results. The problem with this approach is the time required to perform the very long runs, which is likely to restrict the amount of experimentation possible. Indeed, it is not an approach that is used much in practice.

9.6 Selecting the Number of Replications and Run-Length

This section describes methods for determining the number of replications that should be performed with a model and for selecting an appropriate run-length for a long run. The aim in both cases is to ensure that enough output data have been obtained from the simulation in order to estimate the model performance with sufficient accuracy. As part of the discussion on multiple replications there is also a brief explanation of variance reduction. The section concludes with a discussion on the relative merits of using multiple replications and long runs.

9.6.1 Performing multiple replications

As stated in Section 9.3.2, a replication is a run of a simulation that uses specific streams of random numbers. Multiple replications are performed by changing the streams of random numbers that are referenced and re-running the simulation. The aim is to produce multiple samples in order to obtain a better estimate of mean performance. The question is: how many replications need to be performed? Three approaches to answering this question are now described: a rule of thumb, a graphical method and a confidence interval method.

A rule of thumb

Law and McComas (1990) recommend that at least three to five replications are performed. This simple rule of thumb is useful because it makes clear that model users should not rely on the results from a single replication. It does not, however, take into account the characteristics of a model's output. Models with output data that are very varied normally require more replications than models with a more stable output. Indeed, it is not unusual for a model to need more than five replications before a satisfactory estimate of performance is obtained. The two methods below address this issue by inspecting the output data from a model.

Graphical method

A simple graphical approach is to plot the cumulative mean of the output data from a series of replications. It is recommended that at least 10 replications are performed initially. As more replications are performed the graph should become a flat line (minimal variability and no upward or downward trend). The number of replications required is defined by the point at which the line becomes flat. Performing more replications beyond this point will only give a marginal improvement in the estimate of the mean value. If the line does not become flat, then more replications are needed.

The method is best illustrated with reference to an example. Table 9.4 shows the results for the mean time in the system from the user help desk model (Section 9.4). These have been obtained from 20 replications, each of 16 weeks' duration (80 days). In these results the output data from the first 8 days (the warm-up period determined by Welch's method in Section 9.5.1) have been deleted. Because the user help desk model is a non-terminating simulation, there is no natural end-point for a replication. In such cases, Law and Kelton (2000) recommend that the run-length should be "much" longer than the warm-up period, otherwise there may still be some bias in the output data. As a rule of thumb, Banks *et al.* (2001) recommend that the run-length is at least 10 times the length of the warm-up period. For this reason a run-length of 80 days is used in the example.

Figure 9.6 shows a graph of the cumulative mean data. The line becomes flat at around four replications, which is the minimum number recommended. Note that with fewer replications the mean result is an overestimate. Because there is some variation in the line beyond four replications, the model user might make a more conservative estimate that around 10 replications are required. This depends upon the level of certainty in the results needed and the time available for performing the experiments.

Table 9.4 Graphical Method: Results and Cumulative Mean from 20 Replications with the User Help Desk Model.

Replication	Mean time in system	Cumulative mean of mean time in system
1	2484.72	2484.72
2	2354.64	2419.68
3	2396.47	2411.94
4	2196.91	2358.18
5	2321.74	2350.89
6	2247.03	2333.58
7	2489.73	2355.89
8	2396.50	2360.97
9	2207.35	2343.90
10	2530.37	2362.55
11	2358.83	2362.21
12	2321.83	2358.84
13	2346.77	2357.91
14	2223.44	2348.31
15	2276.51	2343.52
16	2310.23	2341.44
17	2302.12	2339.13
18	2418.72	2343.55
19	2339.05	2343.31
20	2193.30	2335.81

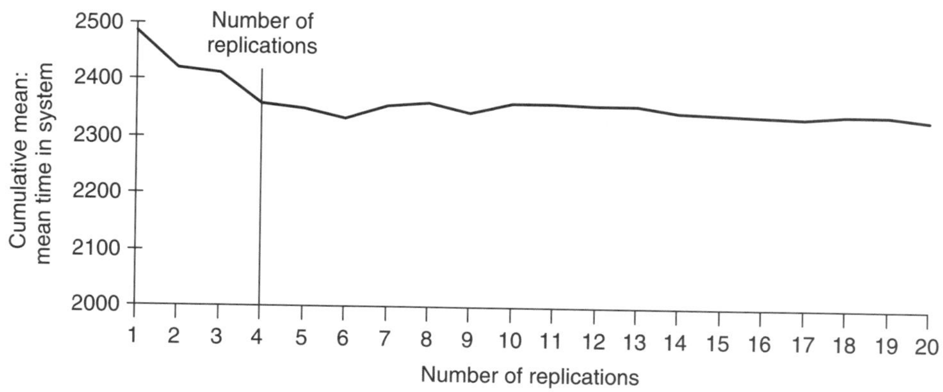

Figure 9.6 Graphical Method: Plot of Cumulative Mean of Mean Time in System.

Confidence interval method

A confidence interval is a statistical means for showing how accurately the mean average of a value is being estimated. The narrower the interval the more accurate the estimate is deemed to be. In general, the more sample data that are included in the interval, the narrower it becomes. When applying confidence intervals to simulation output, more replications (samples) are performed until the interval becomes sufficiently narrow to satisfy the model user (and the clients).

When analysing simulation output data a confidence interval is calculated as follows:

$$CI = \overline{X} \pm t_{n-1,\alpha/2} \frac{S}{\sqrt{n}}$$

where:

$\overline{X}$ = mean of the output data from the replications
S = standard deviation of the output data from the replications (see equation below)
n = number of replications
$t_{n-1,\alpha/2}$ = value from Student's t-distribution with $n-1$ degree of freedom and a significance level of $\alpha/2$

The formula for the standard deviation is:

$$S = \sqrt{\frac{\sum_{i=1}^{n} (X_i - \overline{X})^2}{n-1}}$$

where:

X_i = the result from replication i

A significance level (α) of 5% is often selected. This gives a 95% probability that the value of the true mean (obtained if the model is run for an infinite period) lies within the confidence interval (this is known as a 95% confidence interval). To the contrary, it implies that there is a 5% likelihood that the mean does not lie in the interval. Because the confidence interval provides an upper and a lower limit the significance level is divided by two ($\alpha/2$). So for a 5% significance level, values at 2.5% significance are selected from the Student's t-distribution. Values for the Student's t-distribution are given in Appendix 6. For those wanting a more detailed discussion on confidence intervals, they are described in most elementary and more advanced statistics books (e.g. Wisniewski 2002; Montgomery and Runger 1994).

Table 9.5 shows the 95% confidence intervals for the 20 replications performed with the user help desk model. Again, the data from the warm-up period (8 days) have been deleted from these figures. Figure 9.7 shows the cumulative mean (solid line) and confidence intervals (dashed lines) graphically. Notice how the confidence intervals generally narrow

Table 9.5 Confidence Interval Method: Results from 20 Replications with the User Help Desk Model.

Replication	Mean time in system	Cumulative mean	Standard deviation	95% Confidence interval Lower interval	Upper interval	% deviation
1	2484.72	2484.72	n/a	n/a	n/a	n/a
2	2354.64	2419.68	91.980	1593.27	3246.08	34.15%
3	2396.47	2411.94	66.406	2246.98	2576.90	6.84%
4	2196.91	2358.18	120.414	2166.58	2549.79	8.13%
5	2321.74	2350.89	105.547	2219.84	2481.95	5.57%
6	2247.03	2333.58	103.489	2224.98	2442.19	4.65%
7	2489.73	2355.89	111.392	2252.87	2458.91	4.37%
8	2396.50	2360.97	104.123	2273.92	2448.02	3.69%
9	2207.35	2343.90	110.039	2259.32	2428.48	3.61%
10	2530.37	2362.55	119.333	2277.18	2447.91	3.61%
11	2358.83	2362.21	113.215	2286.15	2438.27	3.22%
12	2321.83	2358.84	108.574	2289.86	2427.83	2.92%
13	2346.77	2357.91	104.005	2295.06	2420.76	2.67%
14	2223.44	2348.31	106.192	2287.00	2409.62	2.61%
15	2276.51	2343.52	103.995	2285.93	2401.11	2.46%
16	2310.23	2341.44	100.813	2287.72	2395.16	2.29%
17	2302.12	2339.13	98.076	2288.70	2389.55	2.16%
18	2418.72	2343.55	96.980	2295.32	2391.78	2.06%
19	2339.05	2343.31	94.253	2297.88	2388.74	1.94%
20	2193.30	2335.81	97.679	2290.10	2381.53	1.96%

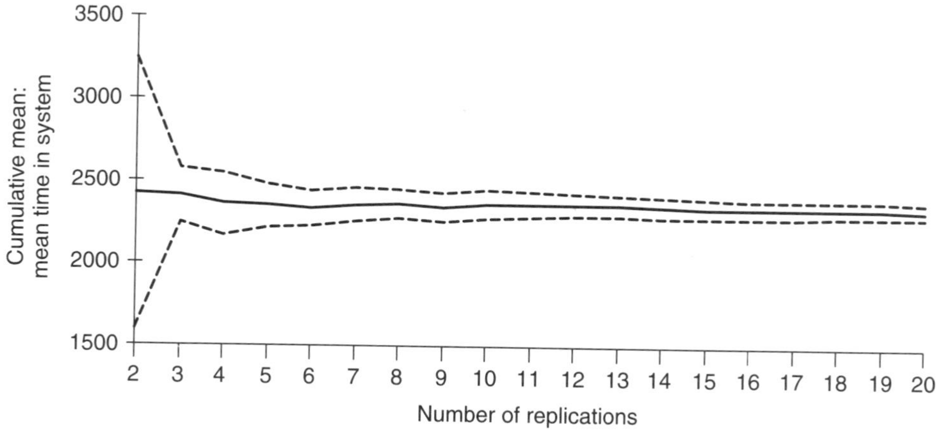

Figure 9.7 Confidence Interval Method: Plot of Cumulative Mean and 95% Confidence Intervals.

as more replications are performed. The final column in Table 9.5 shows the percentage deviation of the confidence interval on either side of the mean. This acts as a measure of the narrowness of the interval. The model user must determine what constitutes a sufficiently narrow interval. The number of replications is selected at the point where the interval reaches and remains below the desired level of deviation. In the example, if less than 10% deviation is seen as satisfactory, then three replications would suffice. If, however, 5% is required, then six replications need to be performed. It is not only important that the interval is sufficiently narrow, but also that the cumulative mean line is reasonably flat (as with the graphical method).

An alternative means for determining the number of replications required is to rearrange the confidence interval formula above so that n (the number of replications) is on the left-hand side, as follows:

$$n = \left(\frac{100St_{n-1,\alpha/2}}{d\overline{X}} \right)^2$$

where:

d = the percentage deviation of the confidence interval about the mean

By performing some initial replications (say five to ten) to estimate S and $\overline{X}$, the number of replications required to achieve a specified percentage deviation (d) can be determined. The accuracy of this method depends, of course, on the accuracy with which S and $\overline{X}$ are estimated from the initial replications. For more details on this approach see Banks *et al.* (2001) and Law and Kelton (2000).

Further issues in selecting the number of replications

For both the graphical and confidence interval method it is important to obtain output data from more replications than are required in order to be sure that the cumulative mean line has flattened and that the confidence interval remains narrow. If there is more than one key response (as defined by the conceptual model, Section 6.2.3), the number of replications should be selected on the basis of the response that requires the most replications.

Because the graphical and confidence interval methods use the output data from the model to draw a conclusion about the number of replications required, they are preferred to the rule of thumb. The confidence interval approach effectively builds on the graphical method by not only enabling an inspection of the cumulative mean line, but also providing a measure of accuracy. As a result, although it requires some more complex calculations, the recommended approach is to use confidence intervals.

As with the selection of a warm-up period, theoretically the number of replications required should be analysed for every experiment performed. In practice the number is determined from an analysis of the base model alone and then applied to all the experiments. As a result, it is worth overestimating the number of replications a little to give a margin of safety. It is also recommended that the number of replications is checked from time to time and especially for the final runs of the simulation.

An Excel spreadsheet (Replications.xls) is provided on the web site (www.wileyeurope.com/go/robinson) that calculates confidence intervals from a series of replications. The user can enter his/her own data and view the cumulative mean, confidence intervals and percentage deviation in both tabular and graphical format.

Multiple replications and simulation software

Most simulation packages provide facilities for performing multiple replications. In most software the replications can be carried out manually by specifying the streams that are to be referenced during a simulation run. Many packages have an experimentation option that allows the user to set up a series of replications that run automatically. In most cases the software also provide facilities for calculating confidence intervals.

9.6.2 Variance reduction (antithetic variates)

One of the aims of variance reduction is to obtain an accurate estimate of model performance while reducing the number of replications required. This is obviously beneficial in that it saves on experimentation time. There is much written about variance reduction and many methods have been proposed. In practice, however, it would appear that only two methods are in frequent use: common random numbers (described in Section 8.3.2) and antithetic variates.

Antithetic variates, proposed by Tocher (1963), are the inverse of the random numbers normally generated by a pseudo random number stream. A pseudo random number stream $\{u_1, u_2, u_3, \ldots\}$ is inverted to become the stream $\{1 - u_1, 1 - u_2, 1 - u_3, \ldots\}$. If samples are being taken from a normal distribution, the use of antithetic variates would have the effect of changing the sample given by the original variate to be on the equal and opposite side of the mean of the normal distribution (Table 9.6). In effect, the samples from the original

Table 9.6 Antithetic Variates and Sampling from a Normal Distribution (mean = 3, SD = 1).

Original samples			Antithetic samples		
Original variate	Normal (3, 1)	Difference from mean	Antithetic variate	Normal (3, 1)	Difference from mean
0.6290	3.33	0.33	0.3710	2.67	−0.33
0.5214	3.05	0.05	0.4786	2.95	−0.05
0.8658	4.11	1.11	0.1342	1.89	−1.11
0.7255	3.60	0.60	0.2745	2.40	−0.60
0.2839	2.43	−0.57	0.7161	3.57	0.57
0.1134	1.79	−1.21	0.8866	4.21	1.21
0.9881	5.26	2.26	0.0119	0.74	−2.26
0.2905	2.45	−0.55	0.7095	3.55	0.55
0.5714	3.18	0.18	0.4286	2.82	−0.18
0.2854	2.43	−0.57	0.7146	3.57	0.57

replication are reversed in the second (antithetic) replication. The theory is that the mean result from the two replications (original and antithetic) gives a better estimate of model performance than from two completely independent replications.

Although the use of antithetic variates is appealing, some words of caution must be given. First, the reversal effect occurs because the normal distribution is symmetrical. If the distribution is not symmetrical, the effect is less marked. For instance, Table 9.7 shows the use of antithetic variates with a negative exponential distribution. Of course, in simulation modelling most of the distributions used are not symmetrical.

Secondly, simulation models normally consist of many random events that interact in a complex fashion. Therefore, it is difficult to predict the effect of inverting the random streams and certainly it cannot be guaranteed that an equal and opposite result will be obtained. Indeed, Law and Kelton (2000) suggest that the use of antithetic variates may actually increase the variance in some circumstances, meaning that more replications are required to obtain a good estimate of model performance.

A third issue is that, although the use of antithetic variates may enable the mean performance of the model to be estimated from fewer replications, the approach by nature restricts the variance in the results. The results cannot, therefore, be used fully to understand the likely spread of model performance (e.g. the standard deviation).

In practice, it is probably reasonable to test the effect of using a mix of original and antithetic variates. If it reduces the number of replications required for a particular model then it is worth continuing to use the approach. If it does not, then all that is lost is the time taken to test the idea. Most simulation software provide a flag for changing random streams to antithetic variates.

For those wishing to investigate the subject of variance reduction further, useful references to give a starting point are Kleijnen and van Groenendaal (1992), Paul and Balmer (1993), Pidd (1998) and Law and Kelton (2000).

Table 9.7 Antithetic Variates and Sampling from a Negative Exponential Distribution (mean = 1).

Original samples			Antithetic samples		
Original variate	Exponential (1)	Difference from mean	Antithetic variate	Exponential (1)	Difference from mean
0.6290	0.99	−0.01	0.3710	0.46	−0.54
0.5214	0.74	−0.26	0.4786	0.65	−0.35
0.8658	2.01	1.01	0.1342	0.14	−0.86
0.7255	1.29	0.29	0.2745	0.32	−0.68
0.2839	0.33	−0.67	0.7161	1.26	0.26
0.1134	0.12	−0.88	0.8866	2.18	1.18
0.9881	4.43	3.43	0.0119	0.01	−0.99
0.2905	0.34	−0.66	0.7095	1.24	0.24
0.5714	0.85	−0.15	0.4286	0.56	−0.44
0.2854	0.34	−0.66	0.7146	1.25	0.25

9.6.3 Performing a single long run

If, instead of using multiple replications, a single long run is to be performed an appropriate length of run needs to be determined. Robinson (1995) describes a graphical method for determining the run-length of a single long run with the aim of ensuring that the results are sufficiently accurate.

Initially, three replications are performed with the model. These should be run for longer than the anticipated run-length. An initial estimate could be made using Banks *et al.*'s (2001) rule of thumb that the run-length should be at least 10 times the length of the warm-up period (Section 9.6.1). Time-series data are generated for the key output data and then cumulative means are calculated for each of the replications. The cumulative means are plotted on a graph. As the run-length increases, it is expected that the cumulative means of the three replications will converge. If the replications were run for an infinite period, they would produce exactly the same result! The level of convergence is calculated as follows:

$$C_i = \frac{Max(\overline{Y}_{i1}, \overline{Y}_{i2}, \overline{Y}_{i3}) - Min(\overline{Y}_{i1}, \overline{Y}_{i2}, \overline{Y}_{i3})}{Min(\overline{Y}_{i1}, \overline{Y}_{i2}, \overline{Y}_{i3})}$$

where:

C_i = convergence at period i
$\overline{Y}_{ij}$ = cumulative mean of output data at period i for replication j

The run-length is selected as the point where the convergence is seen as acceptable. This might typically be at a level of less than 5%. Because of variations in the output data the convergence may temporarily increase with a longer run, particularly when there are only a few observations. It is important, therefore, that the convergence value is not only within an acceptable level, but that it is also fairly steady at the selected run-length. If an acceptable and steady value is not obtained with the output data generated, the run-length should be increased.

It is also recommended that histograms are drawn and compared for the output data from each of the replications. If the model run is sufficiently long the distribution of the output data, as well as the mean, should be reasonably similar. It is expected, however, that the distributions will take longer to converge than the means, and so a very close correspondence is not expected.

Again, the method is illustrated with reference to the user help desk example (Section 9.4). Figure 9.8 shows a graph of the cumulative means of the mean time in the system for 500 days of simulation (following a warm-up period of 8 days). It was found that a run-length of 80 days is insufficient to obtain a convergence that is consistently less than 5%. The first data point is not displayed, since the lines are very divergent and the scale becomes unreadable.

Table 9.8 shows the data for the mean time in the system, the cumulative means and the convergence for days 1 to 10, 241 to 250 and 491 to 500. The convergence is below 5% as early as day 6, but it does not remain consistently below this level until day 246. As the run-length is increased the convergence improves and it is at about the 2% level at day 500.

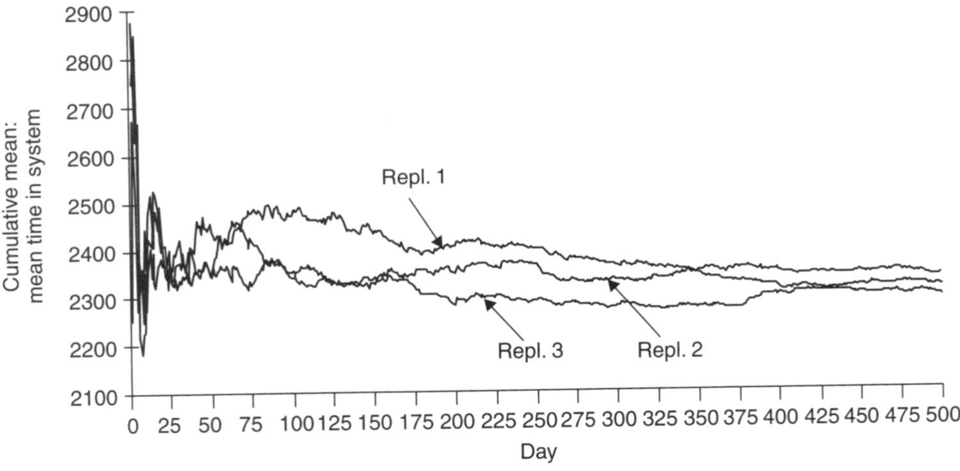

Figure 9.8 Run-Length Selection: Cumulative Means from Three Replications with the User Help Desk Model.

A longer run would be required, however, to confirm that the convergence remains below this level.

Since a run-length of about 250 days gives a convergence of below 5%, the distributions of the output data are now compared for this number of days. Figure 9.9 shows histograms of the daily mean time in the system for the three replications. These include the data from the first 250 days. The histograms are reasonably similar with the exception of the slightly higher frequency in the 1500 to 2000 range for replication 3. It is concluded that a run-length of 250 days is reasonable.

Having selected a run-length, then only one replication needs to be performed during further experimentation. That said, as with the selection of a warm-up period and the number of replications, changes to the model that are made during experimentation may affect the run-length required. Therefore, the run-length should be checked from time to time by applying the method above. This is particularly necessary for the final results.

Further issues in selecting the run-length

The convergence figure should not be confused with a confidence interval. The former is an indicative measure, the latter has a specific statistical meaning. Confidence intervals can be calculated from one long run, but this is more difficult than with independent replications because there are likely to be dependencies in the data; standard confidence interval calculations assume the samples are independent. The batch means method for calculating confidence intervals from a single long run is described in Section 10.3.1. Note that this method could also be applied as a statistical procedure for determining the run-length based on the width of the confidence interval required.

Table 9.8 Run-Length Selection: Results from Three Replications with the User Help Desk Model.

	Replication 1		Replication 2		Replication 3		
Day	Mean time in system	Cumulative mean	Mean time in system	Cumulative mean	Mean time in system	Cumulative mean	Convergence
1	1986.58	1986.58	3628.20	3628.20	2958.04	2958.04	82.64%
2	2521.63	2254.11	2122.12	2875.16	2537.90	2747.97	27.55%
3	3509.34	2672.52	2138.38	2629.57	3052.64	2849.53	8.36%
4	1984.15	2500.43	2769.31	2664.50	2121.98	2667.64	6.69%
5	1368.02	2273.94	2680.11	2667.62	1423.61	2418.83	17.31%
6	3148.23	2419.66	509.45	2307.93	2189.01	2380.53	4.84%
7	1012.93	2218.70	2680.70	2361.18	1960.34	2320.50	6.42%
8	1936.55	2183.43	2017.57	2318.23	1757.50	2250.13	6.17%
9	2563.83	2225.70	3443.61	2443.27	3164.49	2351.72	9.78%
10	2259.49	2229.08	1620.30	2360.98	1594.72	2276.02	5.92%
.	.	.	.	.	.	.	.
.	.	.	.	.	.	.	.
.	.	.	.	.	.	.	.
241	2234.69	2406.46	1995.13	2371.68	1605.38	2287.75	5.19%
242	2021.38	2404.87	1664.38	2368.76	2448.19	2288.41	5.09%
243	2582.38	2405.60	1770.81	2366.29	2224.63	2288.15	5.13%
244	1983.25	2403.87	2320.38	2366.11	1791.38	2286.11	5.15%
245	2000.06	2402.22	3064.00	2368.96	1881.00	2284.46	5.15%
246	1799.31	2399.77	1396.81	2365.00	2602.44	2285.75	4.99%
247	2054.63	2398.37	2931.25	2367.30	2327.56	2285.92	4.92%
248	3361.63	2402.26	1809.63	2365.05	3037.44	2288.95	4.95%
249	1597.56	2399.02	2125.88	2364.09	2055.13	2288.01	4.85%
250	2988.13	2401.38	2150.06	2363.23	2365.63	2288.32	4.94%
.	.	.	.	.	.	.	.
.	.	.	.	.	.	.	.
.	.	.	.	.	.	.	.
491	1744.63	2339.76	1823.63	2317.07	1912.25	2298.90	1.78%
492	1574.75	2338.20	1308.13	2315.02	2075.00	2298.45	1.73%
493	2160.25	2337.84	2620.13	2315.64	2428.13	2298.71	1.70%
494	728.75	2334.59	1982.00	2314.96	1955.50	2298.02	1.59%
495	2359.38	2334.64	2393.38	2315.12	2523.88	2298.47	1.57%
496	2508.38	2334.99	1766.88	2314.02	1289.75	2296.44	1.68%
497	2249.63	2334.81	3036.00	2315.47	1829.00	2295.50	1.71%
498	1558.38	2333.26	2264.25	2315.37	1551.50	2294.00	1.71%
499	2811.38	2334.21	1895.25	2314.52	2084.63	2293.58	1.77%
500	4926.13	2339.40	1998.50	2313.89	1876.00	2292.75	2.03%

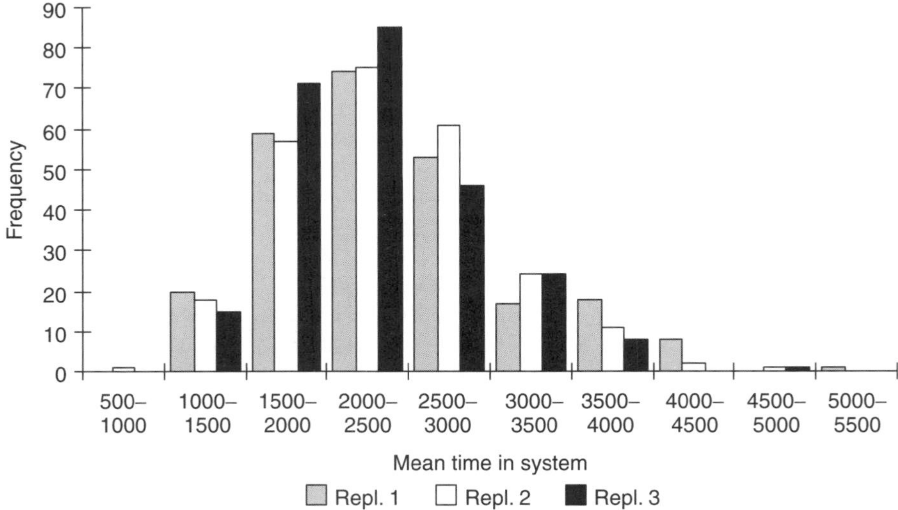

Figure 9.9 Run-Length Selection: Histograms of Results from Three Replications with the User Help Desk Model (250 Observations per Replication).

If there is more than one key response (as defined by the conceptual model, Section 6.2.3), the run-length should be selected on the basis of the response that requires the longest run. So for the user help desk model, other output data should be investigated such as the number of completed enquiries and the utilization of staff.

The discussion above describes the run-length in terms of time. There are occasions on which the run-length might be measured in the number of entities processed, for instance, the number of customers entering or leaving a bank. If this is the case, the same procedures can still be adopted for determining the warm-up period, number of replications and run-length. Rather than drawing time-series, however, the number of entities would be plotted on the *x*-axis of the graphs.

An Excel spreadsheet (Run Length.xls) is provided on the web site (www.wileyeurope.com/go/robinson) that calculates the cumulative means and convergence based on three replications. The user can enter his/her own data and view the results in both tabular and graphical format (time-series and histograms).

9.6.4 Multiple replications versus long runs

For terminating simulations there is no option but to perform multiple replications. For non-terminating simulations, such as the user help desk model, there is an option. The question is whether it is better to perform multiple replications or long runs.

The advantage of performing multiple replications is that confidence intervals can easily be calculated, and they are an important measure of accuracy for simulation results. The disadvantage of multiple replications is that if there is a warm-up period, it needs to be run for every replication that is performed. This wastes valuable experimentation time.

On the other hand, with long runs, the warm-up period is only run once for each experimental scenario. This saves time. Another advantage of long runs is that the results probably appear more intuitive to the model user and the clients, since most operations run week-on-week and they are not constantly returned to the same starting state as with multiple replications. It is not so easy, however, to calculate confidence intervals from a single time-series, since the data are likely to be correlated (Section 10.3.1).

The choice of which approach to use depends upon their relative merits within the context of the simulation study. Is experimentation time very pressured? Are confidence intervals a vital measure of accuracy? Is the intuitive appeal of long runs of particular importance? Ultimately the best approach is to perform multiple replications with long runs. The more output data that can be obtained, the larger the sample, and so the more certainty there can be in the accuracy of the results. Of course, time limitations normally dictate a more economical approach.

9.7 Conclusion

In summary, there are a series of decisions that need to be taken when performing simulation experiments. These are as follows:

- Determine the nature of the simulation model: terminating or non-terminating.
- Determine the nature of the simulation model output: transient or steady-state (steady-state cycle, shifting steady-state).
- Determine how to deal with initialization bias: warm-up period, initial conditions or mixed warm-up and initial conditions. This is an issue for both terminating and non-terminating simulations.
- Determine the amount of output data required: multiple replications or long runs. For terminating simulations the only option is to perform multiple replications. Either approach can be used for non-terminating models.

In this chapter, methods for determining the length of the warm-up period, the number of replications and the length of a long run are described. These methods are further illustrated by the Wardeon Cinema and Panorama Televisions case studies in Appendix 1 (Section A1.6.1) and Appendix 2 (Section A2.6.1) respectively. Now our attention turns to the second issue in experimentation, searching the solution space.

Exercises

E9.1 For the following simulation models identify the expected type of model (terminating or non-terminating) and the nature of the simulation output (transient, steady-state, steady-state cycle).

a) A model of a refrigerator manufacturing plant that aims to determine plant throughput.

b) A model of a chemical plant that tests the production schedule for the next week.
c) A model of a supermarket checkout that aims to determine customer service levels over a typical day.
d) A model of a supermarket checkout that aims to determine customer service levels during a busy period.
e) A model of a hospital emergency unit that aims to determine service levels for patients.

E9.2 The time-series graphs below show typical simulation output. For each graph identify the type of model (terminating or non-terminating) and the nature of the simulation output (transient, steady-state, steady-state cycle).

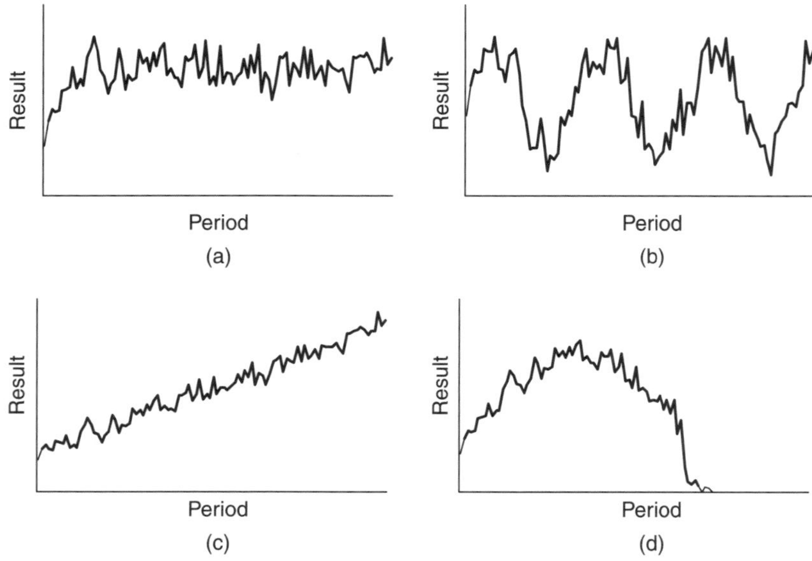

E9.3 Investigate the effect of changing the pseudo random number streams on the results obtained from a simulation model. For instance, experiment with the bank model (described in Chapter 6, Exercise E6.1), or the Wardeon Cinema (Appendix A1.2.1) and Panorama Televisions (Appendix A2.2.1) models.

E9.4 Table 9.9 shows the results obtained for daily throughput from a non-terminating simulation of a manufacturing facility. Five replications have been performed with the model. The results shown are the mean average of the five replications. Determine the warm-up period using:

a) The time-series inspection method
b) Welch's method

Table 9.9 Results from 80 Days of Simulation with a Manufacturing Model (Mean of Five Replications).

Day	Mean t'put	Day	Mean t'put	Day	Mean t'put	Day	Mean t'put
1	0.00	21	198.00	41	174.60	61	184.20
2	0.00	22	217.20	42	157.80	62	202.80
3	40.80	23	210.00	43	150.00	63	238.80
4	208.20	24	190.80	44	160.80	64	250.20
5	195.00	25	130.80	45	124.80	65	202.20
6	181.20	26	145.80	46	177.60	66	181.80
7	156.00	27	184.80	47	195.60	67	135.60
8	148.80	28	193.20	48	215.40	68	158.40
9	101.40	29	139.80	49	226.80	69	117.00
10	124.80	30	218.40	50	205.20	70	169.20
11	102.00	31	210.00	51	208.80	71	237.60
12	195.00	32	203.40	52	198.60	72	220.80
13	192.60	33	213.00	53	183.00	73	214.20
14	190.80	34	238.80	54	190.80	74	207.60
15	209.40	35	234.00	55	228.60	75	176.40
16	214.20	36	205.20	56	227.40	76	191.40
17	202.20	37	180.60	57	222.00	77	172.80
18	189.60	38	136.20	58	230.40	78	182.40
19	196.20	39	231.00	59	216.60	79	190.80
20	219.00	40	214.20	60	208.20	80	174.00

Compare the results obtained using the two methods.
Note: these data are available in a spreadsheet (Exercise9.xls) on the web site (www.wileyeurope.com/go/robinson).

E9.5 Table 9.10 shows the results (mean daily throughput) obtained from 30 replications with the manufacturing model in Exercise E9.4. Each replication has been run for a period of 100 days after the warm-up period, which is deleted from the data. Determine the number of replications that should be performed with the model using:

a) The graphical method.
b) The confidence interval method (assume the client wishes to obtain less than 10% deviation and then less than 5% deviation in the confidence interval from the mean).

Note: these data are available in a spreadsheet (Exercise9.xls) on the web site (www.wileyeurope.com/go/robinson).

E9.6 Artificial time-series data can be created using formula such as:

$$X_t = aX_{t-1} + \text{Normal}(mean = b, SD = b/5)$$

Table 9.10 Results from 30 Replications with a Manufacturing Model (100 Days' Data).

Repl.	Mean daily t'put	Repl.	Mean daily t'put	Repl.	Mean daily t'put
1	179.22	11	190.32	21	206.67
2	202.20	12	171.27	22	189.93
3	199.41	13	182.34	23	140.85
4	156.72	14	201.42	24	194.91
5	199.14	15	203.34	25	182.85
6	183.3	16	188.79	26	201.54
7	146.25	17	203.22	27	202.32
8	172.74	18	184.38	28	173.88
9	160.20	19	184.47	29	187.86
10	148.77	20	196.89	30	164.04

These series include an initial transient and variability. Using the formula above generate 10 series of data, each with 500 observations, in a spreadsheet. Set $a = 0.9$, $b = 1$ and the initial value of X (X_0) $= 0.1$. Determine the warm-up period, number of replications and the run-length for a single long run. Hint: use the "NORMINV" function in Excel to obtain samples from the normal distribution.

Note: an example of these data is available in a spreadsheet (Exercise9.xls) on the web site (www.wileyeurope.com/go/robinson).

E9.7 Try alternative values for the constants in the formula in Exercise E9.6 and see what effect it has on the warm-up period, number of replications and run-length required.

E9.8 Determine the warm-up period and number of replications required with the bank model developed from the case described in Exercise E6.1 (Chapter 6).

E9.9 What are the warm-up, replications and run-length requirements for the Wardeon Cinema model (Appendix 1: Section A1.2.1)?

E9.10 What are the warm-up, replications and run-length requirements for the Panorama Televisions model (Appendix 2: Section A2.2.1)?

E9.11 Test the effect of using antithetic variates with a simulation model. For instance, use the Wardeon Cinema or Panorama Televisions models. What is the effect on the standard deviation of the results obtained from multiple replications? Are fewer replications required to obtain a good estimate of mean performance?

E9.12 Section 9.6.2 discusses the concept of variance reduction. Two methods of variance reduction are introduced in the book, common random numbers (Section 8.3.2) and antithetic variates (Section 9.6.2). A number of other methods of variance reduction have been proposed. Investigate the theory and application of variance reduction in more depth. What approaches are available? When might they be used? What are their strengths and weaknesses? Use the references in Section 9.6.2 as a starting point.

References

Alexopoulos, C. and Seila, A.F. (2000) "Output analysis for simulations". *Proceedings of the 2000 Winter Simulation Conference* (Joines, J.A. Barton, R.R. Kang K. and Fishwick, P.A., eds). Piscataway, NJ, IEEE, pp. 101–108.

Banks, J., Carson, J.S., Nelson, B.L. and Nicol, D.M. (2001) *Discrete-Event System Simulation*, 3rd edn. Upper Saddle River, NJ: Prentice Hall.

Fishman, G.S. (1971) "Estimating sample size in computer simulation experiments". *Management Science*, 18(1), 21–37.

Fishman, G.S. (1973) *Concepts and Methods in Discrete Event Digital Simulation*. New York: Wiley.

Gafarian, A.V., Ancker, C.J. and Morisaku, T. (1978) "Evaluation of commonly used rules for detecting steady-state in computer simulation. *Naval Research Logistics Quarterly*, 25, 511–529.

Goldsman, D., Schruben, L.W. and Swain, J.J. (1994) "Tests for transient means in simulation time series". *Naval Research Logistics Quarterly*, 41, 171–187.

Goldsman, D. and Tokol, G. (2000) "Output analysis procedures for computer simulation". *Proceedings of the 2000 Winter Simulation Conference* (Joines, J.A. Barton, R.R. Kang K. and Fishwick, P.A., eds). Piscataway, NJ, IEEE, pp. 39–45.

Gordon, G. (1969) *System Simulation*. Upper Saddle River, NJ: Prentice-Hall.

Jackway, P.T. and deSilva, B.S. (1992) "A methodology for initialization bias reduction in computer simulation output". *Asia-Pacific Journal of Operational Research*, 9, 87–100.

Kelton W.D. and Law, A.M. (1983) "A new approach for dealing with the startup problem in discrete event simulation". *Naval Research Logistics Quarterly*, 30, 641–658.

Kleijnen, J.P.C. and van Groenendaal, W. (1992) *Simulation: A Statistical Perspective*. Chichester, UK: Wiley.

Law, A. and McComas, M. (1990) "Secrets of successful simulation studies". *Industrial Engineering*, 22(5), 47–72.

Law, A.M. and Kelton, W.D. (2000) *Simulation Modeling and Analysis*, 3rd edn. New York: McGraw-Hill.

Montgomery, D.C. and Runger, G.C. (1994) *Applied Statistics and Probability for Engineers*. New York: Wiley.

Nelson, B.L. (1992) "Statistical analysis of simulation results". *The Handbook of Industrial Engineering*, 2nd edn (Salvendy, G., ed.). New York: Wiley, pp. 2567–2593.

Paul, R.J. and Balmer, D.W. (1993) *Simulation Modelling*. Lund, Sweden: Chartwell Bratt.

Pawlikowski, K. (1990) "Steady-state simulation of queuing processes: a survey of problems and solutions". *ACM Computing Surveys*, 22(2), 123–170.

Pidd, M. (1998) *Computer Simulation in Management Science*, 4th edn. Chichester, UK: Wiley.

Robinson, S. (1995) "An heuristic technique for selecting the run-length of non-terminating steady-state simulations". *Simulation* 65(3), pp. 170–179.

Robinson, S. (2002) "A statistical process control approach for estimating the warm-up period". *Proceedings of the 2002 Winter Simulation Conference* (Yucesan, E., Chen, C.-H., Snowden, S.L. and Charnes, J.M., eds). Piscataway, NJ: IEEE. pp. 439–446.

Robinson, S., Brooks, R.J. and Lewis, C.D. (2002) "Detecting shifts in the mean of a simulation output process". *Journal of the Operational Research Society*, 53(5), 559–573.

Roth, E. (1994) "The relaxation time heuristic for the initial transient problem in M/M/*k* queueing systems". *European Journal of Operational Research*, 72, 376–386.

Schruben, L.W. (1982) "Detecting initialization bias in simulation output". *Operations Research*, 30(3), 569–590.

Schruben, L.W., Singh, H. and Tierney, L. (1983) "Optimal tests for initialization bias in simulation output". *Operations Research*, 31(6), 1167–1178.

Tocher, K.D. (1963) *The Art of Simulation*. London: The English Universities Press.

Vassilacopoulos, G. (1989) "Testing for initialization bias in simulation output". *Simulation*, 52(4), 151–153.

Welch, P. (1983) "The statistical analysis of simulation results. In *The Computer Performance Modeling Handbook* (Lavenberg, S., ed.). New York: Academic Press, pp. 268–328.

White, K.P. Jr. (1997) "An effective truncation heuristic for bias reduction in simulation output". *Simulation*, 69(6), 323–334.

White, K.P. and Spratt, S.C. (2000) "A comparison of five steady-state truncation heuristics for simulation". *Proceedings of the 2000 Winter Simulation Conference* (Joines, J.A. Barton, R.R. Kang K. and Fishwick, P.A., eds). Piscataway, NJ: IEEE, pp. 755–760.

Wilson, J.R. and Pritsker, A.B. (1978) "A survey of research on the simulation startup problem". *Simulation*, 31, 55–59.

Wisniewski, M. (2002) *Quantitative Methods for Decision Makers*, 3rd edn. London: Prentice Hall.

Yucesan, E. (1993) "Randomization tests for initialization bias in simulation output". *Naval Research Logistics Quarterly*, 40, 643–663.

EXPERIMENTATION: SEARCHING THE SOLUTION SPACE

10

10.1 Introduction

The last chapter discusses how accurate results can be obtained when running a single experimental scenario. In this chapter we move on to discuss the selection and comparison of alternative scenarios in experimentation. This involves a search for a solution to the real world problem being addressed by the simulation study. This might mean finding the best scenario or just one that satisfies the clients' requirements. On some occasions it may be no more than developing a better understanding of the real system.

This process is described as searching the solution space. The solution space is the total range of conditions under which the model might be run. Figure 10.1 shows the minimum and maximum values that each experimental factor (five in this example) in a simulation model might take. The solution space is the region that represents all possible combinations of values of the experimental factors. This space, of course, may be very large, in which case looking for a good or optimal scenario is a little like "looking for a needle in a haystack!" As a result, it is important to have efficient procedures for searching the solution space.

The purpose of this chapter is to discuss procedures for searching the solution space and the means by which alternative scenarios can be compared. The chapter starts by describing the nature of simulation experimentation. This is described in terms of the way in which simulations are run and the means by which scenarios for experimentation are identified. Following this, there is a discussion on how the results from a simulation experiment should be analysed. This provides an important foundation for being able to compare alternative scenarios when searching the solution space. The discussion then moves on to cover three key areas in relation to searching the solution space:

- The comparison of results from two or more different scenarios.
- Methods for searching the solution space, covering informal methods, experimental design, metamodelling and optimization.
- Sensitivity analysis.

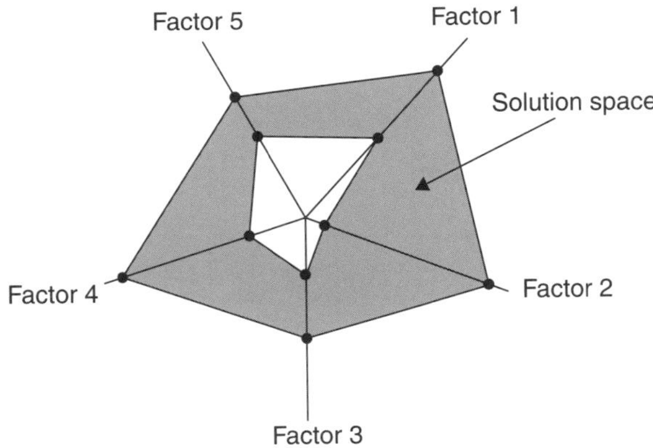

Figure 10.1 Simulation Experimentation: The Solution Space.

Two specific terms are used throughout the chapter. The first is the idea of a *level* for an experimental factor. For quantitative experimental factors (e.g. cycle times, arrival rates) the level is the value of the factor, for qualitative factors (e.g. rules) the level is interpreted as an option. Some quantitative factors can only take on specific discrete values (e.g. employ three, four or five staff) while others are continuous variables (e.g. a cycle time of between 15 and 25 minutes). The second term, *scenario*, is a run of the simulation under a specific set of conditions, that is, levels set for experimental factors. A scenario can be thought of as a specific factor/level combination. By changing the level of one or more experimental factors, the scenario is changed.

It is assumed throughout the chapter that the model user has dealt with the issues of initialization bias (Section 9.5), performing multiple replications and ensuring simulation runs are of sufficient length (Section 9.6). Although much of the discussion centres on a single response, it must be remembered that there may be more than one response of interest. The analyses should, therefore, be repeated for, or extended to, every key response. The reader is also reminded that in experimentation we are learning about the performance of the model and using that understanding to reflect upon the performance of the real system. Determining how well the model performance reflects the real world is an issue for verification and validation (Chapter 12).

Experimentation is an area in which there is a great deal of mathematical and statistical theory. In practice, however, much simulation experimentation is performed in a fairly informal manner. Because much of the benefit in simulation studies comes from developing a better understanding (conceptual learning) rather than obtaining "correct" results (instrumental learning), in many situations informal experimentation is probably satisfactory. That said, the use of rigorous experimental methods should provide a more in-depth understanding of a model's performance as well as instrumental learning. These methods, therefore, should not be ignored. Indeed, their lack of use probably owes more to a lack of understanding among model users than to a lack of utility. This chapter attempts to balance the practical and the theoretical by focusing on the practical issues in experimentation and then describing relevant statistical methods. Meanwhile, references are given throughout that provide a starting point for those wishing to investigate the theory of experimentation further.

10.2 The Nature of Simulation Experimentation

Simulation experiments can take on various forms. These are described here as two pairs: interactive and batch experimentation, and comparing alternatives and search experimentation. The first pair describes the means by which the simulation runs are performed. The second pair describes the means by which the scenarios for experimentation are determined.

10.2.1 Interactive and batch experimentation

Interactive experimentation involves watching the simulation run and making changes to the model to see the effect. For instance, when watching the simulation, the model user might notice a bottleneck in one area of the model. The capacity of that area could be increased (e.g. faster cycle, more machines) and the model run continued to see the effect of such a change. The aim is to develop an understanding of the model (and thereby the real system), the key problem areas and identify potential solutions. Such an approach is very useful for facilitating group decision-making (Section 13.3).

Care must be taken, however, not to let interactive experiments carry too much weight in forming an understanding of the system and opinions about solutions to problems. Because the simulation is being run in front of the user, the run-length is likely to be relatively short. As such, the user probably sees only a small snapshot of potential circumstances and the results are unlikely to be statistically significant. Such experimentation is useful for gaining understanding and for identifying potential improvements, but these should always be tested by more thorough (batch) experimentation, in order to obtain results that have statistical significance.

Batch experiments are performed by setting the experimental factors and leaving the model to run for a predefined run-length (or to a specific event) and for a set number of replications. This requires no interaction from the model user and so the display is normally switched off. This also improves the run-speed of the model. The aim is to run the simulation for sufficient time to obtain statistically significant results. The run-length (including a warm-up period) and the number of replications are determined using methods such as those described in Chapter 9. The majority of the discussion in this chapter centres on batch experimentation.

Simulation software have automatic facilities for performing batch experiments. Also, it is often possible to set up a predefined series of experimental scenarios that can be left to run automatically. This is useful since a number of experiments can be performed overnight or over a weekend. The software should also provide facilities for storing the results from each run, and possibly the status of the model at the end of a run, so further analysis can be performed.

10.2.2 Comparing alternatives and search experimentation

When *comparing alternatives* there are a limited number of scenarios to be compared. These scenarios are often known at the start of the simulation study, for instance, there may be three alternative factory layouts. On other occasions the scenarios emerge as the simulation study progresses. The number of scenarios (the solution space) is often small, although there are occasions when a large number exist.

Meanwhile, in *search experimentation* there are no predefined scenarios. Instead, one or more experimental factors are varied until a target or optimum level is reached. For instance, the aim might be to reach a target throughput or to achieve an optimum level of customer service by balancing the cost of resources with the cost of lost custom. For this type of experimentation there either needs to be a clearly defined target, normally expressed in the objectives of the project, or a well defined function (e.g. cost or profit) to be optimized.

Comparing alternatives and search experimentation are not mutually exclusive. Indeed, a simulation study might involve some comparison of predefined alternatives and also some searching for a target or optimum. The comparison of alternatives is discussed in more detail in Section 10.4 and search experimentation in Section 10.5.

The problem of combinations

In performing simulation experiments it is quite common to find that there are a large number of scenarios to be considered (the solution space is large). This is especially true for search experimentation, but can also be true when comparing alternatives. Take, for instance, a simulation study of a manufacturing plant in which there are four experimental factors. Each factor can be given a number of different levels as follows:

- Factor 1 cycle times: −20%, −10%, as is, +10%, +20% (5 levels)
- Factor 2 buffer sizes: −50%, −25%, as is, +25%, +50% (5 levels)
- Factor 3 machine efficiency: 85%, 90%, 95% (3 levels)
- Factor 4 number of maintenance operators: 4, 5, 6, 7 (4 levels)

In total there are 300 scenarios ($5 \times 5 \times 3 \times 4$). If five replications are performed with each scenario and each replication takes 30 minutes to run, then full experimentation would require 750 hours. That is about four and a half weeks! Bearing in mind that for many simulation studies these figures, particularly for total scenarios, would be quite conservative, it is obvious that full experimentation is often not possible. There are simply too many combinations of experimental factors and levels. Further to this, the situation is often made worse because the experimental factors do not take on discrete levels as suggested above, but they are in fact continuous variables. One of the key issues in (search) experimentation is reducing the number of scenarios to a manageable level. This is an issue that is discussed in Section 10.5.

10.3 Analysis of Results from a Single Scenario

Simulation experiments are performed in order to determine the performance of the model, which is measured by the values of the responses. Section 6.2.3 discusses how appropriate responses are selected for a model. For each response two measures are generally of interest: the average (or point estimate) and the variability.

10.3.1 Point estimates

The average level of a response is most commonly measured by its mean. If a simulation could be run for an infinite time, then it would be possible to obtain an exact value of the mean for each response. Since this is not possible, we must rely upon simulation runs that provide a sample of results. Section 9.6 describes methods for determining the size of the sample. Because simulation experiments provide only a sample of output data it is important that a confidence interval for each mean is reported. A confidence interval provides information on the range within which the population mean (obtained from an infinite run-length) is expected to lie. It is, therefore, the main method for reporting the mean in simulation studies.

Section 9.6.1 describes how a confidence interval can be calculated when multiple replications are being performed. This approach cannot be used with output data from a single long run, however, since it is likely that the data are correlated (confidence intervals rely on the assumption that the samples are independent). Take, for instance, a simulation of a manufacturing plant where the output statistic of interest is daily throughput. The finishing state of the model at the end of any day is likely to affect the throughput in the next day. For example, there may be a machine failure that continues from one day to the next. The throughput on both days will be affected by the failure and therefore there is a correlation between the results for the 2 days. Such problems are even more acute for queuing statistics. The waiting time of a customer is highly correlated to the waiting time of the customer in front. Note also that the confidence interval formula in Section 9.6.1 cannot be used with a single long run because the number of replications (n) is one. The calculation of the standard deviation would, therefore, require a division by zero.

Because single long runs have a number of advantages over performing multiple replications, most notably time saving (Section 9.6.4), it would be useful to be able to construct a confidence interval for the output data. A number of methods have been proposed for achieving this:

- Batch means method
- Overlapping batch means method
- Regenerative method
- Standardized time-series method
- Spectral estimation method
- Autoregressive method

Only the batch means method is described here. For an introduction to the other methods see Alexopoulos and Seila (1998) and Law and Kelton (2000).

Batch means methods for constructing confidence intervals from a single run

In the batch means method the time-series of output data $(Y_1, Y_2, \ldots, Y_n)$ is divided into k batches of length b, such that the mean of each batch is calculated as follows:

$$\overline{Y}_i(b) = \frac{1}{b}\sum_{j=1}^{b} Y_{(i-1)b+j}$$

where:

$$\overline{Y}_i(b) = \text{batch means of length } b$$

Figure 10.2 shows the concept diagrammatically. Obviously, data from the initial transient should be deleted from the time-series.

The idea is that the batches of data are less correlated than the individual observations. For instance, the throughput from week to week in a manufacturing plant is less likely to be correlated than the daily throughput. A machine failure at the end of a week will have less effect on the next week's throughput than on the next day's throughput. Also, as the size of the batches increase so the correlation between the batches should reduce. If the batch size is sufficiently large, it can be assumed that the batches are independent of one another. It is then possible to construct a confidence interval in the normal fashion:

$$CI = \overline{X} \pm t_{k-1,\alpha/2}\frac{S}{\sqrt{k}}$$

where:

S = standard deviation of the batch means
$\overline{X}$ = mean of the individual data
$t_{k-1,\alpha/2}$ = value from Student's t-distribution with $k - 1$ degree of freedom and a significance level of $\alpha/2$

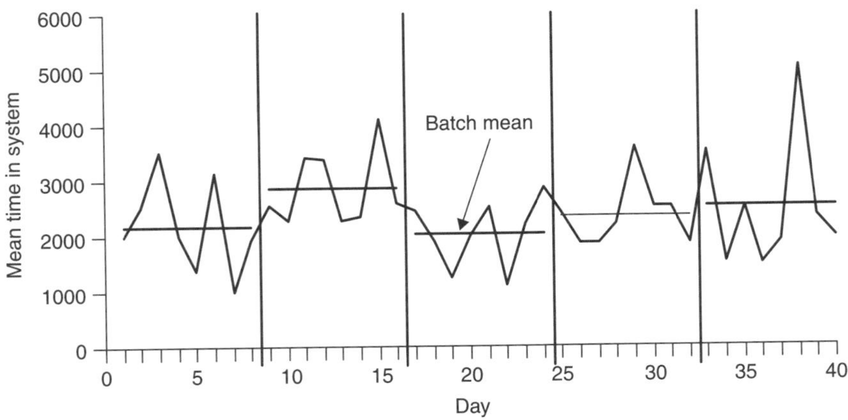

Figure 10.2 Formation of Batch Means from a Time-Series of Output Data (b = 8).

The main problem with the batch means method is determining the batch size. Various methods have been proposed, but none seem completely satisfactory. Schmeiser (1982) suggests that the time-series should not be split into more than 30 batches. He found that the accuracy of the confidence interval does not improve greatly by having more batches. He also recommends that there should be no fewer than 10 batches, since this also affects the accuracy of the interval.

Fishman (1978) proposes a procedure based on the von Neumann (1941) test for correlation. The batch size is doubled until the null hypothesis that there is no correlation in the batch means is accepted. An advantage of the von Neumann test is that it can be applied to small sample sizes (as few as $k = 8$ batches). The details of the test are not given here; the reader is referred to the original references.

Beyond Schmeiser and Fishman, various other procedures have been proposed for determining the batch size. For instance, Banks *et al.* (2001) propose a four-step method and Hoover and Perry (1990) outline an approach that uses the runs test to check for independence. A useful summary of batch means procedures is given in Alexopoulos and Seila (1998) with a more detailed discussion in Fishman (1996).

Table 10.1 shows the batch means (of mean time in the system in minutes) for the user help desk example described in Section 9.4. Based on a single simulation run of 250 days (following a warm-up period of 8 days) and using Fishman's procedure, a batch size of 4

Table 10.1 Batch Means Data for the User Help Desk Model ($b = 4$).

Day	Mean time in system	Batch mean ($b = 4$)
1	1986.58	
2	2521.63	2500.43
3	3509.34	
4	1984.15	
5	1368.02	
6	3148.23	1866.43
7	1012.93	
8	1936.55	
9	2563.83	
10	2259.49	2909.97
11	3424.89	
12	3391.68	
⋮	⋮	⋮
247	2054.63	
248	3361.63	2303.91
249	1597.56	
250	2988.13	
Mean	2401.38	

Table 10.2 **Batch Means Method: 95% Confidence Interval for User Help Desk Model.**

Mean of mean time in system	Standard deviation	95% Confidence Interval Lower interval	95% Confidence Interval Upper interval	Deviation
2401.38	310.73	2322.47	2480.29	3.29%

days is sufficient to remove any correlation from the data. The resulting confidence interval based on 62 batches (samples) is calculated in Table 10.2. Using Schmeiser's approach the batch size could have been doubled to eight, giving 31 batches. Indeed, this yields a very similar result.

Notice how the batch means confidence interval differs slightly from the interval (2224.98 – 2442.19) determined from six independent replications in Section 9.6.1. The two intervals largely overlap, showing that they give a similar result, although the batch means interval is narrower.

A spreadsheet (BatchMeans.xls) that uses Fishman's procedure for determining the batch size is available on the web site (www.wileyeurope.com/go/robinson). The spreadsheet also calculates the resulting confidence interval.

Median and quantile estimation

Another measure of average performance is the median (Appendix A3.2). More generally, we might want to estimate quantiles, that is, the level of performance that can be achieved with a given probability. The median is simply the 0.5 quantile, and the upper and lower quartiles the 0.25 and 0.75 quantiles respectively. Rather than provide only a single value for a quantile, it is useful to calculate a confidence interval based on the sample of data obtained from the simulation. The calculation of confidence intervals for quantiles, however, is not as straightforward as for means. For a discussion see Banks *et al.* (2001) and for quantile estimation from a single long run see Heidelberger and Lewis (1984).

10.3.2 Measures of variability

An average does not provide a complete picture of model performance. Take, for instance, the two histograms in Figure 10.3. Both have the same mean (and indeed mode), but the variability is much greater in the second histogram. In most operations systems a lower level of variability is preferred since it is easier to match resources to the levels of demand. Indeed, a worse average with low variability may be selected in preference to a better average with high variability.

Apart from creating histograms of the output data, useful measures of variability are the minimum, maximum and standard deviation. Be aware of outliers when stating the minimum and maximum, otherwise these measures may be misleading. For a median, quartiles and more generally quantiles provide a measure of variability. Time-series plots are

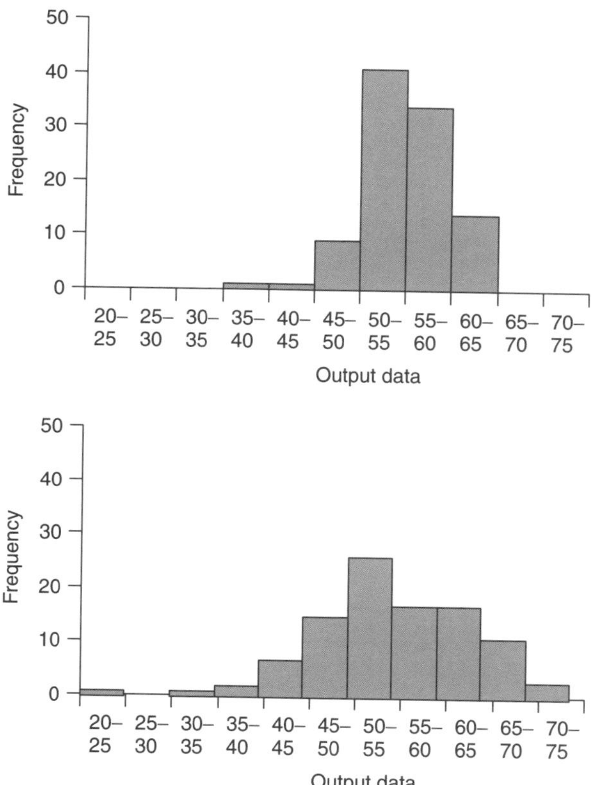

Figure 10.3 Histograms with the Same Mean, but Different Levels of Variability.

also important, since they show the pattern of variability over time, for instance, whether there are cycles in the data. All these reports are discussed in Appendix 3.

10.4 Comparing Alternatives

When comparing alternative scenarios the model user must be able to determine whether one alternative is better than another. This is not simply a case of comparing the mean values of key responses to see which are best. Take, for instance, the case where two scenarios (A and B) are being compared, the key response being daily throughput. Scenario A gives a mean result of 1050 units per day, while the result for scenario B is 1080. Does this mean that scenario B is better than scenario A? Assuming the aim is to increase throughput, then it would initially appear that the answer is in the affirmative. However, apart from the difference in the means, two other factors need to be considered:

- What is the standard deviation of the mean daily throughput for the two scenarios?
- How many replications (or batches) were used to generate the results?

If the data have been generated from only a few replications and there is a lot of variation in the results, this gives little confidence that the difference is significant. If, however, many replications have been performed and the standard deviation is low, there can be more confidence that the difference is real.

A pragmatic approach would be to consider all three factors (the size of the difference, the standard deviation and the number of replications) and make a judgement as to whether the difference in the results is significant. A more rigorous approach relies on forming confidence intervals for the difference between the results.

10.4.1 Comparison of two scenarios

Assuming that common random numbers are being used in the model (Section 8.3.2), a confidence interval for the difference between the results from two scenarios can be calculated using the paired-*t* approach. The confidence interval is calculated as follows:

$$CI = \overline{D} \pm t_{n-1,\alpha/2} \frac{S_D}{\sqrt{n}}$$

$$\overline{D} = \frac{\sum_{j=1}^{n} (X_{1j} - X_{2j})}{n}$$

$$S_D = \sqrt{\frac{\sum_{j=1}^{n} (X_{1j} - X_{2j} - \overline{D})^2}{n-1}}$$

where:

$\overline{D}$ = mean difference between scenario 1 (X_1) and scenario 2 (X_2)
X_{1j} = result from scenario 1 and replication j
X_{2j} = result from scenario 2 and replication j
S_D = standard deviation of the differences
n = number of replications performed (same for both scenarios)
$t_{n-1,\alpha/2}$ = value from Student's *t*-distribution with $n-1$ degree of freedom and a significance level of $\alpha/2$

This formula is basically the same as the confidence interval formula given in Section 9.6.1, except that it uses the difference between two sets of values rather than a single set of values. The resulting confidence interval can lead to one of three outcomes as shown in Figure 10.4.

- *Outcome (a)*: the confidence interval is completely to the left of zero. It can be concluded, with the specified level of confidence (normally 95%), that the result for scenario 1 is less than the result for scenario 2.

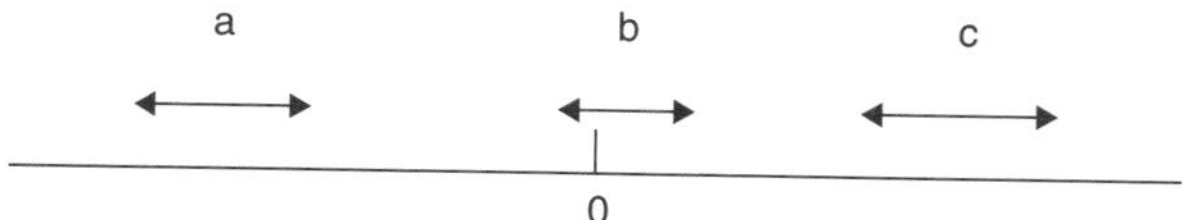

Figure 10.4 Potential Outcomes from a Paired-*t* Confidence Interval.

- *Outcome (b)*: the confidence interval includes zero. It can be concluded, with the specified level of confidence (normally 95%), that the result for scenario 1 is not significantly different from the result for scenario 2.
- *Outcome (c)*: the confidence interval is completely to the right of zero. It can be concluded, with the specified level of confidence (normally 95%), that the result for scenario 1 is greater than the result for scenario 2.

Note also that the extent to which an interval misses zero provides additional information on the size of the difference.

A paired-*t* confidence interval helps to identify the statistical significance of a difference in the results from two scenarios. Banks *et al.* (2001) observe that the *statistical significance* of a difference in the results has a very different meaning from the *practical significance* of a difference. Statistical significance answers the question: is the difference in the results real? Practical significance asks the questions: is the difference sufficiently large to affect the decision? For instance, although scenario 2 may give, say, a 10% improvement over scenario 1, if the cost of scenario 2 is much greater, then the client may opt for scenario 1. In this case the practical significance of the difference is not sufficiently great.

The procedure above assumes that the same number of replications have been performed for both scenarios. Both Law and Kelton (2000) and Banks *et al.* (2001) discuss how confidence intervals for differences can be calculated when unequal numbers of replications have been performed. The confidence interval formula also assumes that common random numbers have been used for the two scenarios (Section 8.3.2). Goldsman and Nelson (1998) describe how a confidence interval can be calculated when common random numbers are not in use, or when they are not working properly (see also the formula in Section 12.4.4). It is noted in Section 8.3.2 that common random numbers are not always effective because changing a scenario may alter the pattern of random number usage. If common random numbers are working properly then it is expected that:

$$S_D^2 < S_1^2 + S_2^2$$

where:

S_D = standard deviation of the differences in the results from scenario 1 and 2
S_1 = standard deviation of the results from scenario 1
S_2 = standard deviation of the results from scenario 2

In other words, the variance (S^2) has been reduced. This test should be performed before going on to calculate a paired-*t* confidence interval. Note that the paired-*t* confidence

Table 10.3 **Paired-*t* Confidence Interval for Two Scenarios from the User Help Desk Model.**

Replication	Scenario 1: mean time in system	Scenario 2: mean time in system	Difference (S1 − S2)
1	2484.72	2120.00	364.72
2	2354.64	2085.46	269.18
3	2396.47	2181.19	215.28
4	2196.91	2017.99	178.92
5	2321.74	2103.86	217.88
6	2247.03	2046.56	200.47
Mean	2333.59	2092.51	241.08
St. dev.	103.491	57.382	67.516
Variance	10710.35	3292.66	4558.44

95% confidence interval for differences		
Lower interval	Upper interval	Conclusion
170.22	311.93	Scenario 1 > Scenario 2

interval approach can also be used on batch means data, as well as multiple replications, simply by interpreting n as the number of batches (k) in each scenario.

Table 10.3 shows a paired-*t* confidence interval for two scenarios simulated with the user help desk model (Section 9.4). Common random numbers are implemented in this model. In the second scenario an additional member of the technical team has been employed. The results show the mean time in the system (in minutes) for six replications with each scenario (as determined in Section 9.6.1). The sum of the variances for the individual scenarios ($10{,}710 + 3293 = 14{,}003$) is much greater than the variance of the differences (4558). It appears, therefore, that the use of common random numbers is working correctly and that it is appropriate to use a paired-*t* confidence interval. Since the confidence interval is a long way to the right of zero this gives a lot of confidence that the result from scenario 1 is greater than the result from scenario 2. Because the aim is to reduce the time in the system, scenario 2 is to be preferred.

A spreadsheet (CompareTwo.xls) is provided on the web site (www.wileyeurope.com/go/robinson) that calculates a paired-*t* confidence interval from a series of replications with two scenarios. It also includes a check as to whether the variance is being reduced by the use of common random numbers.

10.4.2 Comparison of many scenarios

The paired-*t* confidence interval can be extended to enable more than two scenarios to be compared at once by use of the Bonferroni inequality. This states that if we want to make c confidence interval statements with an overall significance level of α, the individual confidence intervals should be formed with a significance level of α/c. For example, if 10 confidence intervals are to be formed for comparison and an overall significance level of 10% (90% confidence) is required, each confidence interval should be calculated with a significance level of 1% (99% confidence).

This is best illustrated with an example. Five scenarios have been simulated with the user help desk model, each with different staffing levels, as follows:

- *Scenario 1*: technical team = 2, help desk staff = 1 (current set-up)
- *Scenario 2*: technical team = 3, help desk staff = 1
- *Scenario 3*: technical team = 4, help desk staff = 1
- *Scenario 4*: technical team = 2, help desk staff = 2
- *Scenario 5*: technical team = 3, help desk staff = 2

In each case six replications have been run and the output data from the initial transient have been deleted. Common random numbers have been employed. The results for the mean time in the system are shown in Table 10.4. If the model user wishes to compare each scenario to the current set-up (base scenario), then four paired-t confidence intervals need to be constructed ($c = s - 1$, where s is the number of scenarios). If the overall level of confidence required is 95% (a significance level of five percent), then the individual significance levels need to be calculated at $5/4 = 1.25\%$.

The four intervals with $\alpha = 1.25\%$ are given in Table 10.5. This clearly shows that scenarios 2, 3 and 5 are all significant improvements (the mean time in the system is less) over scenario 1. Meanwhile scenario 4 is not significantly different from scenario 1. If, instead of comparing each scenario to a base scenario, the model user wishes to compare every scenario to every other, then $c = s(s - 1)/2$. In the example above there are, therefore, 10 ($5 \times 4/2$) confidence intervals to be constructed. In this case, to obtain an overall confidence of 90%, the individual intervals have to be calculated at 1% significance. The resulting confidence intervals are shown in Table 10.6 and the conclusions in Table 10.7.

The use of the Bonferroni inequality is quite effective as long as the number of scenarios remains small. As the amount of scenarios increases, however, the number of confidence intervals can quickly become unmanageable, particularly if a full comparison of all scenarios is required. For instance, a full comparison of 10 scenarios requires 450 ($10 \times 9/2$) intervals.

Table 10.4 User Help Desk Model: Results for Five Scenarios.

Scenario	Mean time in the system
1	2333.59
2	2092.51
3	2010.46
4	2330.86
5	2083.28

Table 10.5 Four Confidence Intervals Comparing Scenarios 2–5 to the Base (Scenario 1) for the User Help Desk Model (Overall Confidence = 95%).

	98.75% confidence intervals for differences		
Comparison	Lower interval	Upper interval	Conclusion
Scenario 1 to 2	136.06	346.09	Scen. 1 > Scen. 2
Scenario 1 to 3	209.89	436.37	Scen. 1 > Scen. 2
Scenario 1 to 4	−60.00	65.45	No difference
Scenario 1 to 5	147.69	352.93	Scen. 1 > Scen. 2

Table 10.6 Confidence Interval Comparison between all Scenarios for the User Help Desk Model (Overall Confidence = 90%).

	99% confidence intervals for differences			
Scenario	2	3	4	5
1	129.94, 352.21	203.28, 442.97	−63.66, 69.11	141.71, 358.91
2		63.32, 100.79	−309.31, −167.39	−23.50, 41.97
3			−406.45, −234.36	−107.39, −38.25
4				169.20, 325.97

Table 10.7 Conclusions from Confidence Interval Comparison between all Scenarios for the User Help Desk Model.

Scenario	2	3	4	5
1	Scen. 1 > Scen. 2	Scen. 1 > Scen. 3	No difference	Scen. 1 > Scen. 5
2		Scen. 2 > Scen. 3	Scen. 2 < Scen. 4	No difference
3			Scen. 3 < Scen. 4	Scen. 3 < Scen. 5
4				Scen. 4 > Scen. 5

Further to this, as more intervals are required, smaller individual significance levels need to be employed in order to maintain a reasonable level of overall confidence. As a result, the individual intervals become much wider, making them less meaningful. Goldsman and Nelson (1998) discuss alternative procedures for multiple comparisons.

The spreadsheet used for comparing two scenarios (CompareTwo.xls) can also be used for comparing multiple scenarios. The user can enter the results from the replications for each pair of scenarios in turn and obtain the correct confidence interval by adjusting the significance level in line with the Bonferroni inequality.

10.4.3 Choosing the best scenario(s)

Beyond comparing scenarios, there is an obvious interest in identifying the best out of a group of scenarios. At the simplest level this can be achieved by inspecting the mean results for each scenario. In the user help desk model, Table 10.4 shows that scenario 3 gives the minimum result for the mean time in the system, and so this appears to be the best scenario.

Of course, simply comparing point estimates does not take account of the standard deviation of the results or the number of replications performed. It is, therefore, better to refer to confidence intervals. In Table 10.7 it can be seen that scenario 3 is in all cases better than the other scenarios. That is, there is a significant difference and the mean time in the system is lower for scenario 3. It is also apparent that scenarios 2 and 5 are next best, although not significantly different from one another. It should be noted, however, that the best scenarios might not always be so easily identifiable using this approach.

Beyond comparing means and using confidence intervals for differences, there are statistical methods for choosing the best scenario known as ranking and selection methods. These are discussed in Law and Kelton (2000). Meanwhile, Goldsman and Nelson (2001) describe six statistical procedures for finding the best scenario.

Finally, we refer back to the earlier discussion on statistical and practical significance (Section 10.4.1). The discussion in this section is centred on identifying the statistically best scenario. The model user and clients need to discuss the practical issues surrounding the decision to determine whether the statistically best scenario is indeed the best decision.

10.5 Search Experimentation

Because there is the potential to have many scenarios (factor/level combinations) in search experimentation, very often it is not possible to simulate every single scenario in the time available in order to determine which meet the target required or provide the optimum result. Consequently, methods need to be found for improving the efficiency of the experimentation process. In broad terms there are three approaches for achieving this:

- *Experimental Design*: identify the experimental factors that are most likely to lead to significant improvements, thereby reducing the total factor/level combinations to be analysed (Section 10.5.2).
- *Metamodels*: fitting a model to the simulation output (a model of a model). Because the fitted model runs much faster than the simulation, many more factor/level combinations can be investigated (Section 10.5.3).
- *Optimization*: performing an efficient search of the factor/level combinations, trying to identify the optimum combination (Section 10.5.4).

There is much written on these approaches and each provides a fertile area for continued research. For our purposes only an outline description is given of the methods for tackling these issues. Although these approaches are described as separate topics, it must be remembered that they overlap with one another and that the approaches can be used in combination during experimentation. Before outlining the formal methods for carrying out search experimentation there is a discussion on some informal approaches.

10.5.1 Informal approaches to search experimentation

Albeit that there is a significant body of theory on search experimentation, anecdotal evidence suggests that most simulation experimentation is performed in an informal manner. The lack of use of formal methods probably results from the need to apply non-elementary statistics when employing them. Many simulation model users do not possess the necessary skills and simulation software generally does not provide much support for search experimentation, with the exception of optimization (Section 10.5.4). On the other hand, informal approaches can be quite effective and have the advantage that the model user is closely involved with the selection of scenarios.

The discussion that follows describes some informal approaches to search experimentation. These are classified under three headings that relate closely to those listed above:

- Identifying important experimental factors (similar to experimental design)
- Developing an understanding of the solution space (similar to metamodelling)
- Searching factor/level combinations efficiently (similar to optimization)

Identifying important experimental factors

When carrying out search experimentation it is often useful to start by identifying the experimental factors that have the greatest impact, that is, give the greatest improvement towards meeting the objectives of the simulation study. Is adding more service personnel more effective than increasing the number of automated service points? Does improving machine cycles have more effect than increasing the buffering between machines? The model user can then concentrate on experimenting with the important factors when searching for the optimum or target.

There are three ways in which the importance of an experimental factor can be identified:

- *Data Analysis*: by analysing the data in a model it is sometimes possible to draw conclusions about the likely impact of a change to an experimental factor. For instance, through data analysis a bottleneck process might be identified. Experimental factors that are likely to relieve this bottleneck (e.g. faster cycle time) could then be classified as important. Of course, such analysis does not provide a complete picture in that it cannot take account of the randomness and interconnections in the model.
- *Expert Knowledge*: subject matter experts, for instance, operations staff, often have a good understanding of the system and the factors that are likely to have greatest impact. It is worth interviewing such people. That said, subject matter experts do not often have a complete understanding of the system. Although they may have a good understanding of isolated sections, their understanding of the total system is unlikely to be complete. If they did have a complete understanding, the simulation study would probably not be required! As a result, care must be taken when relying on the opinions of subject matter experts.

- *Preliminary Experimentation*: changing the levels of experimental factors and running the model to see the effect. Interactive experimentation (Section 10.2.1), if used with caution, may be beneficial in this respect, although it is important to perform batch experiments to test fully the effect of a change to an experimental factor.

Data analysis and expert knowledge have the advantage that they require less time than preliminary experimentation. Preliminary experimentation, however, provides a more thorough means for investigating the effect of a change to an experimental factor.

One problem in identifying important experimental factors is that when factors are changed in isolation they may have a very different effect from when they are changed in combination. Such interaction effects are hard to identify except by more formal means. When using informal methods the model user should be aware of possible interaction effects and test them by changing some factors in combination.

Finally, referring back to the discussion on statistical and practical significance (Section 10.4.1), a change to an experimental factor may have a significant effect on the simulation output (statistical significance), but this does not necessarily mean that it is an important factor. If the change has limited practical significance (e.g. it is too expensive or breaks safety constraints), it cannot be classified as important. Importance requires both statistical and practical significance.

Developing an understanding of the solution space

By simulating a limited number of scenarios (factor/level combinations) it is often possible to form an opinion as to the likely outcome of other scenarios without having to run the simulation. In particular, it may be possible to identify those scenarios that are likely to yield the desired result and those that are unlikely to do so. Through this process the model user forms an understanding of the solution space.

Table 10.8 illustrates the idea for a simple two-factor experiment, with each experimental factor taking on three levels. Rather than simulate all nine scenarios, the model user could run a limited set. In this example it seems reasonable to run the model for the scenarios at the four extremes (corners) and the centre point for confirmation. The results from these runs, which should be reported as confidence intervals, are signified by X_{11}, X_{13}, X_{22}, X_{31} and X_{33}. By simple linear interpolation, the model user could then predict the results for the other four scenarios, denoted by $E(X_{ij})$ for estimated value. This does of course assume

Table 10.8 Understanding the Solution Space: A Two-Factor/Three-Level Experiment.

		Factor 2		
	Simulation output	Level 1	Level 2	Level 3
Factor 1	Level 1	X_{11}	$E(X_{12})$	X_{13}
	Level 2	$E(X_{21})$	X_{22}	$E(X_{23})$
	Level 3	X_{31}	$E(X_{32})$	X_{33}

that the solution space is linear and smooth over the region being investigated, which is probably a satisfactory approximation if the factor levels are reasonably close to each other.

The aim is to form an understanding of the likely outcome for all scenarios without having to simulate every one. Scenarios that are very unlikely to give the desired outcome can be discarded without simulating them. Meanwhile, for scenarios that might give the desired result, simulations should be run to confirm, or otherwise, the expectations. Overall this approach means fewer simulation runs need to be performed, saving time.

For the purposes of illustration Table 10.8 shows how to approach a simple three-dimensional problem (two experimental factors and one response). The idea can be adapted for a greater number of dimensions, possibly with the help of a spreadsheet, although interpretation of the results becomes more difficult as the number of dimensions increases.

Another useful idea is to experiment with an unconstrained model by removing, for instance, the limits to queue capacities or the number of resources available. In this way the maximum requirement for queue capacities and resources can be identified. This, in itself, is useful information, although in practice some constraints are likely to be in place.

It may also be useful to start by performing some experiments with factor levels that are spaced far apart. In so doing, general learning about the solution space can be obtained and the model user can then home in on the areas of interest.

Searching factor/level combinations efficiently

The model user should identify factor changes that have the greatest impact in improving the simulation result or moving the simulation result towards the desired target. The user can then concentrate on continuing to change those experimental factors in the direction that gives the improvement. For instance, if the addition of service personnel leads to the greatest improvement, then further service personnel could be added.

In taking this approach, the model user must be aware of potential interaction effects that occur if multiple factors are changed at the same time and of the need for differences that are practically as well as statistically significant. A further concern is identifying a scenario that appears optimal when a wider search would reveal a better result. This can only be tackled by jumping to quite different factor/level combinations to see if there is a significant improvement.

10.5.2 Experimental design

Experimental design acts as a way of identifying important experimental factors, that is, those factors to which changes are most likely to yield the desired result. It is a formal method for carrying out the preliminary experimentation described in Section 10.5.1. As such, experimental design can be valuable, particularly in the early stages of experimentation, for identifying scenarios that should be simulated.

2^k factorial designs

One approach to experimental design, described by Law and Kelton (2000), is to adopt a 2^k factorial design, where k is the number of experimental factors. Take, for instance,

Table 10.9 2^k Factorial Design with Three Experimental Factors.

Scenario	Factor 1	Factor 2	Factor 3	Response
1	−	−	−	R_1
2	+	−	−	R_2
3	−	+	−	R_3
4	+	+	−	R_4
5	−	−	+	R_5
6	+	−	+	R_6
7	−	+	+	R_7
8	+	+	+	R_8

the example of a simulation with three experimental factors. In a 2^k factorial design each factor is set at two levels denoted by a − and + sign. In our example there are, therefore, a total of eight (2^3) scenarios as shown in Table 10.9. The factor levels chosen might represent the range over which it is expected each factor will be changed. For a quantitative factor, the minimum and maximum value might be chosen. For a qualitative factor, two extreme options might be selected. See the discussion at the end of this sub-section for more comment on the selection of factor levels.

All eight scenarios are then simulated and the results (responses R_1 to R_8) recorded. Based on these results the effect of changing each factor can be computed as the mean average effect on the response of changing a factor from its − to its + level. This is known as the *main effect*. The main effect for factor 1 (e_1) can be calculated as follows:

$$e_1 = \frac{(R_2 - R_1) + (R_4 - R_3) + (R_6 - R_5) + (R_8 - R_7)}{4}$$

In Table 10.9, factor 1 is changed from its − to its + level on four occasions, each time holding the other factors constant. So the difference between R_2 and R_1 shows the effect of changing factor 1 alone. The mean average effect is determined by summing all the differences and dividing by four. Notice that the sign before the response variable (R_i) is the same as the sign in the column for factor 1 in Table 10.9. Taking advantage of this, the formula above can be formed more easily as follows:

$$e_1 = \frac{-R_1 + R_2 - R_3 + R_4 - R_5 + R_6 - R_7 + R_8}{4}$$

The formula for the other main effects can also be formed with reference to the signs in Table 10.9, for instance, for factor 2:

$$e_2 = \frac{-R_1 - R_2 + R_3 + R_4 - R_5 - R_6 + R_7 + R_8}{4}$$

If the main effect of a factor is positive this indicates that, on average, changing the factor from its − to its + level increases the response by the value of the main effect. Similarly a negative main effect identifies a decrease in the response when changing the factor from its − to its + level. If the main effect is close to zero this shows that a change to the factor has a negligible effect. This information indicates the direction in which each factor should be moved in order to achieve the desired effect (increasing or decreasing the response value). The size of the main effect also indicates which factors have the greatest effect on the response and as such helps to identify the most important factors.

Beyond calculating the main effects it is also important to determine the effect of changing more than one factor at a time, known as the interaction effects. For instance, in our example the interaction effect between factor 1 and factor 2 (two-factor interaction effect) is calculated as follows:

$$e_{12} = \frac{1}{2}\left(\frac{(R_4 - R_3) + (R_8 - R_7)}{2} - \frac{(R_2 - R_1) + (R_6 - R_5)}{2}\right)$$

This is half the difference between the mean average effect of changing factor 1 (− to +) when factor 2 is at its + level and the mean average effect of changing factor 1 (− to +) when factor 2 is at its − level. Again, this formula can be formed more simply with reference to the signs in Table 10.9. By effectively multiplying the signs for the two factors under investigation, the sign for each response variable can be determined. For instance for R_1 factor 1 and factor 2 have − signs, giving R_1 a + sign in the formula ($- \times - = +$). Therefore, the formula above can be rewritten as follows:

$$e_{12} = \frac{R_1 - R_2 - R_3 + R_4 + R_5 - R_6 - R_7 + R_8}{4}$$

A positive two-factor interaction effect implies the response is increased by setting factor 1 and factor 2 at the same level (both − or both +). If the interaction effect is negative, then the response is increased by setting the factors at opposite levels (one at − and one at +). An effect close to zero implies that the interaction effect is not significant.

As a simple example, with only two factors, take the experiments performed with the user help desk model in Section 10.4.2. The first factor is the size of the technical team ($- = 2$ and $+ = 4$) and the second is the number of help desk staff ($- = 1$ and $+ = 2$). The experimental design and responses are shown in Table 10.10. Note that the final scenario is an addition to those presented previously.

Table 10.10 User Help Desk Model: Experimental Design.

Scenario	Technical team	Help desk staff	Response
1	−	−	2333.59
2	+	−	2010.46
3	−	+	2330.86
4	+	+	2017.03

The main effects are as follows:

$$e_1 = \frac{(-2333.59 + 2010.46 - 2330.86 + 2017.03)}{2} = -318.48$$

$$e_2 = \frac{(-2333.59 - 2010.46 + 2330.86 + 2017.03)}{2} = 1.92$$

and the interaction effect between the two factors is:

$$e_{12} = \frac{(2333.59 - 2010.46 - 2330.86 + 2017.03)}{2} = 4.65$$

The interaction effect and the effect of the number of help desk staff both appear to be negligible. Meanwhile, the effect of increasing the technical team, on average, reduces the mean time enquiries spend in the system by about 318 minutes. This would seem to be a significant effect. In order to confirm the significance, or otherwise, of the effects, confidence intervals should be reported; see note below.

Three further points should be noted about 2^k factorial designs. First, higher-factor interaction effects can be calculated. For instance, this might mean calculating e_{123} (three-factor interaction effect). The interpretation of interaction effects between more than two factors, however, is quite difficult. Second, although the description above involves only three factors, 2^k factorial designs can be used for simulation models in which there are many more factors. Of course, as the number of factors increases there is a more than proportionate increase in the number of factor/level combinations that need to be simulated. Finally, the responses (R_i) are samples taken from a series of replications performed with each scenario. Therefore, it is best not to give single point estimates for the main and interaction effects. Instead, confidence intervals can be calculated for all effects. This can be done by calculating the effects separately for each replication, and then determining the mean effect and standard deviation. The confidence intervals are then calculated in the usual way. An effect is taken to be statistically significant if the interval does not contain zero.

There are some limitations in using 2^k factorial designs. First, if interaction effects exist then the interpretation of the main effects becomes more difficult. This is because the effect of changing a single factor depends on the levels of the other factors. Secondly, the effects only apply within the bounds of the levels selected. It is dangerous to extrapolate the findings of a 2^k factorial design outside the range of the levels used in the simulation runs. Thirdly, because the approach interpolates between results, a linear model is effectively assumed. This is probably acceptable as long as the two levels chosen for each factor are not too far apart. As a result, the factor levels need to be carefully selected, ensuring that the range is not too great.

It must be remembered that the prime motivation for experimental design is to identify the important experimental factors, those that give the greatest improvement towards meeting the objectives of the simulation study. The calculation of both main and interaction effects helps with this process. Once the important factors have been identified, further simulation experiments can be performed in which the levels of those factors are changed (within the limits of the levels used in the experimental design) to search for the target required or the optimum value for each response.

Other approaches to experimental design

Fractional factorial designs are applied when there are too many factors to enable full experimentation with every factor/level combination. A limited set of factor/level combinations is chosen and conclusions are drawn from an analysis of the results. Law and Kelton (2000) provide an introduction to this topic.

Analysis of variance (ANOVA) provides a more rigorous means for identifying the effect of changes to factors. It involves a series of hypothesis tests in which it is determined whether changes to the experimental factors have an effect on the response. The effect of individually changing factors and of changing factors in combination is tested. Pidd (1998) outlines the use of ANOVA in simulation experiments. Box *et al.* (1978) and Montgomery (2001) discuss the role of ANOVA in experimental design. Meanwhile, most intermediate statistical texts give a more general description of the topic (e.g. Daniel and Terrell, 1995).

There is a large body of theory associated with experimental design with whole books devoted to the subject. The discussion above provides only a brief introduction to the topic, focusing mainly on 2^k factorial designs. More detailed discussion on experimental design for simulation can be found in Law and Kelton (2000), Kleijnen and van Groenendaal (1992) and Kleijnen (1998), with more thorough coverage in Kleijnen (1987). Cheng and Lamb (1998) describe how experimental design can be incorporated into a simulation package through an Excel interface. General texts on the topic of experimental design are also available, for example, Box *et al.* (1978), Box and Draper (1987) and Montgomery (2001). Meanwhile, some statistical software, such as MINITAB (www: MINITAB), provide assistance with experimental design and analysis.

10.5.3 Metamodelling

A metamodel is a model of a model, in our case a model of the simulation output. Because the metamodel is normally an analytical model it runs much faster than the simulation. It is, therefore, possible to investigate many more scenarios with a metamodel than with the simulation itself. The downside is that the metamodel is an approximation of the simulation output and so the results it provides are not as accurate. There is also the overhead of creating the metamodel.

As a starting point in creating a metamodel a series of results, representing a range of factor/level combinations, must be generated from the simulation. Careful selection of the scenarios to be simulated is important in order to assure the greatest accuracy of the metamodel with the minimum number of simulation runs. This requires appropriate experimental design techniques.

Figure 10.5 shows an example for a simulation of a manufacturing plant in which the response (throughput) is plotted against two experimental factors (machine efficiency and buffer size). These data have been generated from 100 scenarios, represented by each point

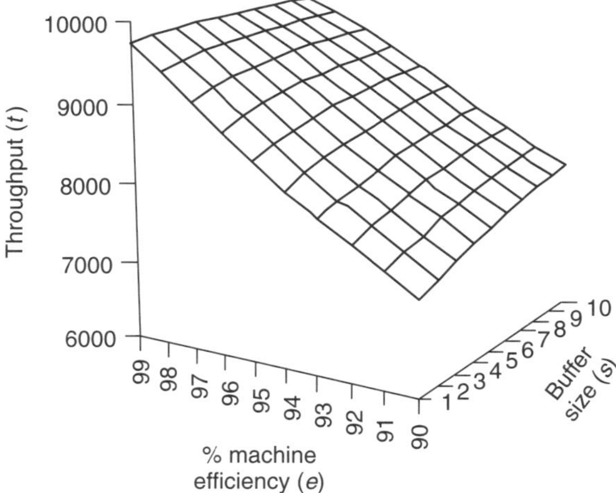

Figure 10.5 Response Surface for Manufacturing Model.

on the graph. The plane is referred to as the *response surface*. If the response surface includes the full range of factor/level combinations that are possible, it represents the complete solution space; otherwise it is a subset of the solution space. Obviously, if there are more than two experimental factors and one response, the response surface cannot be plotted as shown in Figure 10.5.

Once the scenario results have been generated, a model is fitted to the response surface. Most commonly multiple regression models are used where the dependent variable is the response and the independent variables are the experimental factors. Goodness-of-fit issues should be attended to in the normal manner as for any regression analysis (e.g. correlation, residual errors, etc.). If a multiple linear regression model is fitted to the data in Figure 10.5, the following metamodel is generated:

$$t = -15\,386 + 52.57\,s + 251.95\,e$$

This appears to be a good fit with a correlation in excess of 0.99. Of course, this is a simple example and the surface appears to be linear. Such a good fit would not normally be expected and for more complex surfaces more complex regression models would be required.

An alternative metamodelling approach, described by Hurrion (2000), is to use artificial neural networks. The simulated data is used to train the neural network, the experimental factor levels being the inputs and the response values the outputs. The advantage of neural networks is that they are able to deal with non-smooth and discontinuous surfaces more easily than regression analysis.

Once fitted, the metamodel is used for continued experimentation in place of the simulation. In doing so it must be remembered that the metamodel is only an approximation. It should only be used to identify candidate scenarios, which are then run in the full simulation model. It is also dangerous to extrapolate results from the metamodel outside the range of the factor/level combinations used to create the model.

For those wishing to investigate metamodelling further, more detailed introductions can be found in Kleijnen (1998), Law and Kelton (2000) and Banks *et al.* (2001).

10.5.4 Optimization ("searchization")

Simulation optimization is an area on which much research has recently focused. Alongside this, a number of simulation software vendors have released optimization packages. It is probably fair to say that simulation optimization represents the greatest advance in the practice of simulation over recent years.

In simulation optimization the aim is to find the factor/level combination that gives the best value for a response, that is the maximum or minimum value. The problem can be thought of in similar terms to standard mathematical optimization methods. First, there is some objective function to be optimized, typically, cost, profit, throughput or customer service. Secondly, there is a set of decision variables that can be changed; in simulation these are the experimental factors. Finally, there are a series of constraints within which the decision variables can be changed; this is expressed in terms of the range within which the experimental factors can be altered.

The difference from mathematical optimization is that there is no algorithm for guaranteeing an optimum solution. The normal approach in such circumstances is to use heuristic search methods (rules of thumb for directing the search for the best solution). This, indeed, appears to be the most common approach used in simulation optimization. The problem, however, is that a heuristic search requires the simulation to be run, which makes it a time consuming approach. It is, therefore, vital that the search is performed as efficiently as possible.

The heuristic search approach can best be described by reference to a simple example. Figure 10.6 shows a response surface for a simulation model with only one experimental factor. Of course, the shape of the surface is not known to the model user at the start of the experimentation. The aim is to maximize the response value.

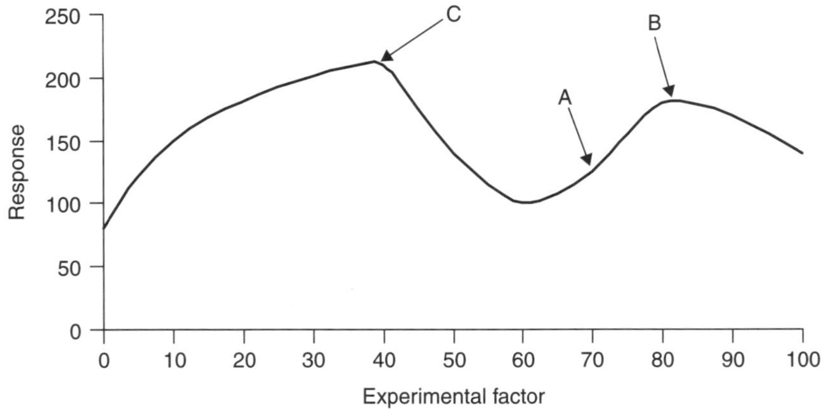

Figure 10.6 Simulation Optimization: Illustration of Simple Heuristic Search.

Assume that the search starts by setting the experimental factor at 70, giving the result at point A. The experimental factor is then reduced and increased by five and the simulation is run twice more (performing multiple replications for both scenarios). In doing so it is found that increasing the factor to 75 improves the value of the response, while reducing it to 65 has the opposite effect. The search then continues by increasing the value of the experimental factor for as long as the response value improves. Eventually, the point B is reached. Using this simple "hill-climbing" search strategy, it would appear that point B is the optimum point.

The problem with such a search strategy is obvious. It can very easily converge to a local and not a global optimum. In Figure 10.6 the global optimum (point C) is completely missed. In order to address this issue a more complex search method needs to be employed. For instance, after a while the search could jump from one value of an experimental factor to another in the hope of finding a better response. Alternatively, from time to time the search might make downhill moves (in a maximization problem) in the hope of finding a larger hill elsewhere. Of course, none of these search mechanisms can guarantee an optimum result, especially when there is only a limited time to perform the search and the solution space is complex.

Many simulation software vendors now provide optimization packages for their software. The majority of these use heuristic search approaches and in particular a set of methods known as meta-heuristics, for example, simulated annealing, genetic algorithms and tabu search (Reeves 1995; Debuse *et al.* 1999). The model user simply specifies the objective function, the experimental factors and the range within which they can be varied. The software then automatically performs the search by running the simulation, inspecting the results, adjusting the experimental factors and re-running the simulation.

As in the discussion above, none of the optimization packages can guarantee that an optimum will be found. This depends upon the time available versus the run-time of the model, the complexity of the solution space and the quality of the search mechanism. That said, the approach is a powerful means for automating an intelligent search of the solution space. Because most optimizers keep a log of all the scenarios simulated, the model user is not only able to see which scenario provides the "best" result, but can also learn about the behaviour of the model from the range of scenarios simulated. A common use of simulation optimizers is to leave them to perform an intelligent search over an extended period, for instance, overnight. Because simulation optimization cannot guarantee the best outcome and because they are often used to perform an intelligent search of the solution space, I prefer the term "searchization" to optimization.

Although simulation optimization provides some significant advantages in terms of searching the solution space, there are also some shortcomings in its use:

- It can lead to a concentration on instrumental learning (what is the result?) rather than conceptual learning (why is that happening?). The latter is a key benefit of simulation.
- It deals with a single objective function when there may be multiple objectives.
- The simulation is a simplification of reality and so it must be remembered that it is the model, not necessarily reality, that is being optimized. Results must be interpreted in the light of wider knowledge about the real world.

- The practical significance of results can be lost in the search for statistically better outcomes.
- The benefits of group debate around the model may be lost as the model user and clients rely too heavily on the optimization process to provide "the result".

Many of these problems can be overcome by careful use of the optimization process and by not relying solely on optimization, but on other experimental methods as well.

The discussion above concentrates on heuristic search methods because these seem to be most commonly in use, particularly in simulation optimization software. Other methods have been devised and research continues into improving optimization methods. Both Fu (2001) and Olafsson and Kim (2002) provide a useful overview of simulation optimization and methods. Other discussions can be found in simulation texts such as Law and Kelton (2000) and Banks *et al.* (2001).

10.6 Sensitivity Analysis

In sensitivity analysis the consequences of changes in model inputs are assessed. In this context model inputs are interpreted more generally than just experimental factors and include all model data. The concept is shown in Figure 10.7. The input (I) is varied, the simulation run and the effect on the response is measured. If there is a significant shift in the response (the gradient is steep), then the response is sensitive to the change in the input. If there is little change (the gradient is shallow), then the response is insensitive to the change.

Sensitivity analysis is useful in three main areas:

- Assessing the effect of uncertainties in the data, particularly category C data (Section 7.3.1).

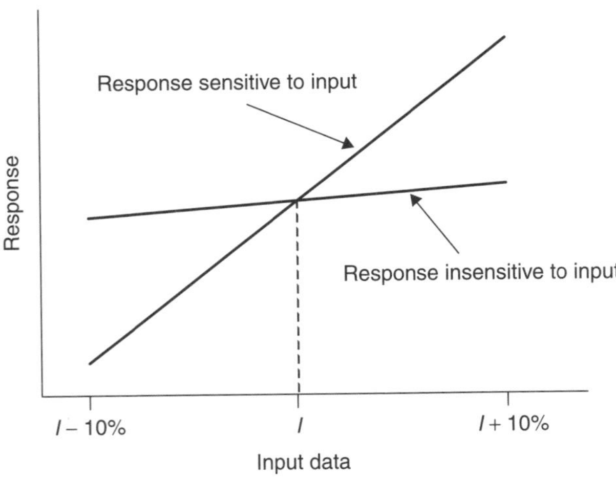

Figure 10.7 Sensitivity Analysis.

- Understanding how changes to the experimental factors affect the responses.
- Assessing the robustness of the solution.

All of these can provide useful information to both the model user and the clients by improving their understanding of the model. The latter is particularly important so the client understands how small changes might affect the proposed solution to the problem being tackled by the simulation study. Indeed, a client may prefer a more robust solution (one that applies across a range of input values) that gives a worse result, to one that is very sensitive to small changes in the inputs, particularly if there are uncertainties about the real system.

The main approach to performing sensitivity analysis is to vary the model inputs, run the simulation and record the change in the responses. Of course, this can be a very time consuming process, especially if there are many model inputs. For this reason, sensitivity analysis should be restricted to a few key inputs, which might be identified as those about which there is greatest uncertainty and which it is believed have the greatest impact on the response. Beyond this, experimental design and metamodelling methods can be useful in helping to perform and speed up sensitivity analysis (Kleijnen 1998; Noordegraaf *et al.* 2003). Perturbation analysis tries to predict the sensitivity of the results from a single run of a simulation model (Glasserman 1991). Because the simulation does not have to be run repeatedly this should save time. It is, however, restricted to quite specific circumstances.

10.7 Conclusion

This chapter describes how simulation experiments are performed and how the results should be reported. Methods for comparing alternative scenarios are described and approaches for searching the solution space are discussed. The key areas and methods that are identified are as follows:

- *The nature of simulation experimentation*: interactive and batch experimentation, comparing alternatives and search experimentation.
- *The analysis of results*: confidence intervals for point estimates (the standard method with multiple replications and the batch means method for a single long run) and measures of variability.
- *Comparison of alternatives*: paired-*t* confidence interval for comparing two alternatives, adjusted by the Bonferroni inequality when more than two scenarios are being compared.
- *Informal search experimentation*: identifying important experimental factors, developing an understanding of the solution space and searching factor/level combinations efficiently.
- *Formal search experimentation*: experimental design, metamodelling and optimization.
- *Sensitivity analysis*

Some of the methods that are described are illustrated by the Wardeon Cinema and Panorama Televisions case studies in Appendix 1 (Section A1.6.2) and Appendix 2 (Section A2.6.2) respectively.

A final note of caution: the experimental methods described tend to focus on finding a solution (a best scenario) and on the statistical significance of the results. The use of experimental procedures, however, should not be to the detriment of developing a better understanding of the real system through the simulation and of understanding the practical significance of the results that are being obtained. Indeed, the proper use of experimental methods, if used alongside these wider considerations, should only enhance this process.

Exercises

E10.1 Ten replications have been performed with a manufacturing model. The mean daily throughput results are shown in Table 10.11 (the warm-up period data have been deleted). Calculate a confidence interval for these results. What does this tell us about the likely value of the mean daily throughput?

E10.2 Table 10.12 shows the daily throughput results from a single run with a manufacturing model (the warm-up period data have been deleted). Using a batch size of four, calculate a confidence interval for these data using the batch means method. What does the confidence interval suggest about the run-length employed?

E10.3 Apply the batch means method to the artificial time-series data created for Exercise 9.6 (Chapter 9). Use the BatchMeans.xls spreadsheet provided on the web site (www.wileyeurope.com/go/robinson).

E10.4 Apply the batch means method to the output data from the Panorama Televisions model (Appendix 2). Use the BatchMeans.xls spreadsheet provided on the web site (www.wileyeurope.com/go/robinson).

Table 10.11 Results from 10 Replications with a Manufacturing Model (Warm-up Period Data have been Deleted).

Replication	Mean daily t'put
1	198.2
2	210.5
3	216.6
4	208.2
5	181.8
6	220.8
7	176.4
8	191.7
9	209.3
10	210.7

Note: these data are available in a spreadsheet (Exercise10.xls) on the web site (www.wileyeurope.com/go/robinson).

Table 10.12 Results from 100 Days of Simulation with a Manufacturing Model (Warm-up Period Data have been Deleted).

Day	T'put	Day	T'put	Day	T'put	Day	T'put
1	111	26	198	51	240	76	201
2	147	27	189	52	240	77	99
3	171	28	240	53	114	78	210
4	51	29	255	54	0	79	249
5	270	30	219	55	0	80	216
6	132	31	258	56	258	81	255
7	114	32	192	57	240	82	225
8	162	33	231	58	225	83	252
9	228	34	126	59	165	84	159
10	210	35	198	60	147	85	174
11	144	36	240	61	237	86	183
12	231	37	219	62	240	87	246
13	90	38	237	63	231	88	258
14	201	39	240	64	222	89	255
15	141	40	255	65	222	90	258
16	0	41	231	66	258	91	258
17	0	42	93	67	195	92	120
18	0	43	171	68	117	93	219
19	0	44	240	69	234	94	258
20	0	45	237	70	183	95	219
21	108	46	213	71	171	96	255
22	234	47	258	72	189	97	258
23	228	48	189	73	147	98	258
24	198	49	228	74	213	99	45
25	258	50	144	75	171	100	171

Note: these data are available in a spreadsheet (Exercise10.xls) on the web site (www.wileyeurope.com/go/robinson).

E10.5 A second set of replications have been run with the manufacturing model in Exercise E10.1, this time with an improvement to the cycle time of a bottleneck process. The results are shown in Table 10.13. Common random numbers have been used for both sets of experiments. Is the new scenario significantly better than the previous one?

E10.6 Perform a series of experiments with the bank model developed from the case described in Exercise E6.1 (Chapter 6). Aim to identify the best combination of ATMs.

E10.7 Perform a series of experiments with the Wardeon Cinema model (Appendix 1: Section A1.2.1). Aim to identify the quantity of resources required.

E10.8 Perform a series of experiments with the Panorama Televisions model (Appendix 2: Section A2.2.1). Aim to achieve the target throughput required.

Table 10.13 Results from a Second Scenario with the Manufacturing Model.

Replication	Mean daily t'put
1	200.1
2	210.6
3	216.6
4	209.9
5	182.4
6	221.0
7	177.7
8	193.5
9	209.4
10	211.5

Note: these data are available in a spreadsheet (Exercise10.xls) on the web site (www.wileyeurope.com/go/robinson).

E10.9 Carry out a sensitivity analysis on a model (e.g. the bank model, the Wardeon Cinema model or the Panorama Televisions model). Select two or three key data and vary them to determine the sensitivity of the results. Vary the data individually and in combination in order to understand their effect on the simulation results.

E10.10 Section 10.5 describes various formal approaches to search experimentation (experimental design, metamodelling and optimization). Carry out some further research into one or more of these areas, identifying the key methods for aiding simulation experimentation. (Hint: use the references in Section 10.5 as a starting point for your research.)

References

Alexopoulos, C. and Seila, A.F. (1998) "Output data analysis". In *Handbook of Simulation* (Banks, J., ed.). New York: Wiley, pp. 225–272.

Banks, J., Carson, J.S., Nelson, B.L. and Nicol, D.M. (2001) *Discrete-Event System Simulation*, 3rd edn. Upper Saddle River, NJ: Prentice Hall.

Box, G.E.P. and Draper, N.R. (1987) *Empirical Model Building and Response Surfaces*. New York: Wiley.

Box, G.E.P., Hunter, W.G. and Hunter J.S. (1978) *Statistics for Experimenters*. New York: Wiley.

Cheng, R.C.H. and Lamb, J.D. (1998) "Interactive implementation of optimal simulation experiment designs". *Proceedings of the 1998 Winter Simulation Conference* (D.J. Medeiros, E.F. Watson, M. Manivannan and J. Carson, eds). Piscataway, NJ: IEEE, pp. 707–712.

Daniel, W.W. and Terrell, J.C. (1995) *Business Statistics for Management and Economics*, 7th edn. Boston, MA: Houghton Mifflin Company.

Debuse, J.C.W., Rayward-Smith, V.J. and Smith, G.D. (1999) "Parameter optimisation for a discrete event simulator". *Computers and Industrial Engineering*, 37, 181–184.

Fishman, G.S. (1978) "Grouping observations in digital simulation". *Management Science*, 24(5), 510–521.

Fishman, G.S. (1996) *Monte Carlo: Concepts, Algorithms, and Applications*. New York: Springer-Verlag.

Fu, M.C. (2001) "Simulation optimization". *Proceedings of the 2001 Winter Simulation Conference* (Peters, B.A., Smith, J.S., Medeiros, D.J. and Rohrer, M.W., eds). Piscataway, NJ: IEEE, pp. 53–61.

Glasserman, P. (1991) *Gradient Estimation via Perturbation Analysis*. Boston: Kluwer.

Goldsman, D. and Nelson, B.L. (1998) Comparing systems via simulation. In: *Handbook of Simulation* (Banks, J., ed.). New York: Wiley, pp. 273–306.

Goldsman, D. and Nelson, B.L. (2001) "Statistical selection of the best system". *Proceedings of the 2001 Winter Simulation Conference* (Peters, B.A., Smith, J.S., Medeiros, D.J. and Rohrer, M.W., eds). Piscataway, NJ: IEEE, pp. 139–146.

Heidelberger, P. and Lewis, P.A.W. (1984) "Quantile estimation in dependent sequences". *Operations Research*, 32, 185–209.

Hoover, S.V. and Perry, R.F. (1990) *Simulation: A Problem-Solving Approach*. Reading, MA: Addison-Wesley.

Hurrion, R.D. (2000) "A sequential method for the development of visual interactive meta-simulation models using neural networks". *Journal of the Operational Research Society*, 51(6), 712–719.

Kleijnen, J.P.C. (1987) *Statistical Tools for Simulation Practitioners*. New York: Marcel Dekker.

Kleijnen, J.P.C. (1998) "Experimental design for sensitivity analysis, optimization, and validation of simulation models". In: *Handbook of Simulation* (Banks, J., ed.). New York: Wiley, pp. 173–223.

Kleijnen, J.P.C. and van Groenendaal, W. (1992) *Simulation: A Statistical Perspective*. Chichester, UK: Wiley.

Law, A.M. and Kelton, W.D. (2000) *Simulation Modeling and Analysis*, 3rd edn. New York: McGraw-Hill.

Montgomery, D.C. (2001) *Design and Analysis of Experiments*, 5th edn. New York: Wiley.

Noordegraaf, A.V., Nielen, M. and Kleijnen, J.P.C. (2003) "Sensitivity analysis by experimental design and metamodelling: case study on simulation in national animal disease control". *European Journal of Operational Research*, 146, 433–443.

Olafsson, S. and Kim, J. (2002) "Simulation optimization". *Proceedings of the 2002 Winter Simulation Conference* (Yucesan, E., Chen, C.-H., Snowden, S.L. and Charnes, J.M., eds). Piscataway, NJ: IEEE, pp. 79–84.

Pidd, M. (1998) *Computer Simulation in Management Science*, 4th edn. Chichester, UK: Wiley.

Reeves, C. (1995) *Modern Heuristic Techniques for Combinatorial Problems*. Maidenhead, UK: McGraw-Hill.

Schmeiser, B. (1982) "Batch size effects in the analysis of simulation output". *Operations Research*, 30(3), 556–568.

Von Neumann, J. (1941) "Distribution of the ratio of the mean square successive difference and the variance". *Annals of Mathematical Statistics*, 12, 367–395.

Internet address

MINITAB: www.minitab.com (July 2003)

IMPLEMENTATION

11

11.1 Introduction

The fourth and final process in a simulation project is implementation. It is in this part of a simulation study that the modelling effort actually has an effect on the real world, either by leading to a tangible change (and hopefully improvement) in the real world, or by giving the clients an improved understanding so they can better manage the real world. This chapter explores the process of implementation in two ways. First, there is a discussion on the meaning of implementation in which three types are identified. Secondly, the interrelationship between implementation and simulation project success is explored along with the factors that lead to success and the means for measuring success.

11.2 What is Implementation?

In its broadest sense implementation means putting something into effect or carrying something out. We think in terms of implementing a programme to restructure an organization or the military implementing a battle plan. In the context of simulation studies, implementation can be interpreted in three ways: implementing the findings from the simulation study, implementing the model and implementation as learning. These are not mutually exclusive and a simulation study may involve implementation in one, two or even all three of these ways.

Implementation should not be seen as something that only happens after a simulation study is completed. It is part of the iterative process described in Section 4.2. Insights gained by the clients throughout the modelling process, even during conceptual modelling, can be implemented while the study is ongoing.

11.2.1 Implementing the findings

In the process of performing a simulation study information and ideas come to light about how to tackle the problem situation being addressed. These findings are derived both as a result of the experimentation and the more general process of enquiry involved in the simulation study. When the simulation study is complete and, indeed, while it is still ongoing, these findings need to be implemented.

If the findings are to be implemented effectively they need to be clearly documented in a final report and an implementation process needs to be put in place. The final report should describe the problem situation and the objectives of the project, provide a summary of the model, describe the experiments performed, outline the key results, list the conclusions and recommendations and make suggestions for further simulation work if it is required. The exact nature and size of the report depends upon the clients' requirements. Apart from providing a written document it is probably useful to present the findings as well, enabling immediate feedback and clarification of issues. Once the findings have been reported, the modeller and model user often cease to have a role as the clients carry forward the implementation process. For this reason, it is vital that the findings are reported with clarity.

In the implementation process the clients determine which of the recommendations from the simulation study will be put into practice. This decision rests on wider issues in the real world situation such as the organizational culture and the finance available. The simulation study is normally just a (small) part of a wider project that is trying to effect some organizational change. It is, therefore, normal for the findings to be interpreted in the light of wider issues. The modeller and model user should not consider the simulation study a failure if some (or even all) of the recommendations are not implemented (Section 11.3.1). The key issue is whether the simulation study has contributed to the wider debate about organizational change.

The implementation process requires its own project team, which may or may not include the modeller and model user. The advantage of keeping them involved is that they have an in-depth understanding of the model as it reflects reality and they are on hand should further information be required from the model. The disadvantage is that their time is taken up when their skills might be required for simulation work elsewhere. If they are external consultants, the expense may detract from their continued involvement.

The implementation process should be monitored throughout to ensure the recommendations are implemented properly. It may be useful to refer back to the simulation from time to time, especially if the real world starts to diverge from the model. The real world is not static and new ideas may come to light that have not been tested in the simulation. For this reason, it may be useful to keep the modeller at least partly involved during the implementation process. If it is envisaged that the simulation will be required frequently during implementation, efforts should be made to keep the model aligned to the real world.

11.2.2 Implementing the model

From the modeller's perspective his/her involvement in a simulation study does not always lead directly to a set of recommendations that are to be implemented. Instead, the model might be handed over to the clients for their own use, in which case the clients become the modeller users. This may be because the clients want to perform their own experiments or because they want to share the experimentation with the modeller. In other cases, the simulation is designed to help make recurring decisions, for instance, determining a weekly production schedule or staff rosters. It is normal, in this situation, for the clients (or at least someone in their organization) to run the simulation as and when decisions are required. At less of an extreme, the clients sometimes prefer the modeller to perform the experiments, but they like to receive and run a copy of the model in order to improve their understanding and confidence in the results. All these circumstances require the hand-over of the model to the clients, otherwise described as implementing the model.

Model implementation requires adequate user documentation (Section 8.4) and training. It is also important to consider continued support for the model users and maintenance of the model. The modeller needs to have time available to help the model users, fix errors in the model, make improvements to the model and keep the model aligned to the real world. If external consultants have been used to develop the simulation, then a contract should be put in place for continued support and maintenance.

Of course, if the clients perform their own experimentation the findings still need to be implemented, even if this simply means putting the weekly production schedule or staff rosters into effect. Therefore, the first form of implementation is still required.

11.2.3 Implementation as learning

The modeller, model user and clients all gain an improved understanding of the real world not just from the results of the simulation experiments, but from the whole process of developing and using the simulation model (Section 1.3.2). This learning is often much wider than the direct focus of the simulation study. It is for this reason that the outcome of a simulation study is described not just as solutions to the problem being tackled, but also as an improved understanding (Section 4.2).

Because this learning is normally intangible rather than explicit, it cannot be identified directly. As a result there is no formal process for implementation. It does, however, lead to a change in management attitudes, beliefs and behaviours. Argyris (1999) describes this as double-loop learning. The importance of such learning, albeit informal and difficult to identify, should not be underestimated. It is a strong argument for keeping the clients involved throughout the modelling process in order to maximize their potential for learning.

11.3 Implementation and Simulation Project Success

For most modellers there is a certain satisfaction in seeing the findings from a simulation study being implemented. From time to time I drive past factories or visit retail outlets and proudly explain to my family how I have helped to design and improve their operations. On the other hand, it is always a disappointment when the results are apparently ignored. It is not surprising, therefore, that a number of studies have focused on implementation and closely allied to this simulation project success. Here this work is classified under three headings: defining simulation project success, achieving simulation project success and measuring simulation project success.

11.3.1 What is simulation project success?

Despite the interest in performing simulation studies successfully and ensuring the findings are implemented, it is hard actually to find a definition of what is meant by success. Balci (1985) states that a simulation study can be considered successful if the "results are credible and are accepted and used by the decision makers". Ulgen (1991) describes a set of criteria for success, including: completion on time and to budget, implementation and measurable financial savings. Meanwhile, Robinson and Pidd (1998) propose the four-stage model of success shown in Figure 11.1. There is a sense of time sequence to the four stages. In the first stage it must be agreed that the simulation study has achieved its objectives, or if this is not the case, that some benefit has been derived from the work. Next, the results should be accepted. This requires more than simply getting the right result (whatever this may mean) and is very much related to the clients' reaction to the findings. Organizational politics can play a significant role in the acceptability of the results. Stage 3 of success involves implementation. Even if the results are accepted, they may not be implemented because, for instance, the finance is not available. The final stage involves checking whether the results of the study were correct once the recommendations have been implemented. This concept is the same as solution validation described in Section 12.4.6. It is notable that the modeller has a decreasing level of control as we move to the right.

11.3.2 How is success achieved?

The definitions of success show a close alignment between implementation and simulation project success. Beyond defining success it is natural to go on and consider how success can be achieved. Various studies have looked at this issue.

In one of the earliest studies, Churchman and Schainblatt (1965) see implementation as a matter of developing the right understanding between the modeller and the clients. They proposed that the modeller and clients should develop a mutual understanding of one another. At the time of writing this was something of departure from practice where at an extreme the modeller's role was simply to provide the clients with "the answer". Today Churchman and Schainblatt's proposition has largely come to fruition, no doubt greatly aided by the power of modern modelling software. Certainly we would argue that developing a mutual understanding is vital to the success of a simulation study.

Tilanus *et al.* (1986) carried out a study of operational research applications in the Netherlands and Belgium and identified the factors in modelling success and failure. Among the success factors are: improved decision-making, good use of data, quick progress,

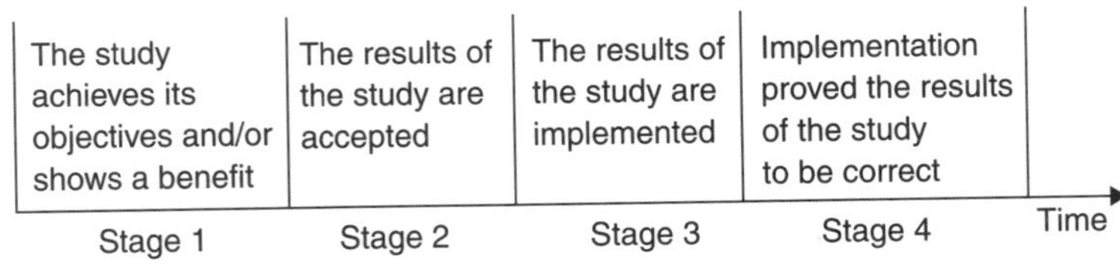

Figure 11.1 Four-Stage Model of Simulation Project Success (Robinson and Pidd 1998).

a simple and clear model, support from senior management and co-operation with the clients. Meanwhile, the causes of failure are very much the reverse of these. Others provide similar lists of factors in success and/or failure, for instance, Annino and Russell (1979), McLeod (1982), Raju (1982), Bean *et al.* (1989), Law and McComas (1989, 1990), Keller *et al.* (1991) and Law (1993). It should be noted, however, that the majority of these lists are based on speculation rather than empirical evidence.

Robinson and Pidd (1998) investigated simulation project success by interviewing both modellers and clients of simulation studies. In doing so they identified 338 factors that contribute to simulation project success. These are classified into the 19 dimensions listed in Table 11.1. To be successful the modeller must pay attention to all these areas. Success, however, does not necessarily require high achievement in every area. Instead, the modeller should concentrate on meeting the clients' expectations. For example, some clients expect frequent, possibly daily, communication with the modeller, while others are content with contact, say, once a week. Later, Robinson (2002) describes a simulation quality trilogy involving the quality of the content, the quality of the process and the quality of the outcome (Figure 11.2). These terms are defined as follows:

- *Quality of the Content*: the extent to which the technical work within the modelling process conforms to the requirements of the study.
- *Quality of the Process*: the extent to which the process of the delivery of the work conforms to the clients' expectations.
- *Quality of the Outcome*: the extent to which the simulation study is useful within the wider context for which it is intended.

The quality of the outcome is seen to derive directly from the former two, hence the diagonal arrows in the diagram. Meanwhile, there is a relationship between the technical work and the process of delivery shown by the horizontal two-way arrows. For instance, better data is likely to be obtained (content quality) if the communication between the modeller and the project team is good (process quality). Based on empirical evidence, Robinson goes on to suggest that in a typical simulation project, performed in a business context, the majority of the clients' quality perceptions are based on process rather than content quality. This is because the clients often do not have sufficient knowledge to judge the technical content of the work.

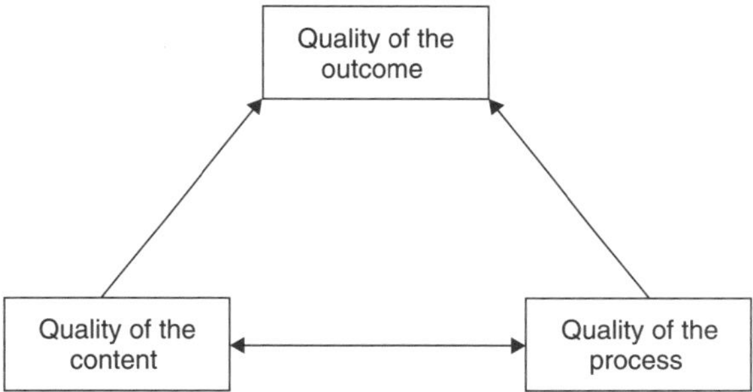

Figure 11.2 Simulation Quality Trilogy (Robinson 2002).

Table 11.1 Dimensions of Simulation Project Quality (Robinson and Pidd 1998).

Dimensions of Simulation Project Quality
The Model: speed, aesthetics, and ease of use
Confidence in the Model: trustworthiness and believability of the model and the results
The Data: availability and accuracy
Software: the proprietary simulation software: ease of use, suitability, flexibility, links to third party software, confidence
Credibility of the Modeller: trustworthiness, believability and honesty of the modeller and his/her organization
Competence of the Modeller: possession of the necessary skills and knowledge by the modeller and his/her organization to perform the simulation project
Professionalism: the modeller's commitment (to the project, to the clients, and to quality), interpersonal skills, and appearance
Reliability of the Modeller: consistency of performance and dependability
Communication and Interaction: frequency, clarity, and appropriateness of communication and interaction with those involved in the simulation project
Involvement: involving everybody (especially the clients) at all stages of the simulation project
Interpersonal: the relationship between the clients and the modeller
Education: the clients learn about simulation and the model as the project progresses
Understanding the Clients: the modeller makes every effort to understand the clients' needs and expectations
Responsiveness: the modeller gives a timely and appropriate response to the clients' needs and expectations
Recovery: recovering from problem situations
Access: approachability and ease of contact of the modeller; accessibility of the model
Fees: correctly charging for the simulation project
The Clients' Organization: the commitment of the clients' organization to the simulation project
Other: cannot be classified under specific dimensions above

11.3.3 How is success measured?

It is good practice to perform a project review at the end of a simulation study. The review should discuss what went well, what could have been done better and what could be improved next time. Some simulation modellers use a questionnaire for this process, while others prefer to hold a post-project review meeting.

Various methods have been proposed that might help with this review process and the measurement of simulation project success. Much of this work centres on assessing the validity of the model and particularly on independent verification and validation. These ideas are discussed in some detail in the next chapter.

Because model validation mainly relates to content quality this means that the assessment of process quality is largely ignored. There is some work, however, that does adopt a wider perspective. In the general context of project management, Slevin and Pinto (1986) develop a questionnaire for measuring the level of success or failure in a project. Meanwhile, Gable (1996) develops a means for measuring success in (operational research) projects performed by external consultants. Quite extensive work has gone into measuring the success of information systems. User information satisfaction is one such measure that concentrates on the users' reactions to a system rather than technical quality (Bailey and Pearson 1983; Ives *et al.*, 1983; Conrath and Mignen 1990; Shirani *et al.*, 1994). Based on these ideas and the concept of service quality, Robinson (1998) designs a questionnaire for measuring the quality of simulation projects. This measures client expectations and modeller performance across a range of the dimensions listed in Table 11.1.

11.4 Conclusion

The term implementation can be interpreted in three ways: implementing the findings from a simulation study, implementing the model and implementing the learning. A simulation study may involve one, two or even all three of these forms of implementation. There is a close alignment between the incidence of implementation and a simulation study being seen as successful. It is apparent that success is achieved not only by being attentive to the technical aspects of the work, but also by paying attention to the process of delivery. Post-project reviews, either in the form of a meeting or a questionnaire, are a useful means for determining whether a simulation study has been successful and how future projects could be improved.

References

Annino, J.S. and Russell, E.C. (1979) "The ten most frequent causes of simulation analysis failure – and how to avoid them!" *Simulation*, 32(6), 137–140.

Argyris, C. (1999) *On Organizational Learning*, 2nd edn. Oxford, UK: Blackwell.

Bailey, J.E. and Pearson, S.W. (1983) "Development of a tool for measuring and analysing computer user satisfaction". *Management Science*, 29(5), 530–545.

Balci, O. (1985) Guidelines for Successful Simulation Studies. Technical Report TR-85-2, Department of Computer Science, Virginia Tech, Blacksburg, Virginia.

Bean, M.F., Brooks, B.M. and Smurthwaite, K. (1989) The Use of Simulation as a Day-to-day Management Tool in Manufacturing Industry. DTI Study Report. PA Consulting Group, Royston, Herts, UK.

Churchman, C.W. and Schainblatt, A.H. (1965) "The researcher and the manager: a dialectic of implementation". *Management Science*, 11(4), 69–87.

Conrath, D.W. and Mignen, O.P. (1990) "What is being done to measure user satisfaction with EDP/MIS". *Information and Management*, 19(1), 7–19.

Gable, G.G. (1996) "A multidimensional model of client success when engaging external consultants". *Management Science*, 42(8), 1175–1198.

Ives, B., Olson, M.H. and Barondi, J.J. (1983) "The measurement of user information satisfaction". *Communication of the* ACM, 26(10), 785–793.

Keller, L., Harrell, C. and Leavy, J. (1991) "The three reasons why simulation fails". *Industrial Engineering*, 23(4), 27–31.

Law, A.M. (1993) "A forum on crucial issues in simulation modelling". *Industrial Engineering*, 25(5), 32–36.

Law, A.M. and McComas, M. (1989) "Pitfalls to avoid in the simulation of manufacturing systems". *Industrial Engineering*, 21(5), 28–69.

Law, A.M. and McComas, M. (1990) "Secrets of successful simulation studies". *Industrial Engineering*, 22(5), 47–72.

McLeod, J. (1982) *Computer Modeling and Simulation: Principles of Good Practice*. Simulation Series, 10(2). La Jolla, CA: The Society for Computer Simulation.

Raju, S.K.S. (1982) Survey of Participants in the SCS Workshop on Model Acceptance: Some Preliminary Results. In: *Computer Modeling and Simulation: Principles of Good Practice* (McLeod, J., ed.), Simulation Series, 10(2). La Jolla, CA: The Society for Computer Simulation, pp. 77–82.

Robinson, S. (1998) "Measuring service quality in the process of delivering a simulation study: the customer's perspective". *International Transactions in Operational Research*, 5(5), 357–374.

Robinson, S. (2002) "General concepts of quality for discrete-event simulation". *European Journal of Operational Research*, 138(1), 103–117.

Robinson, S. and Pidd, M. (1998) "Provider and customer expectations of successful simulation projects". *Journal of the Operational Research Society*, 49(3), 200–209.

Shirani, A., Aiken, M. and Reithel, B. (1994) "A model of user information satisfaction". *Data Base*, 25(4), 17–23.

Slevin, D.P. and Pinto, J.K. (1986) "The project implementation profile: new tool for project managers". *Project Management Journal*, 17(4), 57–70.

Tilanus, C.B., de Gans, O.B. and Lenstra, J.K. (1986) *Quantitative Methods in Management: Case Studies of Failures and Successes*. Chichester, UK: Wiley.

Ulgen, O. (1991) "Proper management techniques are keys to a successful simulation project". *Industrial Engineering*, 23(8), 37–41.

VERIFICATION, VALIDATION AND CONFIDENCE[1]

12

12.1 Introduction

Up to this point very little has been said about model testing. A significant element of any simulation study should involve the verification and validation of the simulation model. Without thorough verification and validation there are no grounds on which to place confidence in a study's results. That said, verification and validation is far from straightforward and it is often not performed as thoroughly as it might be.

In this chapter the concepts of verification and validation are explored as well as some methods for model testing. The chapter is split into four parts. First, the terms verification and validation are defined, and various forms of verification and validation are described and set in the context of the process of performing a simulation study. There is then a discussion on the difficulties that are encountered when trying to perform verification and validation. Thirdly, some useful verification and validation methods are described. Finally, there is a brief discussion on independent verification and validation.

In the chapters on experimentation (Chapters 9 and 10) it is noted that the experimental procedures aim to assure only the accuracy with which the *model performance* is predicted. In those chapters the accuracy with which the *real system performance* is predicted is not taken into account. It is of course verification and validation that aims to determine the accuracy with which the model predicts the performance of the real system.

12.2 What is Verification and Validation?

Verification is the process of ensuring that the model design (conceptual model) has been transformed into a computer model with sufficient accuracy (Davis 1992). Validation, on the other hand, is the process of ensuring that the model is sufficiently accurate for the

[1] This chapter is based on the paper Robinson, S. (1999) Simulation Verification, Validation and Confidence: A Tutorial. *Transactions of the Society for Computer Simulation International*, 16(2), pp. 63–69. Copyright © by Simulation Councils, Inc. Reproduced by permission.

purpose at hand (Carson 1986). Verification has quite a narrow definition and in many respects it can be seen as a subset of the wider issue of validation.

There are two key concepts in validation: the ideas of *sufficient accuracy* and models that are built for a specific *purpose*. By now it should be clear that no model is ever 100% accurate, indeed, a model is not meant to be completely accurate, but a simplified means for understanding and exploring reality (Pidd 2003). In verification and validation the aim is to ensure that the model is sufficiently accurate. Further, this accuracy is with reference to the purpose for which the model is to be used. As a consequence, the purpose, or objectives, of a model must be known before it can be validated. This purpose may have been determined at the start of the simulation study, being expressed through the objectives (Section 6.2.2), or it may be an alternative use for an existing model. Under this definition for validation it is possible to think in terms of absolute validity; a model is either sufficiently accurate for its purpose or it is not. In other words, validity is a binary decision with a conclusion of "yes" or "no". Proving this is a different matter, as is discussed in Section 12.3.

Validity and accuracy are related but separate concepts. While validity is a binary decision, accuracy is measured on a scale of zero to 100%. The relationship between the two concepts can be illustrated with reference to an example. Some years ago I was asked to build a simulation model of a manufacturing plant in order to demonstrate the potential of simulation to an organization (the purpose of the model). A process flow was provided for one of the organization's manufacturing facilities, but no further information was made available. On requesting data on cycle times, breakdowns, travel times and the like, it was suggested that these should be made up! As a result, a model was built that looked something like the manufacturing facility but the data were unrepresentative. Unless I am good at guessing it is probable that the model was completely inaccurate. However, when the model was demonstrated to the client it convinced him of the potential for simulation in his organization, since it showed that his manufacturing facilities could be modelled and that new ideas could be tried in a simulation relatively easily. Although the model was inaccurate it was valid; in other words, it was sufficiently accurate (or inaccurate) for the purpose at hand, that was, to demonstrate the potential of simulation. Obviously a much higher degree of accuracy is normally required for a model to be considered valid. Indeed, the modeller should determine early on in a simulation study the level of accuracy required from the model.

Verification and validation can be further understood by mapping the verification and validation requirements onto the process of performing a simulation study (Section 4.2). Figure 12.1 shows that for each process in a simulation study, at least one verification or validation process is performed in parallel.

Various forms of validation are identified, which can be defined as follows:

- *Conceptual Model Validation*: determining that the content, assumptions and simplifications of the proposed model are sufficiently accurate for the purpose at hand. The question being asked is: does the conceptual model contain all the necessary details to meet the objectives of the simulation study?
- *Data Validation*: determining that the contextual data and the data required for model realization and validation are sufficiently accurate for the purpose at hand. As shown

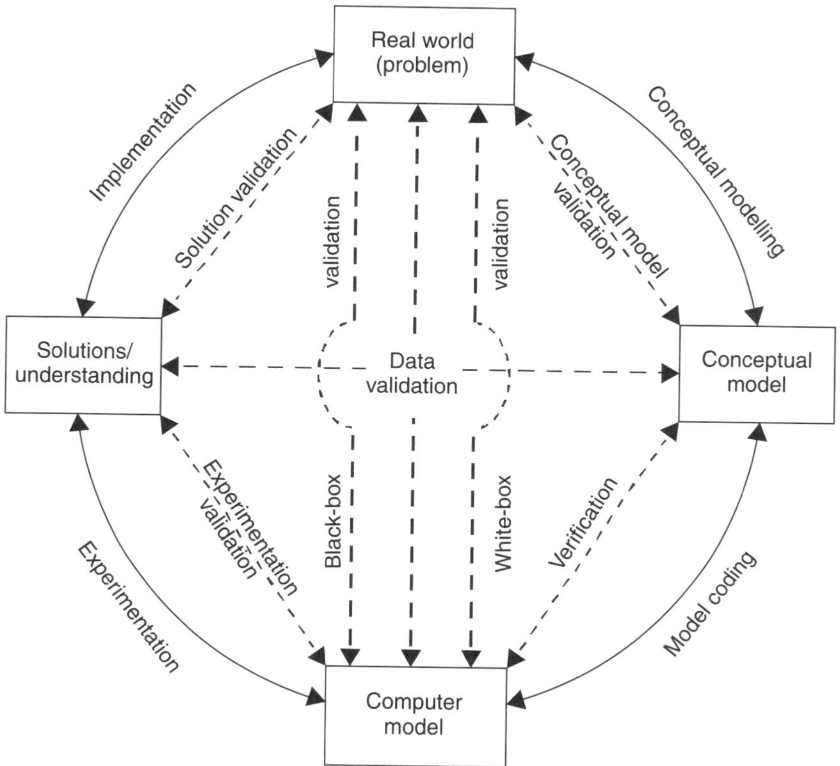

Figure 12.1 Simulation Model Verification and Validation in a Simulation Study (adapted from Landry *et al.* 1983).

in Figure 12.1, this applies to all stages in a simulation study, since data are required at every point.

- *White-Box Validation*: determining that the constituent parts of the computer model represent the corresponding real world elements with sufficient accuracy for the purpose at hand. This is a detailed, or micro, check of the model, in which the question is asked: does each part of the model represent the real world with sufficient accuracy to meet the objectives of the simulation study?
- *Black-Box Validation*: determining that the overall model represents the real world with sufficient accuracy for the purpose at hand. This is an overall, or macro, check of the model's operation, in which the question is asked: does the overall model provide a sufficiently accurate representation of the real world system to meet the objectives of the simulation study?
- *Experimentation Validation*: determining that the experimental procedures adopted are providing results that are sufficiently accurate for the purpose at hand. Key issues are the requirements for removing initialization bias, run-length, replications and sensitivity

analysis to assure the accuracy of the results. Further to this, suitable methods should be adopted for searching the solution space to ensure that learning is maximized and appropriate solutions identified.

- *Solution Validation*: determining that the results obtained from the model of the proposed solution are sufficiently accurate for the purpose at hand. This is similar to black-box validation in that it entails a comparison with the real world. It is different in that it only compares the final model of the proposed solution to the implemented solution. Consequently, solution validation can only take place post implementation and so, unlike the other forms of validation, it is not intrinsic to the simulation study itself. In this sense, it has no value in giving assurance to the client, but it does provide some feedback to the modeller.

Verification is also identified on Figure 12.1 as a test of the fidelity with which the conceptual model is converted into the computer model (as per its definition).

What should be apparent is that verification and validation is not just performed once a complete model has been developed, but that *verification and validation is a continuous process that is performed throughout the life-cycle of a simulation study*. In the same way that modelling is an iterative process, so too is verification and validation. At an early stage in a simulation project a conceptual model is developed. At this point this model should be validated. However, as the project progresses the conceptual model is likely to be revised as the understanding of the problem and the modelling requirements change. As a consequence, the conceptual model also needs to be revalidated. While the conceptual model is being transformed into a computer model, the constituent parts of the model (particularly those recently coded) should be continuously verified. Similarly, the details of the model should be checked against the real world throughout model coding (white-box validation). Black-box validation requires a completed model, since it makes little sense to compare the overall model against the real world until it is complete. This does not imply, however, that black-box validation is only performed once. The identification of model errors and continued changes to the conceptual model necessitates model revisions and therefore further black-box validation. In a similar way, the experimental procedures need to be validated for every revision of the model, including the experimental scenarios. It cannot be assumed that the requirements for experimentation are the same for every model version.

Although white-box validation and black-box validation are often lumped together under one heading, operational validity (Sargent 1999), it is because they are performed as separate activities during a simulation study that a distinction is drawn between them here. White-box validation is intrinsic to model coding, while black-box validation can only be performed once the model code is complete.

12.3 The Difficulties of Verification and Validation

Before discussing specific methods of verification and validation it is important to recognize that there are a number of problems that arise in trying to validate a model.

12.3.1 There is no such thing as general validity

A model is only validated with respect to its purpose. It cannot be assumed that a model that is valid for one purpose is also valid for another. For instance, a model of a production facility may have been validated for use in testing alternative production schedules, however, this does not mean that it is necessarily valid for determining that facility's throughput. A model could only be described as generally valid if it could be demonstrated that it was suitably accurate for every purpose to which it might ever be put. Not only is it unlikely that every potential purpose for a model could be determined, but also such a model would probably be very extensive, requiring vast amounts of code, data and run-time. This goes against the principle of keeping models as simple as possible for the task at hand (Section 5.4.2). Indeed, reality is the only "model" which is generally valid.

12.3.2 There may be no real world to compare against

Much validation requires a comparison of the model to the real system. However, many models are developed of proposed systems, for instance, new production or service facilities. As a consequence, there is no real world to use for comparison. Even if the model is of an existing system, its purpose is to investigate alternative operating practices, for which again no real world exists. The model may be shown to be valid when it is representing the existing operation, but this does not guarantee that it is valid once it represents some change to the system.

12.3.3 Which real world?

Different people have different interpretations of the real world, described as Weltanschauung or world views by Checkland (1981). An employee in a bank may see the bank as a means for earning money, while a customer may see it as a means for safely storing money, or as a means for borrowing money. Depending on who we speak to, we obtain different interpretations of the purpose and operation of the bank. Every day we can read multiple accounts of the same event in our newspapers, each with subtle (or not so subtle!) differences. The event was the same, but the reporters' interpretations vary.

This presents a problem when validating models. If people have different world views, which interpretation(s) should be used for developing and validating a model? A model that is valid to one person may not be valid to another.

12.3.4 Often the real world data are inaccurate

Validation often involves a comparison of some facet of the model, for instance throughput, against real world data. The model is run under the same conditions as the real world to see if it performs in a similar manner. There are two difficulties that arise with this procedure. First, the real world data may not be accurate. Indeed, the purpose of data validation is to determine the accuracy of the data that are being used. If the data are not accurate, however, this creates problems in determining whether a model's results are correct.

Secondly, even if "accurate" real world data do exist, it must be remembered that these are only a sample, which in itself creates inaccuracy. For instance, data may have been collected on the throughput of a production facility over a 10-week period. If, however, data had been collected for a further 10 weeks this would no doubt have changed the distribution of the data. To exacerbate the problem, the simulation itself is providing only a sample: results of, say, 10 weeks of operation. This means that the real world-to-model comparison is a comparison of two samples. Although statistical procedures can be used to determine whether these two samples are similar, these only provide a probabilistic and not a definitive answer.

12.3.5 There is not enough time to verify and validate everything

There is simply not enough time to verify and validate every aspect of a model (Balci 1997). Those that develop software have experienced users breaking what was thought to be perfectly sound code. This is a problem that affects both verification and validation. The modeller's job is to ensure that as much of the model is verified and validated as possible, both in terms of the model details (conceptual model validity, verification, white-box validation and data validation), the overall validity (black-box validation) and the experimental procedures (experimentation validation).

12.3.6 Confidence not validity

The conclusion of this is that although, in theory, a model is either valid or it is not, proving this in practice is a very different matter. Indeed, it is not possible to prove that a model is valid. Instead, it is only possible to think in terms of the confidence that can be placed in a model. The process of verification and validation is not one of trying to demonstrate that the model is correct, but is in fact a process of trying to prove that the model is incorrect. The more tests that are performed in which it cannot be proved that the model is incorrect, the more the clients' (and the modeller's) confidence in the model grows. The purpose of verification and validation is to increase the confidence in the model and its results to the point where the clients are willing to use it as an aid to decision-making. It is also important for the modeller to have confidence that the simulation should be used for decision-making.

12.4 Methods of Verification and Validation

There are many methods of verification and validation available to simulation modellers. Here a summary of some useful approaches is provided. For a detailed review of verification and validation techniques see Balci (1994). It should be noted that good quality documentation (Section 8.4) provides significant help to any verification and validation effort.

12.4.1 Conceptual model validation

There are no formal methods for validating a conceptual model. The project specification (Section 5.5.1) is the prime means available for determining what confidence should be placed in the model. The specification should be circulated among those who have a detailed knowledge of the system and feedback sought on whether the model is appropriate. Where issues occur, these should be dealt with either by adjusting the conceptual model, or by clarifying any misunderstandings. By gaining wide acceptance for the conceptual model the confidence of the modeller and the clients is increased.

It is also useful for the modeller and the clients jointly to assess the assumptions and simplifications for the level of confidence that can be placed in them and their likely impact on the accuracy of the model. Albeit purely based on judgement, such an assessment both ensures that the potential effect of all the assumptions and simplifications is considered and helps identify any areas of particular concern. Those assumptions and simplifications about which there is little confidence, and which it is believed have a high impact, need to be addressed. One approach is to try and remove them by altering the model or investigating the real system further. Alternatively, and when it is not possible to remove them, sensitivity analysis can be performed later in the project to determine their impact.

12.4.2 Data validation

Data are obviously a potential source of inaccuracy in a simulation model and can in their own right move a model from being sufficiently accurate to being invalid. Every effort should be made to ensure that the data are as accurate as possible. The modeller should investigate the sources of data to determine their reliability. The data should be analysed for inconsistencies and any cause for concern investigated. Beyond this, much has to be put down to trust especially when the modeller is simply presented with data. Where problems do occur with the data, these must be dealt with. Section 7.3 describes some methods for dealing with data that are unavailable, inaccurate or in the wrong format.

12.4.3 Verification and white-box validation

Although verification and white-box validation are conceptually different, they are treated together here because they are both performed continuously throughout model coding. Also, they are both micro checks of the model's content. Verification ensures that the model is true to the conceptual model, while white-box validation ensures that the content of the model is true to the real world (in this way it is an indirect form of conceptual model validation). Verification can be performed by the modeller alone, comparing the computer model with the conceptual model description. Meanwhile, white-box validation requires the involvement of those knowledgeable about the real world system. Whereas verification can be performed almost continuously during model coding, white-box validation is performed less frequently since it requires the involvement of more than just the modeller.

Various aspects of the model should be checked during model coding:

- Timings, e.g. cycle times, repair times and travel times.
- Control of elements, e.g. breakdown frequency and shift patterns.
- Control of flows, e.g. routing.

- Control logic, e.g. scheduling and stock replenishment.
- Distribution sampling, e.g. the samples obtained from an empirical distribution.

Three methods of verification and white-box validation are now discussed.

Checking the code

The modeller needs to read through the code to ensure that the right data and logic have been entered. This is especially true for areas of complex logic. A useful idea is to get someone else to read the code, or to explain the code to someone else as a second check. If no modelling experts are available, then most simulation software vendors offer a help-desk service with which specific areas of code could be discussed. Alternatively, by expressing the code in a non-technical format (the documentation could be used for this purpose; Section 8.4) a non-expert could check the data and the logic. This is especially useful for obtaining the opinion of those who have a detailed knowledge of the system being modelled.

Visual checks

The visual display of the model proves to be a powerful aid for verification and validation. By running the model and watching how each element behaves both the logic of the model and the behaviour against the real world can be checked. Various ideas aid this approach:

- Stepping through the model event by event.
- Stopping the model, predicting what will happen next, running the model on and checking what happens.
- Interactively setting up conditions to force certain events to take place.
- Creating extreme conditions, such as a very high arrival rate, to determine whether the model behaves as expected.
- Isolating areas of the model so it runs faster, reducing the time to perform thorough verification and validation.
- Explaining the model as it runs to those knowledgeable about the real system in order to gain their opinion.
- Tracing the progress of an item through the model.

It is useful simply to watch a model running for a period of time. In so doing a lot can be learnt about the behaviour of the simulation. It is also useful to demonstrate the model, formally and informally, to those who have a detailed knowledge of the system. Not only does this enable them to identify any shortcomings in the model, but by involving them this should increase the credibility of the work (assuming that not too many errors are found!).

Inspecting output reports

By inspecting the reports from a simulation run, the actual and expected results can be compared. Of interest in verification and white-box validation is the performance of the individual elements, for example, service point utilizations. Graphical reports of samples from input distributions, for instance, machine repair times, are an aid in checking that they are being modelled correctly. More formal methods for comparing distributions can be employed to provide a more rigorous check (Section 7.5.2).

A report which may be of some use is a 'trace' of a simulation run. This is a blow-by-blow history, normally written to a file, of every event that takes place during a simulation run. Inspecting this report can help to diagnose and rectify any problems.

12.4.4 Black-box validation

In black-box validation the overall behaviour of the model is considered. There are two broad approaches to performing this form of validation. The first is to compare the simulation model to the real world. The other is to make a comparison with another model. The second approach is particularly useful when there are no real world data to compare against.

Comparison with the real system

If confidence is to be placed in a model then, when it is run under the same conditions (inputs) as the real world system, the outputs should be sufficiently similar (Figure 12.2). This concept is expressed as the alternative hypothesis (H_1) in Figure 12.2, since the purpose of validation, the null hypothesis, is to demonstrate that the model is incorrect (Section 12.3.6). The approximation sign shows that the model need only be sufficiently accurate. As already stated, the significant difficulty with this form of validation is that there may not be any accurate real world data with which to perform such a comparison. If this is the case then the comparison can be made against the expectations and intuition of those who have a detailed knowledge of the real system. Comparison against approximate real world data such as these may not give absolute confidence in the model, but it should help to increase confidence.

Historic (or expected) data collected from the real system, such as throughput and customer service levels, can be compared with the results of the simulation when it is run

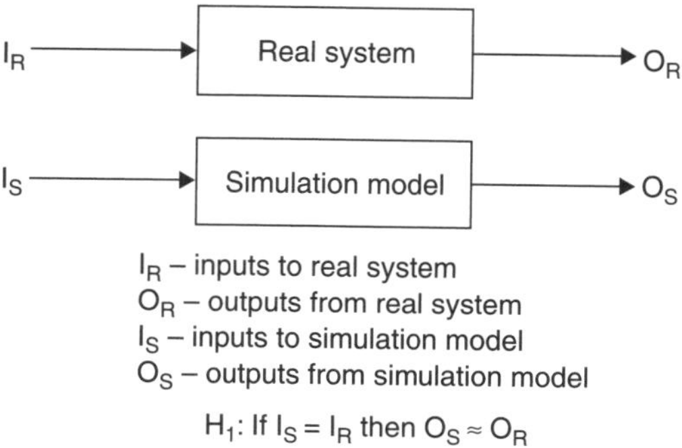

Figure 12.2 Black-Box Validation: Comparison with the Real System.

under the same conditions. It is important to check not only the average levels of these data, but also to compare their spread. This can be performed by judging how closely the averages from the model and the real world match, and by visually comparing the distributions of the data. Various statistical tests also lend themselves to such comparisons (Kleijnen 1995). Assuming that the same quantity of output data is generated from the simulation model as is available from the real system, then a confidence interval for the difference in the means can be calculated as follows:

$$\overline{X}_S - \overline{X}_R \pm t_{2n-2,\alpha/2}\sqrt{\frac{S_S^2 + S_R^2}{n}}$$

where:

$\overline{X}_S$ = mean of simulated output data

$\overline{X}_R$ = mean of real system output data

S_S = standard deviation of simulated output data

S_R = standard deviation of real system output data

n = number of observations (this must be the same for the simulated and real system data)

$t_{2n-2,\alpha/2}$ = value from Student's t-distribution with $2n - 2$ degrees of freedom and a significance level of $\alpha/2$

If the sample size (n) is different then a more complex calculation is required (Montgomery and Runger 1994). Of course, it is probably simpler to delete some observations from the larger sample, in order to make the sample sizes equal. The confidence interval can be interpreted in the same fashion as the paired-t confidence interval described in Section 10.4. Note that a paired-t confidence interval cannot be used for comparing real world data to the simulation model, since the requirement for correlation (achieved in simulation by the use of common random numbers) is not met.

Apart from using a confidence interval to compare the output from the model with the real world, a chi-square test could be used to compare the distributions of the output data (Section 7.5.2). Another powerful approach is to run a simulation from a trace of historic data (Section 7.4.1), enabling a more direct comparison of the model with the real world (Kleijnen 1995; Kleijnen *et al.* 1998, 2001). A paired-t confidence interval would then, in most cases, be appropriate because the two sets of output data should be correlated.

An alternative approach is to compare the relationships between the inputs and outputs in the model and the real world. For instance, if it is known that when an input (e.g. a storage area) is increased by 20% in the real world there is a corresponding 10% increase in one of the outputs (e.g. throughput), a similar relationship should be obtained from the model.

In a Turing Test (Schruben 1980) the model reports are made to look exactly the same as the reports provided by the real system. One or more reports from the model and from the real world are given to someone who is knowledgeable about the system. He/she is then asked to try and distinguish between the two. If he/she is unable to detect any difference, this increases the confidence in the model. If differences are detected, then the reason for these should be investigated and corrected in the model if they are deemed significant. Even if real world reports are not available, it is still worth asking an expert to review the model reports.

Comparison with other models

As an alternative to comparison against the real world, the simulation can be compared with other, normally simpler models (Figure 12.3). This group of methods is particularly useful when no real system data are available. However, this does not preclude their use when these data are available. Indeed, using these in addition to real world comparison can only serve to increase confidence further. One approach is to compare the simulation model against a mathematical model. It is unlikely that a mathematical model is able to predict the outcome of the simulation exactly, otherwise the simulation would probably not have been built. However, for the purposes of comparison a mathematical model may be able to give a crude approximation to the outputs of the real system. Examples of mathematical models that might be used are paper calculations, spreadsheet analysis and queuing theory (Winston 1994). This approach is sometimes referred to as static analysis because it does not (cannot) take into account the full dynamics of the simulation model.

In order to aid comparison it is sometimes useful to simplify the simulation model to the extent that a mathematical model can predict exactly, or at least more exactly, the outcome of the model. One specific, and extreme, case of this is the use of deterministic models. This is a simulation model from which all the random events are removed. In many cases it is possible to determine mathematically the exact outcome of such a model.

Comparisons can also be made against other simulation models of the same or similar systems. For instance, a more detailed model of the system may have been developed for some other purpose. This presupposes, of course, that the other model is itself valid.

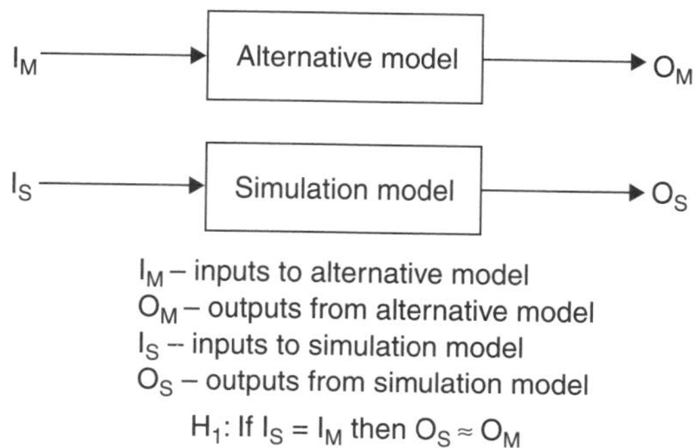

Figure 12.3 Black-Box Validation: Comparison with an Alternative Model.

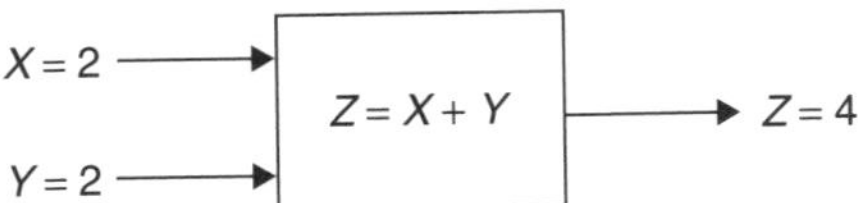

Figure 12.4 Black-Box and White-Box Validation of a Simple Model.

The relation between white-box and black-box validation

Black-box validation is often seen as the primary test for a simulation model where we determine whether the output from the model is sufficiently similar to the real world. Black-box validation, however, should not be relied upon solely, and it is particularly important to test the white-box validity of a model as well. Take the following, very simple, example.

In Figure 12.4 data have been obtained for two inputs (X and Y) and one output (Z). A simple model is proposed, $Z = X + Y$. By checking only the black-box validity it would seem that this model is correct since $X = 2$, $Y = 2$ and $Z = 4$. However, by checking the detail of the model (white-box validation), it might be discovered that the relationship is wrong and in fact it should be $Z = XY$. Albeit that both models give the same result under current conditions, a simple change of the inputs to $X = 3$ and $Y = 3$ would lead to a 50% error in the result if the wrong model is used. This type of error can only be guarded against by testing both white-box and black-box validity.

Another danger in relying on black-box validity alone is it can lead to the temptation to calibrate the model, that is, to tweak the model inputs until the simulation provides the correct output. Although this can be useful if performed in an intelligent fashion, paying attention to white-box validity as well, in isolation it can lead to a simulation that is unrepresentative of the system it is trying to model.

12.4.5 Experimentation validation

Assuring the accuracy of simulation experiments requires attention to the issues of initial transient effects, run-length, the number of replications and sensitivity analysis. Also, the search of the solution space should be sufficient to obtain an adequate understanding and identify appropriate solutions. Methods for dealing with these issues are described in some detail in Chapters 9 and 10.

12.4.6 Solution validation

The aim of all modelling and verification and validation efforts is to try and assure the validity of the final solution. Once implemented, it should be possible to validate the implemented solution against the model's results. This is similar in concept to the comparisons with the real world performed in black-box validation, except that the comparison is between the final model of the proposed solution and the implemented solution. Therefore, the techniques of black-box validation discussed in Section 12.4.4 can be applied.

Solution validity should also involve checking whether the implemented solution is indeed the most suitable. In practice, however, it is unlikely that this is possible, since it is not usually practical to implement alternative solutions to determine their effect; this, no doubt, is the reason for using a simulation in the first place. Neither is solution validation possible if the simulation is only used to develop a better understanding of the real world and not directly to develop a solution. A form of reverse validation, however, may be possible. An improved understanding may lead to the implementation of new ideas. These ideas could then be included in the simulation model and a comparison made to the real world, thereby checking the accuracy of the model.

From discussions with simulation practitioners it is apparent that solution validation is rarely carried out even though it is the only true test of the outcome of a simulation study. A key problem is that the implementation may take many years to complete, by which time the momentum for the simulation work, and possibly the simulation modeller, have long disappeared. Another issue is whether the solution is properly implemented and so whether a meaningful comparison can be made.

12.5 Independent Verification and Validation

Independent verification and validation (IV&V) or verification, validation and accreditation (VV&A) involves an independent third party whose aim is to determine whether a model is suitable for a particular use. Gass (1983) defines model assessment (or evaluation) as "a process by which interested parties (who were not involved in a model's origins, development and implementation) can determine, with some level of confidence, whether or not the model's results can be used in decision-making". He believes that model assessment is necessary in three circumstances:

- When the decision-makers are far removed from the process of developing the model.
- When the model is to be applied to a new set of circumstances other than that originally intended.
- Even if the decision-makers work closely with the analysts during model development, it is unlikely that they have the necessary knowledge and skills to evaluate the model.

Mostly, independent verification and validation is only carried out for large-scale military and public policy models, probably because the costs of the process are prohibitive for most manufacturing and service sector projects which tend to be smaller in scale (Cochran *et al.* 1995). Indeed, writing in 1977, Gass suggests that in selecting a model for major evaluation it should have involved an expenditure of over $250,000 and more than five person-years of effort (Gass 1977). Even for large-scale models, independent verification and validation is not always common practice (Arthur and Nance 1996).

A whole range of procedures for independently assessing simulation models have been proposed over the years, see for instance, Gass (1977, 1983, 1993), Pugh (1977), Gass and Joel (1981), Sargent (1981), Ören (1981), Balci (1985, 2001), Fossett *et al.* (1991), Williams and Sikora (1991), Davis (1992), and Kneppel and Arangno (1993). Most of these procedures outline a set of criteria that need to be assessed. The majority of these criteria involve model verification and validation, although other factors such as documentation and training are also considered to be important. Gass and Joel (1981), for instance, use seven criteria:

- Model definition
- Model structure
- Model data
- Computer model verification
- Model validation
- Model usability
- Model pedigree

For each of the criteria either a subjective score is given (e.g. on a scale of 1–5) or a set of qualitative statements is made. Where subjective scores are given, then some overall score can be calculated, possibly taking into account the importance of each criteria (Gass and Joel 1981). The overall score indicates the level of confidence that can be placed in the model for its intended purpose. Balci *et al.* (2002) describe software that aids the evaluation process.

12.6 Conclusion

It is not possible to prove that a model is absolutely correct. Therefore, model verification and validation is concerned with creating enough confidence in a model for the results to be accepted. This is done by trying to prove that the model is incorrect. The more tests that are performed in which it cannot be proved that the model is incorrect, the more confidence in the model is increased. For verification and validation the general rule is: the more testing the better.

Of course, the modeller and the clients may have different thresholds for confidence. Some clients may derive their confidence simply from the model's display, others may require more in-depth verification and validation before they are willing to believe the results. The modeller is responsible for guiding the clients and ensuring that sufficient verification and validation is performed.

Finally, the modeller should remember that the acceptance of a simulation study and its results does not rest solely on the validity of the model. Verification and validation assures (content) quality in the sense that the model conforms to the clients' technical requirements for a model and a set of results that are sufficiently accurate (Section 11.3.2). What it does not determine is the extent to which the simulation study meets the clients' expectations concerning the process of project delivery (process quality). This issue is addressed in Section 11.3.

Some of the methods of verification and validation described in this chapter are illustrated by the Wardeon Cinema and Panorama Televisions case studies in Appendix 1 (Section A1.5) and Appendix 2 (Section A2.5) respectively.

Exercises

E12.1 Compare and contrast the difficulties that might be encountered in validating a simulation model of:

a) An existing manufacturing plant
b) A unique construction project

E12.2 Table 12.1 shows the results (mean customer waiting time) obtained from 10 replications with a simulation model of a bank. Each replication was run for a period of one day. It also shows the data collected by observing 10 days of operation of the bank. Does this data give confidence in the validity of the model?

E12.3 Obtain and read some simulation case studies (see Exercise E1.3 in Chapter 1 for potential sources). Identify the methods used to verify and validate the models. Can you identify any ways in which the verification and validation could be improved upon?

E12.4 Carry out some verification and validation tests with the bank model developed from the case described in Exercise E6.1 (Chapter 6).

E12.5 Carry out some verification and validation tests with the Wardeon Cinema model (Appendix 1: Section A1.2.1).

E12.6 Carry out some verification and validation tests with the Panorama Televisions model (Appendix 2: Section A2.2.1).

Table 12.1 Simulation Results and Real World Data for Mean Customer Waiting Time (minutes) at a Bank.

Replication/Day	Simulation result (mean customer waiting time)	Bank data (mean customer waiting time)
1	1.06	0.97
2	1.02	1.01
3	1.06	1.00
4	1.03	1.01
5	1.01	0.98
6	1.11	1.03
7	0.98	1.02
8	1.08	0.95
9	1.06	1.00
10	1.02	1.06
Mean	1.04	1.00
St. dev.	0.04	0.03

References

Arthur, J.D. and Nance, R.E. (1996) "Independent verification and validation: a missing link in simulation methodology?" *Proceedings of the 1996 Winter Simulation Conference* (Charnes, J.M., Morrice, D.J., Brunner, D.T. and Swain, J.J., eds). Piscataway, NJ: IEEE, pp. 230–236.

Balci, O. (1985) Guidelines for Successful Simulation Studies. Technical Report TR-85-2, Department of Computer Science, Virginia Tech, Blacksburg, VA.

Balci, O. (1994) "Validation, verification, and testing techniques throughout the life cycle of a simulation study". *Annals of Operations Research*, 53, 121–173.

Balci, O. (1997) "Principles of simulation model validation, verification, and testing". *Transactions of the Society for Computer Simulation*, 14(1), 3–12.

Balci, O. (2001) "A methodology for certification of modeling and simulation applications". ACM *Transactions on Modeling and Computer Simulation*, 11(4), 352–377.

Balci, O., Adams, R.J., Myers, D.S. and Nance, R.E. (2002) A Collaborative Evaluation Environment for Credibility Assessment of Modeling and Simulation Applications. *Proceedings of the 2002 Winter Simulation Conference* (Yucesan, E., Chen, C.-H., Snowden, S.L. and Charnes, J.M., eds). Piscataway, NJ: IEEE; pp. 214–220.

Carson, J.S. (1986) "Convincing users of model's validity is challenging aspect of modeler's job". *Industrial Engineering*, 18(6), 74–85.

Checkland, P. (1981) *Systems Thinking, Systems Practice*. Chichester, UK: Wiley.

Cochran, J.K., Mackulak, G.T. and Savory, P.A. (1995) "Simulation project characteristics in industrial settings". *Interfaces*, 25(4), 104–113.

Davis, P.K. (1992) Generalizing concepts of verification, validation and accreditation (VV&A) for military simulation. R-4249-ACQ, October 1992, RAND, Santa Monica, CA.

Fossett, C.A., Harrison, D., Weintrob, H. and Gass, S.I. (1991) "An assessment procedure for simulation models: a case study". *Operations Research*, 39(5), 710–723.

Gass, S.I. (1977) "Evaluation of complex models". *Computers and Operations Research*, 4, 27–35.

Gass, S.I. (1983) "Decision-aiding models: validation, assessment, and related issues for policy analysis". *Operations Research*, 31(4), 603–631.

Gass, S.I. (1993) "Model accreditation: a rationale and process for determining a numerical rating". *European Journal of Operational Research*, 66, 250–258.

Gass, S.I. and Joel, L.S. (1981) "Concepts of model confidence". *Computers and Operations Research*, 8(4), 341–346.

Kleijnen, J.P.C. (1995) "Verification and validation of simulation models". *European Journal of Operational Research*, 82(1), 145–162.

Kleijnen, J.P.C., Bettonvil, B. and Groenendaal, W.V. (1998) "Validation of trace-driven simulation models: a novel regression test". *Management Science*, 44(6), 812–819.

Kleijnen, J.P.C., Cheng, R.C.H. and Bettonvil, B. (2001) "Validation of trace-driven simulation models: Bootstrap methods". *Management Science*, 47(11), 1533–1538.

Knepell, P.L. and Arangno, D.C. (1993) *Simulation Validation: A Confidence Assessment Methodology*. Monograph 3512–04. Los Alamitos, CA: IEEE Computer Society Press.

Landry, M., Malouin, J.L. and Oral, M. (1983) "Model validation in operations research". *European Journal of Operational Research*, 14(3), 207–220.

Montgomery, D.C. and Runger, G.C. (1994) *Applied Statistics and Probability for Engineers*. New York: Wiley.

Ören, T.I. (1981) "Concepts and criteria to assess acceptability of simulation studies: a frame of reference". *Communications of the ACM*, 28(2), 190–201.

Pidd, M. (2003) *Tools for Thinking: Modelling in Management Science*, 2nd edn. Chichester, UK: Wiley.

Pugh, R.E. (1977) *Evaluation of Policy Simulation Models*. Washington DC: Information Resource Press.

Sargent, R.G. (1981) An Assessment Procedure and a Set of Criteria for Use in the Evaluation of Computerized Models and Computer-Based Modelling Tools. RADC-TR-80-409, Rome Air Development Center, Air Force Systems Command, Griffiths Air Force Base, NY.

Sargent, R.G. (1999) "Validation and verification of simulation models". *Proceedings of the 1999 Winter Simulation Conference* (Farrington, P.A. Nembhard, H.B. Sturrock, D.T. and Evans, G.W., eds). Piscataway, NJ: IEEE, pp. 39–48.

Schruben, L.W. (1980) "Establishing the credibility of simulations". *Simulation*, 34(3), 101–105.

Williams, M.L. and Sikora, J. (1991) "SIMVAL minisymposium–a report". *PHALANX, Bulletin of the Military Operations Research Society*, 24(2), 1–6.

Winston, W.L. (1994) *Operations Research: Applications and Algorithms*, 3rd edn. Belmont, CA: Duxbury Press.

THE PRACTICE OF SIMULATION

13

13.1 Introduction

The preceding chapters describe in some detail the process of performing a simulation project. This description outlines key principles and methods for performing a simulation study. It is apparent from case studies and investigations of simulation practice, however, that each simulation study has its own unique features. For instance, while some models have only a short life, others can be used for many years. Some models need a high level of accuracy while others do not. Some simulation modellers are highly skilled at developing software, other modellers are more concerned with managing the simulation process.

In this final chapter, various types of simulation practice are identified. This is first described in terms of model types and then in terms of the way that simulation models are developed and used (modes of practice). Although the concepts that are presented are generalizations, they are useful for giving a modeller some guidelines for adopting the appropriate simulation practice when faced with a problem to be tackled by simulation.

13.2 Types of Simulation Model

Within organizations simulation models are employed in a variety of ways. Five types of simulation model are identified here: throwaway, ongoing use, regular use, generic and reusable. The first three types relate to the frequency with which a model is used and the latter two to the number of problem situations that can be addressed by a model. Apart from describing each of these model types, the discussion that follows also identifies the implications for the process of performing a simulation study.

It should be noted that a single model may take on more than one of these types. Also, a model may evolve from one type to another. For instance, a model that was originally intended to be thrown away at the end of a study may be used on an ongoing basis or may become a generic model that is used in other organizations.

Throwaway models

A throwaway model is used for the duration of a simulation study and then never used again. Such models are developed to investigate one or more issues of concern to the clients. Once these issues have been resolved, either by the model or by some other means, the model ceases to have any relevance and so it is no longer required. This is probably the most common use for a simulation model.

Such models can be highly focused on the issues being addressed, making it easier to reduce the scope and level of detail in the model to a minimum. Elegant user interfaces are less likely to be required, especially if the model is only to be used by the modeller. Model documentation plays a secondary role to the need for project documentation, since it is the latter that provides an enduring record of the work. Verification and validation is only concerned with the immediate purpose of the model.

Ongoing use models

Some models are used on an ongoing basis. This is most likely when the wider project within which the model is being used requires continued use of the model to answer a variety of questions and to determine the effect of changes to the real system. These models differ from throwaway models in terms of their longevity and the changing role they might play as time progresses.

Because the role of these models can change through time they tend to have a wider focus than throwaway models. The model evolves as time progresses. As a result, it is more difficult to control the scope and level of detail and much effort must go into keeping the model as simple as possible for the task at hand. If not, there is a danger that the scope and level of detail continually increase, which may lead to a model with lower utility.

Careful documentation of the simulation becomes vital both for keeping a record of the model as it evolves and because the modeller and model users can easily change over the model's lifetime. Meanwhile, the model needs to be continuously verified and validated in response to changes in the real system and the changing role of the model.

Regular use models

Some simulations are developed for operational use, that is, aiding decision-making on a regular basis (e.g. scheduling decisions). These are described as models for regular use. Such models may require a high level of accuracy, especially if they are intended to download real-time data from the real system. Although these models are used on a long-term basis, the model development is largely carried out before hand-over to the user. From this point on developments mostly involve keeping the model in line with the real system.

Although these models are often focused on helping to answer only one or two questions, they may require a high level of accuracy to assure the quality of the decisions that are made based on their results. This probably requires a detailed model. Much effort must also go into model validation. An elegant user interface is probably required as the model user may not have any simulation expertize. For the same reason user documentation is important. Procedures for maintaining the model and supporting the model users on a long-term basis need to be put in place. To ensure continued maintenance and support it is important that the model is well documented.

Generic models

A generic model is a simulation of a particular context that can be used across a number of organizations. For instance, a generic model could be developed of a check-in desk area at an airport. The same model could be used for other parts of the airport and for other airports. These models are normally quite focused, aiming to address only a limited number of issues, for instance, effects of different departure schedules and staff rosters.

A key problem with developing generic models is being able to represent a system across a range of organizations. On the surface one check-in desk is much the same as another. Dig a little deeper and some important differences may emerge, for instance, the time before departure at which passengers are expected to check in and the queuing system (single or multiple queues). The difficulty is not necessarily in representing these differences, but in identifying them and so being able to create a truly generic model.

Both model and user documentation are important so the model can be supported and maintained over a period of time. The model interface also needs to be user friendly as the simulation is likely to be adopted by a range of users with differing modelling skills. The model must also be validated each time it is introduced to a new situation. Indeed, a key problem with giving models to third-party users is that they may employ it for purposes for which it was not designed, never testing its validity. Like any other model, a generic simulation cannot be assumed to be generally valid. Also, in simulation studies much of the benefit comes from the learning gained during the process of developing the model. If clients are simply handed a complete model, this learning may be lost.

Reusable models/components

Generic models are a special case of reusable models/components. A reusable model implies that a complete model is used in another context and/or for another purpose to that for which it was originally intended (note that proper use of a generic model entails using a model in another context for the same purpose as originally intended). A reusable component involves using a part of a model, normally as part of a new simulation model, in another context and/or for another purpose.

There is much interest in software reuse generally because of the potential to save time and money in developing new software, especially with the ability to share and obtain code across the world wide web. Indeed, visual interactive modelling systems (Section 3.3.3) are an example of component reuse. The software provides a set of low level components, such as machines and queues, that are reused again and again by simulation modellers.

There are, however, a number of problems with the reuse of simulation models and components (Pidd 2002; Taylor and Paul 2002). The producer of the model or component pays the cost of writing, documenting, verifying and validating the code. Unless a charging mechanism is put in place the beneficiary does not cover this cost. What incentive is there to share models and components? Beyond the economic issue there is the question of validity. How can the modeller be sure that the model or component is valid for the context in which it is to be reused? This requires thorough documentation or a revalidation effort. How can appropriate models and components be found? Without a central library of code, modellers are reliant on stumbling upon what they require. Even if appropriate code can be found, it is unlikely that it exactly matches the modeller's requirements and so some re-coding is required. Overall, it must be questioned whether reuse, particularly of full models, does save time. Perhaps the most successful examples of reuse are with low level components and where efficient mechanisms for sharing code have been put in place within an organization who both bear the cost and gain the benefits of reuse.

13.3 Modes of Simulation Practice[1]

Having looked at the different types of model, our attention now turns to the ways in which simulation models are developed and used (modes of practice). From discussions with simulation modellers it is clear that there are differences in simulation practice. It is useful to highlight these differences to gain an understanding of the alternative ways in which simulation studies can be performed. From personal observation, discussions with simulation modellers and descriptions of simulation modelling in the literature, three modes of practice are now identified. The first two modes seem to be predominant. Meanwhile, there is little evidence of significant practice of the third mode and, as such, it represents a potential future for simulation modelling. It should be noted that these modes are derived from, and relate to, simulation modelling as it is practised in business and the military. That is not to say that they are exclusive to these domains, or that other practices do not exist. Certainly, these modes can be identified in simulation modelling of say, health care, transport and computer systems.

13.3.1 Three modes of practice

Mode 1: Simulation as software engineering

Simulation as *software engineering* is typified by lengthy projects, possibly taking years to complete, that are performed by teams of modellers. The users of the models are often far removed from the development process, and may become involved only when a specific problem is to be tackled with the completed model. The prime motivation of such projects is the accurate representation of the real world. In some cases this is to such an extreme that a model is developed without having a specific problem to be tackled, leading to models looking for a problem. Ginzberg (1978), writing about operational research, argues that this approach places the modeller in the role of a purveyor of a product (the model).

[1] This section is based on the paper: Robinson, S. (2003) "Modes of simulation practice: approaches to business and military simulation". *Simulation Practice and Theory*, 10, 513–523. Copyright (2003). Reprinted with permission from Elsevier.

The section is also based on the paper: Robinson, S. (2001) "Modes of simulation practice in business and the military". *Proceedings of the 2001 Winter Simulation Conference* (Peters, B.A., Smith, J.S., Medeiros, D.J. and Rohrer, M.W., eds). Piscataway, NJ: IEEE, pp. 805–811.

Mode 2: Simulation as a process of organizational change

In simulation studies that are a *process of organizational change* the role of the modeller is as an agent of change, whose task it is to help the user (who may better be described as a client) perform his/her job better. The modeller works with the client to help him/her better understand the nature of the organization's problems and to identify actions that may lead to an improvement. The prime motivation for such projects is problem understanding and problem solving. These projects tend to be short, typically a few weeks, are performed by a lone modeller, and require high levels of client involvement. In describing similar types of operational research intervention, Ginzberg (1978) uses the term "process of social change". The term organizational change is preferred here, since social change has a strong and wider meaning among social scientists. Ginzberg argues that if the social (organizational) change view is adopted, then the modeller's role is one of providing a service.

Mode 3: Simulation as facilitation

Mode 3, simulation as *facilitation*, can be seen as a special, but extreme, case of simulation as a process of organizational change. Here a model is developed and used (in an interactive manner) in a group meeting as a means for understanding the real world and for promoting discussion on potential improvements. The prime motivation is understanding and provoking a debate about the problem situation. Model accuracy is potentially of little significance as long as it is useful for promoting the group discussion. There is much similarity between this mode of practice and that described by Vennix (1996) for group decision-making with system dynamics (Section 2.2.3).

Robinson (2001) describes a case study performed in this fashion. He also argues that when simulation is used in this manner it has much in common with "soft" (qualitative) operational research; the other modes described above have more in common with "hard" (quantitative) operational research. Beyond this, it is hard to find examples of simulation used in this way, although anecdotal evidence suggests a growing interest and use of this approach. Indeed, the increasing power of computer hardware and availability of visual interactive modelling systems have made this approach more feasible.

13.3.2 Facets of the modes of simulation practice

The descriptions above provide brief outlines of the three modes of practice. A more detailed description, outlining various facets of these modes of practice, is given in Table 13.1. The facets are split into three groupings relating to the simulation model, the modelling process and the modellers. Many of the descriptions of the facets are self-explanatory. Those requiring more explanation are discussed below. Note that these descriptions are generalizations that identify the predominant approach; there will, of course, be exceptions.

In the software engineering approach the model is developed with a view to being used by a number of different users, possibly for quite different problems. At a lower level, component reuse is an important issue in enabling time to be saved when developing new models. The validity of the model is primarily judged by its representativeness during development, although once a specific use for the model has been found, its fitness for

Table 13.1 **Facets of the Modes of Practice.**

	Simulation as:		
Facet	Software engineering	A process of organizational change	Facilitation
1. Simulation Model			
Prime motivation	Representation	Intervention in a problem situation	Understanding and provoking debate about a problem situation
Size of the model	Large-scale	Small-scale	Quick-and-dirty
Longevity of model	Long-term (years)	Short-term (months/weeks)	Short-term (weeks/days)
Model use	Ongoing use (reusable?)	Throw-away, possibly after some ongoing use	Throw-away
Validity of the model	Representativeness (during development) Fitness for use (during use)	Sufficient accuracy for its purpose	Usefulness
Software for the model	Programming language/simulation software	Simulation software/visual interactive modelling system	Visual interactive modelling system
2. Modelling Process			
Purpose	Many questions could be asked of the model	Specific questions to be answered	Vague questions to be answered
Length of the project	Years	Months/weeks	Weeks/days
Iteration through stages in the project	Limited iteration	Frequent iteration	Highly iterative
Beneficiaries	"Users"	"Clients"	"Actors"
Beneficiaries' involvement	Experimentation only	High at times, e.g. conceptualization, validation and experimentation	Very high throughout
Learning	From experimentation with the model	From the modelling process	From the debate surrounding the modelling process
Validating the model	Modeller and independent assessment	Modeller and client	Modeller and actors
Cost	High	Medium	Low
3. The Modellers			
Number of modellers	Many	One	One
Predominant skill	Software development	Modelling	Process management

purpose becomes paramount. In terms of the modelling process, many questions could be asked of the model, which may not all be defined prior to model development. There is a certain amount of iteration through the stages of the project, but efforts are made to limit this by, for instance, having a detailed specification for the model prior to model coding. The beneficiaries are typically described as "users", who tend to only become involved at the experimentation stage (although some may aid with the specification of the model). Because the users are only involved during experimentation with the model, their learning is largely restricted to the information obtained from the results of the experiments. The model is validated by the modeller and sometimes by an independent third party before use. The users have little involvement with validation. Because of the nature of these projects, the predominant skill of the modellers is in software development.

When simulation is performed as a process of organizational change, because the model is developed to answer specific questions about a specific problem situation, it has no wider applicability. Therefore, it is essentially thrown away after the simulation study is complete (although in some cases the model might be used on an ongoing basis to perform further investigations). It is unlikely that the model could be used for a different problem situation because the questions are likely to be different, and each problem situation is likely to be unique. There may be some notion of component reuse, albeit at a very low level, for instance, a workstation. Validation is considered in terms of whether the model is sufficiently accurate for its purpose and is performed by the modeller in conjunction with the clients. There is a high level of iteration in the modelling process, with limited efforts at formalizing the process. The beneficiaries are typically described as "clients", because they are direct beneficiaries from the whole modelling process. Indeed, the clients are highly involved at many stages of the modelling process, gaining benefits from all stages in terms of an improved understanding as well as the solutions that may be derived from experimentation with the model. The predominant skill of the modeller needs to be in modelling rather than software development.

The facets for simulation as facilitation are more extreme versions of those for simulation as a process of organizational change. The model's validity is judged primarily on whether it was useful, with quite possibly little concern for its accuracy. The questions to be answered may be very vague, particularly because there may be a poor understanding of the problem situation, the motivation for the model being to improve this understanding. The beneficiaries may be thought of as "actors" because of their very high involvement in the modelling process. Their learning is derived not so much from the results obtained from the model (which may be very inaccurate!), but from the debate that takes place during the modelling process. By nature, simulation performed in this manner will require a great deal of iteration between the stages in the process, and as a result, the modeller needs to be skilled in process management.

13.3.3 Modes of practice in business and the military

Figure 13.1 places business and military simulations on a continuum from the software engineering mode of practice, through the process of organizational change mode, to

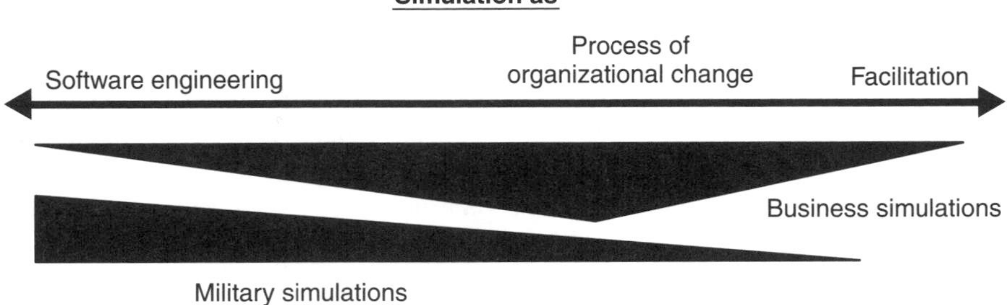

Figure 13.1 Modes of Simulation Practice in Business and the Military.

simulation as facilitation. The height of the shape indicates the frequency of practice within a certain mode.

It is apparent in reviewing the literature on military simulation that the mode that predominates is that of simulation as software engineering. Most models are large-scale, require many man-years of development and are expected to be used (and reused) over a long period of time. This is not to say that simulation is never performed as a process of organizational change, but that this, and facilitation, are much less frequent in the military.

There are a number of reasons why mode 1 predominates in the military, among them are probably:

- The investments being considered, and so the risks and potential savings, are generally large (counted in $millions and $billions as well as lives saved), making large modelling efforts more cost beneficial.
- Decision-making tends to take place over a long period of time, giving time for large-scale model development.
- Models are seen to be useful for many decision situations, requiring model longevity.
- The nature of the real world being modelled involves many complex interactions, leading to large-scale models.
- Plentiful finance tends to be available as most models are financed from the public purse, making larger-scale developments more possible.

In contrast, business simulations are primarily performed as a process of organizational change. The models are generally small-scale and require a few weeks or months to develop (Cochran *et al.* 1995). The models are often used in only one project and are rarely reused. As already stated, at present there is little evidence of simulation being used for facilitation in business, although it is anticipated that the improvements in computing power will make this mode more and more possible in the future. Business simulations are sometimes performed in the software engineering mode, for instance, some detailed enterprise models (Love and Barton 1996) and some real-time simulations (Drake and Smith 1996).

Mode 2 probably predominates in the business context because:

- The investments being considered, and so the risks and potential savings, are generally smaller than in the military (counted in the $thousands and $millions), making large modelling efforts less cost beneficial.
- Decision-making tends to take place over a short period of time, giving no time for large-scale model development.
- Models are seen to be useful for single decision situations, therefore, model longevity is not required.
- The nature of the real world being modelled involves fewer complex interactions than in the military, leading to smaller-scale models.
- Most models are privately financed, restricting the availability of funds and so making larger-scale developments less possible.

One area of simulation modelling that does not fit directly with these archetypes is simulation for gaming, either for war games or business games. The models themselves are probably developed in the software engineering mode, the experimentation (gaming), however, is more akin to simulation as facilitation. As such, a model can move from one mode to another during its life, in this case, in a very deliberate way.

A less deliberate way of moving from one mode to another sometimes occurs with simulation in business. A model that was developed for a specific purpose is then developed into a generic model that can be used by the same business, or others, to look at a similar class of problems. An example might be a model of a specific retail outlet that is later transformed into an application orientated simulation package (Section 3.3.3) for modelling retail outlets. The original model was developed in the process of organizational change mode, but later its development takes on some of the characteristics of the software engineering mode.

13.4 Conclusion

Simulation models are developed and used in quite different ways. This chapter explores some of these differences in terms of model types and in terms of the way in which simulation models are developed and used (modes of practice). Five model types are identified: throw-away, ongoing use, regular use, generic and reusable. Three modes of practice are described: software engineering, process of organizational change and facilitation. The predominant modes of practice adopted in business and the military are identified. These modes can also be seen in other sectors such as health, transport and computer systems. The aim of this discussion is to provide a modeller with some guidelines for adopting the appropriate simulation practice.

References

Cochran, J.K., Mackulak, G.T. and Savory, P.A. (1995) "Simulation project characteristics in industrial settings". *Interfaces*, 25(4), 104–113.

Drake, G.R. and Smith, J.S. (1996) "Simulation system for real-time planning, scheduling, and control". *Proceedings of the 1996 Winter Simulation Conference* (Charnes, J.M., Morrice, D.J., Brunner, D.T. and Swain, J.J., eds). Piscataway, NJ: IEEE, pp. 1083–1090.

Ginzberg, M.J. (1978) "Finding an adequate measure of OR/MS effectiveness". *Interfaces*, 8(4), 59–62.

Love, D. and Barton, J. (1996) "Evaluation of design decisions through CIM and simulation". *Integrated Manufacturing Systems*, 7(4), 3–11.

Pidd, M. (2002) "Simulation software and model reuse: a polemic". *Proceedings of the 2002 Winter Simulation Conference* (Yucesan, E., Chen, C.-H., Snowden, S.L. and Charnes, J.M., eds). Piscataway, NJ: IEEE, pp. 772–775.

Robinson, S. (2001) "Soft with a hard centre: discrete-event simulation in facilitation". *Journal of the Operational Research Society*, 52(8), 905–915.

Taylor, S.J.E. and Paul, R.J. (2002) "What use is model reuse: is there a crook at the end of the rainbow?" *Proceedings of the 2002 Winter Simulation Conference* (Yucesan, E., Chen, C.-H., Snowden, S.L. and Charnes, J.M., eds). Piscataway, NJ: IEEE, pp. 648–652.

Vennix, J.A.M. (1996) *Group Model Building: Facilitating Team Learning using System Dynamics*. Chichester, UK: Wiley.

APPENDIX 1

WARDEON CINEMA

A1.1 Introduction

The Wardeon Cinema case presents an example of simulation applied to a service operation, in this instance a telephone information and ticket booking service. The purpose of the case is to show how the modelling principles described in the book can be applied to a semi-realistic problem situation. The description that follows goes through the key processes of conceptual modelling, data collection and analysis, model coding, verification and validation, and experimentation. Obviously this provides something of a linear explanation of how the problem would be tackled. In practice, and indeed in setting up this example, there would be a great deal of iteration between these processes as the model is developed and used.

A1.2 Conceptual Modelling

A1.2.1 The problem situation

Wardeon Cinemas own and manage multiplex cinemas in the United Kingdom. Their Nottingham complex has been open for 5 years and is very successful in attracting clientele, despite fierce competition in the region from other cinema groups. Recently, however, there have been a number of complaints about the telephone enquiries and booking service.

The telephone system was installed at the time the complex was opened. It provides a message service giving information on film times and an option to seek further information or book tickets by speaking to a booking clerk. Initially this service was adequate, but with rising demand the telephone queues are now often full, particularly on the busiest days (Saturdays). As a result, callers either balk (give up having received an engaged tone) or wait for some time and then hang up (abandon) having obtained neither the information nor the booking they require. Meanwhile, the booking clerks are regularly lambasted by irate customers who have waited up to 15 minutes or more for a response. The cinema's managers are obviously concerned about the loss of goodwill and custom.

Wardeon Nottingham has decided to purchase and install a more modern telephone system. They have obtained various quotes for the system, the favoured choice being from a local company, Dodgey Phones Ltd. The proposed system uses digital technology, allowing customers to use their telephone keypads to choose from an automated menu system. As a result, it is believed that customers will be able to obtain the information they require from the recorded message service more rapidly. Further to this, the system will also provide facilities for booking tickets via the telephone keypad, without the need to speak to a booking clerk. Because some members of the public still wish to speak to a member of staff, particularly if they require further information or would rather book tickets in person, then there will be an option to speak with a customer service representative (CSR). Dodgey have also suggested increasing the capacity of the system from its present level and playing soothing music to customers should they have to wait for a response.

Figure A1.1 shows a schematic of the system proposed by Dodgey. Calls enter the system via a call router (or automatic call distributor, ACD), where the callers enter a number 1, 2 or 3 on their keypad for the service they require (information, ticket sales or CSR respectively). Calls are then routed to the appropriate service. Having completed a call with one of the automated services, callers will be given the option to return to the call router to select another service. The plan is to install four lines for each of the services including the call router. It is unlikely, however, that Wardeon will employ four CSR staff; the current intention is to employ three staff during the busiest periods. Wardeon have the option to purchase extra lines for each service, in blocks of two, albeit at some additional expense.

Wardeon's aim is to resource the system sufficiently so that less than 5% of calls are lost (balk or abandon), even on busy days. They also want the total waiting time, that is the sum of waiting times in all queues, to be less than 2 minutes for at least 80% of calls and the mean to be less than 1 minute. There are a number of concerns,

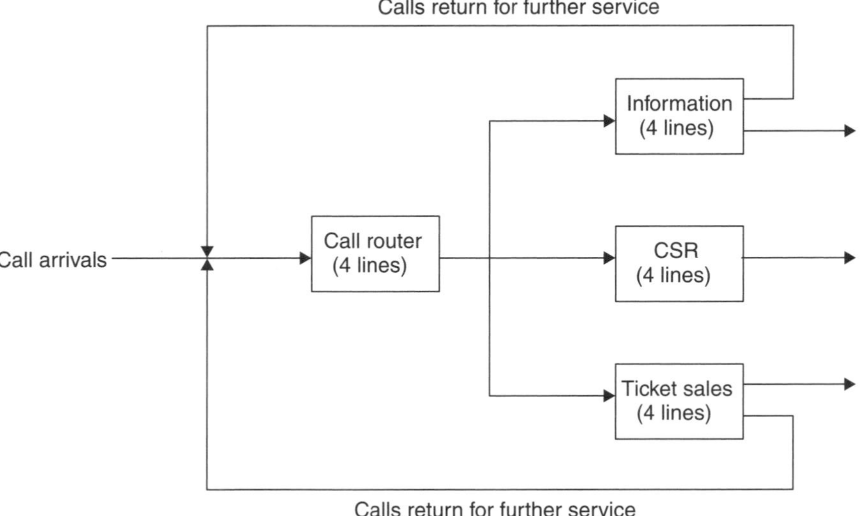

Figure A1.1 Wardeon Cinema New Telephone System.

however, with the system that is being proposed (apart from the name of the supplier!), in particular:

- Whether there are sufficient information lines.
- Whether there are sufficient ticket sales lines.

Wardeon are quite happy with the current plan to have four call router lines because of the short time it takes calls to be handled by this part of the system. They would also like to know how many CSR staff to have available at different times of the day.

In the future Wardeon are planning to expand the Nottingham cinema complex. As a result, it is expected that the demand on the telephone system will continue to grow. They would therefore like to know the maximum capacity of the telephone system so they are able to identify the demand level at which further expansion will be needed.

The management board are meeting in 3 weeks and need to make a decision as to whether to go ahead with the Dodgey proposal, or not. The intention is to have the results of the simulation ready for that meeting. It should be noted that a number of the managers at Wardeon are sceptical concerning the need for a simulation. They have never used it before and will need convincing that the tool is useful.

A1.2.2 Modelling objectives

The purpose of the simulation model is for the management at Wardeon Nottingham to assure itself that the telephone system proposed by Dodgey will provide a satisfactory level of service.

Specific objectives are to:

1. Determine the number of resources (information lines and ticket sales lines) required so that less than 5% of calls are lost (balk or abandon) on busy days and total waiting time is less than 2 minutes for 80% of calls (the mean waiting time to be less than 1 minute).
2. Determine the maximum capacity of the system (number of calls that can be handled), while maintaining the required service level.

Note: The question concerning the number of CSR staff required is not addressed by these objectives. This is because time-scales are pressing and so there is insufficient time. This phase of work will concentrate on the physical equipment required. Staff requirements can be determined following the board meeting in a second phase of work.

General project objectives

- *Time-scale*: a final report must be available in 3 weeks.
- *Nature of model display*: 2D schematic, showing flow of calls through the system.
- *Nature of model use*: by modeller.

The visual display needs to be representative, but not over-intricate, since some managers are sceptical about the use of simulation.

A1.2.3 Model inputs and outputs

Experimental factors

- Number of information lines (range: 4, 6, 8)
- Number of ticket sales lines (range: 4, 6, 8)
- Call arrival rate (no defined range)

Responses (to determine achievement of objectives)

- Percentage of lost calls (= number of lost calls (balked or left)/total number of calls received) for the full system.
- Percentage of completed calls with a total waiting time of less than 2 minutes.
- Histogram of total waiting time for all completed calls, including mean, standard deviation, maximum and minimum.

Notes:

- Balking is defined as a call attempting to enter any of the queues (call router, information, ticket sales, CSR) and being unable to because the queue is already full of pending calls. This is a failure of the system.
- Leaving calls are defined as callers who hang up while waiting in a queue. This is a decision of the caller.
- Total waiting time will be recorded for all completed calls and will be the total time the call has spent in all of the queues.

Responses (to determine reasons for failure to meet objectives)

- Percentage of lost calls by area
- Queue sizes: mean, minimum and maximum
- Resource utilization (cumulative percentage)
- Time-series of calls arriving at call router by hour
- Time-series of mean resource utilization by hour
- Time-series of mean size of each queue by hour

Notes:

- The three time-series can be compared to see if there are particular periods where the rate of call arrivals and resource availability are not well matched. This will be demonstrable by resource under/over-utilization or excessive queue lengths.
- Reports on queue sizes and resource utilization will point to specific areas where problems occur.

A1.2.4 Model content

Model scope

Component	Include/exclude	Justification
Calls	Include	Flow through the telephone system.
Service processes:	Include	All processes need to be modelled to give full statistics on queues and resource utilization.
Call router	Include	Connects call arrivals to other service processes and affects total waiting time response.
Information	Include	Experimental factor.
Ticket sales	Include	Experimental factor.
CSR	Include	Affects total waiting time response.
Queues for each service process	Include	Required for waiting time and queue size response.
CSR staff	Include	Affects total waiting time response.

Note there is no scope reduction. The only potential scope reduction is to remove the CSR, but this would lead to an inaccuracy in the total waiting time response. Since some managers are already sceptical about the use of simulation, the exclusion of the CSR would probably reduce the credibility of the model. The CSR also needs to be included if a second phase of modelling is carried out in which the number of CSR staff is considered.

Model level of detail

Component	Detail	Include/exclude	Comment
Calls	Customer inter-arrival times, rate varying by hour of the day	Include	Modelled as a distribution with changing parameters every 2 hours. Required for flow of calls into the system and call arrival response.
	Customer inter-arrival times, rate varying by day of week	Exclude	Only model the busiest period, on a Saturday.
	Customer inter-arrival times, rate fixed	Include	Experimental factor for determining system capacity. Modelled as a distribution with fixed parameters.

Component	Detail	Include/exclude	Comment
	Nature of call	Include	Randomly sampled to determine service process required. Re-sampled after information and ticket sales to enable re-circulation of calls.
Service processes	Number of lines	Include	Affects speed of service.
	Service time	Include	Modelled as a distribution, taking account of variability in callers' requirements and speed of use.
	Failures	Exclude	Occur very rarely.
	Routing out	Include	Based on nature of the call.
Queues for each service process	Capacity	Include	Affects balking. Required for lost calls response.
	Queue priority	Include	Affects individual waiting times.
	Leaving threshold	Include	Standard waiting time after which a call will abandon a queue. Required for lost calls response.
	Individual caller behaviour	Exclude	Behaviour not well understood, so rely on leaving threshold above.
CSR staff	Number	Include	Represent as total CSR lines available.
	Staff rosters	Exclude	Assume constant number of staff (3) available for this version of the model.

Assumptions

- There are sufficient call router lines.
- There is no requirement to increase the number of CSR lines.
- The arrival pattern defined in 2-hour slots is sufficiently accurate.
- Lost customers returning later are already accounted for in the arrival data, so do not need to be modelled explicitly.
- Equipment failures occur rarely and so do not need to be modelled.
- No attempt should be made to model individual customer behaviour (e.g. individual waiting time thresholds), since no data are available. Use a single threshold time for leaving queues.
- Data obtained on call arrivals and the nature of calls from the previous telephone system at the Nottingham cinema is sufficiently accurate for predicting future demand.

Simplification

- Only model the busiest period (Saturday). If the resources are able to cope with the busiest period, then they are able to cope with quieter periods.
- Staff rosters are not to be modelled. It is assumed that there are three CSR staff available throughout the day. The interest at this stage is in the capability of the system rather than the staffing of the system, which can be considered in a second phase of the work.

A1.3 Model Data

All times are in minutes unless otherwise stated.

Calls

Mean arrival rates and inter-arrival times for recent Saturdays (busiest period). Inter-arrival data used as the mean of a negative exponential distribution.

Time of day	(a) Mean arrival rate per hour	Mean inter-arrival time (minutes) 60/(a)
08:00–10:00	120	0.5
10:00–12:00	150	0.4
12:00–14:00	200	0.3
14:00–16:00	240	0.25
16:00–18:00	400	0.15
18:00–20:00	240	0.25
20:00–22:00	150	0.4

Note: opening hours are 8:00–22:00

Nature of call:

Information	60%
Ticket sales	30%
CSR	10%

Call router

Number of lines	4
Service time	Lognormal (*location* = 0.71, *spread* = 0.04) giving *mean* = 0.5, *SD* = 0.1

Information

Number of lines	4
Service time	Erlang ($mean = 2, k = 5$)
Routing out:	
Leave	73%
Ticket sales (via call router)	25%
CSR (via call router)	2%

Ticket sales

Number of lines	4
Service time	Lognormal ($location = 1.09, spread = 0.02$) giving $mean = 3.0$, $SD = 0.4$
Routing out:	
Leave	98%
CSR (via call router)	2%

CSR

Number of lines	4
Service time	Erlang ($mean = 3, k = 3$)

Queues

Capacity	10
Queue priority	First-in-first-out
Leaving threshold time	3 minutes

CSR staff

Number	3

A1.4 Model Coding

A simulation model of the Wardeon case can be downloaded from the web site (www.wileyeurope.com/go/robinson). Versions of the model are available for various simulation packages.

A1.5 Verification and Validation

To illustrate the concept of verification and validation, two validation tests are performed on the Wardeon Cinema model. The first is a deterministic test and the second a comparison between the simulation and a mathematical model. Both are methods of black-box validation. Obviously much more testing, particularly other forms of verification and validation, would be required to give a reasonable level of confidence in the model.

Deterministic model

All random elements of the model are removed, that is, variations in inter-arrival times, routings and service times. All calls leave the system after receiving their first service and so there is no re-routing following a service at information and ticket sales. The arrival rate is fixed to the mean value over the day, 214 per hour (inter-arrival time of 60/214 = 0.28 minutes). The service times at each service point are fixed to their mean values, for instance, 0.5 minutes at the call router. From the router six in 10 calls are routed to the information lines, three in 10 to ticket sales and one in 10 to the CSR lines. Based on these values it is possible to predict exactly the utilization of each of the service points (Table A1.1).

Note that the arrival rate at the information lines is higher than the service rate. This in itself points to the need for more information lines. It is expected that the information line queue will grow at a rate of 8.4 calls per hour.

Table A1.2 shows the results from a simulation run of 100 hours with the deterministic model. A warm-up period of 1 hour has been used in order to let work-in-progress feed through to each of the service points. The utilization results match the calculated results exactly. The queue length at the information lines is also correct. The total run length, including the warm-up period, is 101 hours, giving an expected queue length of 8.4 × 101 = 848.4. Obviously this needs to be an integer value! Note that the restriction on the capacity of the queue has been removed and that having joined the queue it is assumed no calls will abandon the queue.

Table A1.1 Deterministic Model: Expected Service Point Utilizations.

Metric	Calculation	Call router	Information	Ticket sales	CSR
Arrival rate per hour (a)	Total calls per hour × proportion of calls going to service	214 × 1.0 = 214	214 × 0.6 = 128.4	214 × 0.3 = 64.2	214 × 0.1 = 21.4
Calls handled per hour (b)	60 minutes/service time × number of lines	60/0.5 × 4 = 480	60/2 × 4 = 120	60/3 × 4 = 80	60/3 × 3 = 60
Utilization	a/b	214/480 = **44.58%**	128.4/120 > 100%	64.2/80 = **80.25%**	21.4/60 = **35.67%**

Table A1.2 Wardeon Cinema: Simulation Results for the Deterministic Model.

Service point	Utilization
Call router	44.58%
Information	100% (Queue length = 849)
Ticket sales	80.25%
CSR	35.67%

Comparison to mathematical models

Rather than remove all the random events from the simulation, with only a few simplifications to the simulation it is possible to obtain a reasonable prediction of how the model should perform. Three simplifications are made:

- There is no re-routing following a service at information and ticket sales.
- Queue size restrictions are removed.
- Calls cannot abandon a queue.

With these simplifications the predictions in Table A1.1 still apply because they are based on the mean values of the arrival and service time distributions. Due to the randomness in the model it is not expected, however, that there will be an exact correspondence between the predictions and the simulation results.

Table A1.3 shows the results of running the simplified simulation for seven replications of one day in length (see Section A1.6.1 for discussion on replications). The predicted result only falls within the confidence interval of the simulated result for the router. It is close to the confidence interval, however, for both ticket sales and CSR. The main discrepancy is for the information lines, where the simulated utilization is well below the predicted 100%. The reason for this is that, due to the randomness in the model, during a short simulation run the information line queue does not build up and so there are periods during which the information lines are idle. It is expected that once the queues have built up, then the utilization will be much closer to the predicted 100%. Indeed, a simulation run of a few days (rather than one day) shows this to be the case.

It is difficult to predict the performance of the full simulation model using mathematical calculations due to the re-circulation of calls, balking and leaving. The first will increase the utilization of the service points, while the latter two will reduce it. Despite this, it is worth comparing the results of the full simulation model with the predictions made in Table A1.1, although some discrepancies are expected. Such a comparison will raise concerns about the validity of the model if the simulation results are very different from the predictions and the differences cannot be explained.

Table A1.4 shows the results for the full simulation model. For the router, ticket sales and CSR there is about a 5% discrepancy, in each case the simulated result is higher. This would suggest the effect of re-circulating calls dominates over leaving and balking. The difference

Table A1.3 Wardeon Cinema: Simulation Results for the Simplified Simulation Model.

	Replication	Router	Information	Ticket sales	CSR
	1	43.33	89.05	76.31	35.66
	2	45.08	90.07	78.99	37.20
	3	44.53	87.70	75.70	37.91
	4	44.42	89.05	79.72	36.97
	5	44.83	88.15	79.68	36.50
	6	44.90	89.13	79.41	40.31
	7	46.20	91.51	79.61	36.35
	Mean	44.75	89.24	78.49	37.27
	St. dev.	0.86	1.26	1.72	1.52
95% confidence interval	Lower	43.96	88.07	76.89	35.87
	Upper	45.55	90.40	80.08	38.67
	Expectation	44.58	100.00	80.25	35.67

Table A1.4 Wardeon Cinema: Simulation Results for Full Simulation Model.

	Replication	Router	Information	Ticket sales	CSR
	1	48.90	82.91	84.10	39.46
	2	50.73	84.75	86.46	42.25
	3	49.86	83.07	85.73	42.82
	4	50.07	85.99	87.62	41.61
	5	50.32	84.99	85.48	40.10
	6	50.48	84.53	87.00	44.16
	7	52.40	88.10	88.26	40.11
	Mean	50.39	84.91	86.38	41.50
	St. dev.	1.06	1.77	1.41	1.70
95% confidence interval	Lower	49.41	83.26	85.08	39.93
	Upper	51.38	86.55	87.68	43.08
	Expectation	44.58	100.00	80.25	35.67

is greater for the information lines for the reasons discussed above. These differences do not seem unreasonable, particularly because an explanation can be found.

Conclusion

The deterministic test shows an exact correspondence between the deterministic model and the calculated results. There is a satisfactory match between the results of the simplified simulation and the results predicted by the mathematical model, as there is for the full simulation. Some differences are expected and those that occur can be explained.

This testing provides some level of confidence that the model is sufficiently accurate for predicting system performance. More testing, particularly looking at queuing results (the key performance measures), would help to increase this confidence further.

A1.6 Experimentation

A1.6.1 Obtaining accurate results

The nature of the simulation model

The Wardeon Cinema model is a terminating simulation. The termination point is after 1 day of operation (08:00–22:00), that is 14 hours.

The nature of the simulation model output

There are three key output statistics (Section A1.2.3):

- Percentage of lost calls
- Percentage of calls completed with a total waiting time of less than 2 minutes
- Mean total waiting time

The output is expected to be transient since the arrival rate changes throughout the day. A graph of the percentage of lost calls (Figure A1.2) shows that these output data rise to a peak and then fall. This seems to confirm that the output is transient.

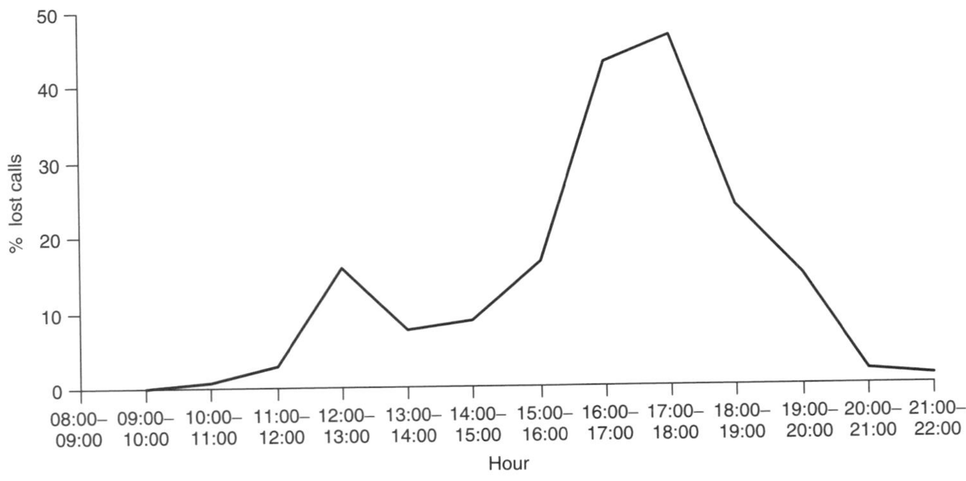

Figure A1.2 Wardeon Cinema: Time-Series of the Percentage of Lost Calls.

Dealing with initialization bias

The model starts in a realistic initial condition with no calls in the system. There is no need for a warm-up period or specific initial conditions.

Amount of output data required

Since the model is terminating, multiple replications have to be performed. The number of replications needs to be determined. Tables A1.5 to A1.7 show the results from 10 replications of 14 hours for the three key output statistics. As well as the result, the cumulative mean and confidence intervals are also calculated. The cumulative mean and confidence intervals are shown graphically in Figures A1.3 to A1.5.

The cumulative mean in all the graphs is reasonably flat throughout. The confidence intervals narrow fairly rapidly. For the latter two statistics the deviation is less than 5% at four replications, although it does rise marginally above this level at replication seven for the mean total waiting time. The interval narrows a little slower for the percentage of lost calls and the deviation is not less than 5% until the seventh replication. Therefore, seven replications will be performed with the model for experimentation.

A1.6.2 Searching the solution space

Objective 1: Number of resources

Wardeon have the option of increasing the number of information lines and ticket sales lines. In total this gives nine scenarios for experimentation as shown in Table A1.8. Rather than run all nine scenarios, only the five shown in bold are performed initially.

Table A1.9 to A1.11 show the results (mean and 95% confidence intervals) for the percentage of lost calls, the percentage of calls with a total waiting time of less than 2

Table A1.5 Wardeon Cinema: Results for Percentage of Lost Calls.

				95% confidence interval		
Replication	% lost calls	Cumulative mean	Standard deviation	Lower interval	Upper interval	% deviation
1	19.20	19.20	n/a	n/a	n/a	n/a
2	20.27	19.73	0.758	12.92	26.55	34.53%
3	19.04	19.50	0.670	17.84	21.16	8.54%
4	17.65	19.04	1.073	17.33	20.75	8.97%
5	19.12	19.05	0.930	17.90	20.21	6.06%
6	18.17	18.91	0.907	17.96	19.86	5.03%
7	20.35	19.11	0.992	18.20	20.03	4.80%
8	19.12	19.11	0.918	18.35	19.88	4.02%
9	20.66	19.29	1.002	18.52	20.06	3.99%
10	19.77	19.33	0.957	18.65	20.02	3.54%

Table A1.6 Wardeon Cinema: Results for Percentage of Calls Completed with a Total Waiting Time of less than 2 Minutes.

Replication	% calls completed in 2 mins	Cumulative mean	Standard deviation	95% confidence interval Lower interval	Upper interval	% deviation
1	65.00	65.00	n/a	n/a	n/a	n/a
2	61.70	63.35	2.335	42.37	84.33	33.11%
3	61.96	62.89	1.837	58.32	67.45	7.25%
4	65.33	63.50	1.935	60.42	66.58	4.85%
5	63.85	63.57	1.683	61.48	65.66	3.29%
6	66.13	64.00	1.834	62.07	65.92	3.01%
7	58.66	63.23	2.621	60.81	65.66	3.83%
8	63.18	63.23	2.426	61.20	65.26	3.21%
9	59.65	62.83	2.564	60.86	64.80	3.14%
10	64.92	63.04	2.506	61.25	64.83	2.84%

Table A1.7 Wardeon Cinema: Results for Mean Total Waiting Time.

Replication	Mean total wait time	Cumulative mean	Standard deviation	95% confidence interval Lower interval	Upper interval	% deviation
1	1.40	1.40	n/a	n/a	n/a	n/a
2	1.47	1.44	0.048	1.01	1.87	29.83%
3	1.48	1.45	0.042	1.35	1.56	7.18%
4	1.40	1.44	0.044	1.37	1.51	4.91%
5	1.43	1.44	0.039	1.39	1.48	3.33%
6	1.34	1.42	0.052	1.37	1.48	3.88%
7	1.60	1.45	0.082	1.37	1.52	5.22%
8	1.46	1.45	0.076	1.38	1.51	4.37%
9	1.57	1.46	0.082	1.40	1.52	4.30%
10	1.39	1.45	0.080	1.40	1.51	3.95%

minutes and the mean total waiting time respectively. For the scenarios not run (scenarios 2, 4, 6 and 8), the results have been determined by interpolation, for example, scenario 2 = (scenario 1 + scenario 3)/2. The tables provide a very simple metamodel.

The results for the percentage of lost calls (Table A1.9) show that only scenario 9 gives the required result. Although the interpolated results for scenarios 6 and 8 do not quite meet the objective of less than 5%, they are worth exploring further. Inspection of Table A1.10 shows that scenario 9 again meets the objective (more than 80%) and suggests

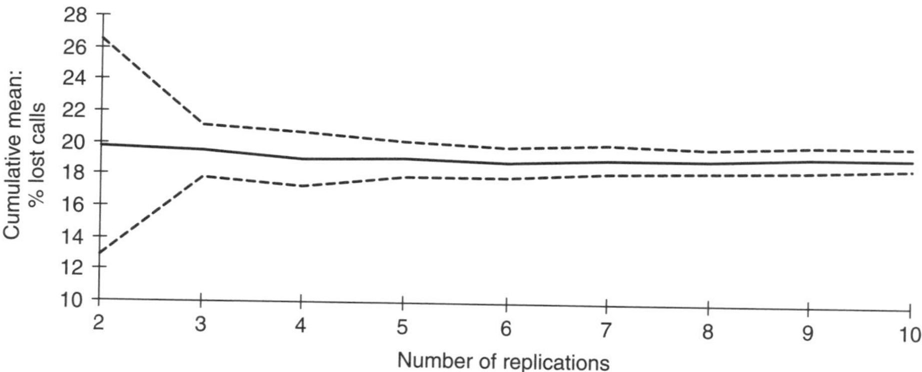

Figure A1.3 Wardeon Cinema: Mean and Confidence Intervals for Percentage of Lost Calls.

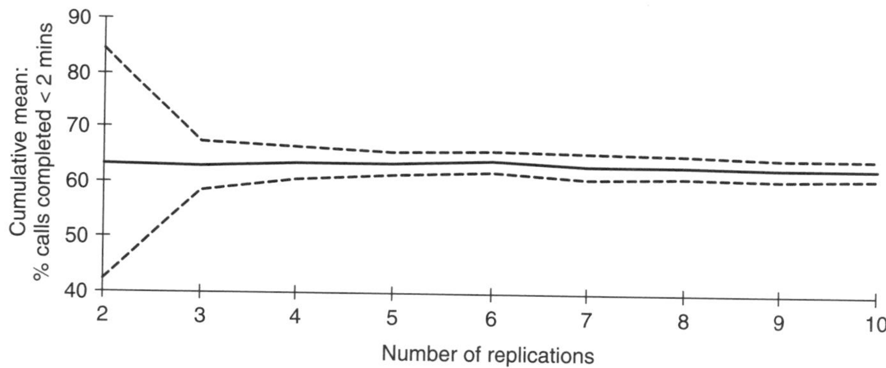

Figure A1.4 Wardeon Cinema: Mean and Confidence Intervals for Percentage of Calls Completed with a Total Waiting Time of less than 2 Minutes.

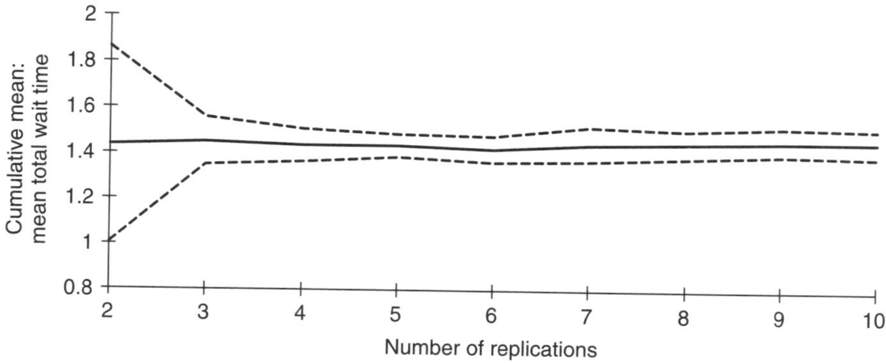

Figure A1.5 Wardeon Cinema: Mean and Confidence Intervals for Mean Total Waiting Time.

Table A1.8 Wardeon Cinema: Scenarios for Number of Resources.

		Information lines		
		4	6	8
Ticket sales lines	4	**Scenario 1**	Scenario 2	**Scenario 3**
	6	Scenario 4	**Scenario 5**	Scenario 6
	8	**Scenario 7**	Scenario 8	**Scenario 9**

Table A1.9 Wardeon Cinema: Percentage of Lost Calls (Mean and 95% Confidence Interval).

		Information lines		
		4	6	8
Ticket sales lines	4	19.11 (18.20, 20.03)	*14.98*	10.84 (10.21, 11.47)
	6	*15.27*	6.70 (6.21, 7.20)	*6.26*
	8	11.43 (10.50, 12.37)	*6.56*	1.69 (1.25, 2.13)

Table A1.10 Wardeon Cinema: Percentage of Calls with Total Waiting Time of less than 2 Minutes (Mean and 95% Confidence Interval).

		Information lines		
		4	6	8
Ticket sales lines	4	63.23 (60.81, 65.66)	*71.54*	79.85 (78.64, 81.07)
	6	*70.25*	80.23 (78.96, 81.51)	*85.30*
	8	77.27 (74.82, 79.72)	*84.01*	90.75 (89.09, 92.41)

that scenarios 6 and 8 will also do so. The confidence intervals for scenarios 3 and 5 both straddle 80%, so they either give or are close to giving the required result. Meanwhile the results in Table A1.11 show a similar pattern. Note that for this set of results the confidence interval for scenario 7 shows that it may also meet the objective of a mean of less than 1 minute. More replications would be required to confirm this.

Table A1.11 Wardeon Cinema: Mean Total Waiting Time (Mean and 95% Confidence Interval).

Ticket sales lines	Information lines: 4	6	8
4	1.45 (1.37, 1.52)	*1.15*	0.85 (0.82, 0.89)
6	*1.20*	0.88 (0.83, 0.93)	*0.67*
8	0.96 (0.89, 1.03)	*0.73*	0.49 (0.44, 0.55)

Table A1.12 Wardeon Cinema: Results for Scenarios 6 and 8.

Result	Scenario 6	Scenario 8
Percentage of lost calls	4.38 (3.78, 4.98)	4.26 (3.97, 4.55)
Percentage of calls with total waiting time of less than 2 minutes	85.86 (84.18, 87.53)	85.36 (84.41, 86.31)
Mean total waiting time	0.67 (0.61, 0.73)	0.69 (0.65, 0.73)

As a result of these findings, simulations are performed for scenarios 6 and 8, in order to determine whether they meet the objectives. The results are shown in Table A1.12. This demonstrates that both scenarios meet the requirements of Wardeon Cinema. Further to this, paired-t confidence intervals show no significant difference between the results for the two scenarios. Meanwhile, a comparison of scenarios 6, 8 and 9 (Table A1.13) shows that scenario 9 is a significant improvement over the other two scenarios. Note that common random numbers have been implemented in the model, making the calculation of a paired-t confidence interval valid.

Figure A1.6 shows the variability in the total waiting time for enquiries in the three scenarios. What it shows is that the majority of enquiries wait for less than 1 minute in total, with some waiting for up to 7 minutes. Close inspection of the data shows that the maximum total wait in all replications for these scenarios is about 9 minutes. There is very little difference between the scenarios except that more enquiries wait for less than 1 minute in scenario 9 (eight information and ticket sales lines), which is to be expected.

Based on these findings, the management of Wardeon need to decide whether to adopt scenario 6 (eight information lines and six ticket sales lines) or scenario 8 (six information lines and eight ticket sales lines). They may, of course, prefer to adopt scenario 9 (eight information and ticket sales lines), especially as there are plans to expand the cinema

Table A1.13 Wardeon Cinema: Paired-*t* Confidence Interval Comparison of Scenarios 6, 8 and 9 (98.33% Intervals giving Overall Confidence of 95%).

Percentage of Lost Calls

Scenario	98.33% confidence intervals			
	8		9	
6	−0.56, 0.80	No difference	2.25, 3.13	Scen. 6 > Scen. 9
8			2.12, 3.03	Scen. 8 > Scen. 9

Percentage of Calls with Total Waiting Time of less than 2 Minutes

Scenario	98.33% confidence intervals			
	8		9	
6	−1.38, 2.37	No difference	−6.61, −3.17	Scen. 6 < Scen. 9
8			−7.16, −3.61	Scen. 8 < Scen. 9

Mean Total Waiting Time

Scenario	98.33% confidence intervals			
	8		9	
6	−0.07, 0.05	No difference	0.13, 0.23	Scen. 6 > Scen. 9
8			0.13, 0.25	Scen. 8 > Scen. 9

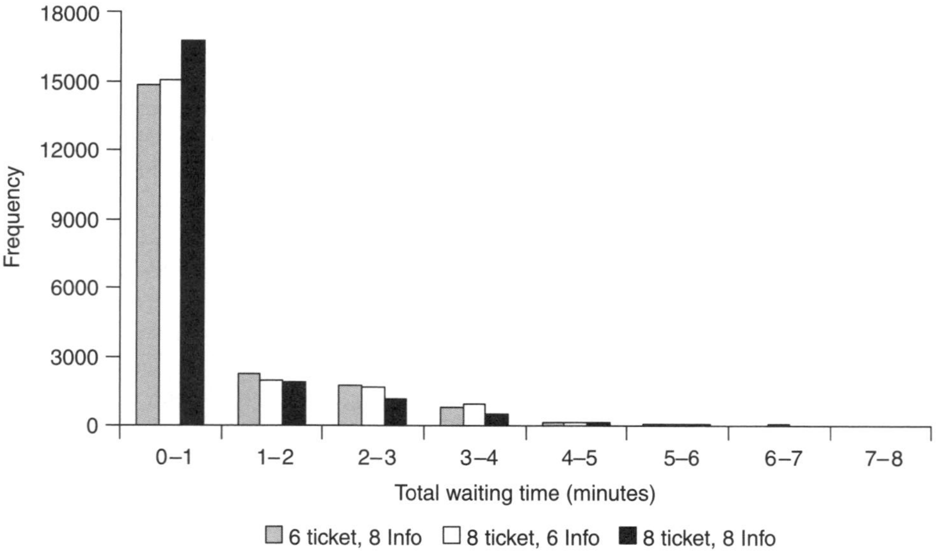

Figure A1.6 Wardeon Cinema: Variability in Total Waiting Time in Scenarios 6, 8 and 9.

complex. The results above give information on the statistical significance of the results. Management must determine their practical significance.

Objective 2: Maximum capacity

To investigate the maximum capacity of the system, scenario 9 (eight information and ticket sales lines) is used. Sensitivity analysis is performed, steadily increasing the arrival rate of customers by applying a multiplier to the inter-arrival time profile. The arrival rate is increased in steps of 5% up to a 40% increase. Figures A1.7 to A1.9 show the mean and confidence intervals for the three key results. The objectives for waiting time are still met right up to an increase of 40% in arrivals. However, the objective for lost calls ceases to be met with an increase in arrivals of around 20%. If demand is expected to rise further, additional information and ticket sales lines would be required.

A1.7 Conclusions and Recommendations

Under expected levels of demand, Wardeon require either six information lines and eight ticket sales lines, or eight information lines and six ticket sales lines. The model predicts that the performance of the system is indifferent between the two options.

The model predicts that the maximum capacity of the system (with eight information lines and eight ticket lines) is reached when demand is about 20% higher than currently predicted. Further expansion in demand would require additional resources if performance objectives are still to be met.

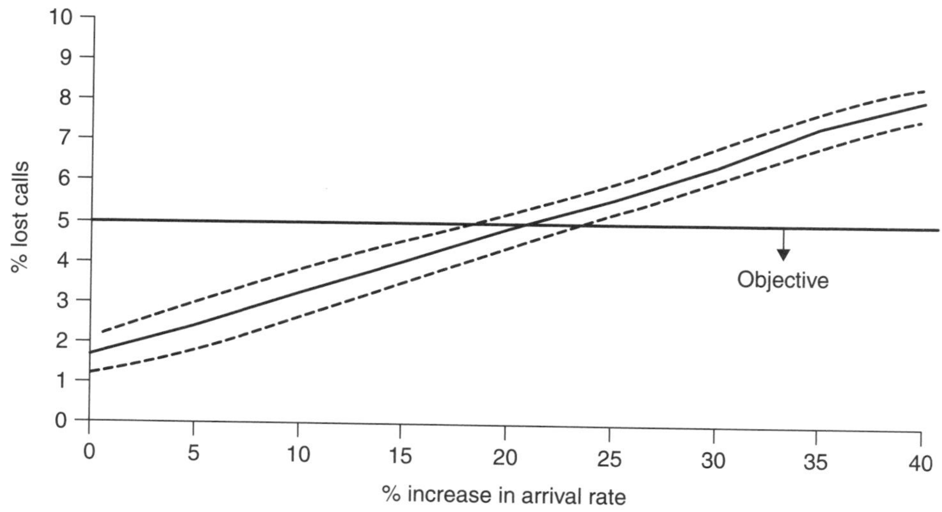

Figure A1.7 Sensitivity Analysis on Increased Arrivals: Mean and 95% Confidence Intervals for Percentage of Lost Calls.

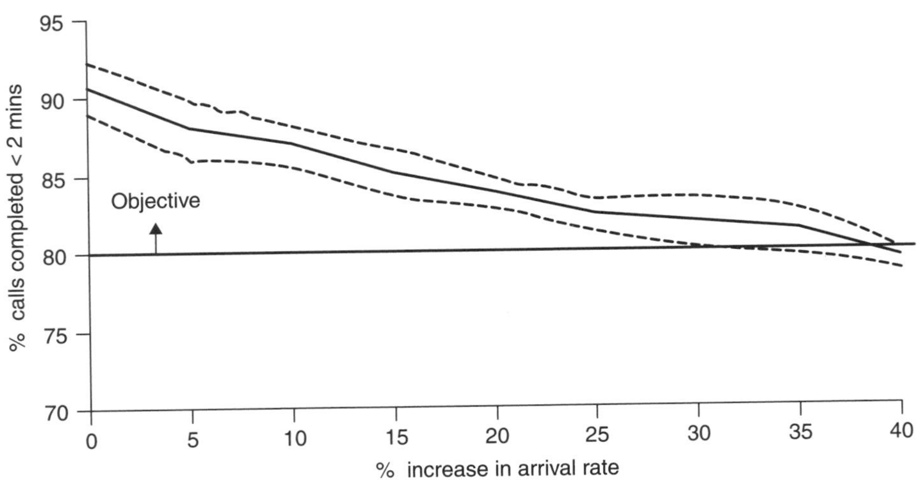

Figure A1.8 Sensitivity Analysis on Increased Arrivals: Mean and 95% Confidence Intervals for Percentage of Calls with Total Waiting Time of less than 2 Minutes.

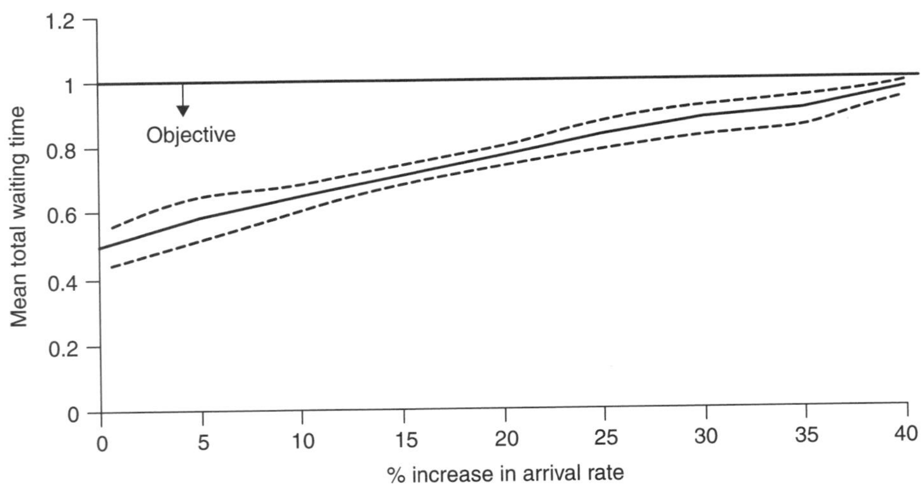

Figure A1.9 Sensitivity Analysis on Increased Arrivals: Mean and 95% Confidence Intervals for Mean Total Waiting Time.

In the light of these findings it is recommended that:

- The system is set up with at least either six/eight or eight/six information and ticket sales lines respectively.

- To allow for increased demand in the future the system should be set up with eight information and ticket sales lines.
- If demand is expected to grow by more than 20%, further information and ticket sales lines are required.

Further work should investigate the number of CSR staff to have available at different times of the day.

APPENDIX 2

PANORAMA TELEVISIONS

A2.1 Introduction

The Panorama Televisions case presents an example of simulation applied to a manufacturing operation, in this instance a television assembly line. The purpose of the case is to show how the modelling principles described in the book can be applied to a semi-realistic problem situation. The description that follows goes through the key processes of conceptual modelling, data collection and analysis, model coding, verification and validation, and experimentation. Obviously this provides something of a linear explanation of how the problem would be tackled. In practice, and indeed in setting up this example, there would be a great deal of iteration between these processes as the model is developed and used.

A2.2 Conceptual Modelling

A2.2.1 The problem situation

Panorama Televisions have been involved in the manufacture of electrical goods since the early days of the radio. They now concentrate on the production of high quality, premium priced televisions for the international market. There are four televisions in their product range: small, medium, large and flat screen.

Panorama's manufacturing site is shown in Figure A2.1. Cathode ray tubes (CRT) are assembled in one facility and then transported, by overhead conveyor, to the television assembly plant. Once the televisions are assembled and fully tested they are taken to the warehouse, stored and then shipped to the customer. Two forklift trucks transport the televisions from the assembly plant to the warehouse.

Last year, to meet increased demand, Panorama invested in a new television assembly plant. Also, after some negotiation with the unions, all areas of the site moved to continuous working over a 5-day week. However, the plant has never achieved its target throughput of 500 units per day. In fact, daily throughput is only just over 400 units.

The plant is shown in Figure A2.2. Plastic moulded boxes are loaded to a pallet by an operator at OP10. A production schedule, which is based on projected demand, determines

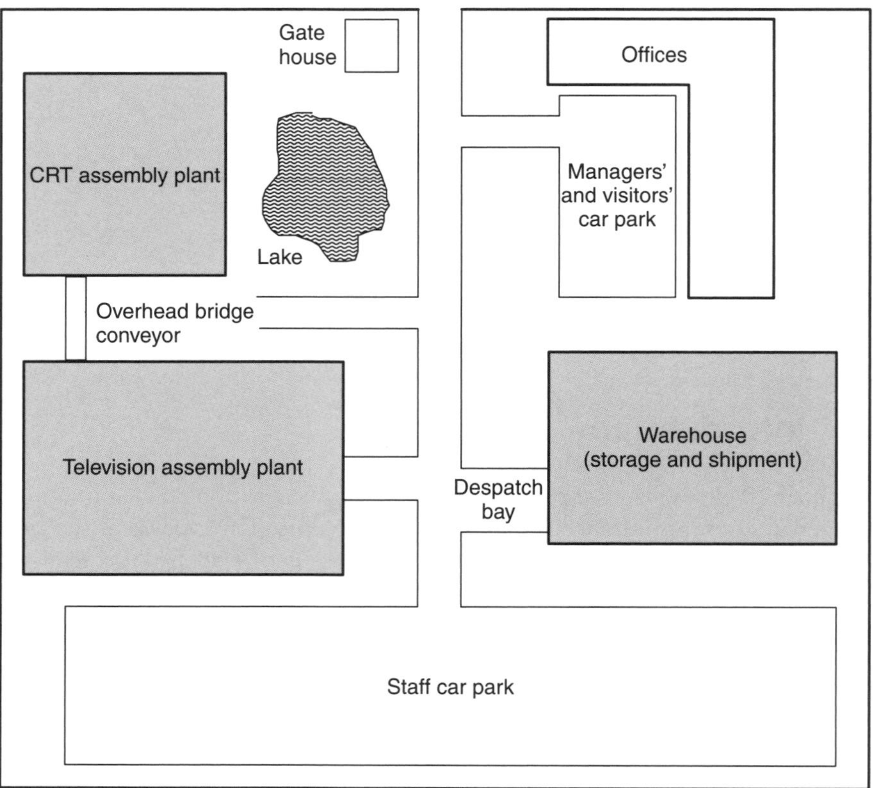

Figure A2.1 Panorama Televisions: Manufacturing Site.

the type of box to be loaded (small, medium, large or for flat screen). At OP20 the CRT is assembled to the box before the electric coil is added at OP30. The televisions travel on a conveyor and five manual operators assemble the electrical equipment, OP40. The television is then tested and any failures go to the rework area. Good televisions have the back assembled at OP50 and are unloaded from the line at OP60 by an operator. The empty pallets are returned by conveyor to OP10 and the televisions are stored on a circular sling conveyor. A television is taken from the conveyor when a final test booth becomes available. Televisions failing this test are sent for final rework. Televisions passing are stored on another sling conveyor and are packed at OP70. Packed televisions are transported to the warehouse by forklift truck.

The final test and packing area are often short of work and there is enough spare capacity to achieve 500 units per day. The management at Panorama believe that the throughput problem is a result of the number of stoppages on the main assembly line. There are a significant number of breakdowns, and set-ups are required every time there is a change of

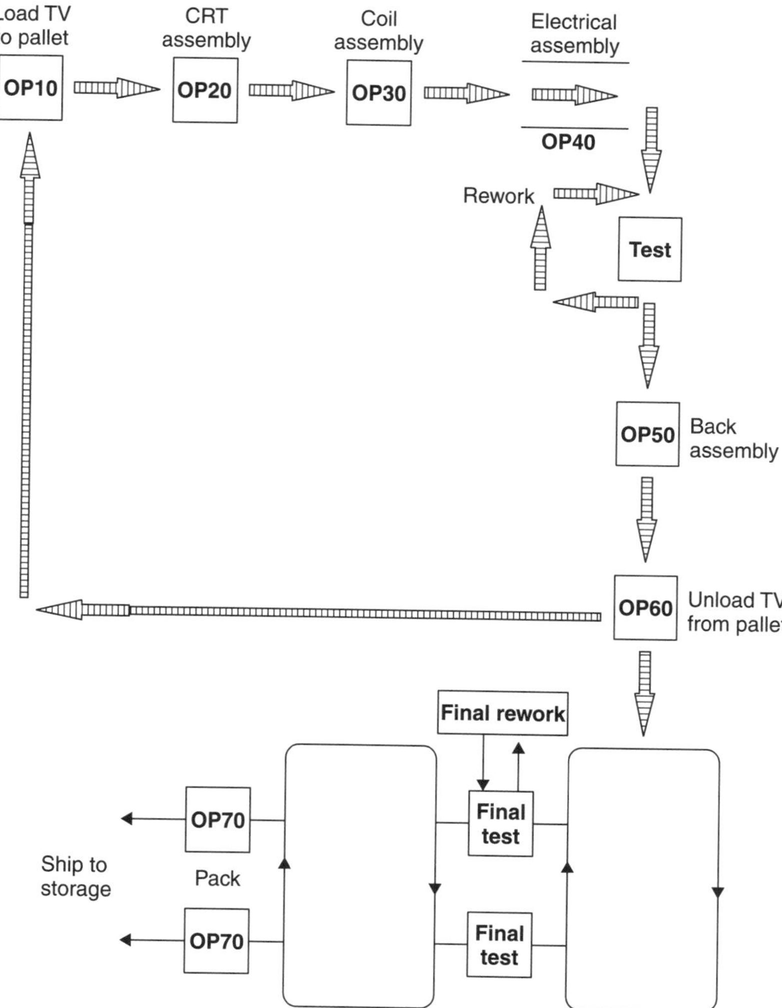

Figure A2.2 Panorama Televisions: Television Assembly Plant.

product in the production schedule. However, there seems little opportunity to improve the efficiency of the machines, nor can the production schedule be changed since it is driven by customer demand. The solution being considered is to increase the buffering between the operations to dampen the effects of stoppages. Design engineers have considered this proposal and believe that, due to physical constraints on space, the buffering could be increased by a maximum of 200%. This will also require further pallets to be bought. In fact, there is some uncertainty as to whether enough pallets are currently being used.

Increasing the number of pallets may provide a solution without the need for further storage.

Extra storage is expensive, so before investing Panorama want to be sure it is necessary. Also, special pallets have to be used at a cost of $1000 each, so it is important to minimize the number required. Target throughput must be achieved, but expenditure should be kept to a minimum. The management at Panorama would like some proposals on how to improve the line within 10 working days.

A2.2.2 Modelling objectives

Panorama's overall aim is to achieve a throughput of 500 units per day from the television assembly line. Therefore, the specific modelling objective is to:

- Determine whether 500 units per day can be achieved with additional pallets only.

If this cannot be achieved with the current design, then the objective is to:

- Identify the additional storage and pallets required to achieve 500 units per day.

General project objectives

- *Time-scale*: 10 working days
- *Nature of model display*: simple schematic
- *Nature of model use*: by modeller

The model is largely required for performing experiments and obtaining results, communication is not a major need. Therefore, the level of visual impact need only enable effective model testing and experimentation.

A2.2.3 Model inputs and outputs

Experimental factors

- The number of pallets (range 30–200)
- The size of the buffers (conveyors) between the operations (maximum 200% increase)

Responses (to determine achievement of objectives)

- Time-series of daily throughput
- Histogram of daily throughput
- Mean, standard deviation, minimum and maximum daily throughput

These three reports will enable an analysis of the distribution of daily throughput and its behaviour over time.

Responses (to determine reasons for failure to meet objectives)

- Percentage machine utilization: idle, working, blocked, broken and set-up

A2.2.4 Model content

Model scope

Component	Include/exclude	Justification
Televisions	Include	Production schedule influences capacity through machine set-ups.
Pallets	Include	Experimental factor.
Operations:		
OP10–OP60 including rework	Include	Key influence on throughput.
Final test–OP70	Exclude	Capacity known to be sufficient, pallets do not enter this area.
Buffering (conveyors):		
OP10–OP60 plus pallet return	Include	Experimental factor.
Final test–OP70 with sling conveyors	Exclude	Capacity known to be sufficient, pallets do not enter this area.
Labour:		
Operators	Exclude	Required for operation of manual processes (OP10, OP40, OP60, Rework), but always present and so they cause no variation in throughput.
Maintenance	Include	Required for repair of machines. A shortage of staff would affect throughput.

The main opportunity for scope reduction comes from the exclusion of the sling conveyors, final test and OP70. This is because there is spare capacity in this section of the line and so it is not acting as a bottleneck. Also, this section is separate from the main line and the pallets (an experimental factor) are not used in this area. Because the problems centre on the television assembly plant, there is no need to model the CRT assembly plant or the warehouse.

Model level of detail

Component	Detail	Include/exclude	Comment
Televisions	Production schedule	Include	Schedule describes number and type to be produced in a sequence.
Pallets	Number	Include	Experimental factor.
OP10–OP60 (inc. rework)	Cycle time	Include	Automatic ops: fixed time. Manual ops: distribution.
	Breakdown	Include	Time between failure distribution.
	Repair	Include	Repair time distribution.
	Set-up	Include	Frequency and distribution for set-up time.
	Rework	Include	Percentage failure at test station
Conveyors	Cycle time	Include	Fixed cycle.
	Capacity	Include	Experimental factor.
	Type	Include	Fixed/accumulating.
	Breakdowns	Exclude	Occur only infrequently so have little effect on throughput.
Maintenance labour	Number	Include	
	Repair and setup tasks	Include	Which operations each operator attends to repair breakdowns and set up machines.
	Other tasks	Exclude	Assume machine repair is a priority and so other tasks do not interfere.

Assumptions

- Conveyor breakdowns are infrequent, therefore they are not modelled.
- The plant works continuously for 5 days a week, therefore no shifts are modelled.
- No work, including repair to machines, takes place over a weekend.
- Capacity of final test and OP70 is sufficient.
- Machine repair is the priority task for maintenance staff.

Simplifications

- Sub-components, such as television boxes and cathode ray tubes, are 100% available, and so are not modelled.

A2.3 Model Data

All times are in minutes.

Televisions

Production schedule (repeating):

Small TV	20
Medium TV	30
Large TV	40
Flat screen TV	20

Pallets

Number of pallets	30

OP10

Cycle time	Normal (*mean* = 1.9, *SD* = 0.19)

OP20

Cycle time	2.1
Breakdowns:	
Time between failure	Negative exponential (*mean* = 300)
Repair time	Triangular (*min* = 5, *mode* = 25, *max* = 60)
Set-ups on changeover of TV type:	
Set-up time	Normal (*mean* = 5.0, *SD* = 0.5)

OP30

Cycle time	2.0
Breakdowns:	
Time between failure	Negative exponential (*mean* = 450)
Repair time	Erlang (*mean* = 35, *k* = 3)
Set-ups on changeover of TV type:	
Set-up time	Normal (*mean* = 5.0, *SD* = 0.5)

OP40

Cycle time — 2.0 per station
5 stations

Test

Cycle time — 1.5

Breakdowns:
- Time between failure — Negative exponential (*mean* = 250)
- Repair time — Since the data gives a bimodal distribution, an empirical distribution is used:

Repair time	Frequency
0.0–10.0	10
10.0–20.0	25
20.0–30.0	20
30.0–40.0	7
40.0–50.0	5
50.0–60.0	17
60.0–70.0	14

Set-ups on changeover of TV type:
- Set-up time — Normal (*mean* = 3.0, *SD* = 0.3)

OP50

Cycle time — 2.1

Breakdowns:
- Time between failure — Negative exponential (*mean* = 370)
- Repair time — Triangular (*min* = 10, *mode* = 30, *max* = 80)

Set-ups on changeover:
- Set-up time — Normal (*mean* = 5.0, *SD* = 0.5)

OP60

Cycle time — Normal (*mean* = 1.9, *SD* = 0.19)

Rework

Percentage test failures — 5.0%
Rework times — Negative exponential (*mean* = 35)

Conveyors

Mainline conveyors:

Capacity	5
Transfer times	2.5
Type	Accumulating

Pallet return conveyor

Capacity	40
Transfer times	20.0
Type	Accumulating

Maintenance labour

Total number of repair/set-up labour 1
Operations attended for repair and set-up:

OP20, OP30, Test, OP50

A2.3.1 Validation data

Throughput data have been collected over a recent period of 50 days. The daily throughput data are given in Table A2.1.

A2.4 Model coding

A simulation model of the Panorama case can be downloaded from the web site (www.wileyeurope.com/go/robinson). Versions of the model are available for various simulation packages.

Table A2.1 Panorama Televisions: Historic Data on Daily Throughput over 50 Days.

Day	T'put	Day	T'put	Day	T'put	Day	T'put	Day	T'put
1	432	11	333	21	396	31	385	41	390
2	411	12	428	22	386	32	402	42	381
3	447	13	387	23	433	33	427	43	416
4	447	14	462	24	485	34	437	44	401
5	389	15	424	25	485	35	442	45	393
6	396	16	431	26	435	36	472	46	449
7	453	17	459	27	395	37	433	47	409
8	356	18	420	28	458	38	489	48	398
9	407	19	439	29	384	39	394	49	397
10	392	20	433	30	380	40	421	50	351

A2.5 Verification and validation

To illustrate the concept of verification and validation, two validation tests are performed on the Panorama Televisions model. The first is a deterministic test and the second a comparison between the model results and the historic data on daily throughput presented in Section A2.3.1. Both are methods of black-box validation. Obviously much more testing, particularly other forms of verification and validation, would be required to give a reasonable level of confidence in the model.

Deterministic model

All random elements of the model are removed, that is, breakdowns, set-ups, television repairs and variations in operation cycles. It is then possible to predict exactly the throughput from the model as follows:

$$\text{Throughput} = \frac{\text{Run length}}{\text{Longest cycle time}}$$

OP20 and OP50 have the longest cycle times (2.1 minutes). Therefore, the expected throughput over (say) 5 days is:

$$\text{Five days throughput} = \frac{1440 * 5}{2.1} = 3428$$

When the deterministic simulation is run for a period 5 days, following 1 day of warm-up (Section A2.6.1), it gives a throughput of 3428 as predicted.

Comparison to historic data

The simulation model is run for a period of 50 days and the results are compared with the historic data given in Section A2.3.1. Table A2.2 shows the frequency distribution, the mean and standard deviation of daily throughput for the real system and for the model. Histograms for the two frequency distributions are shown in Figure A2.3. The means and standard deviations are fairly similar. The shape of the frequency distribution for the real system is quite different from the distribution derived from the simulation model. That said, the range of the data is similar. With only 50 samples the two distributions are not expected to match exactly.

Calculation of a confidence interval for the differences in the means (Section 12.4.4) shows that it is unlikely that the means are different. At 95% confidence the interval is in the range from −18.58 to 9.42. Since zero is within the interval, it appears that there is no difference in the means of the two distributions.

Figure A2.4 shows a probability–probability plot (Section 7.5.2) that compares the distributions of daily throughput derived from the model and the real system. There is some divergence from the 45-degree line showing that there are differences in the distributions. Indeed, a chi-square test (Section 7.5.2) concludes that there is a significant difference between the two distributions.

Table A2.2 Panorama Televisions: Comparison of Model Results for 50 Days of Simulation against Historic Data from the Real System.

Daily throughput	Frequency real system	Frequency model
320–339	1	2
340–359	2	3
360–379	0	4
380–399	16	6
400–419	6	13
420–439	13	11
440–459	7	7
460–479	2	4
480–499	3	0
Mean	417.40	412.82
St. dev.	34.46	36.08

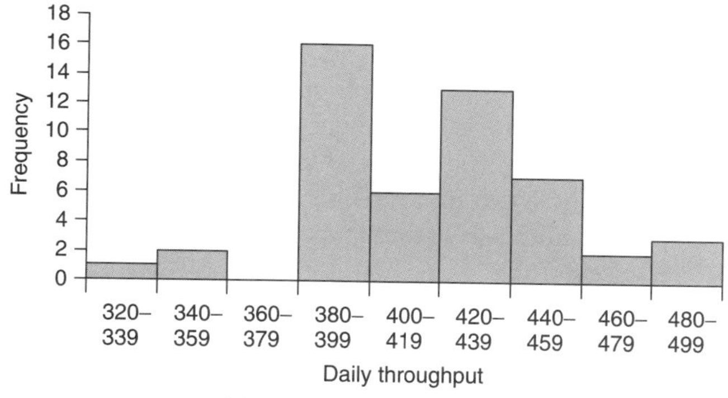

(a) Historic data from the real system

Frequency
0
2
4
6
8
10
12
14
320–339
340–359
360–379
380–399
400–419
420–439
440–459
460–479
480–499
Daily throughput

(b) Result from the simulation model

Figure A2.3 Panorama Televisions: Comparison of Model Results for 50 Days of Simulation against Historic Data from the Real System.

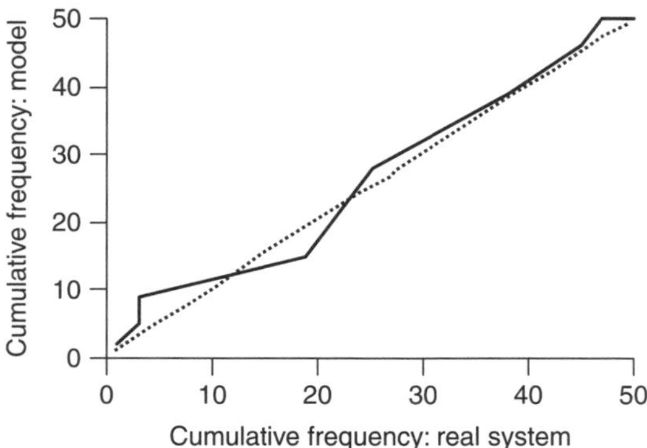

Figure A2.4 **Probability–Probability Plot Comparing Simulated and Real System Data.**

Conclusion

The deterministic test demonstrates, as expected, an exact match between the deterministic model and the calculated result. Meanwhile, a comparison of the full simulation model with the historic data demonstrates a close correspondence in the mean daily throughput, but there are some differences in the throughput distributions. These differences are not unexpected when the sample size is quite small and so this does not significantly reduce confidence in the model. These two tests provide some level of confidence that the model is sufficiently accurate for predicting the throughput of the system. More testing would help to increase this confidence further.

A2.6 Experimentation

A2.6.1 Obtaining accurate results

The nature of the simulation model

The Panorama Televisions model is a non-terminating simulation.

The nature of the simulation model output

There is one key output statistics: daily throughput (Section A2.2.3). Because the input data are constant throughout a simulation run, the output is expected to reach a steady state. Note that although there is a rolling production schedule, changing the product only causes relatively short stoppages and it does not affect the speed of the line. It is also expected that an initial transient exists, since the model starts from an unrealistic state of containing no work-in-progress. Figure A2.5 shows a time-series of daily throughput which

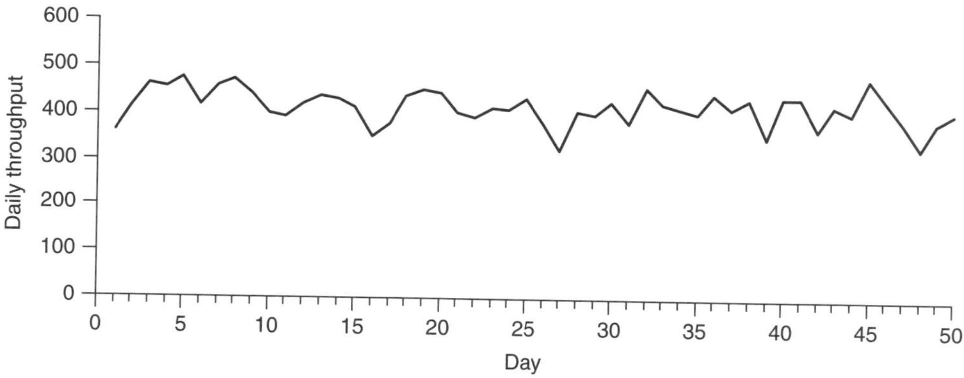

Figure A2.5 Panorama Televisions: Time-Series of Daily Throughput.

seems to confirm that the output is steady-state. There is, however, little evidence of any initialization bias.

Dealing with initialization bias

Although the time-series of daily throughput shows little evidence of initialization bias, it is known that the model starts from an unrealistic state of containing no work-in-progress. Therefore, the initialization bias is investigated using a smaller observation interval of hours in order to see if a pattern emerges. Figure A2.6 shows a time-series for the mean hourly throughput from five replications of 120 hours. This again does not show a clear initialization bias apart from a low throughput in the first hour.

Using Welch's method on the data in Figure A2.6, the line does not become smooth until a window size of about 30 is applied. The moving average line is shown in Figure A2.7.

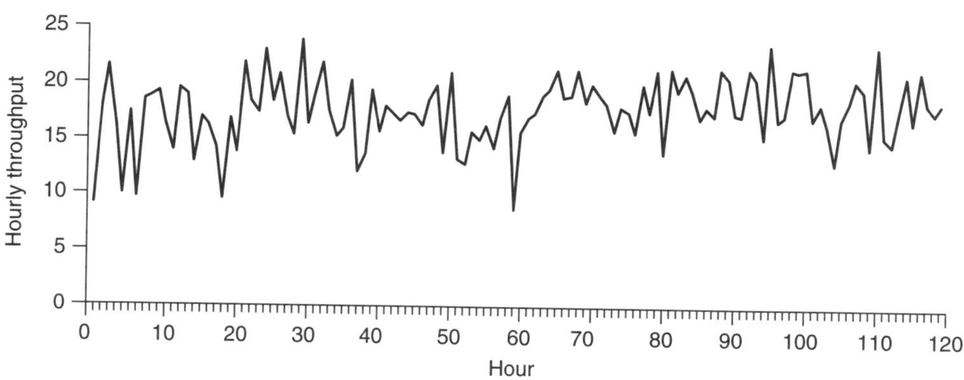

Figure A2.6 Panorama Televisions: Time-Series of Hourly Throughput (Mean of Five Replications).

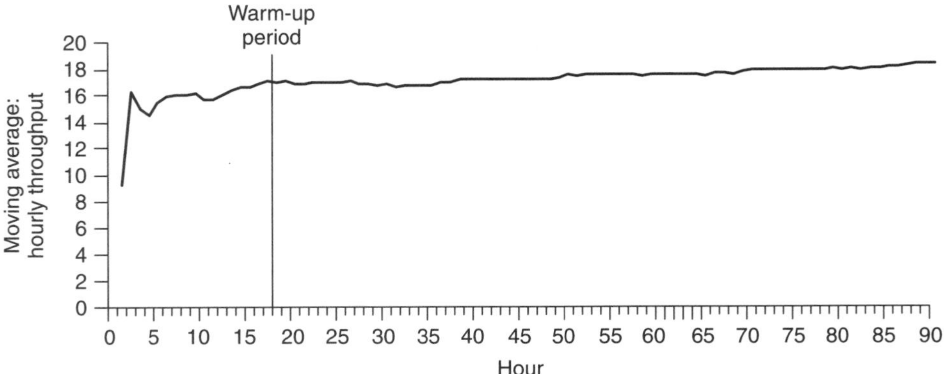

Figure A2.7 Panorama Televisions: Welch's Method with Window Size (w) of 30.

The line becomes flat at around 17 to 18 hours. This figure is rounded up to 24 hours in line with the normal observation interval (days). This also gives a margin of safety for when alternative scenarios are run. A warm-up period of 1 day will be used for experimentation.

Amount of output data required

Since the Panorama Televisions model is a non-terminating simulation, a single long run will be used. Table A2.3 shows the results for daily throughput from three replications of 60 days (this is following a 1-day warm-up period). The cumulative means of the daily throughput and the convergence are calculated. Figure A2.8 shows the cumulative mean data graphically. The data appear to have settled at about 30 days with the convergence remaining close to or below 1% and the three lines remaining fairly flat. The distributions of daily throughput for the three replications (shown in Figure A2.9) also seem reasonably similar at 30 days. Therefore, a run-length of 30 days will be used for experimentation.

A2.6.2 Searching the solution space

Preliminary experimentation

The first experiments focus on increasing the number of pallets as per the first objective. Table A2.4 shows the results of increasing the number of pallets from its current level of 30. The mean and standard deviation of the daily throughput are given; the latter providing a measure of variability. In the final column a confidence interval for the mean daily throughput is shown. This is calculated using the batch means method for which a batch size of two is found to be adequate. Indeed, a batch size of two is adequate for all the results reported below.

Table A2.3 Panorama Televisions Run-Length Selection: Cumulative Means and Convergence for Three Replications.

	Replication 1		Replication 2		Replication 3		
Day	Daily throughput	Cumulative mean	Daily throughput	Cumulative mean	Daily throughput	Cumulative mean	Convergence
1	359	359.0	417	417.0	432	432.0	20.33%
2	414	386.5	406	411.5	468	450.0	16.43%
3	461	411.3	467	430.0	435	445.0	8.18%
4	453	421.8	428	429.5	442	444.3	5.33%
5	476	432.6	379	419.4	365	428.4	3.15%
6	417	430.0	415	418.7	444	431.0	2.95%
7	458	434.0	406	416.9	456	434.6	4.25%
8	470	438.5	471	423.6	469	438.9	3.60%
9	441	438.8	441	425.6	363	430.4	3.11%
10	400	434.9	399	422.9	342	421.6	3.15%
11	393	431.1	401	420.9	410	420.5	2.51%
12	421	430.3	417	420.6	347	414.4	3.82%
13	437	430.8	363	416.2	441	416.5	3.51%
14	430	430.7	418	416.3	462	419.7	3.47%
15	412	429.5	383	414.1	390	417.7	3.72%
16	350	424.5	434	415.3	373	414.9	2.30%
17	379	421.8	457	417.8	438	416.3	1.33%
18	437	422.7	439	418.9	479	419.8	0.89%
19	452	424.2	435	419.8	441	420.9	1.05%
20	443	425.2	460	421.8	390	419.4	1.38%
21	402	424.0	362	419.0	430	419.9	1.22%
22	391	422.5	417	418.9	410	419.4	0.88%
23	412	422.1	384	417.3	401	418.6	1.14%
24	408	421.5	385	416.0	436	419.3	1.32%
25	433	422.0	352	413.4	303	414.7	2.06%
26	377	420.2	418	413.6	459	416.4	1.60%
27	324	416.7	463	415.4	364	414.4	0.54%
28	406	416.3	369	413.8	416	414.5	0.60%
29	398	415.7	429	414.3	405	414.2	0.36%
30	426	416.0	437	415.1	444	415.2	0.22%
31	382	414.9	391	414.3	379	414.0	0.22%
32	458	416.3	414	414.3	438	414.8	0.48%
33	423	416.5	412	414.2	402	414.4	0.54%
34	414	416.4	404	413.9	412	414.3	0.60%
35	404	416.0	374	412.8	417	414.4	0.79%
36	443	416.8	357	411.2	437	415.0	1.35%
37	411	416.6	439	412.0	397	414.5	1.13%
38	433	417.1	410	411.9	367	413.3	1.25%
39	349	415.3	419	412.1	384	412.5	0.78%

(*continued overleaf*)

Table A2.3 (*continued*)

	Replication 1		Replication 2		Replication 3		
Day	Daily throughput	Cumulative mean	Daily throughput	Cumulative mean	Daily throughput	Cumulative mean	Convergence
40	437	415.9	387	411.5	427	412.9	1.06%
41	437	416.4	438	412.1	412	412.9	1.03%
42	369	415.2	440	412.8	436	413.4	0.59%
43	418	415.3	336	411.0	408	413.3	1.05%
44	402	415.0	368	410.0	401	413.0	1.21%
45	477	416.4	422	410.3	423	413.2	1.48%
46	434	416.8	428	410.7	414	413.2	1.48%
47	385	416.1	388	410.2	424	413.5	1.44%
48	330	414.3	409	410.2	370	412.6	1.01%
49	384	413.7	492	411.8	406	412.4	0.45%
50	405	413.5	444	412.5	425	412.7	0.25%
51	437	414.0	422	412.7	420	412.8	0.31%
52	452	414.7	415	412.7	422	413.0	0.48%
53	398	414.4	426	413.0	385	412.5	0.46%
54	467	415.4	441	413.5	389	412.0	0.80%
55	403	415.1	435	413.9	358	411.1	0.99%
56	407	415.0	447	414.5	468	412.1	0.71%
57	427	415.2	370	413.7	445	412.6	0.62%
58	428	415.4	446	414.2	484	413.9	0.37%
59	416	415.4	461	415.0	439	414.3	0.27%
60	379	414.8	393	414.7	376	413.7	0.28%

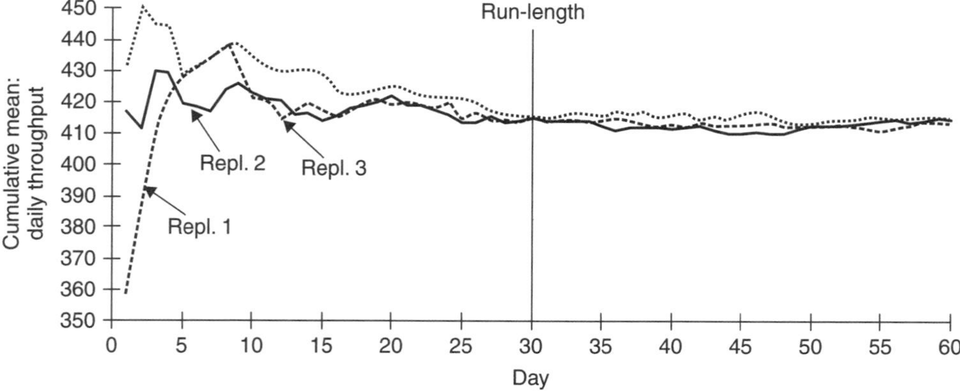

Figure A2.8 Panorama Televisions Run-Length Selection: Cumulative Means for Three Replications.

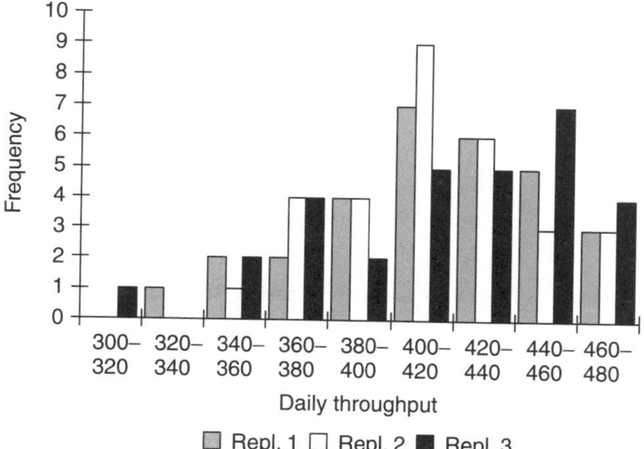

Figure A2.9 Panorama Televisions Run-Length Selection: Histograms of 30 Days' Results for Three Replications.

Table A2.4 Panorama Televisions: Increasing the Number of Pallets.

Number of pallets	Mean daily throughput	Standard deviation of daily throughput	Batch means 95% confidence interval
30 (current set-up)	414.17	36.54	395.34, 433.00
50	431.00	40.02	415.21, 446.79
75	424.77	44.99	406.81, 442.73
100	0.00	0.00	n/a

It is clear that the throughput is well below the target level of 500 units per day for all scenarios. The throughput is zero with 100 pallets because there are too many pallets in the system and the production facility becomes completely blocked.

Since it is not possible to achieve the required throughput by increasing pallets alone, some initial experiments are performed in which the buffering is increased as well (objective two). Table A2.5 shows the effect of increasing the buffers by 100% and 200%. The number of pallets is also increased to take advantage of the additional buffering. Even with an increase of 200%, the throughput is well below the target of 500 units per day.

In order to investigate the reasons why the target throughput is not being achieved the report on machine utilization is inspected (Table A2.6). These results are obtained from the simulation run with a 200% increase in buffering. It is notable that the operations (particularly Test and OP50) are waiting for a considerable time for maintenance labour. This implies that the machine is broken or waiting for set-up while the maintenance operator is working on another machine. It would, therefore, seem advisable to employ an additional maintenance operator.

Table A2.5 Panorama Televisions: Increasing the Buffer Sizes (and Number of Pallets).

Increase in buffer size	Number of pallets	Mean daily throughput	Standard deviation of daily throughput	Batch means 95% confidence interval
100%	100	439.93	44.06	422.38, 457.48
200%	150	440.60	42.58	424.61, 456.59

Table A2.6 Panorama Televisions: Machine Utilization Report (with 200% Buffer Increase and 150 Pallets).

Operation	% working	% idle	% blocked	% set-up	% broken down	% waiting for maintenance labour
OP10	58.06	0.00	41.94	0.00	0.00	0.00
OP20	64.24	0.00	20.79	5.55	5.58	3.84
OP30	61.19	1.23	22.63	5.60	6.04	3.30
OP40	61.20	1.76	37.04	0.00	0.00	0.00
Test	48.29	0.09	24.67	9.75	6.80	10.41
Rework	57.76	42.24	0.00	0.00	0.00	0.00
OP50	64.26	2.80	0.00	15.73	5.96	11.25
OP60	58.15	41.85	0.00	0.00	0.00	0.00

Final experimentation

Final experimentation is performed with two maintenance operators. In effect this means that a third experimental factor has been introduced to the simulation study. Table A2.7 shows the results obtained from different combinations of buffer size increase and numbers of pallets. It is immediately obvious that the addition of a maintenance operator has led to an increase in throughput.

For a specific buffer size, the throughput rises as the number of pallets is increased. If the number of pallets is increased too far, however, the throughput falls. This result is expected and is due to increased blocking as the system becomes clogged with pallets.

The maximum throughput achieved is with a 200% increase in the buffer size and with either 125 or 150 pallets. With these levels for the experimental factors we are 95% certain that the mean throughput is between 475 and 503 units per day. This suggests it is quite unlikely that the throughput will meet the target level, but this can only be confirmed by increasing the run-length or performing more replications, thereby narrowing the confidence interval. A run of 200 days gives a mean of 490.14 and a 95% confidence interval of 485.67 to 494.61, lending more weight to the conclusion that the target throughput cannot be achieved.

Table A2.7 Panorama Televisions: Increasing the Buffer Sizes and Number of Pallets (with Two Maintenance Operators).

Increase in buffer size	Number of pallets	Mean daily throughput	Standard deviation of daily throughput	Batch means 95% confidence interval
0%	50	460.10	36.12	443.80, 476.40
0%	75	447.40	36.16	432.25, 462.55
100%	50	461.60	33.80	447.23, 475.97
100%	75	477.97	38.81	461.76, 494.17
100%	100	478.23	38.89	461.97, 494.50
100%	125	478.03	36.31	462.76, 493.30
100%	150	407.10	40.78	388.96, 425.24
200%	100	487.93	31.41	474.28, 501.59
200%	125	489.33	32.37	475.44, 503.23
200%	150	489.33	32.37	475.44, 503.23
200%	175	488.50	31.11	474.73, 502.27
200%	200	478.50	36.65	462.54, 494.46

A note on the experimental approach

The experimentation described above is performed in an informal fashion, searching for potential improvements. During this informal search a third experimental factor (the number of maintenance operators) is identified. A more formal experimental approach could be adopted, possibly using experimental design to determine the effect of the initial two experimental factors and optimization to look for the combination of pallets and buffer sizes that maximizes throughput. Without identifying the need to employ more maintenance operators, however, such experimentation would not be very informative.

A2.7 Conclusions and recommendations

Based on the experiments performed, the following conclusions are reached:

- An additional maintenance operator is required.
- Increasing the buffer sizes and number of pallets improves the throughput.
- A mean throughput of around 490 units per day (485 to 495 with 95% confidence) can be achieved with a 200% increase in buffer sizes and 125 pallets.
- It does not appear that target throughput can be achieved by increasing the number of pallets and buffer sizes (within defined limits) alone.

Since the target throughput cannot be achieved, it is recommended that additional policies should be considered. For example, increasing the buffering by more than 200%, improving preventative maintenance to reduce the number of breakdowns, and changing the production schedule to reduce the number of set-ups. It is possible that the latter two policies would reduce the need for additional buffering and pallets. These could be investigated as part of a further simulation study.

APPENDIX 3

METHODS OF REPORTING SIMULATION RESULTS

A3.1 Introduction

There are many ways to present the results of a simulation. It is important that the right method is chosen to ensure that the results can be interpreted correctly and communicated effectively. The aim of this appendix is to describe various methods of presenting the results and to give some advice on the advantages and disadvantages of each. Two broad approaches to reporting results are described: numerical reports and graphical reports. There is also a brief discussion on methods of viewing the reports.

Before discussing specific methods of reporting, there are some general issues to address. First, many of the reports described below should be used in collaboration with each other and not in isolation. For instance, when a histogram is being used, the mean, standard deviation, maximum and minimum should normally be reported too. Secondly, most simulation packages give facilities for producing many of the reports outlined below. In some cases reports are given automatically, in others they may have to be defined by the modeller. Finally, account should always be taken of the way in which the results are presented in the real world. If a pie chart is normally used, it is probably best to provide one in the model to take advantage of their familiarity.

A3.2 Numerical Reports

Cumulative total and percentage

It is useful to know the cumulative total of some responses, for example, total throughput, total work in progress or total time spent serving customers. On other occasions the total can be expressed as a percentage, for instance, the percentage of customers served within 5 minutes of arrival or the percentage of time a machine is idle. A shortcoming of these numerical reports is that no indication of variation is given, while modelling variability rates among the major reasons for performing a simulation study.

Mean average and standard deviation

The mean average is commonly referred to as just the average. For example, the mean daily throughput is calculated at the end of a simulation run as an indication of the facility's average throughput. The mean is calculated as follows:

$$\overline{X} = \frac{\sum_{i=1}^{n} X_i}{n}$$

where:

$\overline{X}$ = mean average
X_i = individual values
n = number of individual values

In itself, the mean gives no indication of the amount by which the individual responses vary. This is useful information. For example, there is a significant difference between a system that gives a steady throughput and one where the throughput varies greatly, even though the mean may be the same. The standard deviation is the normal means for reporting the variability about the mean. The formula for the standard deviation (S) is:

$$S = \sqrt{\frac{\sum_{i=1}^{n} (X_i - \overline{X})^2}{n-1}}$$

The mean and standard deviation are the most commonly used measures of the average and spread. Most simply, they provide a useful means for inspecting and comparing the results from different experiments. They are also the basis for performing more complex statistical analysis such as calculating confidence intervals (Section 9.6.1 and Chapter 10).

Median average and quartiles

An alternative way of expressing the average is to use the median. This is the most central measurement. If all the responses are arranged in order of magnitude then the median is the middle value. For example:

Values:	345	398	503	420	457	234	367
Arranged values:	234	345	367	398	420	457	503
				↑ Median			

If there are an even number of observations, the median is calculated as half-way between the two central values.

In the same way that the standard deviation describes the spread of responses about the mean, so quartiles express the spread around the median. A quarter of the values lie below the lower quartile while three-quarters of the values lie below the upper quartile. The difference between the upper and the lower quartile is known as the inter-quartile range. This is a useful measure of the spread.

Beyond identifying quartiles, quantiles provide a more general measure of spread. The 0.9 quantile, for instance, defines the point below which 90% of the data lie. The lower and upper quartiles are simply the 0.25 and 0.75 quantiles respectively.

A frequency chart of daily throughput is shown in Figure A3.1 from which a cumulative frequency chart has been constructed. The median, lower quartile and upper quartile are all shown.

The median is a useful measure when the responses are likely to be significantly skewed. When looking at the average size of a queue it might be that the queue is frequently small

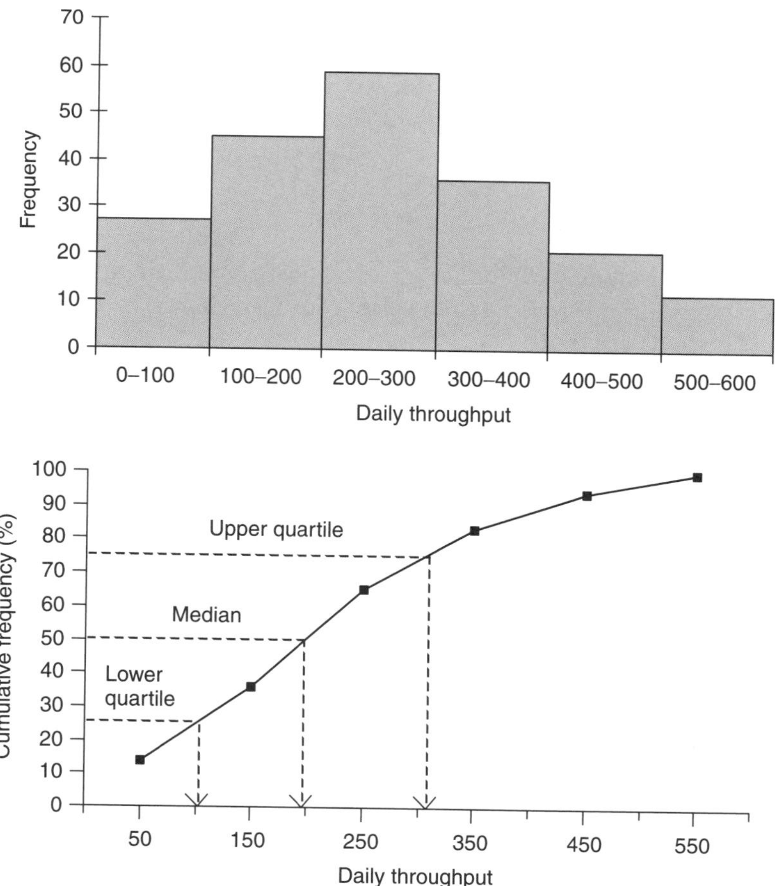

Figure A3.1 Median and Quartiles of Daily Throughput.

and just occasionally it is very large. The mean would tend to give a lot of weight to the large values while the median would not. Therefore, the median might be the preferred measure in this case. The main disadvantage of the median is that, unlike the mean, there is little in the way of further statistical analysis that can be performed with it.

Modal average

The third way of expressing the average is the mode. This is the value that occurs most frequently. So, in the example above, the mode would be the most frequent size of the queue. This again is useful if the distribution of responses is skewed, pointing to the value that is most likely to occur. It is not possible, however, to perform any further statistical analysis with the mode.

Minimum and maximum

The simplest way of measuring spread is to report the maximum and minimum responses obtained. These are very useful when shown in conjunction with other measures of spread such as the standard deviation. However, the possibility of outlying values giving an extreme maximum or minimum means that these measures should not be reported in isolation.

Statistical analysis

It is often useful to perform some further statistical analysis on the results obtained from a simulation. In particular, it is useful to calculate confidence intervals. These are discussed in Section 9.6.1 and Chapter 10.

A3.3 Graphical Reports

Time-series

A time-series records the level of some response at regular intervals of time, such as hourly, daily or weekly. They are often used by the press for reporting key economic data such as unemployment figures and inflation rates over the past 12 months, although they are rarely referred to as time-series in this context. Figure A3.2 shows an example of their use in a simulation showing the daily throughput of two products and the total.

Time-series are one of the most useful reports in a simulation, showing, for example, the changes in throughput, work-in-progress and average queue sizes over time. They are especially useful in showing the history of a simulation run, which can in turn identify periods when problems occur, for instance, a period of low throughput. Time-series also indicate the variability of a response, which is important when modelling the variability in a system.

The main disadvantage of using time-series is that only an indication of variability is given. They do not show a response's distribution. Also, if a simulation is run for a

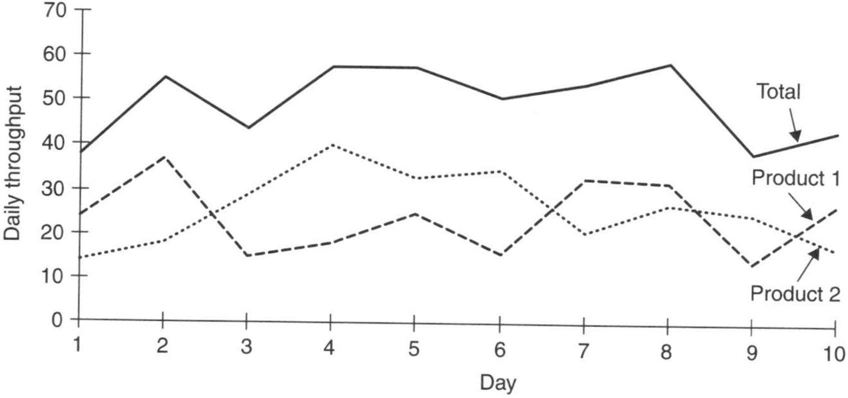

Figure A3.2 **A Time-Series Showing Daily Throughput.**

long period, there is a danger that important patterns in the data are lost in the mass of information.

Histograms

A histogram records the variation in the level of a response, in other words, its distribution. They are also known as frequency charts, bar charts and column charts. Figure A3.3 is an example showing the distribution of waiting times for customers at a supermarket checkout.

Stacked bar charts can be used to show additional information about the responses recorded in a histogram. Each bar is split into a number of ranges and either shaded or coloured differently. In Figure A3.4, the histogram shown in Figure A3.3 is shaded to show the waiting times at each individual checkout.

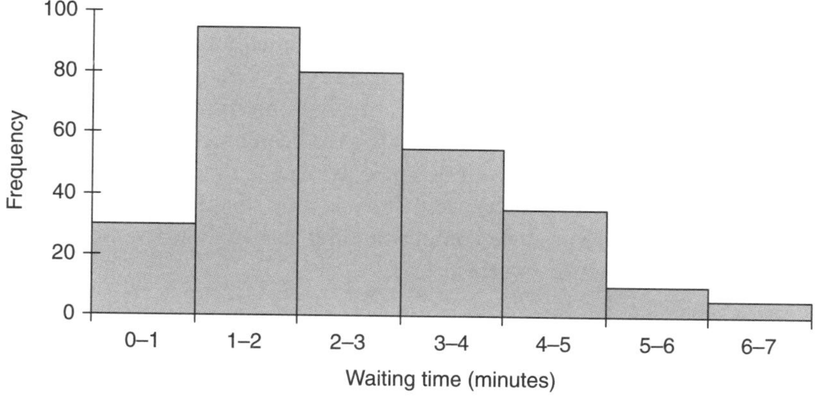

Figure A3.3 **A Histogram Showing Waiting Time at a Supermarket Checkout.**

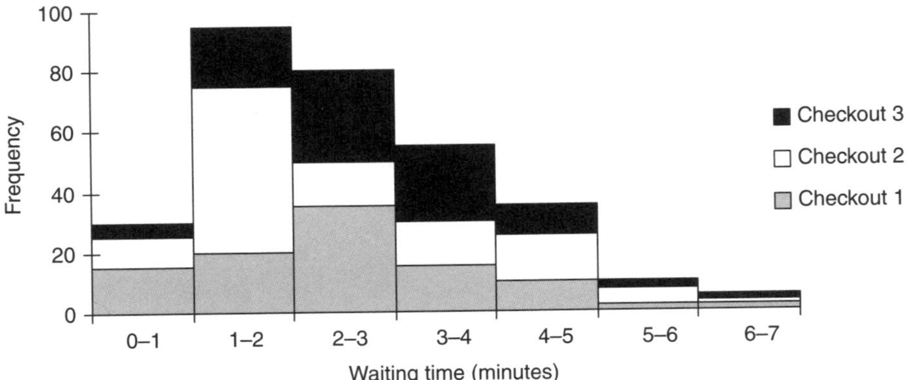

Figure A3.4 A Stacked Bar Chart Showing Waiting Time at each Individual Supermarket Checkout.

Histograms clearly show the variability in a model. They are often used to complement a time-series, showing, for instance, the distribution of daily throughput. Histograms are also used for recording responses that cannot be collected at regular intervals of time, for example, the repair times of a machine. A major use is to validate the samples taken from an input distribution, say the inter-arrival times of customers. The histogram is then compared with the data that were entered into the model.

Their main disadvantage is that no record is taken of the time at which an event occurred. As a result, the history of events is lost. It is useful to have such a record, since it is then possible to re-run the simulation at times when events of interest occurred to gain an understanding of their cause. For this reason, when it is applicable, the use of a time-series with a histogram is recommended.

Gantt charts

A Gantt chart shows the utilization of resources over time, building up a detailed history of a simulation run. An example is shown in Figure A3.5. The utilization of, for instance, machines, labour and power can all be traced. Gantt charts are also used to show the sequence of jobs performed, for example, the products that have been processed by a machine.

Unlike a time-series, recordings are not made at regular time intervals, but whenever some change takes place. As a result, the history is more detailed. However, since large quantities of information are produced, understanding and analysis are more difficult. The user may suffer from information overload.

Pie charts

Pie charts show the proportional split of some response. Figure A3.6 is an example. Typical uses are to show a resource's utilization, or the percentage split of customer types or product

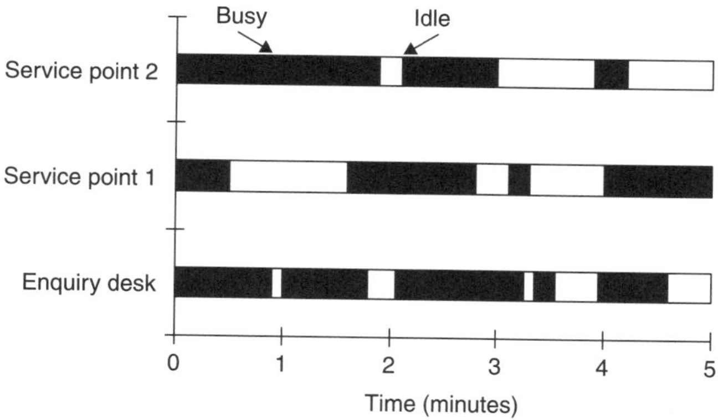

Figure A3.5 A Gantt Chart Showing the Utilization of Service Points.

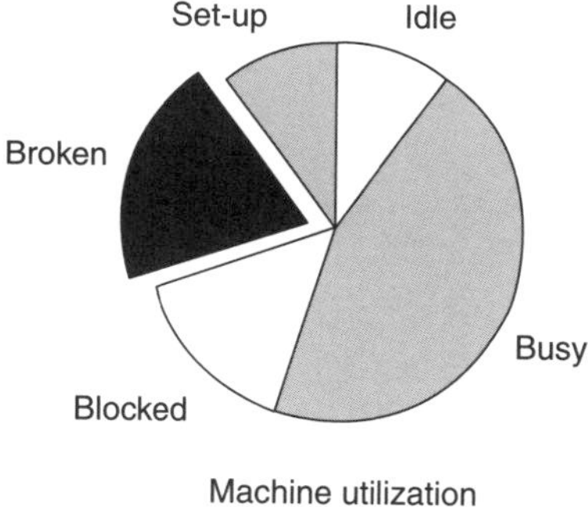

Figure A3.6 A Pie Chart Showing the Utilization of a Machine.

variants. Their shortcoming is that only an aggregate representation is given with no account of variability or time.

Scatter diagrams

A scatter diagram shows the association, or correlation, between two values and is useful for indicating whether a relationship might exist. If the values are associated, then the points on the diagram form a relatively straight line, otherwise the points are widely dispersed. The first diagram in Figure A3.7 shows an example of data that are closely associated. In this case the waiting time of a customer in a queue appears to be related to the waiting time of the previous customer (as would be expected). The second diagram is an example of data that are not closely associated. The length of a breakdown on a machine appears not to be related to the previous repair time.

Scatter diagrams are particularly useful in testing assumptions about the relationship between two values. In this respect they can act as an aid to model validation by testing that

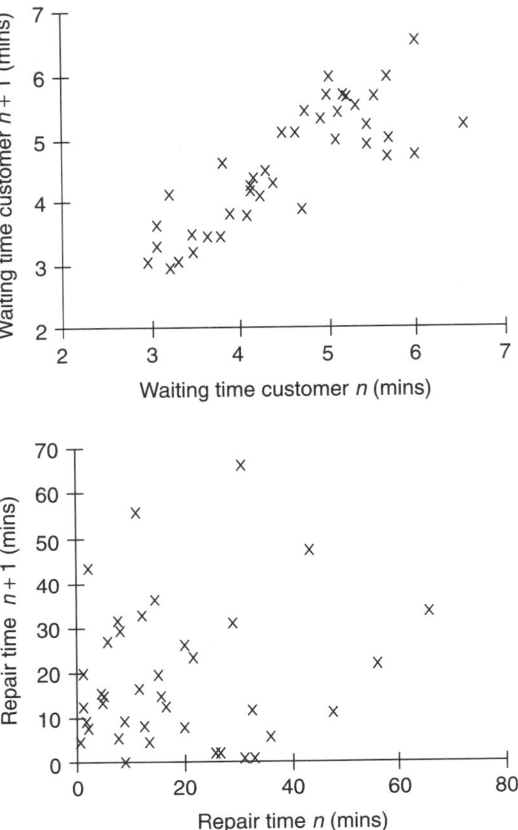

Figure A3.7 Scatter Diagrams of Customer Waiting Times and Machine Breakdowns.

the output from a model relates closely to data from the real world system (Section 12.4.4). Another application is to ensure that the occurrence of random events in a model does appear to be truly random (no association).

A3.4 Viewing Reports

Four methods of viewing reports can be used. In practice it is likely that a mixture of the methods will be adopted. Indeed, none of the methods are mutually exclusive.

Dynamic display

Tables and graphs can be displayed on the simulation screen, changing as the simulation runs. These dynamic reports can prove very useful, especially for demonstrations and when the model is being used as a training tool. The disadvantages are that there is limited space on the screen and it is not always possible to directly print these reports to presentation standards.

Interactive reports

The provision of interactive menus, through which the reports are viewed, can overcome the difficulties of having a dynamic display, particularly the limitations on space. However, it is no longer possible to see the reports change as the model runs.

Data files

In both of the methods above, further manipulation of the results is not possible. Writing the results to external data files enables this to be done. It is also a useful means of maintaining a permanent record of a run.

Third party software

Having written the results to a data file, they could be imported to a spreadsheet, database or other third party software. Indeed, many simulation packages enable data to be sent directly from the simulation to a third party package. This enables further analysis and the use of presentation graphics.

APPENDIX 4

STATISTICAL DISTRIBUTIONS

Listed below are many of the distributions that are useful in simulation modelling. They are grouped under four headings: continuous, discrete, approximate and other distributions. No preference is implied by the order of the distributions, which are listed alphabetically within each group. For each distribution under the first three headings, the parameters, shape, potential applications, mean, standard deviation and range of values are described. Under the fourth heading, just the potential applications are given. A more detailed discussion on some of these distributions and on the selection of appropriate distributions can be found in Chapter 7.

An Excel spreadsheet (Distributions.xls) that displays the shapes of the distributions described under the first two headings is provided on the web site (www.wileyeurope.com/go/robinson). The user can enter a distribution's parameters and see how its shape, mean and standard deviation alter.

A4.1 Continuous Distributions

Beta (shape₁, shape₂)

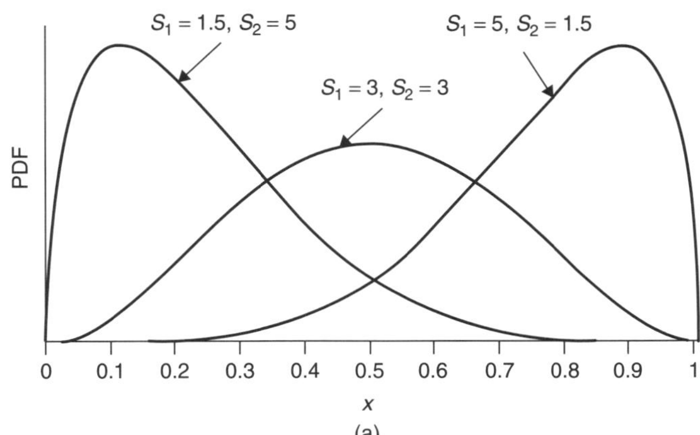

(a)

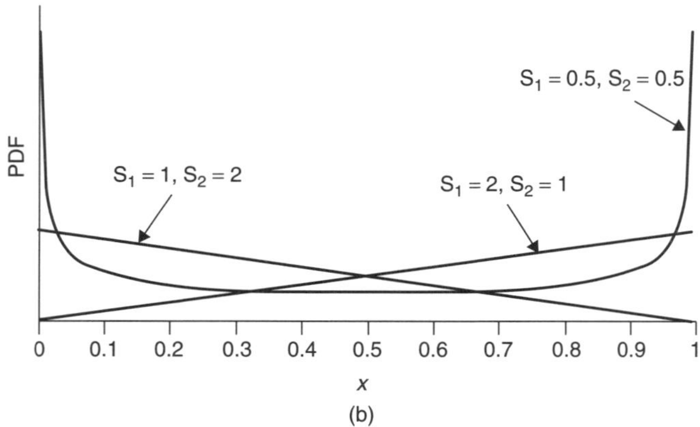

(b)

Potential applications:	time to complete a task; proportions (e.g. defects in a batch of items); useful as an approximation in the absence of data
Mean:	$\frac{shape_1}{shape_1 + shape_2}$
Standard deviation:	$\sqrt{\frac{shape_1 \times shape_2}{(shape_1 + shape_2)^2(shape_1 + shape_2 + 1)}}$
Range of values:	$0 < x < 1$ (use a multiplier to extend the range)
Comments:	the beta distribution is used for task times in PERT networks (Ackoff and Sasieni 1968)

Erlang (mean, k)

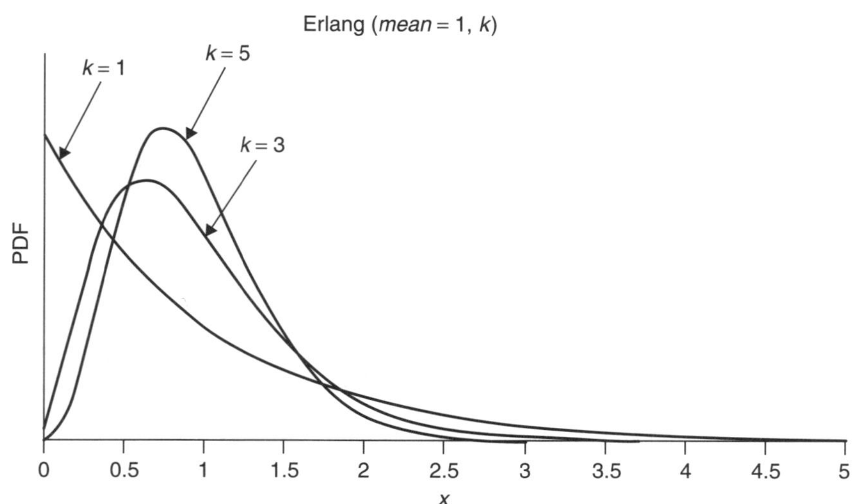

Potential applications: time to complete a task; inter-arrival times (e.g. customer arrivals); time between failure

Mean: *mean*

Standard deviation: $\frac{mean}{\sqrt{k}}$

Range of values: $0 < x < \infty$

Comments: k is an integer; the Erlang distribution is a specific form of the gamma distribution: Erlang (*mean*, k) = gamma (k, *mean*/k); an Erlang (*mean*, 1) = negative exponential (*mean*); the Erlang distribution is used in queuing theory (Winston 1994)

Gamma (shape, scale)

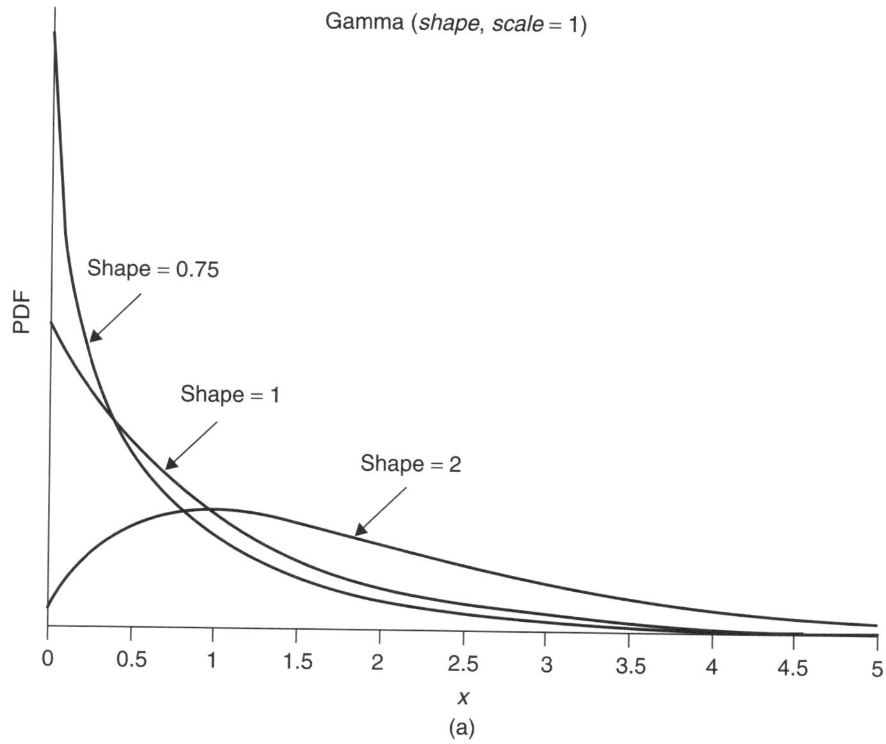

(a)

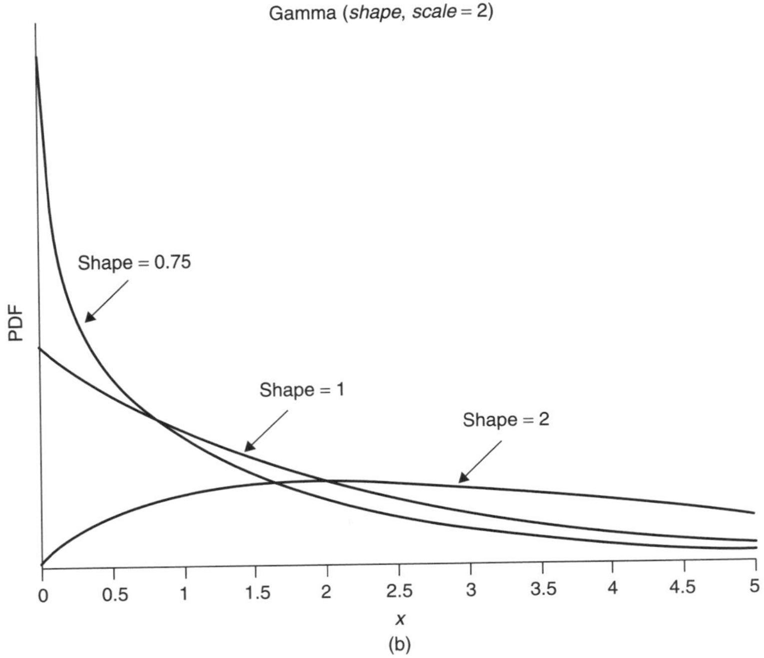

(b)

Potential applications:	time to complete a task; inter-arrival times (e.g. customer arrivals, time between failure)
Mean:	*shape* × *scale*
Standard deviation:	$\sqrt{shape} \times scale$
Range of values:	$0 < x < \infty$
Comments:	gamma (1, *scale*) = negative exponential (*scale*)

Lognormal (location, spread)

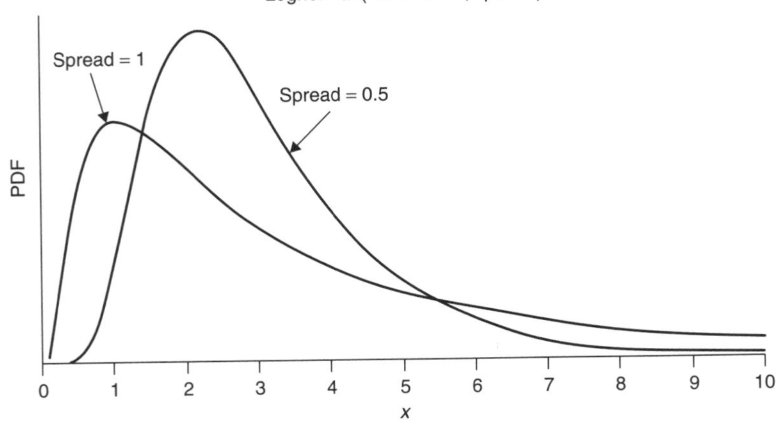

Potential applications: time to complete a task

Mean: $e^{location+spread/2}$

Standard deviation: $\sqrt{e^{2location+spread}(e^{spread} - 1)}$

Range of values: $0 < x < \infty$

Comments: the hump of the lognormal can be higher than the gamma (or similar) distribution, giving a greater probability to values around the mode; in most simulation software the mean and standard deviation are entered as the parameters of the distribution, rather than the less intuitive location and spread

Negative exponential (mean)

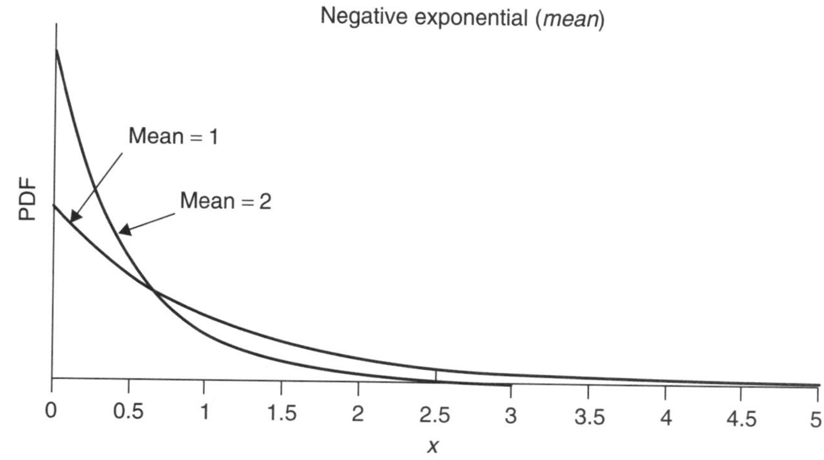

Potential applications: inter-arrival times (e.g. customer arrivals, time between failure); time to complete a task

Mean: *mean*

Standard deviation: *mean*

Range of values: $0 <= x < \infty$

Comments: also referred to as the exponential distribution; limited value for representing the time to complete a task because of high probability of near zero values; the negative exponential distribution is used in queuing theory (Winston 1994)

Normal (mean, standard deviation)

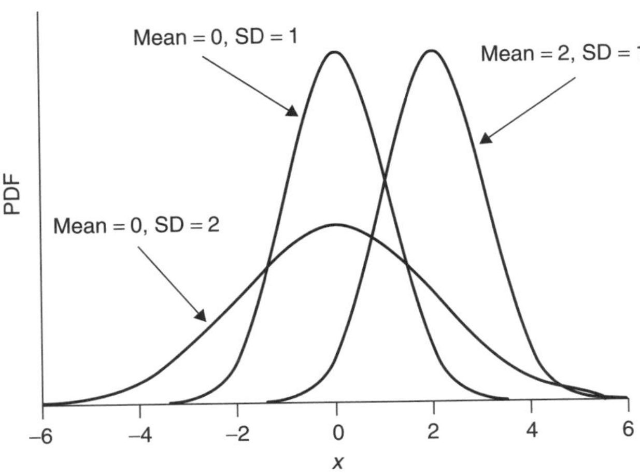

Potential applications:	errors (e.g. in weight or dimension of components)
Mean:	*mean*
Standard deviation:	*SD*
Range of values:	$-\infty < x < \infty$
Comments:	it is possible to sample negative values and so care must be taken (e.g. when sampling times)

Truncated normal (mean, standard deviation, lower limit, upper limit)

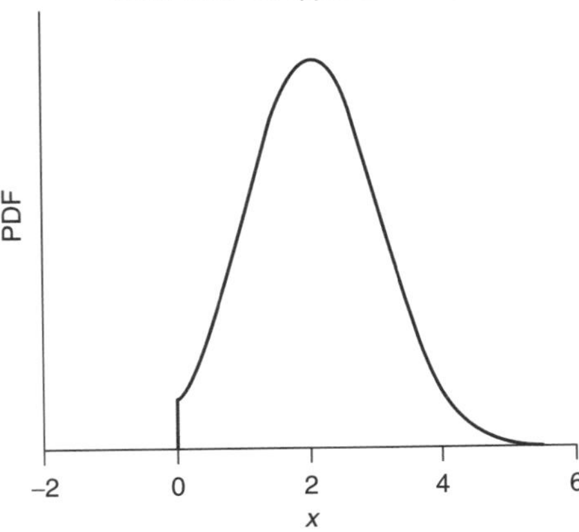

Potential applications:	similar to normal distribution but avoids problem of extreme values (e.g. negative values)
Range of values:	if lower limit specified: *lower limit* <= $x < \infty$ if upper limit specified: $-\infty < x <=$ *upper limit* if both limits specified: *lower limit* <= x <= *upper limit*
Comments:	other distributions can also be truncated by re-sampling if the value of x is outside the required range

Weibull (shape, scale)

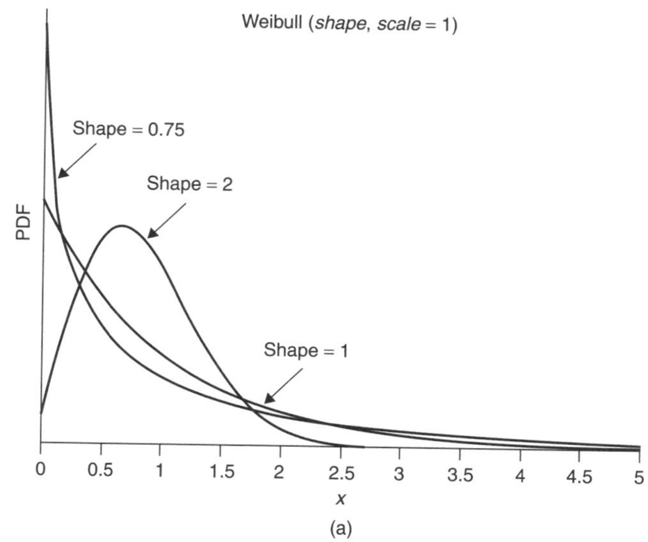

(a)

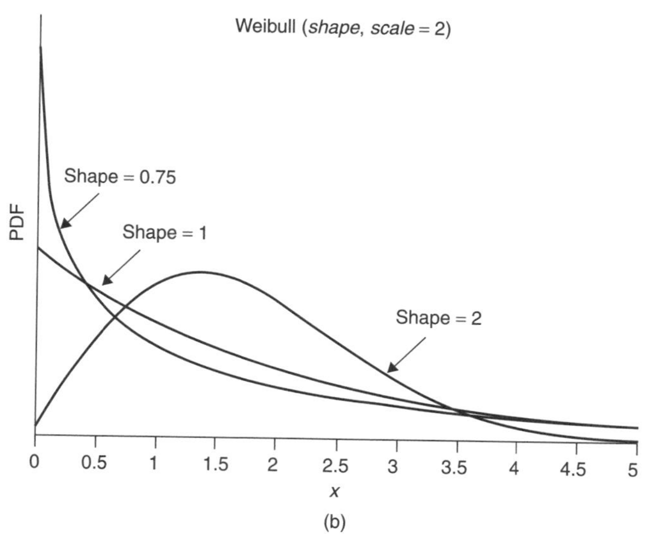

(b)

Potential applications: time between failure; time to complete a task

Range of values: $0 < x < \infty$

Comments: in quality management the Weibull distribution is used for modelling equipment failures (Dale 1994; Juran and Godfrey 1999); Weibull (1, *scale*) = negative exponential (*scale*)

A4.2 Discrete Distributions

Binomial (trials, probability)

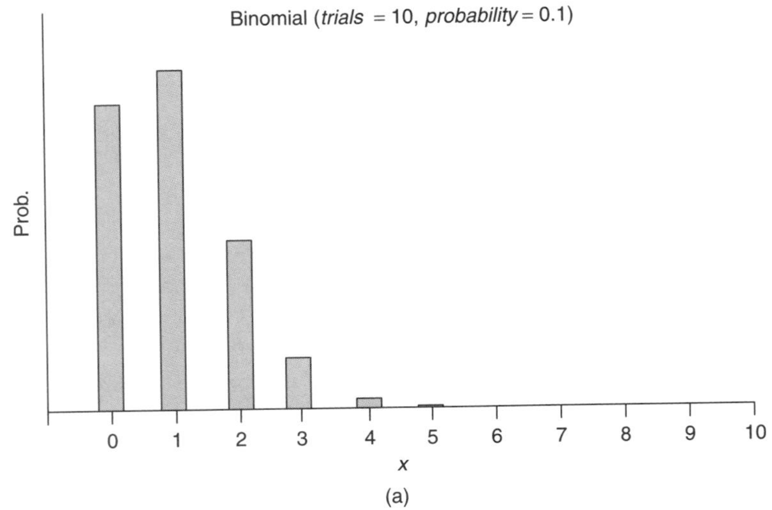

(a)

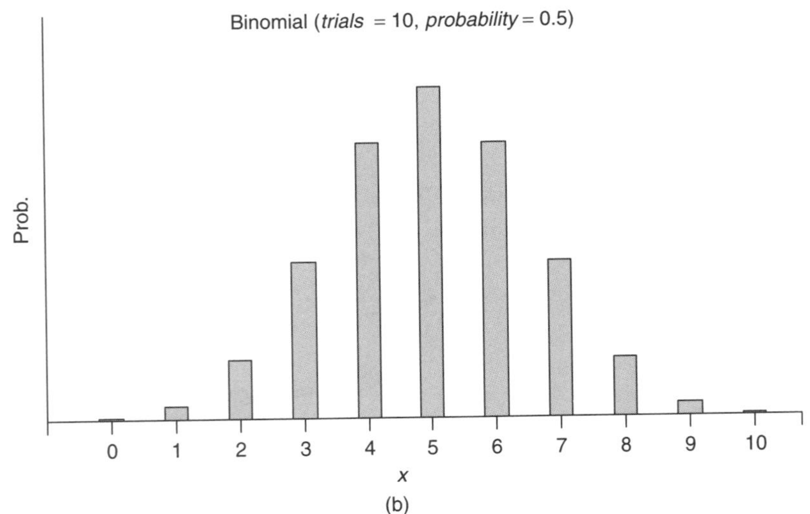

(b)

Potential applications: total "successes" in a number of trials (e.g. number of defective items in a batch); number of items in a batch (e.g. size of an order)

Mean $trials \times probability$

Standard deviation: $\sqrt{trials \times probability\ (1 - probability)}$

Range of values: $0 <= x <= trials$, x is an integer

Poisson (mean)

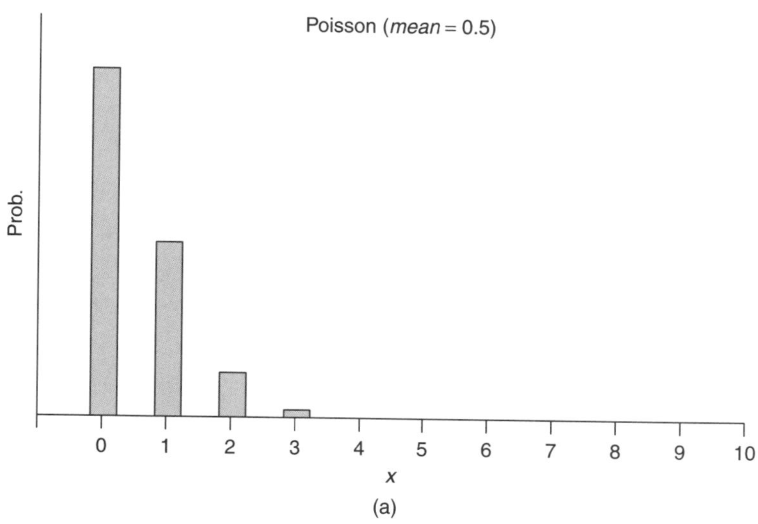

(a)

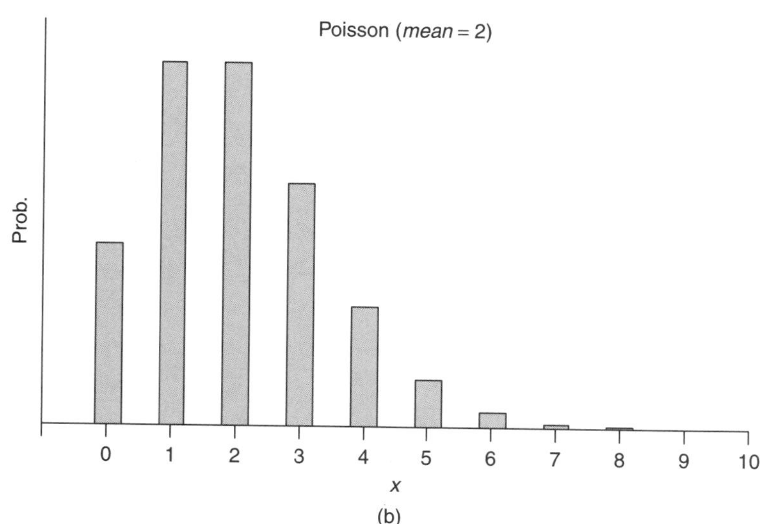

(b)

Potential applications:	number of events in a period of time (e.g. customer arrivals in an hour); number of items in a batch (e.g. size of an order)
Mean:	*mean*
Standard deviation:	$\sqrt{mean}$
Range of values:	$0 <= x < \infty$, x is an integer

A4.3 Approximate Distributions

Integer Uniform (min, max)

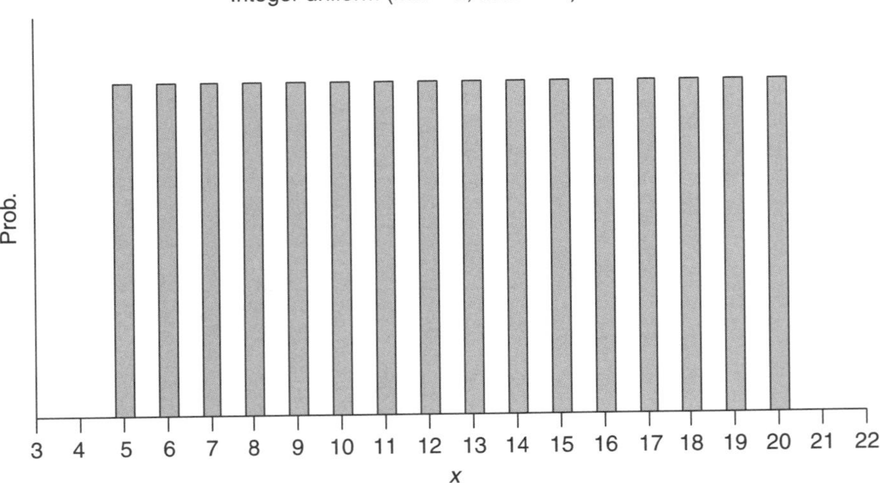

Potential applications:	useful as an approximation when little is known other than the likely range of values
Mean:	$\frac{\text{min} + \text{max}}{2}$
Standard deviation:	$\sqrt{\frac{(\text{max} - \text{min} + 1)^2 - 1}{12}}$
Range of values:	$min <= x <= max$, x is an integer
Comments:	integer random numbers (range 0–99) are an example of values generated from an integer uniform ($min = 0$, $max = 99$)

Triangular (min, mode, max)

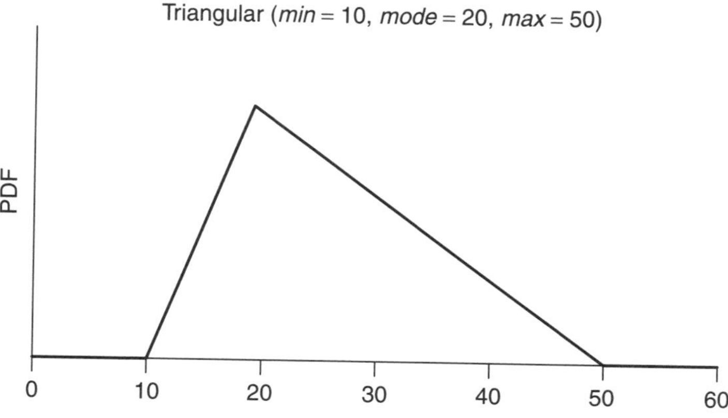

Potential applications:	useful as an approximation when little is known other than the likely range of values and the most likely value (*mode*)
Mean:	$\frac{\text{min} + \text{mode} + \text{max}}{3}$
Standard deviation:	$\sqrt{\frac{\left(\begin{array}{c}\text{min}^2 + \text{mode}^2 + \text{max}^2 - \\ (\text{min} \times \text{mode} + \text{min} \times \text{max} + \text{mode} \times \text{max})\end{array}\right)}{18}}$
Range of values:	*min* <= *x* <= *max*

Uniform (min, max)

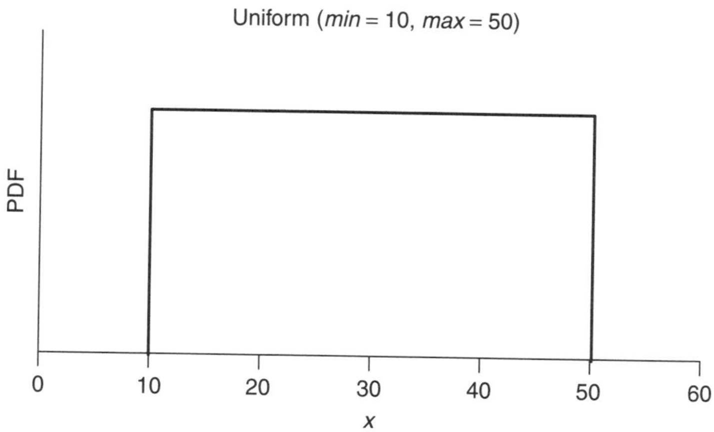

Potential applications: useful as an approximation when little is known other than the likely range of values

Mean: $\frac{\text{min} + \text{max}}{2}$

Standard deviation: $\frac{\text{max} - \text{min}}{\sqrt{12}}$

Range of values: $min <= x <= max$

Comments: random numbers (range 0–1) are an example of values generated from a uniform ($min = 0$, $max = 1$)

A4.4 Other Distributions

The distributions listed above are those that are perhaps most commonly used in simulation models. There are a number of other distributions that may be used on some occasions. These distributions are listed below as well as their potential applications. For further details on these distributions see Law and Kelton (2000).

- *Geometric*: number of failures before success, number of successes before failure, number of items in a batch.
- *Log-logistic*: time to perform a task.
- *Negative binomial*: number of failures before success, number of successes before failure, number of items in a batch.
- *Pearson type V*: time to perform a task.
- *Pearson type VI*: time to perform a task.

References

Ackoff, R.L. and Sasieni, M.W. (1968) *Fundamentals of Operations Research*. Chichester, UK: Wiley.

Dale, B.G. (1994) *Managing Quality*, 2nd edn. Hemel Hempstead, UK: Prentice Hall.

Juran, J.M. and Godfrey, A.B. (1999) *Juran's Quality Handbook*, 5th edn. New York: McGraw-Hill.

Law, A.M. and Kelton, W.D. (2000) *Simulation Modeling and Analysis*, 3rd edn. New York: McGraw-Hill.

Winston, W.L. (1994) *Operations Research: Applications and Algorithms*, 3rd edn. Belmont, CA: Duxbury Press.

APPENDIX 5

CRITICAL VALUES FOR THE CHI-SQUARE TEST

Degrees of freedom	Level of significance	
	5%	1%
1	3.8415	6.6349
2	5.9915	9.2104
3	7.8147	11.3449
4	9.4877	13.2767
5	11.0705	15.0863
6	12.5916	16.8119
7	14.0671	18.4753
8	15.5073	20.0902
9	16.9190	21.6660
10	18.3070	23.2093
11	19.6752	24.7250
12	21.0261	26.2170
13	22.3620	27.6882
14	23.6848	29.1412
15	24.9958	30.5780
16	26.2962	31.9999
17	27.5871	33.4087
18	28.8693	34.8052
19	30.1435	36.1908
20	31.4104	37.5663

Degrees of freedom	Level of significance 5%	1%
21	32.6706	38.9322
22	33.9245	40.2894
23	35.1725	41.6383
24	36.4150	42.9798
25	37.6525	44.3140
26	38.8851	45.6416
27	40.1133	46.9628
28	41.3372	48.2782
29	42.5569	49.5878
30	43.7730	50.8922
40	55.7585	63.6908
50	67.5048	76.1538
60	79.0820	88.3794
70	90.5313	100.4251
80	101.8795	112.3288
90	113.1452	124.1162
100	124.3421	135.8069

APPENDIX 6

CRITICAL VALUES FOR THE STUDENT'S *t*-DISTRIBUTION

Degrees of freedom	Level of significance	
	2.5%	0.5%
1	12.7062	63.6559
2	4.3027	9.9250
3	3.1824	5.8408
4	2.7765	4.6041
5	2.5706	4.0321
6	2.4469	3.7074
7	2.3646	3.4995
8	2.3060	3.3554
9	2.2622	3.2498
10	2.2281	3.1693
11	2.2010	3.1058
12	2.1788	3.0545
13	2.1604	3.0123
14	2.1448	2.9768
15	2.1315	2.9467
16	2.1199	2.9208
17	2.1098	2.8982
18	2.1009	2.8784
19	2.0930	2.8609
20	2.0860	2.8453

Degrees of freedom	Level of significance	
	2.5%	0.5%
21	2.0796	2.8314
22	2.0739	2.8188
23	2.0687	2.8073
24	2.0639	2.7970
25	2.0595	2.7874
26	2.0555	2.7787
27	2.0518	2.7707
28	2.0484	2.7633
29	2.0452	2.7564
30	2.0423	2.7500
40	2.0211	2.7045
50	2.0086	2.6778
60	2.0003	2.6603
70	1.9944	2.6479
80	1.9901	2.6387
90	1.9867	2.6316
100	1.9840	2.6259

INDEX